Human Rights in
Global Politics

Edited by

Tim Dunne and Nicholas J. Wheeler

PUBLISHED BY THE PRESS SYNDICATE OF THE UNIVERSITY OF CAMBRIDGE
The Pitt Building, Trumpington Street, Cambridge, United Kingdom

CAMBRIDGE UNIVERSITY PRESS
The Edinburgh Building, Cambridge, CB2 2RU, UK
40 West 20th Street, New York, NY 10011–4211, USA
477 Williamstown Road, Port Melbourne, VIC 3207, Australia
Ruiz de Alarcón 13, 28014 Madrid, Spain
Dock House, The Waterfront, Cape Town 8001, South Africa

http://www.cambridge.org

© Cambridge University Press 1999

First published 1999
Ninth printing 2006

Printed in the United Kingdom at the University Press, Cambridge

Typeset in 10/12pt Plantin   [G C]

A catalogue record for this book is available from the British Library

Library of Congress Cataloguing in Publication data

Human rights in global politics / edited by Tim Dunne, Nicholas J. Wheeler.
      p.   cm.
ISBN 0 521 64138 1 (hb) – ISBN 0 521 64643 X (pb)
1. Human rights.   I. Dunne, Timothy, 1965–   .   II. Wheeler,
Nicholas J.
JC571.H769524   1999
323 – dc21   98-35137   CIP

ISBN 0 521 64138 1 hardback
ISBN 0 521 64643 X paperback

Human Rights in Global Politics

There is a stark contradiction between the theory of universal human rights and the everyday practice of human wrongs. This timely volume investigates whether human rights abuses are a result of the failure of governments to live up to a universal human rights standard, or whether the search for moral universals is a fundamentally flawed enterprise which distracts us from the task of developing rights in the context of particular ethical communities. In the first part of the book, chapters by Ken Booth, Jack Donnelly, Chris Brown, Bhikhu Parekh and Mary Midgley explore the philosophical basis of claims to universal human rights. In the second part, Richard Falk, Mary Kaldor, Martin Shaw, Gil Loescher, Georgina Ashworth, Andrew Hurrell, Ken Booth and Tim Dunne reflect on the role of the media, global civil society, states, migration, non-governmental organisations, capitalism, and schools and universities in developing a global human rights culture.

TIM DUNNE is a Lecturer in the Department of International Politics at the University of Wales, Aberystwyth. He has published several journal articles on international relations theory, and is author of *Inventing International Society: A History of the English School* (1998).

NICHOLAS J. WHEELER is a Senior Lecturer in the Department of International Politics at the University of Wales, Aberystwyth. He has published widely on human rights and humanitarian intervention, and is presently writing *Saving Strangers: Humanitarian Intervention in International Society*.

Contents

Contributors

GEORGINA ASHWORTH, Director of CHANGE, London

KEN BOOTH, Professor of International Politics, University of Wales, Aberystwyth

CHRIS BROWN, Professor of International Relations, London School of Economics

JACK DONNELLY, Professor of International Studies, University of Denver

TIM DUNNE, Lecturer in International Politics, University of Wales, Aberystwyth

RICHARD FALK, Professor of International Law and Practice, Princeton University

ANDREW HURRELL, Fellow of Nuffield College and Lecturer in International Relations, University of Oxford

MARY KALDOR, Reader in Contemporary European Studies, University of Sussex

GIL LOESCHER, Professor of International Relations, University of Notre Dame

MARY MIDGLEY, former Senior Lecturer in Philosophy, University of Newcastle and currently writer and broadcaster

BHIKHU PAREKH, Professor of Political Theory, University of Hull

MARTIN SHAW, Professor of International Relations and Politics, University of Sussex

NICHOLAS J. WHEELER, Senior Lecturer in International Politics, University of Wales, Aberystwyth

Preface and acknowledgements

Human Rights in Global Politics developed out of a conference which brought together some of the leading theorists and activists working on human rights. We asked them to reflect on the growing disparity between the almost globally accepted standard for the protection of universal human rights and the daily denial of those basic rights to millions of people.

The Department of International Politics at Aberystwyth was an appropriate venue for the conference. After all, the first ever endowed chair in the field was instituted to advance 'a truer understanding of civilisations other than our own', a theme which recurs in this volume. We wanted to harness this normative ambition to new thinking in international theory. Our guide in this respect was an earlier conference entitled 'After Positivism' – later published by Cambridge as *International Theory: Positivism and Beyond* and edited by Steve Smith, Ken Booth and Marysia Zalewski – held in Aberystwyth seventy-five years after the birth of the discipline. We are delighted that Cambridge University Press is publishing the revised proceedings of this second in a series of conferences. Throughout the preparation of the volume, John Haslam has been a very encouraging commissioning editor. He attended the original conference and has stood by the project from the outset.

Our aim to gather together some of the most influential scholars in the world was made possible in large measure by the Cadogan Research Initiative of the Higher Education Funding Council for Wales. Generous financial support from the University also enabled us to extend the scope of the conference beyond the contributors to include a number of distinguished guests: Hayward Alker, James Der Derian, Michael Freeman, Andrew Linklater, James Mayall, Radmilla Nakarada, Margo Picken, Hidemi Suganami, Ann Tickner and R. B. J. Walker. We recorded the conversations generated by the panels and have drawn from them in the course of producing this book.

As ever in a project of this kind, we have benefited enormously from the support of colleagues in the Department. In particular, we owe a special thank you to Steve Smith for his guidance during the planning stages, his overall contribution to the occasion and his constant probing of our assumptions about the metatheoretical foundations of the human rights discourse. We would also like to thank Michael Cox for the characteristically discerning advice he provided during the completion of the book. Our other two debts can also be traced back to the history of this Department since both of the individuals in question were 'Inter Pol' students in the early 1960s.

R. J. Vincent's book on *Human Rights and International Relations* has had a profound influence on our thinking on this subject. In this and in his later work, Vincent combined a cosmopolitan moral awareness with a keen sense that political power is concentrated at the level of states. We have often expressed our personal regret that his tragic and premature death denied us the opportunity of hearing his reflections on human rights in global politics some ten years after his *magnum opus*. As a mark of our admiration for his work, we dedicate this book to his memory.

John Vincent's contribution to the 'academy', as he liked to call it, is celebrated annually in the form of a memorial lecture given at Keele University. Ken Booth gave the second R. J. Vincent Memorial Lecture on 'Human Wrongs and International Relations'. Although an admirer of Vincent's contribution to the discipline, Booth expressed disquiet about the capacity of sovereign states to enhance human rights. The difference between Booth and Vincent can be framed in terms of whether international society is a civilising or a corrupting force. Our introduction to *Human Rights in Global Politics* examines whether it is possible to steer a course between these two positions. Additionally, it provides a sustained discussion of the unifying themes of the volume.

Not only has Ken Booth been one of the foremost influences on the eventual shape and content of the book, he has also been typically generous with his time despite the clamour of other commitments. Both of us would like to thank Ken warmly for his unstinting support and for demonstrating that, when it comes to human rights, the professional is the personal.

Descending from the summit of the intellectual influences that have guided our thinking on the subject, we would like to acknowledge all those who have assisted in the publication of the book. The anonymous referees provided very important comments and constructive criticisms, as did Marysia Zalewski on chapter 10. A special thank you to Elaine Lowe, whose patience and technical skill are apparently limitless. In addition, Pauline Ewan provided us with valuable assistance in the final production of the manuscript. Lastly, the other members of the

Department provide an environment in which research is prized and ideas matter. Tim would also like to thank Caroline for not allowing academic matters to get in the way of life.

At the outset, we took the view that the royalties from the book should find an appropriate destination. All the contributors agreed to our suggestion that we should donate the money to Sight Savers International, a non-governmental organisation committed to the elimination of blindness and visual impairment. With this, it is our hope that reading human rights may in a small way be eliminating human wrongs.

TIM DUNNE AND NICHOLAS J. WHEELER
Aberystwyth, June 1998

Introduction: human rights and the fifty years' crisis

Tim Dunne and Nicholas J. Wheeler

The humanitarian principles embodied in the UN Charter and the Universal Declaration of Human Rights marked the beginnings of a full-blown global human rights regime. The Declaration, signed fifty years ago, established a standard of civilised conduct which applies to all governments in the treatment of their citizens. For example, the Declaration requires states to provide subsistence needs and basic welfare provision as well as a panoply of civil and political rights. Although the latter assumed prominence in the subsequent history of the post-1945 regime, it is important to underscore that from the outset, *universal* human rights encompassed a concern for positive rights (such as collective provision of education and healthcare) as well as negative rights (freedom from repressive government policies).

The framers of these basic documents assumed that there was no necessary conflict between the principles of sovereignty and non-intervention and respect for universal human rights. This represented a historic evolution in the norms of international society which from the seventeenth century onwards had maintained that the domestic practices of governments were not a subject of international concern. According to the Westphalian conception of legitimacy, a government's claim to be recognised as sovereign was not dependent upon how it behaved towards its own citizens. As a consequence of the experiences of totalitarianism, governments recognised that there was a need to challenge the Westphalian model of unlimited sovereignty. In these emerging human rights norms, there was a clear consensus that states must be made accountable for their behaviour.

Underlying the evolution of human rights principles was the conviction held by the framers of the Charter that there was a clear link between good governance and the maintenance of international peace and security. It was believed that the aggressive foreign policies of the Axis powers were caused by the militaristic nature of their political systems. Diplomats and state leaders in the early post-1945 period endorsed the 'democratic peace' thesis which has been rejuvenated in

1

the theory and practice of international relations since the end of the Cold War.

The manifesto for human rights and international security contained within the Charter and the Declaration represented, therefore, a radical assault on the existing principle of international legitimacy. Sovereignty remained the constitutive norm of the society of states, but the meaning that was given to sovereignty had been modified. In R. J. Vincent's words, the way a government treats its people exposes 'the internal regimes of all the members of international society to the legitimate appraisal of their peers'.[1]

Since the first wave of standard-setting, successive decades have seen the growing codification of human rights into both treaty and customary international law. Alongside this strengthening of the regime, there has emerged a growing moral awareness among world public opinion of human rights issues and concerns, reflected in the existence of NGOs like Amnesty International which act as the conscience of the regime. An informed and active citizenry has a crucial role to play in monitoring state behaviour for the reason that there is a disjuncture between the declaratory commitments of governments to protect and promote human rights and their compliance with these standards. For example, Amnesty International pointed out in its 1997 Report that of the world's 185 sovereign states, 123 routinely practise torture.[2] Even more striking is the fact that the crime of genocide which is outlawed by the 1950 Genocide Convention has not been banished from the practice of world politics, as the appalling tragedy of Rwanda illustrated in April 1994. In short, governments – many of whom drafted and signed the 'international bill of rights' – have massively defaulted on their normative commitments.

One of the principal purposes of *Human Rights in Global Politics* is to reflect critically upon the stark contradiction between the idea of universal human rights and practices of human wrongs. To this end, we have brought together a distinguished group of scholars and practitioners to engage with the question: why are there all these human rights standards but the bodies keep piling up? The assumption here is that there is a universal standard of human rights but states fail to live up to it. However, a recurring theme in the volume is the questioning of the foundation of this universal standard. Perhaps another reason for this compliance gap is that political communities interpret universal human rights very differently. On this reading, the explanation for the fifty years' crisis in the human rights regime is expressed succinctly by E. H. Carr: 'the question is not who are the standard-bearers, but *what* is the standard?' Two possible responses suggest themselves. First, different societies 'sign up' to the idea of universal human rights but disagree over the meaning and priority to be accorded to these rights. This intersocietal critique, when wielded by non-liberal states, becomes an assault on the West's understanding of what counts as human rights. Second, and more subversive from a human rights perspective, is whether there is a shared discourse of human rights *per se*. In the course of this Introduction we provide an overview of the explanations given by our contributors for the existence of the compliance gap and their prescriptions for closing it.

The five chapters in Part I of the volume by Booth, Donnelly, Brown, Parekh and Midgley, have two general purposes: first, to critically assess orthodox attempts to justify human rights in terms of grand narratives of reason or nature; second, to evaluate the theoretical possibilities for constructing a form of universal values which is *not* pre-given by either of these narratives. The guiding question is whether human rights practices can exist without presupposing an essential human nature. Part II of the volume provides a detailed empirical investigation of specific practices of global human wrongs, as well as exploring how international human rights norms might be strengthened. Richard Falk, Mary Kaldor, Martin Shaw, Gil Loescher, Georgina Ashworth, and Ken Booth and Tim Dunne focus on the issue areas of genocide, ethnic cleansing, mass murder, refugees, women's human rights, and the right to education, whilst Andrew Hurrell considers the tensions between universalism and particularism in relation to the normative structures of the society of states. With the exception of Hurrell, the contributors to Part II share the view that the compliance gap stems from normative failures on the part of states. Hurrell's questioning of a universal standard brings us back to the importance of the philosophical investigations in the first part of the volume.

Developments in postmodern social and political theory challenge the very quest for moral certainty which underpinned the vision of the post-1945 human rights regime. Postmodernists tell us to be incredulous towards metanarratives such as 'humanity': surely, they argue, the presumption of universal human rights is but another example of Enlightenment mythology. An underlying theme of this volume is to reflect upon the implications for the practice of human rights of the contention, made by postmoderns, that the architecture of the human rights regime has no epistemological warrant for the foundations it assumes.

Historically, the idea of rights has embodied two foundational claims. First, that there is an identifiable subject who has entitlements; and secondly, that to possess a right presupposes the existence of a duty-bearer against whom the right is claimed. R. J. Vincent expresses this relationship with characteristic clarity:

Ontology

		Cultural relativism	Universalism
Epistemology	Anti-foundationalism	Communitarian pragmatism	Cosmopolitan pragmatism
	Foundationalism	Traditional communitarianism	Liberal natural rights

Figure 1. Background social theories of human rights.

A right in this sense can be thought of as consisting of five main elements: a right-holder (the subject of a right) has a claim to some substance (the object of a right), which he or she might assert, or demand, or enjoy, or enforce (exercising a right) against some individual or group (the bearer of the correlative duty), citing in support of his or her claim some particular ground (the justification of a right).[3]

It is this last point, that there is 'some particular ground' upon which rights-holders can justify their claim to rights, which has framed the dominant discourse on human rights.

Figure 1 identifies four key metatheoretical positions in the human rights discourse. The lower-right cell is occupied by natural rights theorists who hold onto the liberal view of human rights as universal rights. The ontological underpinning of this position, as we describe in more detail below, is the belief that morality exists by virtue of our built-in humanity.

The idea of *human* rights, for a liberal natural rights theorist, is that we all have rights by virtue of our common humanity. Individuals have certain kinds of rights as members of particular communities, but human rights belong to humanity and do not depend for their existence on the legal and moral practices of different communities. Thus, even if individuals are denied rights by the laws of a particular state, they still can make a claim to rights by virtue of their membership of common humanity. What, then, philosophically grounds such a claim to universality?

One attempt to furnish a defence of common morality historically has been made by the natural law tradition. At its core, natural law maintains that there is a unity among all peoples of the world irrespective of cultural difference. For Vitoria, writing in the sixteenth century, humankind was governed by natural laws of love and amity. Later society-of-states theorists recognised the intrusion of the 'law of nations' into the idea of a cosmic moral law, but nevertheless hold on to the idea that natural law provides an underlying moral foundation. Whilst classical thinking on natural law placed duties at the centre of its moral deliberations, the challenge for contemporary advocates is to show how natural law can support a theory of universal rights.

Epistemology plays a central role in discerning the content of natural rights. Claims to know what is right are founded on 'those basic precepts of common morality [which] are accessible to human reason, they can be known by anyone capable of thought and action'.[4] Thus, the faculty of reason which is assumed to be transcultural enables individuals to deduce the correct moral code by which to live their lives. This is an appealing idea but the fundamental weakness of 'practical reason' is that it cannot easily explain why moral practices vary within and between cultures.

Recognising that natural law is a problematic justification for human rights, we nevertheless agree with Chris Brown's contention that 'some idea of natural law must underlie all genuinely universal approaches to human rights'.[5] Contemporary liberal universalists like R. J. Vincent and Henry Shue find themselves occupying the same epistemological terrain as the natural law tradition (our lower-right cell) but put rights rather than duties at the centre of their moral reasoning. The kernel of this natural rights position is that all individuals have certain basic rights because they share the same essential human nature. Shue's understanding of 'basic rights' develops out of the idea that without the satisfaction of needs such as 'subsistence' and 'security' it is impossible to enjoy all other rights.[6] However, as Vincent argues, some natural rights thinkers identify 'a second, and deeper, appeal not to our physical but to our moral nature'.[7] 'It is in this context', Vincent continues, 'that human rights are sometimes called "inalienable".'[8]

Liberal natural rights thinking has underpinned the development of the international legal regime on human rights. For evidence of the widespread acceptance of the discourse of 'natural rights', we need look no further than the United Nations Charter which seeks 'to reaffirm faith in fundamental human rights'. Similarly, the Preamble to the 1948 Universal Declaration of Human Rights states that the 'recognition of the inherent dignity and of the equal and inalienable rights of all members of the human family is the foundation of freedom, justice and peace in the world'.[9] The fundamental problem with defending the human rights regime in terms of natural rights thinking is the failure of its advocates to provide a convincing theory of human nature which would ground notions of human dignity.[10]

In chapter 1 of the volume, Ken Booth argues that defending the idea of human rights in terms of a fixed theory of human nature corrupts our thinking about the possibilities for humanity at the end of the millennium. For Booth, the question 'Are human rights universal?' is an unhelpful one because it is too soon in human history to give a definite answer. By locating the subject of human rights at the interface of the disciplines of International Relations and Anthropology, Booth is able to identify three tyrannies that oppress the theory and practice of human rights: 'presentism', 'culturalism' and 'positivism'. 'Presentism' views the social world as natural and immutable, whereas social anthropology tells us that humanity is constantly evolving and that appeals to human nature as the 'clinching argument' are always overturned by changing social relations. This for Booth is the starting point for thinking about the question of the universality of human rights.

The second tyranny is 'culturalism' – the belief that cultures can be black-boxed in the same way that realists in International Relations black-box states. Booth rejects the exclusivity of cultures on the grounds that it privileges traditional values at the expense of emancipatory ones. The claim of cultural authenticity should not be allowed to stop the conversation on human rights anymore than the appeal to a particular view of human nature should close discussion on the possibility of a warless world. In the past, Booth has cautioned against the dangers of ethnocentrism – seeing other cultures through the prism of one's own sense of cultural superiority – but he argues that sensitivity to the cultural values of others should not be allowed to degenerate into the dogma of culturalism.

The idea of emancipation is the only effective escape from regressive human rights thinking but Booth acknowledges that this raises as many questions as it answers. The final part of the chapter tries to answer some of these questions through a critique of the third tyranny of 'objectivity' and a defence of human rights as universal values. The problem with claims to objectivity in the social world is that they naturalise the existing order as given and immutable. As Booth argues, this is threatening to human rights because by leaving power where it is, the daily round of human wrongs is reproduced. Cultural relativists and postmodernists argue for toleration of diversity, but Booth thinks that we should change the focus to asking 'how much diversity should be tolerated?' The people who have to be heard are not governments, journalists or even human rights NGOs; rather, they are the victims of world politics who should be placed at the centre of theory and praxis in world politics. In deciding how much diversity is tolerable in world politics, Booth argues that a good place to start would be to 'ask the victims' whether they want to remain hungry and oppressed. If the answer is no, then he claims that 'there is no intelligible reason for saying "this is not my concern."'

In response to the question of what are the foundations for human rights, Booth follows Geoffrey Warnock and Mary Midgley in asserting that it is wrong to torture, starve, humiliate and hurt others. Human rights are not a matter of opinion, cultural prejudice or one community's story as opposed to another's; they are a response to these 'universal social facts'. These derive, according to Booth, 'from our animal nature (the need for food and shelter) and from our social character and potentiality'. Human rights, then, are an idea whose time has come, and this is reflected in the almost universal acceptance of the language of universal human rights.

Reading the human rights story as part of the moral evolution of the human race is echoed in chapter 2 by Jack Donnelly. Like Booth, Donnelly identifies a critical relationship between the ideas of human rights and human dignity. Historically, societies have secured human dignity through other mechanisms than human rights, but Donnelly shows how the idea of human rights emerged as a specific historical response to the challenges of modernity. Rather than depending upon an ahistorical account of the subject, he advances the claim that human rights arose in the West in the early part of the twentieth century as a way to overcome threats to human dignity posed by repressive political and economic structures.

Donnelly's willingness to side-step the question of how we ground universal human rights reflects his belief, like Booth's, that any attempt to resolve the metaethical foundations of human rights is a distraction. What matters for Donnelly is the 'remarkable international normative consensus on the list of rights'[11] found in the Universal Declaration, the 1966 International Covenants on civil/political, and economic/social rights and the 1993 Vienna Declaration. He supports this contention by appealing to the cross-cultural consensus on basic rights such as 'the rights to life, liberty, security of the person; the guarantee of legal personality; and protections against slavery, arbitrary arrest, detention, or exile and inhuman or degrading treatment'.[12] What further strengthens Donnelly's claim that there is a normative consensus underlying the human rights regime is the fact that in the daily round of diplomacy, state leaders justify their human rights policies in terms of these standards.

Whilst arguing that the various legal instruments which constitute the international bill of rights command 'a remarkable international normative consensus',[13] Donnelly recognises that states do not always uphold these standards. Individuals claim human rights against their state because states are the only bearers of correlative duties, but they frequently fail to fulfil these duties. It is this discrepancy between the human rights commitments of states and their actual practices which Donnelly sees as the central *problématique* of the contemporary human rights regime. The challenge then is to close the gap between the standard embodied in the regime and states' compliance with it. Liberals like Donnelly are cautiously optimistic that the regime can be mobilised by its supporters as a means to pressurise those states which transgress its rules and flout its conventions. Through public censure, promises of rewards for good behaviour, threats of economic sanctions and, ultimately, armed intervention, the society of states has the potential to use human rights as a civilising force against repressive governments.[14]

In stark contrast, Chris Brown argues in chapter 3 that the existence of the standard is itself the problem. Rights, in short, are a consequence of the civilised practices of liberal polities and not the *cause* of these. Therefore, Brown argues forcefully, any attempt by international society to close the compliance gap is a 'near-impossible task'. Brown criticises defenders of the regime from a communitarian perspective which holds that we have rights by virtue of our community and *not* some abstract notion of 'common humanity'. This is an argument that has traditionally been mobilised by cultural relativists, a position represented in the lower-left cell of figure 1. The central claim here is that morality is culturally bound and values can only be grounded in tradition. The idea, then, of individuals possessing inalienable rights which they claim against the state is unthinkable in many societies where the individual is embedded in a complex network of communal duties and familial responsibilities. Following Molly Cochran, we interpret cultural relativism as a form of moral discourse which '*founds* and enables the ethical discourse in which social judgements are possible'.[15]

Cultural relativists are often accused of being unable to judge between competing values. Brown's chapter shows the difficulties that relativists have in responding to this criticism. He argues that whilst 'some kind of lowest common denominator' might be present in diverse cultures, such a moral standard lacks a 'critical cutting edge' because it is reducible to these cultural practices. He qualifies this by recognising that certain human wrongs like genocide and mass murder will be caught by this moral minimalism. Although this 'general moral standard' provides a means to judge and criticise egregious regimes like Hitler's Germany, Pol Pot's Cambodia and Amin's Uganda, Brown argues that it is unable to deal with more routine human rights abuses.

In showing the difficulties that relativists have in criticising other cultures, Brown does not argue for a universalist position. Instead, he seeks to transcend the debate between relativists and universalists by arguing that the problem with both positions is their dependence upon epistemological foundationalism: the problem with universal critiques of relativism is that they assume that there is some non-relativist position upon which to stand. It is this claim which Brown rejects and he does so by drawing on the arguments of the postmodern philosopher Richard Rorty. For a pragmatist like Rorty, the idea that reason or science can access 'justified true belief' (epistemology) is nothing but a myth. Our beliefs are no more than contingent preferences which help us to cope with the complexities of late modern life. Rights, for Rorty, are nothing more than a story that liberal societies have decided to 'tell' and, as a consequence, it is only liberal societies which provide an epistemological context for human rights justifications.

The rejection by pragmatists of all narratives which posit universal truths would appear, at first sight, to sound the death-knell for defenders of human rights. However, Rorty argues that the jettisoning of epistemological foundationalism does not mean that liberals cannot defend human rights values. Rather, he argues that it is 'we twentieth-century liberals' who have the responsibility to nurture and strengthen the 'human rights culture' which is a fact of the post-Holocaust world. Crucially for Rorty, this culture 'seems to owe nothing to increased moral knowledge, and everything to hearing sad and sentimental stories'.[16] What human solidarity depends upon is the manipulation of the sentiments such that 'we liberals' come to realise that our differences with others are less important than our shared capacity to experience pain and suffering. As Brown points out, Rorty's position has nothing to say to those societies which have not undergone a process of 'education of the sentiments'. Thus, Rorty tells us that there is no knockdown argument against those Bosnian Serbs who choose to construct Bosnian Muslims as sub-human. He does not want to call these people inhuman or morally wrong as this implies the existence of a universal human nature; instead, he wants to argue that they have been deprived of the conditions in which to develop feelings of human solidarity. Brown recognises Rorty's position 'does not solve all the problems of relativism' and sentimentality is an 'inadequate' response to human wrongs but reluctantly admits that 'it is difficult to see what other moral vocabulary is available to us once we reach the limits of an ethical community'.

The strength of Brown's position – which we label 'communitarian pragmatism' in figure 1 – is his attempt to hold on to human rights whilst jettisoning their philosophical foundations. What the debate between the upper-left side of figure 1 and the upper-right illustrates is that dispensing with epistemological certainty has not resolved key questions about the nature and limits of an ethical community within which rights claims are situated. Whilst the contours of this new post-pragmatist debate between cosmopolitanism and communitarianism are not as clear-cut as between traditional communitarianism and natural rights theory, the conversation between communitarian and cosmopolitan pragmatism – represented in this volume by Brown on the one hand and Booth, Parekh and Midgley on the other – contributes to recent philosophical reflections on the possibilities for universal values in the wake of the Enlightenment.

In chapter 4, the moral philosopher Bhikhu Parekh argues for a conception of universal values which steers a course between the opposites of moral relativism and foundationalist claims of an essential and knowable human nature. Parekh agrees with Booth that the fundamental problem with relativism is 'that we have no means of judging a society's moral beliefs and practices'. At the opposite pole to relativism stands 'moral monism', a position which maintains that 'we cannot only judge other societies but also lay down what way of life is the highest or truly human' (lower-right cell in figure 1). Parekh finds this equally unsatisfactory because it assumes an essential human nature which can be revealed after the superstructure of cultural embeddedness has been stripped away.

Between these two extremes lies 'minimum universalism' which recognises the fact of moral diversity but believes 'that moral life can be lived in several different ways, but insists that they can be judged on the basis of a universally valid body of values'. He identifies this position with H. L. A. Hart, Michael Walzer, John Rawls, Stuart Hampshire and Martha Nussbaum. Although this theoretical position has more to commend it than the other two, Parekh argues that it does not overcome the following objections. First, it relies on an account of human nature which brings it perilously close to monism; secondly, contrary to Donnelly, it is questionable whether there is a normative consensus on prohibiting even the most cruel and inhumane practices; and thirdly, universal principles are either too abstract or too weak to provide the possibility of judgement across cultures. Parekh is dissatisfied with all three existing approaches, advocating a theory of non-ethnocentric universal values. These, he contends, can only be constructed by means of a dialogue between equals. It is important to pause and reflect on what Parekh means by a dialogue and why we think it represents 'cosmopolitan pragmatism':

The point of a cross-cultural dialogue is to arrive at a body of values to which all the participants can be expected to agree. Our concern is not to discover values, for they have no objective basis, but to agree on them . . . Values are a matter of collective decision, and like any other decision it is based on reasons. Since moral values cannot be rationally demonstrated, our concern should be to build a consensus around those that can be shown to be rationally most defensible.

In emphasising that universal values can have no 'objective basis', Parekh can be located in the top half of figure 1. Universal values *are* possible but have to be decided through argumentation. What he is espousing is a very different position to that articulated by Rorty and Brown who reject the idea that reason can arbitrate between rival validity claims. As we saw in Brown's chapter, communitarian pragmatists can supply us with an account of how we should live, but their justification is only intelligible within the limits of an ethical community. In contrast, Parekh's cosmopolitan pragmatism (upper-right cell) believes it is possible to recognise the reality of cultural embeddedness whilst leaving open the possibility for a transcultural consensus which is more than just 'the lowest common denominator of different cultural traditions'.

How, then, does Parekh try to balance the centrifugal tendencies of ethnocentrism and universalism? Towards the end of the chapter, he shifts the focus to the 'Asian values' debate as a way of exploring how non-foundational universal values can be arrived at through cross-cultural dialogue. In contrast to Booth's critique of the language of 'Asian values', Parekh welcomes the fact that Singapore and China, as participants in the human rights dialogue, bring to the 'table' their own ethnocentric biases. Singapore's challenge to Western values rests upon a defence of a different form of life which privileges communal values over individual rights. Parekh argues that this alternative understanding of human dignity 'is fully consistent with universal values'. By contrast, China's rejection of the fundamental freedoms which underpin the human rights regime, such as free speech, freedom of association and political participation, 'offends' against universal values. The key question here is why is Singapore's ethnocentrism acceptable and China's not? As we have seen above, Parekh wants to differentiate his position from that of minimum universalism but his criteria for judging between the moral practices of Singapore and China seem to rely on a conception of universal values which precedes the dialogue. He argues that there are certain 'universal constants' such as human dignity, worth, equality and fundamental interests which '*generate* appropriate universal values' (our emphasis). If these constants are already built in to the structure of all societies, Parekh's attempt to derive a cosmopolitanism without foundations through dialogue is vulnerable to the criticism that he is presupposing the very foundations which he seeks to deny.

Parekh argues that an outsider's judgement of another society's interpretation of universal values is strengthened if there is internal criticism of the justifications which its own government puts forward. He cites Chinese human rights activists who argue that torture, arbitrary arrest and imprisonment without proper trial are not compatible with the language of universal human rights which Chinese state leaders proclaim. Whilst internal critique adds legitimacy to the West's moral condemnation of China's human rights practices, it raises the broader issue as to whether the criticisms of outsiders are only valid in those situations where values are internally contested. Ultimately, this is not an acceptable position because it denies the validity of outsiders making moral judgements in the absence of internally disputed values and practices.

A good illustration of this problem is the case of Koranic punishments in Islamic societies. The practice of amputation of the right hand for theft is morally abhorrent in the West, but Muslim societies defend this cultural practice on the grounds that however severe the punishment might seem, 'it is in fact extremely lenient and merciful in comparison to what the offender will suffer in the next life should the religious punishment not be enforced in this life'.[17] The Sudanese human rights scholar An-Na'im argues that whilst the values of the Koran are open to interpretation and contestation in relation to some practices, there is no interpretation of Islam which would prohibit this religious punishment for theft. This essentialist view of Islam is open to the critique mobilised by Booth in chapter 1.

An-Na'im argues that Muslim governments see no incompatibility between this cultural practice and their acceptance of the right (embodied in the Universal Declaration and the International Covenants) that 'no one shall be subjected to torture or to cruel, inhuman or degrading treatment'.[18] But if the amputation of limbs is consistent with universal human rights norms, then where does the concession to cultural diversity stop? If the regime is to have any normative force, it must provide an independent moral standard which is not reducible to cultural particularism.

The case of Koranic punishments challenges advocates of cross-cultural dialogue. Whilst such a dialogue would provide an opportunity for Islamic societies to justify their legal practices as being in accord with internationally agreed human rights standards, conversation requires that the participants be open to changing their practices. However, states endorsing Islamic law have been reluctant to reflect critically on their religious practices and this has prevented any meaningful cross-cultural dialogue.

A further area of dispute where ethnocentric biases have hitherto proved resistant to genuine dialogue is that between the United States and China. This issue is emerging as a key foreign policy challenge for the United States at the end of the twentieth century, and it presents scholars working in the human rights field with a case which illustrates the ideological and practical constraints acting upon negotiators. How should we characterise the US/China debate on 'rights'? It is often argued that 'rights talk' is alien to Chinese culture and traditions.[19] An example cited in support of this argument is the radically different social relations found in Chinese society. In place of Western ideas of independence, equality and liberty, Chinese culture has developed a very different set of moral and communal relations emphasising hierarchy, deference and interdependence. This picture of the 'self' which underpins Chinese culture is radically at odds with the West's understanding of what it means to be human. From a Chinese perspective, it does not make sense – so the argument runs – to speak of humanity as an attribute of an individual; rather, 'an individual can only become a human being in community'.[20]

Whilst cultural difference has played some part in shaping China's response to the human rights regime, it is an inadequate explanation. In the first instance, an obvious danger with this line of argument is that it counterposes two distinct and homogeneous 'Chinese' and 'Western' identities. It is not clear that the cultural differences between the USA and China are greater than those which exist between the USA and other non-liberal states which publicly endorse the human rights regime.[21] More to the point, it is up to defenders of difference to show *how* the incorporation of universal human rights into Chinese traditions would undermine their culture.

The belief that China is different led the Beijing government to criticise the discourse of human rights. Their stance was clearly spelt out in a 'White Paper' entitled 'Human Rights in China', published in 1991. It argued that China was a developing country with limited resources and a huge population. For this reason, social turmoil could threaten the people's most important right, 'the right to subsistence'. Although rejecting the emphasis upon civil and political rights, China is at the same time appealing to a collective right to subsistence which is more minimalist than the economic and social rights contained in the Covenant. The implication of this position is that the state has a moral responsibility to curtail individual freedoms and political participation in the name of the higher good of the community. Moreover, China rejected any international criticism of its human rights record since this constituted interference in its internal affairs.

What should we make of these arguments put forward by the Chinese government? China's position is open to two possible interpretations. Either China is part of the dialogue over universal values – albeit advancing a very different conception of what it means to be a human being than in traditional rights-based discourse – or China is using the language of human rights as a foreign policy instrument designed to deflect criticism of the regime (whilst promoting economic interests in the bargain). Even if China is sincere in its aim to promote a particular form of life, it is difficult to see why we should value this type of political order if it 'treats fundamental human rights with contempt'.[22]

The Clinton Administration made it clear that China's human rights practices were unacceptable, but fell short of pursuing a policy of diplomatic and economic isolation. In the aftermath of the UN Human Rights Commission's decision not to debate China's human rights record, Secretary of State Madeleine Albright warned in April 1997 that the United States will continue to 'shine the spotlight' on violators. 'China is changing', she added, 'but the Chinese Government's repression of political dissent has not'.[23] Despite these strong words, the Clinton Administration relegated human rights beneath commercial interests on the foreign policy agenda. Al Gore's visit to China typified the Democrat's Janus-faced attitude to China. Following the agreement to buy Boeing aircraft, worth £425 million, Gore genuflected to his guests with the words 'we are greatly honoured by this order from our valued customer and old friend'.[24] It would be unreasonable to single out the United States for prioritising commercial diplomacy over human rights. Despite the efforts of progressive small states like Denmark to cajole their fellow European Union members into 'getting tough' with China, few European states supported the Danish proposal to censure China at the UN Commission. During the same week that the resolution was rejected, the Chinese premier Li Peng gave a timely speech to the International Chamber of Commerce in Shanghai, in which he dangled the carrot of $300 billion of business opportunities in China before 2000.[25]

Western states might respond to this criticism of elevating commercial interests over human rights concerns by arguing that the two are pulling in the same direction. The idea behind the Clinton policy of 'commercial engagement' is that it is better to trade and criticise a recalcitrant state than to isolate it. This was essentially Clinton's justification for the renewal of China's most favoured nation trade privileges. 'I believe if we were to revoke normal trade status it would cut off our contact with the Chinese people and undermine our influence with the Chinese Government.'[26] Yet this begs the obvious question why Clinton imposed economic sanctions on Burma, which has an equally appalling human rights record to that of China? The US President repeatedly criticised the Burmese government, calling it a 'gangster state' in his keynote address to the ASEAN Regional Forum meeting in Manila in 1997. Critics of this move, particularly in the Asia region, contrast the tough stand against Burma with the lukewarm relations maintained with the equally repressive, albeit far richer, China.[27]

In addition to the above commercial and geopolitical considerations, one further reason why China escaped moral censure at the 1997 Human Rights Commission in Geneva was its muted indication that it might be about to sign the 1966 Covenants. Such a move would be further evidence of China's progressive enmeshment in the human rights discourse. The key turning point here was its decision to sign the 1993 Vienna Declaration on Human Rights. In signing, China consented to Paragraph 3 which states that 'all human rights are universal, indivisible and inter-related'.[28] An important implication of this is that under-development cannot be 'invoked to justify the abridgement of internationally recognised human rights'. By publicly endorsing a position which was at variance with its 1991 White Paper, China has unwittingly left itself open to criticism of its continuing human rights abuses.

China's entanglement in the diplomacy of human rights has had some effects in legitimising human rights practices, but in no way can this interaction be called a dialogue in the sense understood by Parekh. China is playing a tactical game designed to deflect Western threats to its regime, but it shows little sign of fully participating in the post-Cold War conversation on human rights. Evidence in support of this claim can be seen in the statement by the head of the Chinese delegation to the Vienna Conference, Liu Huaqiu, who argued 'one should not and cannot think of the human rights standard and model of certain countries as the only proper ones and demand all other countries to comply with them'.[29] The problem here is that China has signed up to a universal human rights standard at Vienna and at the same time has justified its stance on human rights by claiming there is no standard, and that those who seek to enforce one are playing the game of power politics.

In order to have a dialogue on the content of non-foundationalist universal values, participants must be prepared to reflect critically on whether their human rights practices are 'rationally defensible'. As we have seen from the above, neither Chinese nor Western state leaders have been prepared to empathise with the ethnocentrism of the other. Instead, each party has used the diplomacy of human rights to try and convert the other to its position. What is required is for the United States and China to enter into the conversation in the knowledge that they must be open to changing their position.

How, then, should we respond to states which refuse to enter into a dialogue and which continue systematically to abuse basic rights? Mary Midgley, in chapter 5 argues that the moral vocabulary of human rights provides a compass for finding our way in the world. She argues that public opinion in the West has a responsibility to protest against global human wrongs and that no-one can claim to be an innocent bystander. Although Midgley recognises that there are always limits to the possibilities for ethical conduct, she warns against accepting the 'common sense' of realism with its impoverished conception of the moral imagination. Instead, she argues for an expansion of our moral horizons such that we come to recognise that '[w]e can often do enormously more than we are inclined to claim'.

At the heart of her critique of realism's moral boundaries is the conviction that we all have moral duties to come to the aid of 'distant humans'. Midgley supports this claim by drawing on her own recollections of what it meant to be a concerned citizen living in Britain in the 1930s. The victims of Nazism were not distant strangers in faraway places; rather, their suffering 'mattered to everybody'. Buttressing her belief that there is always space for moral agency, she argues that 'we in the West' should have put more pressure on the Nazi state. The key question raised by Midgley's discussion of the moral implications of the Nazis is of why we should go to the rescue of 'distant humans'? One answer is that we all share a common humanity, but this only brings us back to the philosophical conundrum of how we ground this ethical position. Rorty's communitarian pragmatism (upper-left in figure 1) leads him to argue that the rescuers – those who risked their lives inside Nazi Germany and occupied Europe to save Jews – did not do so because of a belief in a shared humanity but because of more particularist identifications with those whom they rescued.[30] Set against this is the personal testimony of the rescuers that they acted because of a belief that the Jews were their fellow-humans (lower-right in figure 1).[31] The philosophical question of why we have duties to 'distant humans' is important, but the salient fact is that these metatheoretical disputes did not prevent people from becoming rescuers in Nazi Germany.

The experience of the Holocaust – which, in Midgley's words, 'altered the colour of the sky for everyone' – led to the emergence of the global human rights regime. The collective determination to never again repeat the terror of the Nazi death camps led to the signing in 1948 of the Genocide Convention. As with the general language of human rights, the importance of the Convention is that it sharpens our moral awareness and makes us conscious of our responsibilities to 'distant humans'. If the assumption was that the existence of the Genocide Convention would safeguard humankind from this terrible crime, Richard Falk in chapter 6 of the volume argues that the genocidal experiences in Cambodia, Bosnia and Rwanda reveal the hollowness of the cry 'never again'.

The general moral indifference shown by the Western powers to Nazi Germany's treatment of the Jews has been, according to Falk, paradigmatic of the responses of the society of states to the practice of genocide in post-1945 world politics. Despite establishing criminal accountability for political leaders engaging in acts of genocide, international society has not been prepared to pay the price and bear the burden of collective armed intervention to enforce compliance upon those states and political groups breaking the rules of the Convention. Indeed, the terrible tragedy of Rwanda in 1994, where the international community stood by and watched as hundreds of thousands were slaughtered in a matter of weeks, illustrates how far we are away from what Falk has elsewhere called an 'anti-genocide capability and culture'.[32]

The ineffectual response to genocidal politics, argues Falk, is evidence of the 'low priority accorded to moral dimensions of foreign policy by the governments and elites of leading states'. He recognises that armed humanitarian intervention might fail for operational reasons and this could be one of the factors contributing to the reluctance of decision-makers to intervene. However, he rejects this rationale for non-intervention because states have not allowed logistical considerations to prevent them from intervening when important geopolitical interests are at stake.

Falk identifies two key factors which explain the poverty of the moral imagination exhibited by statist elites. The first is the grip of the realist mind-set on policy-makers which limits armed intervention to instances where strategic interests are paramount. This might have helped the people of Kuwait in the oil-rich Persian Gulf, but it left millions in Cambodia, Burundi, Bosnia and Rwanda to perish.

The second factor contributing to the persistence of genocidal politics is the deleterious effect of the global market on the moral capacities of governments and civil societies. Falk worries that the impact of globalisation is narrowing our moral horizons by reducing 'the overall capacity and will of governments to address human wrongs either within their own society or elsewhere'. If Falk's prognosis is correct, economic globalisation is likely to compel societies to turn inwards thereby depleting the resources that can be devoted to the amelioration of poverty and malnutrition on a global scale. The slow death of millions in the South who are deprived of basic subsistence rights has been named the 'holocaust of neglect' by Henry Shue, and Falk's chapter alerts us to the importance of widening our category of genocidal politics to include these victims of global human wrongs.

In the face of these powerful ideological barriers against the development of an ethical foreign policy, Falk follows Booth and Midgley in arguing that 'moral purpose' must be injected into foreign policy decision-making. Here, he identifies an important role for global civil society in promoting values of human rights, non-violence and democracy as a counter to the hegemonic ideologies of realism and *laissez-faire* economics.

The role of transnational civil society in holding state leaders and political groups accountable for their exercise of power is the theme which Mary Kaldor addresses in chapter 7. She focuses on the changing role of transnational civil society in the 1980s and 1990s. Her central thesis is that having achieved the liberalisation of authoritarian state structures in Eastern Europe through the process of 'detente from below', the challenge facing transnational civil society in the 1990s is how to cope with the human suffering produced by the collapse of state structures brought about by the triumph of ethnic and exclusivist conceptions of identity.

The starting point for 'detente from below' was the 1975 Helsinki Final Act. At the time, the Soviet Union's signing of the human rights provisions of Basket 3 was seen as little more than a rhetorical commitment. However, as Kaldor shows, what the Soviet Union and its Eastern European allies interpreted as 'paper commitments' were pivotal in legitimising the human rights struggle of groups like Charter 77 in Czechoslovakia, KOR in Poland and the Democratic Opposition in Hungary. Furthermore, the emergence of the Peace Movement in Western Europe added a further transnational impetus to this process. The opposition groups in East-Central Europe, and the peace activists in the West, developed a dialogue based on the shared values of dismantling the militarised structures of the Cold War and developing democratic forms of politics. Kaldor argues that it was transnational social movements which made possible the emergence of Gorbachev, which in turn facilitated the revolutions of 1989 and the ending of the Cold War.

In her chapter, Kaldor makes a convincing case for the capacity of transnational social movements to civilise state institutions. Whilst this was decisive in dismantling the Iron Curtain, she argues that these agents were ineffective in stopping the descent into barbarism in the former Yugoslavia. She points out that before war broke out in Bosnia in April 1992 there were groups and individuals committed to the defence of civic values across the former Yugoslavia, but these supporters of civil society could not survive without the protection afforded by the rule of law.

Like Midgley, Kaldor believes that the language of human rights is a powerful tool in promoting the rights of distant humans, but she argues that we need to add to human rights the idea of civil society because it makes concrete the idea of 'individual responsibility for respect of human rights through political action'. But if the lesson of the war in Bosnia is that local supporters of civic values can only succeed if they have 'outside support and access to those international organisations that can influence governments', Kaldor leaves unanswered the question of how the voices of the victims of ethnic and political violence are to be heard in the foreign offices of the leading Western states.

This is the central issue which is investigated by Martin Shaw in chapter 8 of the volume. His point of departure is a comparison between the zone of contentment in the West, where war has become virtually unthinkable, and the series of humanitarian crises which have afflicted large parts of the developing world as a consequence of state disintegration and civil war. Shaw agrees with Falk that left to their own devices, Western states will not intervene for humanitarian reasons unless there are clear strategic interests at stake. However, Shaw's thesis is that where there is extensive television coverage of human suffering, Western governments will come under pressure to come to the aid of innocent civilians.

In support of this argument, the main body of his chapter focuses on the rationale for the international rescue of the Kurds. The initial position of the United States and British governments was that they were not responsible for the fate of the Kurds after their failed uprising. In the course of the unfolding refugee crisis, Western state leaders were forced to shift their ground. None of this would have been possible, Shaw argues, without the mobilising power of television which 'took up the plight of the Kurds in an unprecedented campaign which successfully forced governments' hands'. Bush and Major tried to act as though they did not have responsibility for what was happening in the mountains of Northern Iraq, but television journalists were determined to hold these leaders accountable for the consequences of their actions during the war and their incitement to the Iraqi people to revolt against Saddam. It was this exposure by television of the contradiction between their words and deeds which led Major and Bush to move decisively behind the calls for intervention.

In arguing that it was the televisual media and not newspapers or transnational social movements which constituted the Western intervention in northern Iraq, Shaw recognises that television as a medium for representing victims has important limitations. The most basic is that television depends upon the presence of journalists. Where were the cameras, Shaw asks, when the Iraqi Republican Guard brutally suppressed the Shi'ite rebellion? Or scores of other long-term humanitarian crises which did not receive televisual attention, such as the civil wars in Tadjikistan, Georgia, Angola, Liberia and Sierra Leone? The presence of television journalists is clearly a key factor in mediating responses to human suffering, but extensive coverage of the atrocities in Bosnia did not lead Western governments to intervene militarily. This suggests that televisual coverage is a necessary but not a sufficient condition for governments to intervene. A second limitation is that television rarely allows the victims of global human wrongs to speak for themselves. Rather, as in the case of the Kurds, it is the 'authoritative voices' of foreign journalists who determine whether and how victims are represented. The cries for help on the part of Kurdish refugees, trapped and dying on the Iraqi–Turkish border, were heard because their plight was a direct consequence of Western intervention in Iraq. But as Gil Loescher reminds us in chapter 9, the refugee crisis in northern Iraq in 1991 represents the tip of the iceberg of the global challenge posed by the millions of asylum-seekers and internally displaced peoples.

Loescher charts the development of the international refugee regime from its inception in 1951, showing how the United Nations High Commission for Refugees (UNHCR) has broadened its mandate beyond individual asylum-seekers to include groups seeking third-party resettlement who have been dispossessed from their homelands because of armed conflict. Loescher argues that a major challenge facing the regime in the 1990s is the problem of peoples who are trapped within their state in war-torn societies. Traditionally, UNHCR has tried to settle refugees in third countries. But the scale of the current refugee problem, the growing unwillingness of Western governments to accept asylum-seekers, and the fact that the internally displaced do not qualify for refugee status has forced UNHCR to search for new ways of coping with this crisis.

The new approach of UNHCR, discussed in the chapter, is to resolve the internal conflicts and severe human rights abuses which produce a refugee crisis. However, Loescher is not optimistic about UNHCR succeeding in this crisis prevention role. It lacks the resources, logistics, training and expertise necessary, and requires the support of governments which remain jealous of their sovereign prerogatives. Additionally, Western states are reluctant to invest money in long-term programmes designed to prevent conflict and promote development in war-torn societies. Instead, they seem to prefer to cope with humanitarian emergencies when they occur. But the effect of this is to channel the scarce resources of the international donor community into emergency short-term aid which addresses the symptoms of violent conflict but does little to tackle its underlying causes.

The way forward, Loescher argues, is for UNHCR to recognise that the problem of refugees cannot be separated from those of human rights, economic development, international security, and migration. In particular, he argues that the existing human rights machinery needs to be strengthened and applied more effectively to deal with refugees, particularly with regard to state compliance with the 1951 Convention. However, the increasing emphasis on short-term emergency aid has ensured that no extra funds have been provided for the UN's human rights regime 'despite its potential to strengthen civil society, promote democratic and pluralistic institutions and procedures and, thereby, to prevent human rights abuses and mass displacements'.

To compensate for their unwillingness to incur the costs of developing an integrated approach to the global refugee crisis, donor governments increasingly fund NGOs to act as agents of humanitarian relief and development, as well as contribute to early-warning human rights monitoring and conflict prevention. Loescher recognises the value of NGOs as agents of humanitarian assistance, protection, mediation and conflict resolution, but cautions more generally against too much faith being placed in the preventative approach to the global refugee crisis. He is worried that the belief that the problem can be addressed at source will reinforce the growing practice of Western governments to see 'asylum-seekers as an unwanted burden and as an unnecessary inconvenience'.

This view of asylum-seekers confirms Richard Falk's prognosis that economic globalisation is producing 'compassion fatigue' on the part of Western states and societies. The asylum-seeker is a distant human who has now become the stranger knocking at the door. The response of the 'culture of contentment' to these victims of global human wrongs shows the limits of Rorty's idea of 'sentimental education' because our moral imaginations are failing to realise 'what it is like to be in her situation – to be far from home, among strangers'. It is instructive that Rorty should talk about 'her', because the majority of refugees *are* women, and the tragic fact is that many of these suffer physical and sexual abuse at border crossings from those charged with responsibility to protect them.

But as Georgina Ashworth shows in chapter 10, it is not only refugee women who are violated and treated as sub-human. Rather, ordinary women are victims of a gender bias in global politics which produces systematic violations of their rights. In addition to suffering the same kinds of human wrongs that are inflicted upon men, many women are victims of specific crimes such as enforced prostitution, domestic violence, rape (including rape in war) and physical (or emotional) mutilation. Given the widespread practices of physical violence against women, graphically portrayed by Ashworth, it is perhaps not surprising that feminists claim that 'violence against women is perhaps the most pervasive yet least recognised human rights abuse in the world'.[33]

What explanations does Ashworth provide for the screaming silences of the regime in the face of this litany of human rights abuses towards women? As the opening sentence of her chapter suggests, one of the enduring problems has been the assumption that 'human rights are gender neutral' (an assumption which is severely undermined by the list of gender-based human wrongs). Added to the presumption of neutrality in the regime itself is the persistent silencing of women's voices in mainstream academic approaches to politics, sociology, economics and law. In recent years, however, Ashworth recognises that women's human rights issues are beginning to be heard, in part as a consequence of the interdisciplinary dialogue which many feminist academics have pioneered across the social sciences.

In the body of the chapter, Ashworth points to the progressive coalitions which women's human rights groups have forged, and the relative success they have had in articulating the need for a gender-sensitive regime. For feminist human rights activists, the prime objective is to expose the contradictions between the Universal Declaration's claim to universality and the specific practices of human rights abuses against women, thereby bringing these violations within the remit of the human rights regime. What is particularly important about the story Ashworth tells is the immanent possibilities which exist for transnational social movements to cajole the UN regime into bringing the regime into line with its own standards. An example of this is the way in which NGOs like CHANGE pressurised the regime in the Vienna Declaration to recognise the human rights of women and the girl child as an 'inalienable, integral and indivisible part of universal human rights'.[34]

The victories that women's human rights groups achieved in Vienna, and more recently at the World Conference on Women in Beijing, must be tempered with the recognition that there are more battles to be won. NGOs will play a crucial role in monitoring the new gendered dimension of human rights in the daily practices of states and international institutions. The question of state compliance with human rights norms is an issue taken up by Andrew Hurrell in chapter 11. Human rights concerns are often subordinated to other foreign policy goals, but Hurrell argues that governments find it increasingly difficult to ignore their human rights obligations. The human rights regime, he argues, works through the 'mobilisation of shame' on the part of governments, NGOs and domestic groups fighting for human rights. The effect of this, Hurrell argues, is to make states increasingly sensitive to 'reputational concerns'. He points to China's carrot-and-stick strategy which it employed to avoid censure at the UN Commission on Human Rights.

An important debate at the end of the Cold War concerns the question of whether the society of states should coercively enforce compliance with the human rights standard. A key development here is the way in which the UN Security Council is, in the 1990s, defining human rights abuses and humanitarian concerns as a threat to 'international peace and security' thereby legitimising coercive intervention under Chapter VII of the UN Charter. Whilst UN authority has provided a degree of legitimacy for armed intervention, Hurrell is sensitive to the criticisms of many non-Western states about the risks of double-standards and of self-interest being cloaked in humanitarian garb. He argues that recent collective interventions illustrate the trade-off between 'short-term effectiveness' measured in terms of the relief of human suffering and the dangers of 'a long-term erosion of legitimacy'. The chapters by Falk, Kaldor, Shaw, Loescher and Ashworth in Part II of the book share the underlying belief that the problem of global human wrongs stems from the failure of statist elites to comply with the global human rights standard. However, Hurrell's chapter returns us to the central *problématique* discussed in Part I: is the claim to universality masking the particular interests and values of its exponents, and is it increasingly contested as a consequence of the rise of new power centres in world politics? Hurrell explores this question in terms of the relationship between human rights and power in the debate between the West and Asia.

He argues that the 'Asian values' challenge to the West reflects the growth of the economic and political power of states like China, Malaysia and Singapore, which interpret human rights concerns on the part of the West as a manoeuvre in the competition for relative gains. Even if the discourse of Asian values is 'manipulated and abused by governments' as part of traditional power politics, Hurrell argues that the debate reveals 'real and genuine conflicts over the nature of human rights'. As a consequence he suggests that instead of worrying about the 'foundations' of our human rights claims, we should 'build on and develop the human rights culture and community that has evolved in practice – the element of consensus visible in the actual practice of states'.

In searching for a human rights culture without foundations, Hurrell is explicitly recognising the impact that postmodernism has had on the contemporary human rights debate. His acceptance of this, and the fact of cultural heterogeneity places Hurrell towards the upper-left corner of our matrix. The only values which morally divergent states can agree on are the norms of sovereignty and non-intervention. Like Hedley Bull, Hurrell is dissatisfied with the limits of a pluralist conception of international morality, and looks to the possibility of moving to a more solidarist society of states. A key component of this vision is that state leaders should act as 'guardians of human rights everywhere'.[35] But the question which Hurrell leaves unanswered is how can the society of states deal with 'gangster' states unless it is prepared to condemn those who commit human rights abuses behind the walls of sovereignty.

ASEAN's decision in 1997 to accept Burma into its regional forum despite extensive pressure from the United States and the European Union illustrates the moral limitations of a pluralist society of states. Western states argued that Burma's human rights record should disqualify it from admission, but this was countered by a number of ASEAN member states on the grounds that the primary rule of the organisation was the right of each member state to sovereign jurisdiction. The metaphor often invoked by ASEAN state leaders, when under pressure from Western states, is that all member states agree not to peer into each other's 'back yard'.

A further problem with Hurrell's contention is suggested by Parekh earlier in this volume. As we have seen, Parekh's notion of a human rights dialogue assumes all participants try to empathise with the ethnocentric biases of their partners. In allowing sovereignty and non-intervention to trump substantive values, Hurrell is leaving open the possibility that conversationalists will veto any moves towards a consensus which offends against their cultural predilections and interests.

Although Hurrell's attempt to build bridges between procedural and substantive conceptions of legitimacy is problematic, he provides a more convincing account than Parekh of why the Asian values debate has become a prominent issue at the end of the Cold War. Drawing on a tradition of thinking about the practices of statecraft, Hurrell alerts us to the constant intrusion of power in shaping the contours of moral discourse in international society. Hurrell cites Singapore's spokesman for foreign affairs, Kishore Mabhubani, who commented in 1995 that 'All human rights covenants were created when the West was in power'. A precondition for a genuine dialogue is equality, according to Parekh, but the Asian values debate illustrates the limits of an ideal conversation in the hierarchy of states.

The theoretical and empirical investigations into the possibility of a diplomatic dialogue on human rights is predicated on the assumption that states have agency. This returns us to Jack Donnelly's central contention that the only duty-bearing agents are states, but this assumes that states which fail to comply with human rights norms can be pressurised into changing their behaviour. What is interesting about the final part of Hurrell's chapter is the suggestion that the traditional approach to viewing the state as violator needs to take on board that the culpability 'of state authorities may be difficult to demonstrate, or may indeed be wholly absent'.

If we cannot rely on states to combat human wrongs, either because they are the problem (the view espoused by Booth and to some extent Falk) or because they may not be *able* to be the solution (Hurrell), then we are driven back to considering the emancipatory potential of transnational civil society (Kaldor, Shaw, Ashworth). What sustains the latter is an active citizenry campaigning for cosmopolitan values. In the concluding chapter of the volume, Ken Booth and Tim Dunne examine the role that education can play in sustaining these values. They open their discussion by pointing to the link between education and promoting the 'good life' which has been an undercurrent in Western philosophy since Plato; virtuous citizens of the cosmopolis *had* to be educated in philosophy and ethics. With the rise of modernity, pedagogy has increasingly been redefined as a process where technical knowledge is imparted rather than discovered through an intellectual encounter. Booth and Dunne argue that this spirit needs to be revived if generations of students are going to grow up believing in universal human rights values.

From the outset, education has been an important part of the human rights regime. Article 26 of the Universal Declaration proclaimed that education was a universal human right, a commitment which has been refined in subsequent human rights documents. The regime goes beyond stipulating a right to an education in so far as it begins to adumbrate the need for an education *in* human rights. By this, the UN system means the promotion of 'understanding', 'tolerance', 'respect for fundamental freedoms' and 'friendship'. In other words, to conform to the spirit of the regime, states would have to promote human rights values in the curriculum as well as meet the standards for provision embodied in the regime. Booth and Dunne make a persuasive case for thinking about both aspects of the regime instead of the traditional emphasis upon the provision (rather than the content) of education.

Consistent with many of the contributions to this volume, the concluding chapter on education and human rights illustrates the contradiction between the host of principles, declarations, conventions and programmes of action, and the stark fact that there are almost 1 billion people in the world who are illiterate. In addition to the problem of compliance, there is also the question addressed by Booth, Brown, Parekh and Midgley, as to how we promote *universal* values in a deeply divided world. The latter part of the conclusion defends a form of ethnocentrism because education, like all ideas and values, must be a view from somewhere. But crucially, Booth and Dunne argue that a key requirement of such an education is to avoid the parochialism and intolerance that a sense of cultural difference can breed. Building on the arguments of contributors to the volume, the authors offer a list of cosmopolitan values which they believe to be integral to nurturing a global human rights culture.

Notes

1 R. J. Vincent, *Human Rights and International Relations* (Cambridge University Press, 1986), p. 152.
2 *Amnesty International Annual Report 1997* (London: Amnesty International, 1997).
3 Vincent, *Human Rights*, p. 8. Vincent acknowledges his debt for this definition to Alan Gewirth.
4 Joseph Boyle, 'Natural law and international ethics', in Terry Nardin and David R. Mapel (eds.), *Traditions of International Ethics* (Cambridge University Press, 1992), p. 129.
5 Chris Brown, 'Universal human rights: a critique', this volume, p. 106.
6 Henry Shue, *Basic Rights: Subsistence, Affluence, and US Foreign Policy* (Princeton University Press, 1980), pp. 18–22.
7 Vincent, *Human Rights*, p. 14.
8 *Ibid.*
9 Antonio Cassese, *Human Rights in a Changing World* (Cambridge: Polity Press, 1990), p. 189.
10 This argument is traced in Jack Donnelly, *Universal Human Rights in Theory and Practice* (Ithaca: Cornell University Press, 1989), p. 23.
11 *Ibid.*
12 *Ibid.*, p. 122.
13 *Ibid.*, p. 23.
14 Jack Donnelly, 'Human rights: old scepticisms, new standards', *International Affairs* 47 (1998): 1–25.

15 Molly Cochran, 'Cosmopolitanism and communitarianism in a post-Cold War world', in Andrew Linklater and John Macmillan (eds.), *Boundaries in Question* (London: Pinter, 1995), p. 48. Emphasis added.

16 Richard Rorty, 'Human rights, rationality and sentimentality', in Stephen Shute and Susan Hurley (eds.), *On Human Rights: The Oxford Amnesty Lectures* (New York: Basic Books, 1993), p. 133.

17 Abdullahi Ahmed An-Na'im, 'Toward a cross-cultural approach to defining international standards of human rights: the meaning of cruel, inhuman, or degrading treatment or punishment', in An-Na'im (ed.), *Human Rights in Cross-Cultural Perspectives: A Quest for Consensus* (Philadelphia University Press, 1992), p. 35.

18 Article 5 of the Universal Declaration of Human Rights and Article 7 of the International Covenant of Civil and Political Rights. Quoted in An-Na'im, 'Toward a cross-cultural approach', p. 41.

19 In 1991, the Chinese government produced a paper which sought to justify their opposition to the discourse of universal human rights. It was claimed that '[o]wing to tremendous differences in historical background, social system, cultural tradition and economic development, countries differ in their understanding and practice of human rights'. *Human Rights in China* (Beijing: Foreign Languages Press, 1991), vol. I, p. 2, footnote 2.

20 Roger T. Ames, 'Continuing the conversation on Chinese human rights', *Ethics and International Affairs* 11 (1997): 177–205, at 193.

21 We are defining 'publicly endorse' to mean the signing and ratification of the 1966 International Covenants.

22 See Amnesty International, 'China: No One is Safe', report on China, 26 April 1997, p. 1. This report provides extensive documentation of Chinese human rights abuses.

23 'Albright vows to maintain rights ire', *Sydney Morning Herald*, 17 April 1997.

24 'Gore China trip reaps trade bounty', *Electronic Telegraph*, 26 March 1997.

25 This was said to be an important factor in Australia's failure to back the resolution. See 'When it comes to pressure, Beijing has the (trade) numbers', *Sydney Morning Herald*, 12 April 1997.

26 'Trade rewards for human rights reversal', *Sydney Morning Herald*, 22 May 1997.

27 The US government tried to prevent Burma's inclusion in ASEAN. The State Department spokesman, Nick Burns, put the US position clearly: 'We're trying to use our influence with the ASEAN partners to make the point that Burma should be given a stiff message that it's not welcome.' *Sydney Morning Herald*, 28 April 1997.

28 See Vienna Declaration And Programme of Action, 25 June 1993, p. 6.

29 Quoted in James T. H. Tang, *Human Rights and International Relations in the Asia Pacific* (London: Pinter, 1995), p. 214.

30 Richard Rorty, *Contingency, Irony and Solidarity* (Cambridge University Press, 1989), pp. 189–98.

31 See Tony Kushner, *The Holocaust and the Liberal Imagination: A Social and Cultural History* (Oxford: Blackwell, 1994); Norman Geras, *Solidarity and*

the *Conversation of Humankind: The Ungrounded Liberalism of Richard Rorty* (London: Verso, 1995), pp. 7–43; and Samuel P. Oliner and Pearl M. Oliner, *The Altruistic Personality: Rescuers of Jews in Nazi Europe* (New York: Free Press, 1992).

32 Richard Falk, 'The lesson of Bosnia', in *The UN's War* (special issue of the Balkan War Report), p. 27.

33 Lori Hesse, 'Violence against women: the missing agenda', in M. Koblinsky, J. Timyan and J. Gay (eds.), *The Health of Women* (Boulder: Westview Press, 1993), p. 171.

34 See Vienna Declaration and Programme of Action, 25 June 1993, para. 18 of the Preamble.

35 The term is Hedley Bull's. See H. Bull 'The Grotian conception of international society', in Martin Wight and Herbert Butterfield (eds.), *Diplomatic Investigations* (London: Allen and Unwin, 1966).

Part I

Theories of human rights

1   Three tyrannies

Ken Booth

Another race is only an other, strolling
on the far side of our skin, badged with his weather

Carol Rumens

A few weeks after the conference which led to this book I was in
Cracow, south-east Poland, unable to sleep. My insomnia had less to
do with how I thought I would feel in the morning – as a day-tourist in
Auschwitz – than with the noise being made by a succession of student
revellers in the street below. By a strange coincidence, one of the books
I picked up to pass the time contained the poem 'Outside Oswiecim' by
Carol Rumens, two of whose lines are quoted above.[1] In a few words
she gives poetic legitimisation to the point of my paper at the conference from which this chapter is derived. In her rejection of the fashionable definite article and capitalisation (*The Other*) in favour of the lower
case and indefinite article (*an other*), Rumens is rejecting the politics of
the concentration camp in favour of a common humanity ontology, *an
other* regarding politics. It is an inclusivist rather than an exclusivist
view of being human, human being. *The Other* is an alien: *an other* is all
of us. Words – even small words like definite and indefinite articles –
can be tyrants; they can both kill and set free. Who we are and what we
might become is in a word. Whether one was inside or outside Auschwitz
at a certain period, permanently, was in a word.

The purpose of this chapter is to discuss the language of human
rights, and in particular three tyrannies in the way we conceive, approach and talk about human rights. The discourse of human rights is
potentially crucial to human history because it is part of the language of
the human species' self-creating emancipation from natural and societal
threats. There are well-known difficulties in according rights such centrality in the human story. They are neither a panacea for overcoming
injustice nor do they exhaust ethical possibilities; duty and responsibility also have a place.[2] Nevertheless, I believe that the self-interest inherent in the idea of entitlements is better calculated to encourage reciprocity

Table 1. *The three tyrannies*

Tyranny	Danger	Escape
The present tense ('presentism')	Common sense	Sociality theory
Cultural essentialism ('culturalism')	Traditionalism	Emancipation
Scientific objectivity ('positivism')	Relativism	Universality

and the extension of moral obligation, especially across borders, than appeals to duty and responsibility at this stage of global history.

I will label the three tyrannies around which the chapter is organised the tyranny of the present tense ('presentism'), the tyranny of cultural essentialism ('culturalism') and the tyranny of scientific objectivity ('positivism'). Together, these constitute sets of attitudes, almost an ideology, which imprison human rights potentialities in a static, particularist and regressive discourse, reproducing prevailing patterns of power rather than the reinvention of the politics of human possibility. In place of this negative ideology – whose proponents, ironically, tend to have a self-image of sense, sensitivity and sophistication – I want to argue for a discourse of human rights embedded in the potentialities of human sociality, a politics of emancipation, and a philosophy of universality. The framework for the chapter is summarised in table 1.

The tyranny of the present tense

In this section I want specifically to address the historical implication of the 'common sense' view that human rights are reflections of what is often seen as the so-called human condition – a world made up of people(s) with essentially 'tribal souls'.[3] Human rights from this perspective derive from communitarian values; not only is this so, but it must be the case, for rights can only develop on the bedrock of the values of distinct ethical communities. This view attacks the very heart of the idea of universal human rights, asserting that – because we do not have a 'universal ethical community' we cannot have 'universal human rights'. One counter is sociality theory. Sociality exposes and emphasises the openness of human social potential; it challenges the assertive *is*, with its implications both of a full knowledge of the world ('we describe the world as it is') and of timelessness ('this is how it is').

The provocation to think of the present tense as a *tyranny* when discussing International Relations came from reading Michael Carrithers' book, *Why Humans Have Cultures. Explaining Anthropology and Social Diversity.*[4] He describes the problems in anthropological work caused by phrasing disclosures about societies in the present tense (what he calls the 'ethnographic present'). This tendency, which became well established before the Second World War, came to be called 'presentist', and was associated with the adoption of ahistorical perspectives on societies and cultures. It was subsequently criticised for underestimating the complexity of the social world, for producing unfruitful generalisations, for disregarding the historical character of social experience, and for reducing the understanding of human relatedness across the globe. I want to argue that presentism has had a similar impact on human rights thinking, and that it should be criticised for a similar range of reasons.[5]

Running through Carrithers' argument is his belief that anthropologists have thought too much in terms of humans as animals with cultures, and not enough as animals with history.[6] This has revealed itself in the tendency of anthropologists to represent cultures in the present tense, as was evident, for example, in the study of his own special interest, the ancient Hindu sect of the Jains. 'Jains do this and Jains do that', he reports some anthropologists as saying, a formulation which easily leads to the belief that Jains have always done this and have always done that. Carrithers' own work has shown that this has not necessarily been the case. We can see exactly the same tendency in the way some people talk about human rights: they look around, and observe that humans do this and humans do that – usually focusing on the nastier side of human behaviour – which then quickly leads them to the conclusion that humans have always done this and have always done that – and always will.

The tyranny of presentism, which produces and reproduces ahistorical perspectives in both Anthropology and human rights, can be countered by adopting a macro-historical approach. The latter underlines the persistence of change. Historical anthropology shows that each society reproduces itself, but not as an exact copy. We inherit scripts, but we have scope – more or less depending on who, when and where we are – to revise them. The result, in Carrithers' words, is that:

We had thought that humans were just animals with cultures . . . intelligent, plastic, teachable animals, passive and comfortable to the weight of tradition. Now we see that humans are also active, they are also animals with history. They are inventive and profoundly social animals, living in and through their relations with each other and acting and reacting upon each other to make new relations and new forms of life.[7]

These brief points emphasise the mutability of human experience – plasticity, change, temporality, metamorphosis, interactivity – all related to the sociality wired into the consciousness of the human animal. It is from this perspective, thinking of humans as 'animals with history' rather than from the perspective of temporal parochialism as well as ethnocentrism, that we should contemplate the question: 'Are human rights universal?'

The best response to such a question is to refuse to start from here (this place, this time). How do we know whether human rights are universal? It is too soon in history to say. Once we start thinking along these lines, future history becomes more open; if at the same time we begin to recognise how open it was in the past – and not allow our knowledge of the historical outcome to dominate our understanding of the possibilities at the beginning – then our perspective on human rights should alter radically. The key move is to anthropologise and historicise human rights, and to see the culture of human rights as one aspect of our species' cultural evolution. To do otherwise is to be oppressed by presentism, and its twin, ethnocentrism, and so miss the potential open-endedness of politics and the freedom inherent in human consciousness.

But there is yet a more fundamental counter than macro-history to the problems of presentism and that is sociality theory. At the very beginning of his book Carrithers puts together two questions. The first is that of Socrates: 'How should one live?' The second is that of the anthropologist: 'How do we live together?'[8] Underlying one's answers to these questions must be one's assumptions about the capability of humans to make history, including human rights. For physical anthropologists a century ago it was race that lay at what Gananath Obeyesekere called the 'muddy bottom' of human nature.[9] Then came culture. My own preference is what Carrithers calls a 'mutualist' view of what makes our history, which stresses sociality, defined as 'a capacity for complex social behaviour'. From this perspective, sociality trumps culture, civilisations, race and other candidates for being at the 'muddy bottom' of social behaviour.

The record of the past 2.5 million years, since the early hominids began to invent responses to the world rather than act solely through biological instinct, confirms in myriad ways that complex social behaviour is so basic as to be definable as natural. And because it is so basic, change has been an inevitable consequence. So we must agree with Carrithers that we should place 'change, not permanence, at the centre of our vision'.

Presentism produces conservativism by constraining our political imaginations, and by encouraging us to generalise from an historical moment. If, as students of International Relations, we lift our eyes above the traditional skyline of our subject ('International Relations Since

1945' or, at best, 'International Politics in the Twentieth Century') and instead look at the evolution of life on earth, what becomes immediately striking is 'the incessant mutability of human experience [and] the temporality woven into all human institutions and relationships'.[10] Macro-history should teach us to expect radical surprises. Scholars in feudal Europe did not conceive a world organised around the political identity of nationhood, and peasants in the Age of the Divine Rights of Kings could not dream that one day they would help choose their ruler by marking an X on a ballot paper. Politically speaking, one generation's truth becomes a not-very-distant relative's historical curiosity. The rise and spread of nations, democracy and sovereignty illustrates the mutability of human experience and the temporality of institutions.

The human race, in evolutionary time, has only just begun. To try and predict whether human rights will universally strike deep roots in practice as well as theory is the equivalent of predicting who will win a race, just after its start. Furthermore, in this case, the answer must depend on the weight of future responses given to the normative question of Socrates: how should we live – in this case globally? For the past fifty years a struggle for hegemony has taken place between communitarian common sense, with its conservative power, and proponents of universalist conceptions of human rights.[11] Since 1945 the hegemonic ideology in the discipline of International Relations has been political realism, which of course has not been comfortable with the idea of human rights, while the hegemonic idea in global power politics, since recorded time, has been communitarian not cosmopolitan.[12] Together, these forces have created the context in which human rights get thought about and practised.

The preceding discussion about presentism is not meant to lead to any teleological conclusion about history, such as the triumph of universal human rights. It has been a ground-clearing argument, to try to establish several points before we can talk more sensibly about human rights on a global scale. The argument has tried to show that change is the only constant in human society; that humans are capable of enormous social diversity; and that the political and intellectual hegemony to date has favoured communitarian rather than cosmopolitan versions of politics. The argument is not that a strong universal rights culture will happen, only that there are no grounds – historically or anthropologically – for saying that it will not. Sociality theory demonstrates the human potentiality for complex social relations, and it remains to be seen what this might mean, worldwide, under conditions of globalisation and the radically different material conditions of the decades ahead. Presentism is the tyranny of an ahistorical, indeed anti-historical human rights discourse, which serves traditionalist values and power structures by promoting communitarian common sense. From the perspective of historical humanity we are not destined, as a species, to be what we are; rather, we might be what we strive to become. Race is not the muddy bottom of the human story; 'human nature' is not a clinching argument about how we might live; 'tribal souls' are social constructs; communitarian philosophies are only snapshots; and cultures are the means not the mover, and so cannot be allowed to have the last word. Nevertheless, the tyranny of the present tense continues to produce the kind of communitarian common sense which can be expressed by adapting an equation of Yehezkel Dror from Strategic Studies, namely: Is equals Was equals Will Be.[13] Snapshots are turned into timeless definitions of the human condition. I want to argue that the futures made possible by sociality will always trump the temporality of any communitarian political theory. Political and communitarian common sense comes and goes; sociality is the only permanent 'is'.

The tyranny of cultures

The tyranny of cultures expresses itself as culturalism, by which I mean the reduction of social and political explanations to culture and to the black-boxing of cultures as exclusivist identity-referents. There have been many factors contributing to this tendency, in the worlds of politics and academic inquiry. With regard to the latter, Anthropology has historically positioned itself against the idea of universal values by its methodological localism – what Richard Wilson calls its 'prolonged love affair with local culture' and Jack Donnelly calls a 'radical cultural relativism' in which 'culture' becomes the supreme ethical value and 'sole source of the validity of a moral right or rule'.[14] There is an obvious comparison between this culture-centric outlook and state-centric perspectives in orthodox International Relations. Culturalism is a strong form of the interrelated approaches of cultural essentialism (or reductionism), cultural determinism and cultural relativism. It turns culture – or cultures – into the trump card in any debate about human rights, or indeed world politics.

What is emphasised by culturalism is the uniqueness and exclusivity of each culture. Cultures are (more or less) carefully studied from a holistic perspective, in terms of their particular social logics, cultural rhythms and world-view. As a counter to ethnocentric generalisations, cultural relativism represented progress in Anthropology. A powerful argument developed that the particularity of each culture was such that 'its' values and ways of behaving (the quotation marks signify how

easily we are drawn into reifying cultures) can and should be interpreted only in terms of the particular values, beliefs and rationalities of
the culture concerned. The aim was to try and understand each culture
'from the inside', so that those who belong to particular cultures are
seen as they see themselves, or wish to be seen (or, invariably, how the
most powerful in particular cultures see themselves). Cultural relativism argues that each culture or society possesses its own rationality,
coherence and set of values, and it is in these terms only that one can
properly interpret the organisation, customs and beliefs (including ideas
about human rights) of that culture or society.

In terms of the anthropology of human rights – and so the wider
project of developing a human rights culture – there are three main
problems with culturalism. First, it takes away the basis for comparison
between cultures and societies, which has philosophical and ethical
implications. Secondly, it exaggerates the self-contained nature of societies – especially modern societies and cultures – in which their unique
social and ethical values are supposed to be embedded. And thirdly, it
privileges traditionalism, which is often a means by which elites maintain their privileges. I will address the latter two points here, leaving the
first for the final section.

Culturalism, by giving a totalising picture of specific cultures, produces a false view of the world. Inventing and black-boxing units of
analysis has been a problem to which both International Relations specialists and anthropologists have been prone. Historical sociologists have
tried to show International Relations specialists that the 'state' is a
historical construct, not the ready made textbook unit many assume.
Likewise, many anthropologists have tended to see and describe societies as 'unchanging and traditional', making assumptions about the
past that have turned out to be false.[15] Carrithers argues that we must
'reassemble' our pictures of human society 'without the sharp boundaries or the unalterable tradition'. Humans are 'conformable' to the
weight of tradition, but as 'animals with history' they are 'inventive and
profoundly social animals, living in and through their relations with
each other and acting and reacting upon each other to make new relations and new forms of life'.[16] If this is the case, what constitutes the
'cultural authenticity' to which all values, including human rights, should
be relative? Culturalism is tempting – as is state-centric International
Relations – because it simplifies, and makes complexity easier to handle.
Instead of getting into the bureaucratic politics, for example, behind a
phrase such as 'France decided . . .', we take a short-cut instead, and
make France some-one-thing. Such short-cuts are even less defensible
when we come to 'cultures', for nobody speaks for cultures in the way

governments presume to do for states, and cultures in the modern world are interpenetrated. We hear about 'the Islamic position' or 'Asian values', but who speaks for Islam, or Asia? Nobody does: yet at the same time many people, organisations and states do. Invariably, when it comes to cultures, it is the loudest, the most powerful or the most fundamentalist who speak, and claim authenticity. Authenticity becomes not simply a cultural matter: it becomes profoundly political.

Cultural authenticity is an important prize over which to fight, for being seen to possess it might help in any struggle for political and social power, including helping to determine whose interpretation of human rights will dominate within particular cultural regimes. Cultural-ism assumes there is an objective reality to cultural authenticity, but it can be shown in practice that these ostensible Archimedean points are invariably contested from *within*. If authentic cultural traditions and outlooks are disputed *within*, and human rights are supposed to be *relative* to the traditions and outlooks of particular cultures, to what, or whom, within that disputed culture are human rights supposed to be relative? This argument is a fundamental challenge to those who criticise universality in human rights theories and practices.

Political programmes should not be built on the basis of cultural reductionism, for what is defined as authentic in a culture is more an expression of the prevailing balance of forces, rather than the discovery of an Archimedean point.[17] How much importance should we attach to *culture* as the defining referent (as opposed to nation, gender, class or other identity) when British Anglicans are split over the authenticity of women being ordained as ministers of religion? Or when Muslims dis-agree over the *fatwa* issued legitimising the murder of Salman Rushdie? Or when the British Jewish community argues over the validity of the concept of 'Jewish sperm'? Or when the Taliban in Afghanistan seem to believe that Shi'ites in Iran are dangerous liberals and modernisers? Or when some believe that were Confucius alive today – a key figure in the development of Chinese cultural traditions – he might well be jailed as a dissident? Or, when the idea of a 'Muslim woman' means different things in terms of status, role and contribution across Africa, Asia and the Middle East – not to mention Europe? Or when Malaysia extends Islamic compassion to white believers from Bosnia, but not black be-lievers from Bangladesh? Or when Jews in Israel argue over Zionism? Or when Muslims in Egypt disagree over whether female genital muti-lation is an 'Islamic practice'? Or when Islamic feminists in Iran attack a film endorsing multiple marriages (for men)? Or when Arafat and other Islamic leaders tried to gag Palestinian women criticising domestic violence and the unequal treatment of women under local laws at the

Beijing Women's Conference? Or when Afghan feminists challenge the Taliban decrees against women working? Or when some Japanese, looking back, rethink their code of honour with regard to the way they treated prisoners of war in the Second World War? Or when republican opposition to the Windsor family is seen as perfectly compatible with Britishness? Or when, in Sierra Leone, women clash over whether female genital mutilation is essential for the initiation into womanhood and so its defenders are upholders of important traditions, or whether it is brutalising and its critics are agents of the West? In all these cases the question is the same: what is doing the important work? Is it class, gender, nation, society, generation or culture? For some reason, these days, culture is privileged above all, and especially when human rights is the subject. Against those who assert that human rights must be embedded in an ethical community, I would say: which 'ethical community' – that of culture (which usually means traditionalism) or that of class, gender, nation, generation, or some other category such as the 'poor', 'the hungry', 'the oppressed' – the victims? To whom or what has human rights relativism to be relative?

The main problem with culturalism is traditionalism, the propagating of traditions to serve (conservative) power interests; this often includes special reverence for practices based in a society's religion (though we often find that revered religious traditions have even more distant pre-religious roots). Traditionalism holds that knowledge – and indeed Truth – is derived from past revelations – be they divine or otherwise – and are transmitted by tradition. Culturalism produces, or more accurately re-produces, traditionalism, and this can have several regressive consequences for the theory and practice of human rights. But to reject traditionalism is not to reject traditions. Indeed, traditionalism can be seen as the enemy of positive traditions and culture in some senses. Traditions are obviously important; they help cement societies, and they are sometimes all the wretched have to give their lives any meaning.

What concerns us are the functions that cultural practices – many of them 'invented' relatively recently but now seen as primordial – serve in society. Some of these are relatively benign, as in the narrowly 'cultural' forms of social cement discussed by Hobsbawm, such as the *gorsedd* of druids in Wales.[18] On the other hand, some can be profoundly threatening. Traditionalist practices, for example, invariably translate into masculinist values hostile to women, thereby legitimising domestic violence, *suttee* and all those practices of patriarchal society that led Yoko Ono to describe woman as 'the nigger of the world'. Traditionalism can equally serve class interests, through the spreading of the idea that birth is destiny, that people should know their place, and that the meek shall inherit the earth. A blatant example of class interest served by enshrining traditionalism has been the perpetuation of the caste system in India.[19] Traditionalism was evident in the way Nazi Germany romanticised history to try and create an image of a continuous racial and national spirit, running through the heroes of the past to the Hitler regime. In a less malignant form, there was also the Major Government's 'Back to Basics' campaign in the early 1990s which aimed to create an image whereby that insecure government became seen as the true inheritor of all that had put the great in Great Britain. In such ways traditionalism is a means by which a particular political group, class, elite, gender or government seeks to achieve and maintain ascendancy. Not surprisingly, the fundamentalists of any political or religious persuasion are drawn to traditionalism as a lever in the political process. As Robert Cox said about theory, all traditionalism is *for* somebody or *for* some purpose.[20]

Culturalism must not be allowed to tyrannise human rights – to trump all other arguments and control the agenda – for culturalism and traditionalism perpetuate certain values and power structures. At this point in history they are regressive in human rights terms, because the values and structures they perpetuate are those of patriarchy, class, religious traditionalism, ethnic values and so on. Inevitably, therefore, huge numbers of people are marginalised, both locally and globally. Against these regressive human rights forces I want now to argue the case for emancipation as the preferred discourse for human rights. This concept is controversial, and raises as many questions as it settles, but these are not good reasons for rejecting it. For one thing, such is the destiny of all our most important human concepts, such as justice or love. For another, it would be surprising if there were no controversy about what can be conceived as the politics of inventing humanity.

In a formal sense, emancipation is concerned with freedom from restraint: in Latin *emancipare* meant 'to release from slavery or tutelage'. Expressed more fully, it might be defined as the freeing of people as individuals and groups from those physical and human constraints which stop them carrying out what they would freely choose to do; this means identifying and struggling against oppressive structures or power, and creating new structures and power relationships that promise to enhance human potentialities. Originally, as implied in the Latin roots of the term, emancipation was more concerned with struggling *against*; historically, this meant against legal and other constraints, notably slavery and religious oppression. In the twentieth century, emancipation became not only struggle *against* oppression but also, more coherently, struggle *for* new visions of society. In this way it became more closely identified with 'Left' politics and with the creation of a different social, human, political and international order. Emancipatory politics have been evident in the ebb and flow of historical transformation, which has involved expanding the potential for what Guy Bois called 'individual realisation'.[21] This focus on the individual does not mean, as critics assert, that what is envisaged is an 'atomised' liberal human being. On the contrary, individual realisation is not possible except in the context of society – that is, with others. Otherwise, individuality is psychotic.

Before trying to explain what emancipation is, it is useful to stress what it is not. Here it is useful to make a distinction between 'true' and 'false' emancipation. First, true emancipation cannot be defined in some timeless fashion, as some-one-thing at the end-point of the human story; secondly, true emancipation cannot be at somebody else's expense (except, that is, at the expense of the beneficiaries of oppression, and even here I would argue that to be freed of being an oppressor is a step on the road to becoming more humane, and therefore is emancipatory);[22] and thirdly, true emancipation cannot be considered to be synonymous with Western ways of thinking and behaving (though neither are 'Western' ways necessarily antithetical to emancipation). If emancipation is seen as timeless, at the expense of others, or simply a cloak for Westernisation, it is *false* emancipation.

Emancipation is not a static concept

True emancipation is not a fixed idea of what the world would be like – some distant end-point Utopia. A properly historicised conception of emancipation recognises that every emancipation creates a new margin, just as every major technological fix creates new problems (such as the new ethical problems raised by medical breakthroughs). Emancipation contains a theory of progress, but also recognises that life is one thing after another. Because emancipation must be continuously contextual, because material and other conditions change, it has to be an open and flexible vision. In terms of practical politics it is better to use the adjective, as in *emancipatory* policies, which implies movement, rather than the noun, *emancipation*, which implies a static state. The reality of emancipation is best likened to a political horizon: something to aim for, something that establishes perspective, but something that by definition can never be reached. Emancipation is not a state of being; it is the condition of becoming.

Emancipation must not be at the expense of others

We must always be sensitive to the question 'Whose emancipation?', for any step that is at somebody's expense would constitute false emancipation. True emancipation is based on the belief that 'I cannot be emancipated until you are' – whoever the I. In practice this raises complex political calculations and trade-offs. Clearly, all oppression cannot be abolished at the same time. Different parts of the human convoy must perforce move at different speeds, but the important thing is that they are moving in the same direction, towards human flourishing and away from oppression. Thus, contingent politics have to determine the lines of advance because emancipation cannot proceed at the same speed in all settings. So, for example, it is justifiable for women's emancipation to be sought in the West, even while the West (including the emancipating woman) benefits from a world capitalist system in which there are gross and unjustifiable inequalities. Likewise, the emancipation of South Africa from apartheid cannot be criticised on the grounds that it took the attention of anti-racists away from other struggles. Emancipation *before others* is not in itself the same as emancipation *at the expense of others*, as long as those who are emancipated use that privilege to help secure the emancipation of others (a theme developed in the final chapter).

Emancipation is not synonymous with Westernisation

The conception of emancipation advanced here recognises many contributions made within 'the West' in the development of ideas about human flourishing, including human rights. But we need also to recognise the dark side, and therefore eschew the idea that emancipation should simply be equated with Westernisation. Such a conclusion would be contrary to the spirit of emancipation. We may have been living through several centuries in which Western ideas about emancipation have flourished, but that does not make it an historical imperative, or politically desirable. But neither does it mean that some ideas are not to be preferred over others, even 'Western' ones. The spirit of emancipation is that there are no final answers and that nobody has a monopoly of ultimate truth (even if we conceive an omniscient god, who taught her all she knows?). There is no reason to suppose that what is taken as Western society today represents the best of all possible worlds, not least because that society does not attain its own best standards, is full of hypocrisy, and in relation to the rest of the world, many of its citizens flourish without questions in the midst of injustice.

The three points above have criticised false emancipation – as finite, exclusivist and particularist. In this next stage I want to identify the three roles of true emancipation.

Emancipation as a philosophical anchorage

We all need some grounding for knowledge, though the term 'ground-ing' implies very demanding requirements. My preference is for 'an-chorages'. The idea of conceiving emancipation as an anchorage means that we can talk about what constitutes valid knowledge in terms of emancipatory potential. This is the view that there is no ultimate truth in the social world, only a pragmatic truth, created intersubjectively. The concept of emancipation gives us a point of reference from which we can assess and criticise where we have come from (locally and globally) and from which we can contemplate the future of the human story – convinced that 'we do not have to live like this'.[23]

The metaphor of an anchorage implies a resting point in a dynamic process. As such it gives space for Critical Theory's concept of immanent critique, that is, the attempt to recognise better possibilities inherent in an existing situation; and it also suggests a crossover point in a dialectic, as humans struggle from one anchorage to another, buffeted by all the material and other changes that history throws up. Without a concept of betterment, one cannot have any critical distance to assess one's existing position – or indeed think about the different ways of getting to a better state of affairs. One arrives at a notion of betterment through theorising – even fantasising – and in this way the next step is taken. The story of politics, in a sentence, has evolved from a small group considering the advantages of moving from one environment to another, perhaps from one cave to another, to the issue of the management of the global environment for the whole species. Over time, emancipation has become deeply imprinted into human consciousness. The biological instinct for survival evolved over time into a culture of reason, which in turn became the politics of emancipation.

Emancipation is therefore an historically contingent idea around which people can begin to discuss what to do next in politics. It is a basis for saying whether something is 'true' – whether claims to knowledge should be taken seriously. In this first global age, human rights constitute a crucial aspect of this discussion, for they are concerned with ideas about creating space for the self-realisation of individuals, and the invention of a more inclusive and loving humanity as a whole.

Emancipation as a strategic process

By strategic process I underline the point made earlier that emancipation is to be considered not as a static end-point, but rather as a dynamic concept. A very useful distinction here is that of Joseph Nye, between 'end-point utopias' and 'process utopias'.[24] This distinction emphasises the desirability of dynamic rather than static conceptions of the future. Instead of blueprints (a worked-out model of world government for the twenty-second century, for example) when history would come to an end, the argument is that politics is about travelling hopefully. It is futile to try and overmanage the future, because of possibly radical changes in the material conditions. Consequently, the best way ahead is through benign and reformist steps calculated to make a better world somewhat more probable for future generations. As Albert Camus argued, the means one uses today shape the ends one might perhaps reach tomorrow.[25]

As a strategic process, some would criticise the idea of emancipation, and say that the concept of progress is flawed, particularly when it comes to making judgements about the lives of others. This argument will be discussed more fully in the final section; here I want to argue that there is always one position that is more emancipatory than another – though in particular circumstances it might not be clear at the time. The transcultural judgement of history – a portentous term, but useful here – is stronger than the relativist argument. Peter Singer gives various examples of the debates about human betterment that history has judged: the struggle against slavery; the unionising of workers against terrible working conditions; the giving to women the right to vote, be educated, hold property; the fight against Hitler; the civil rights movement in the United States in the 1960s.[26] If we take a sufficiently long-term perspective, Singer argues, 'it is not difficult to see that on many issues, there *has* been a right side'. He calls it, after Henry Sidgwick, 'the point of view of the universe',[27] and gives as examples of being on the 'right side' today: helping the poorest in developing countries; promoting the peaceful resolution of conflicts; extending ethical concern beyond our species; and protecting the environment.[28]

The idea of progress is not fashionable in some circles, but there is positive and negative evidence suggesting that the great mass of people in the world think differently. Positively, there is the evidence of what might be called the spirit of 1989. By this I mean the global responsiveness and solidarity in relation to the savagery in Tiananmen Square (and particularly the image of the lone individual standing against a column of tanks), the ending of the Cold War (and particularly the image of ordinary people standing on the Berlin Wall, while at the same time destroying it with picks and hammers) and the surrender of apartheid in South Africa (and particularly the image of the dignified and inspirational Mandela emerging from prison and calling for reconciliation). Negatively, 'progress' is legitimised because nobody is calling for the return of mutilating cultural practices (such as foot-binding in China) or the freedom of not being able to read.

At times, critics of emancipation are not arguing against the principle so much as against Westernisation. As a reality check, we should look at what they stand for in practice, on issues such as slavery and racism. Scratch a Western relativist, and one always finds a closet believer in progress underneath. In other parts of the world what is underneath is likely to be a supporter of a local tyranny.

Emancipation as a tactical goal

In the previous two points, emancipation has been identified as a philosophical anchorage and a strategic process; but politics require policies, and emancipatory ideas need to be turned into effective action. Emancipation is intimately concerned with praxis, and not simply critique: it must be attentive to real people in real places, seeking to better their conditions while at the same time changing world politics in structural ways which help improve local conditions. For a guiding idea, we can usefully turn to Critical Theory and its aim to build 'concrete utopias' out of possibilities which are immanent in particular situations.[29] This is process utopias in action – 'pushing the peanut forward' as Singer describes it. On what basis can we decide what constitutes a concrete utopia? There are two clusters of ideas that may help. One is to advance on as many fronts as possible, with policies informed by the World Order goals and principles advanced so powerfully over the years by Richard Falk and others: non-violence, humane governance, economic justice, human rights and environmental sustainability.[30] A second set of ideas for thinking about concrete utopias is Etienne Balibar's notion of égaliberté, which recognises equality and liberty as mutually constitutive conditions for human emancipation. For Balibar égaliberté is therefore a 'formula for permanent revolution, for the continuous radicalisation of the Enlightenment'.[31] This, I believe, is the spirit of true emancipation. Tactical goals based on World Order values and the principle of égaliberté are positive guides for emancipatory advances, locally and globally. But principles can only help so far: turning abstract concepts into concrete utopias under specific historical conditions is another matter. Emancipation also needs clever and committed human agency.

In conclusion we can see that the answer to the question 'What is emancipation?' is both easy and difficult. Emancipation is easy because we know what it is not; it is difficult because we do not know with the same confidence what it looks like in terms of specific struggles. But the three functions of emancipation, just discussed, show that when compared with culturalism and traditionalism, it offers a theory of progress for politics, it provides a politics of hope, and it gives guidance to a politics of resistance. Emancipation is the theory and practice of inventing humanity. It is the discourse of human self-creation, and the politics of trying to bring it about. At this stage of human history, marked by the interplay of globalisation, patriarchy, world capitalism, industrialisation, population densification, environmental stress, widening disparities between haves and have-nots and so on, the growth of a universal human rights culture must be central to emancipatory policies. If sociality is the only permanent 'is', emancipation is the only permanent hope of becoming.

The first section of this chapter argued that the ability to make complex social relations lies at the muddy bottom of the human rights story, and that this sociality is the only permanent 'is'. In the present section it has been argued that emancipation should be the guiding idea for escaping the regressive human rights implications of culturalism and traditionalism: human becoming is the only permanent form of being, and emancipation is the politics of that reality. In the final section, discussing the tyranny of objectivity, it will be argued that in this first truly global age, human rights is an essential aspect of that becoming, and that the only intelligible perspective to adopt is universalist.

The tyranny of scientific objectivity

The argument in this section of the chapter has two main steps. The first is to explain the attraction that scientific objectivity has had for students of Anthropology and the Social Sciences in general, and the resultant danger of positivism; in particular how the latter manifests itself in ways that strengthen the problems of culturalism by reifying what is essentially porous and changeable, and by strengthening cultural and ethical relativism – all of which impact adversely on human rights. Secondly, a defence of universality will be mounted. I want to criticise the cultural relativist perspective on universality, and defend the latter as the only true way of thinking about human rights, by showing that such an approach is possible, desirable and logical, can avoid all the relativist criticisms, and can be based on the secure but sad fact of universal human wrongs.

Objectivity has been the gold standard of modernist Social Science. It opens up not only issues of epistemology but also controversial questions about the proper role of the academic and of how – if at all – value-laden subjects such as human rights should be approached. Just

as the natural scientist is supposed to look objectively down the microscope at some specimen, and describe it with scholarly detachment, so
social scientists are supposed to look down their microscopes at aspects
of the human world, and describe them with comparable scientific
detachment. Many students of International Relations now believe this
approach, loosely called positivism, to be faulty: for one thing, 'objectivity' in the sense intended is thought to be unattainable, for values
infuse the mind of the observer looking down the microscope at human
social practices (the observer can never escape the set of theories which
he or she believes); secondly, what is observed on the specimen slide –
humans – are self-aware in a way natural objects are not, and so can
add another dimension to the observer/observed problem; and finally, a
value-free approach would not leave students of International Relations
with much to discuss (we might count voting patterns in the General
Assembly on human rights issues, but would leave all the most interesting political and philosophical issues aside). Positivism expresses the
naturalist fallacy in the social sciences[32] and this expresses itself in the
reproduction of the hygienic order of neo-realist International Relations.[33]
One problem of objectivity is the way that it separates the-attempting-
knower and that-which-is-to-be-known in such a way as to endow the-
attempting-knower with distinct authority deriving from science. But as
Gaston Blanchard has put it: 'We have only to speak of an object to
think that we are being objective. But, because we chose it in the first
place, the object reveals more about us than we do about it.'[34]

So, the stakes are high, as Steve Smith has argued so forcefully, in
the debate about epistemology and method. Positivism has been important, he argues, because of its role 'in determining, in the name
of science, just what counts as the subject matter of international relations.'[35] This in turn is important because it helps determine what
counts as knowledge in the subject, who are the serious players in the
discipline, and, because of the relationship between theory and practice, how things might get done in the 'real world' of international
affairs.[36] In short, the epistemology of human rights is a political as
much as it is a philosophical issue. The ideal of objectivity, and of
positivism, can therefore be threatening to human rights in a variety of
ways. What purports to be value-free/objective/apolitical/positivist analysis
can merely be a cloak for status quo thinking (and therefore values).
This can be seen most clearly in the relationship between positivism
and crude realism, which together purported, unselfconsciously, to describe the world 'as it is' for nearly half a century after the Second
World War, yet all the time did so through the ethnocentric lenses of
Anglo-American, masculinist, capitalist and nationalist mind-sets (but

such mind-sets were not the only ones attracted to positivism: much of the first generation of Peace Research was also heavily positivist). However, for the most part positivism has tended to be closely identified with the disciplinary dominance of realism in academic International Relations. What is of most concern here is the role positivism has played in Anthropology, and so has fed how many think about the cultural dimensions of International Relations.

McGrane has argued provocatively, but persuasively, that the rise and history of what we now call Anthropology has been grounded in 'the positivistic faith'. By this he means 'the belief that the criterion of truth and the historical progress and perfection of our scientific theories lies in their ever closer approximation to an autonomous reality'.[37] This autonomous reality has come in the twentieth century to be identified with cultures (and particularly 'primitive cultures'). By definition, this categorisation produces units that are 'relative' to each other, constituting a global ordering of one-among-many.[38] McGrane sees this move as 'a supreme manifestation of the Western tradition', namely the tendency of 'the Western mind to identify itself as separate from what it perceives as external to itself'. Leaving aside McGrane's unhelpful reification of 'the Western mind' – how could he as a Westerner make his critique if the Western mind were so totalising? – the key argument is that culture has been *invented* as necessary for the *praxis* of Anthropology. (The 'prior and autonomous existence' of culture was necessary for modern Anthropology, we might argue, just as the prior and autonomous existence of textbook states were for realist International Relations. The disciplines of Anthropology and International Relations have therefore both shared an interest in maintaining the conditions of their own possibility, namely autonomous units of analysis – cultures and states.) 'Culture' does not emerge, in McGrane's argument, as a 'decisive and almost inescapable part of our world' until the twentieth century.[39] Only then did difference between Europe and the non-European 'Other', between the familiar and the alien, come to be seen for the first time in terms of cultural difference/diversity. Anthropologists became identified as 'purveyors of exotica'. In the nineteenth century, McGrane argues, difference/diversity had been defined in terms of evolutionary development through progressive stages of civilisation; in the Enlightenment it had been seen in terms of the modalities of science and ignorance; and in the Renaissance it had been between the Christian and the infernal. This argument opens up many significant issues for students of human rights, notably the relatively short time that 'culture' has been a key referent, the significance of the view that the conceptualisation of difference tells us more about ourselves than the subject conceptualised, the interest of Anthropology in the 'external' world rather than in examining its own theories, the role of academic 'disciplines' as discourses of domination, and the invention of culture as a relative concept. Anthropology invented culture for the social sciences, and in so doing played a part in what Rhoda Howard has called the 'romantic communitarianism'[40] which now affects so many dimensions of global life and confronts students of human rights with so many problems.

Cultural relativism, as defined earlier, consists of the attempt to interpret another culture in its own terms, by careful and thorough investigation from the inside, eschewing one's own ethnocentric bias. Cultural relativism can be seen as both a by-product and characteristic error of positivism: an attempt is made to achieve objectivity by stepping outside one's own culture, but in so doing one then stands firmly inside another. At the heart of both positivism and cultural relativism is the ideal of 'scientific detachment'. It has a number of analytical uses, as suggested earlier. It is crucial, if one is to try to understand a culture and see it from inside to any meaningful degree, to try and transcend or eliminate ethnocentric bias for the period of observation. However, there are at least two major criticisms of cultural relativism which are significant in terms of human rights.

Cultural relativism is empirically falsifying

Cultural relativism tends to posit self-contained socio-cultural entities, which have developed their own unique thoughtways and systems and which are coherent and unchanging. Here is a case where an epistemological assumption – the culturalist one – has enormous ontological consequences.[41] One of the themes of this chapter has been to challenge the hygienic order of culturalism on empirical as well as normative grounds. It is in terms of the former that William McNeill, among others, has criticised Huntington's billiard-ball model of civilisations. McNeill argues that when local habits and customs have been threatened, 'withdrawal and reaffirmation' have been the first and most elemental reactions; however, history shows that borrowing 'foreign ideas and practices' and adapting them to local use has been far more important. In his opinion, 'the net effect of successful borrowing and adaptation was to increase human wealth and power by enlarging our niche in the ecosystem. This, in fact is, and has always been, the central phenomenon of human history.' When the 'bunker mentality' dominates, McNeill argues that the result is for a people to be 'disastrously left behind'; even a civilisation as vast and successful as that of China had to face up to this fact in the last century, and has yet to recover its self-esteem.[42]

If the very notion of 'cultures' is as problematical as the earlier argument suggests, there is a strong case for abandoning 'culture' as a political referent and instead regarding culltures as dangerous political myths, like the term 'race'. The similarity in the terms is worth elaborating, for racial classifications are as various and vague as are the referents used in discussions about human rights: to what is relativism in human rights to be relative to – states, nations, cultures, societies, civilisations, communities (national or subnational) or what? Cultures, like race, have more political purchase than scientific validity. Some scientists have identified five racial sub-species, others fifty, while yet others have argued that the concept of race has no scientific validity whatever, pointing out that the human species in genetic terms is remarkably homogeneous compared with other animals, that there is more genetic variation within one human 'race' than between that race and another, that genetic variation from one individual to another of the same race 'swamps' the average differences between racial groupings, that human diversity within Africa in terms of DNA is nearly three times that of Europe, and that 'black' races contain as much genetic variation as the rest of humanity put together. Race, then, is an idea that is the product of history and politics. Racial groupings, in the words of Chris Stringer, 'are simply the end points of old trade routes'.[43] The fact that both race and culture are contestable terms – but not contested enough – does not prevent them from being powerful political myths – useful for some, and consequential for all.

Cultural relativism is ethically flawed

Cultural relativism is a parent of ethical relativism. The latter, which derives from what in one sense is a laudable attempt to judge cultures in their own terms, denies the appropriateness of anyone from one culture making meaningful moral judgements about behaviour or attitudes in another – whatever the oppression, exploitation, discrimination or subordination. The relativist position is flawed when it comes to thinking about human rights for three main reasons: first, because of the radical uncertainty of the appropriate referent to which particular values are supposed to be relative – the point argued earlier; secondly, because there are no sensible lines which we can draw when faced by suffering and say 'this is nothing to do with me' – an argument to be elaborated later; and thirdly, because relativism would take away the ability to condemn human wrongs. The relativist position is confused, and also infused with moral nihilism.[44] From an ethical relativist perspective one could not easily describe some traditional practices as 'torture not culture',[45] or argue that beheading, amputation or prolonged stays on 'death row' are not civilised ways of dealing with criminals. Relativism, taken to its ultimate asks one not to intervene, and to leave judgement to those on the inside, who (ostensibly!) share the same values and thought-worlds. It is a form of what Callinicos calls 'ethnocentric blindness'.[46] Power corrupts, and cultural relativism helps; no wonder tyrants dislike the light shone by monitoring groups, inside and outside, committed to universal standards of human rights.

The corollary of the argument that cultural relativism is ethically flawed is not that the West is Best. Western liberal triumphalists need to recognise the continuing relevance of Gandhi's comment, when asked what he thought about Western civilisation: 'I think it would be a good idea'. Some in the West are in a position to criticise certain practices in other parts of the world, but what is taken to be the West in a political sense can rarely preach to the rest of the world, because while there are things that the West has got right – the abolition of hunger, the rule of law, democracy and so on – there is also plenty that is wrong, from possessive individualism to the selfish exploitation by the West of the world's resources, and many of its people. Cultural relativism is flawed, but so is the idea that any single political power knows best about everything.

Cultural relativism is flawed as an approach to politics, but cultural sensitivity must inform all we do, including how we think about universal perspectives on human rights. In the following five points I will synthesise a range of critical views about universality, from cultural relativists, post-structuralists and realists.

Universalism is based on an essentialist view of human nature

This criticism is based on the widespread view that those who advocate universality do so because they believe that humans share a common nature, which is identifiable. One such universalist view, often criticised, is the natural law tradition. This posits that there is a *natural law* which exists independently of the positive laws of polities, to which all humans are subject, and which derives from nature – or god. This set of laws is discernible through reason. Such a tradition rests on an essentialist argument, as does the definition of human rights which states that human rights are the rights one has simply because one is a human. Both these views are tautologous. I want to argue that we should have human rights not because we are human, but to make us human. The only element of essentialism in this argument is that these rights should apply to our biological species.

The defence of universality here is akin to Philip Allott's social idealism, which seeks to open up the human future,[47] free of humanly constructed 'essentialisms' and 'false necessities'.[48] Allott's social idealism regards human society as self-constituting. Societies change, or not, as do the people who are made in them, as a result of the historical interplay of particular social, economic, political and other theories in precise settings. The key is human consciousness, and human evolution is the evolution of human consciousness. The point is that humans are not essentially born, they are socially made, and that human rights are part of what might make them at this stage of world history. We have human rights not because we are human, but because we want the species to become human.

The universality of human rights is an ideology which is a cover for the imposition of Western values

It is not surprising at the end of the twentieth century that universalist or cosmopolitan thinking about human rights appears to be the smuggling in of Westernism. Part of the strength of relativism comes from sensitivity about the success and excess of Western imperialism. It is important to remember this history, but we should not allow guilt about historical injustices (for which we had no direct responsibility) and anxieties about cultural insensitivity, to lead us into bad arguments and worse politics – which might add yet further to the sum of human misery.

The most trivial point anybody can make about human rights is that they come from 'somewhere'. Of course they do. Are we to take from the values-from-somewhere position that geography is therefore destiny? If so, where do we stop? How local should we go? If, for example, there is a clash between the values of the family and the values of one's religion, or between the values of the state and the values of one's ethnic culture, which values-from-somewhere should be privileged? Once again, the problem of the multiple and uncertain referent rears its head. So-called cultures and communities may seem bounded, but they are not gagged, and some values travel rather well. All groups, I believe, have a concept of hospitality. Hospitality is not rejected because it originated, somewhere, in a faraway cave about which we know nothing. Love, in its many varieties, also finds a place in all societies and cultures; though its precise expressions vary, we all know it when we see it, or should do. We do not reject love, just because it was invented 'somewhere', in humankind's evolutionary struggles. Indeed, most people celebrate love in its varied forms, as the highest purpose in life. Equally, torture was also invented, 'somewhere', and is now – though it was not always – almost as universally condemned as love is valued.[49] That a world of love is better than no love, and love is better than torture, are cultural universals. How these are expressed are details, arising from time and space. To say that human rights come from somewhere – and the West is not the only geographical expression claiming to be a parent[50] – should never be allowed to be the end of the story: it is only a starting point for discussion of how we should live, as humans, on a global scale.

Cultural relativism has been a powerful idea in International Relations since the late 1980s as a result of the influence of a strange mix of bedfellows comprising postmodernists, liberals trying to adopt a culturally sensitive position on human rights, and civilisation *realpolitikers* who argue that the world has slid seamlessly from a Cold War to a 'clash of civilisations'. The effect has been a tendency to naturalise or even valorise the relationship between cultural space, ethical communities and values. One of the problems with the communitarian perspective is that it emphasises the territoriality of values, as with geopolitical human rights blocs.[51] This is a profoundly conservative move, embedded in ideas about sovereign space. If we adopt this perspective, the chessboard of international relations – and hence the politics of human rights – will be entirely synonymous with the geography of meaning. Spatial relationships are undoubtedly of fundamental importance in human society, but geography is not destiny. Spatial 'realities' are frequently altered by changes in technology and sociology. A river might be impassable in one era but bridgeable in another; it might be a line that divides people or a resource that brings together an economy. The ideology that the geography of meaning is more important, more consequential, than history is redolent of the spurious ideology of geopolitics in the 1930s.

Behind the criticism of universality is concern about the relationship between the spread of ideas and associated material and political power.[52] Expressed crudely, and adopting Mao's famous line, the assumption seems to be that cultural power grows out of the barrel of a gun. If this argument is accepted, and 'power' is seen to be doing all the work, then the real choice is not between power (external) and culture (local) but simply between different sites of power, local or external. It is not always obvious why local power is necessarily to be preferred, in terms of the values it imposes on those it can reach. Clearly, there is often a direct relationship between the spread of values and the gradient of political power: the Bible followed the flag. But material and political power are not always decisive. The history of religions points elsewhere, and suggests that some ideas *become* powerful as a result of the power of the idea, as opposed to the material and political power of the holder. That is, power may be immanent in the idea, rather than the idea being immanent in the power. Ideas can become powerful 'when their time has come'. Christianity spread in the Roman Empire because the powerless believed it. Likewise, Islam grew because it spoke to the poor. The cries of *Liberté, Egalité, Fraternité* did not sweep France as a result of the material and political power of the sansculottes. And the idea of the equality of the sexes did not grow out of the barrel of a gun. In all these cases, whatever their subsequent history, the moral commitment of powerless people, rather than the material power of states or elites, was the decisive factor. In the beginning it was the power in the idea that moved people, not the material power pushing the idea.

The spread of a human rights culture, I believe, cannot simply be explained in power political terms – by the domination of the West. Human rights speak to the age of industrialisation, dislocation and globalisation in some fundamental sense, as being right, as other life-enhancing ideas have spoken to other people at other times. The twentieth century may have represented a period of history when for the West there seemed no limits to growth, including the spread of liberalism. Some were led to trumpet The 'end of history'.[53] In the next century the growth of limits may be much more evident. And it may be that under the pressure of population growth, environmental decay and Asian power that the idea of individual freedom, so central now, will seem irresponsible. Human rights as now conceived in the West are by no means set to head the agenda through the rest of history. There are also ideas whose time has passed.

The argument that universal human rights are simply a continuation of Western imperialism by other means can be turned on its head. Peter Baehr, for example, has argued that the *failure* to think of applying human rights to non-Western societies reflects a 'rather paternalistic way of thinking'.[54] Baehr writes that those who say that people in the 'developing world' are not ready for, or would not appreciate, political freedoms are not only being patronising but are also playing into the hands of repressive regimes who want to deny civil and political rights as long as there is economic underdevelopment. This view ignores the victims of repression (who rarely argue for the right of their government to repress them), and fails to recognise that the denial of such rights might also be dysfunctional in terms of achieving economic and social development.

Western opinion, and governments, often regard themselves as exemplars of human rights. In practice the West has no grounds for complacency or self-satisfaction. Not only has the job not been completed at home, but there are major hypocrisies and silences. Structuralist theorists, for example, argue that the power of the North depends upon the weakness of the South, that Northern wealth depends on the South's poverty, and that the enjoyment of its rights depends on the wrongs it inflicts. Worthies of previous eras enjoyed and trumpeted their good life while living more or less comfortably on the backs of slaves: we are no different. In this circumstance Western complacency and hypocrisy is overwhelming. There are some ethnocentric (originally Western) values for which we should not apologise, but there are plenty for which we should.

Universality would produce an unhealthy sameness

Universalism sets standards, but that need not be the same as sameness or cultural homogeneity. Just because an examination sets standards (for example, requiring certain minimum levels of grammar, logic and knowledge) it does not mean that every essay on Shakespeare has to be identical. As far as values are concerned, arguments are usually framed in the form of negative injunctions – 'Thou shall not . . .'. A whole series of such injunctions still allows considerable freedom in which people can express themselves. There is scope for diversity within standards. This is the nature of democracy, for example.

Furthermore, universal standards may indeed sustain diversity rather than the opposite. The spread of feminism and gay rights breaks up the universal transcultural presence of patriarchy, and without universal principles, it is difficult to see how indigenous peoples have any chance of surviving. Here, the work of Western (universalist) organisations such as Survival, for example, is important. If left to sovereign governments, the future of indigenous peoples and their land would look even bleaker than it does today. Universal feminism allowed women's rights to develop in different countries more quickly than if there had been no transnational and transcultural feminist solidarity. And if a debate still goes on within feminism about the meaning of 'woman', this is surely of far less urgency than the daily abuses of women (a word postmodern feminists cannot avoid). The anxieties of some Western academics about 'sameness' seems a trivial and patronising concern when compared with the anxieties of women in desperate circumstances, needing a hand. If left exclusively to local patriarchal power-brokers, that hand will be the traditional fist.

The politics of cultural relativism can be expressed as 'the tolerance of diversity'. Few would oppose diversity in principle – except those, perhaps, who believe that a Disney theme park represents the best of all possible worlds. But the key question is: how much diversity should be tolerated? Even if we understand all, does it mean that we have to forgive all? Cultural relativists and postmodernists will argue against universal ideas – 'metanarratives' – while valuing tolerance as a universal. Clearly, there are no non-universalists. Even the total rejection of universal human rights is a universalist position on human rights. If we accept the argument that ideas and values are culturally specific, then presumably postmodern ideas will not travel beyond their urban Western privileged origins – or is the argument another of postmodernism's smuggled-in metanarratives? In any case, their ideas are not seen as relevant by the victims of world politics, who often look for salvation to universalist ideas such as human rights. In circumstances when there may simply be no final philosophical argument for settling whether particular universals are regressive or emancipatory, a good place to start thinking about politics is to ask the victims. Generally, the victims see universal solidarity as more of a promise than they see sameness as a threat. As a Westerner, I believe that the risk of being thought to be an imperialist in some circumstances is justifed in the face of local fascism. Commenting on recent Indonesian history, Baehr has written that: 'The acceptance of the universality of human rights standards is a notion that may be uncomfortable to oppressive governments. It is, however, generally adhered to by their victims.'[55] A general commitment to the tolerance of diversity must therefore be tempered, in order to overcome human wrongs, by a diversity of tolerance in application.

Universalist ideas, like emancipation, are sometimes criticised for denying 'the other's otherness'. If homogenisation is the fear, the record suggests that we should worry about it locally before universally. Why is the eradication of difference in the face of (local) communitarian power less worth struggling for than any eradication of difference as a result of external 'imperialism'? Genocide, for example, is a human wrong which is more likely to take place within a sovereign entity than between sovereign entities. An approach to world politics dominated by imperial local conceptions of 'us' and *The Other* (a dominant nation in a multination state, for example) erodes diversity in the name of sovereignty. It is my belief that it is only by recognising our human sameness in *an other* regarding universal solidarity that we will actually protect human diversity and reduce human wrongs.

*Any idea aiming at universality is Utopian, totalitarian
and dangerous*

All human ideas have their dark side, and universality is no exception;
but universality is not necessarily negative in its consequences, and
human rights is a shining example. An important distinction here, as with
emancipation, is between 'true' and 'false' universality. False universality
can appear to be Utopian (in the sense that it aims to produce a better
world) but can end up being totalitarian and dangerous. Local politics
can also be the latter with more likelihood of achieving success, as the
history of the twentieth century attests. These warnings are important
for those aspiring to universal standards, but equally the warning is for
those who believe that small is always beautiful. The lesson to be drawn
in both cases is the desirability of democracy within and between countries – as captured in the notion of 'cosmopolitan democracy'.[56] Cosmopolitan democracy, if operationalised, would be a stronger safeguard
against totalitarian and dangerous sameness than the ideals of Westphalia.

It is not therefore primarily a matter of trying to settle once and for
all the philosophical argument between relativism and universalism in
a globally satisfying way. This is probably impossible; rather, the task
is to operationalise cosmopolitan democracy. This is the idea which at
the present stage of history is best calculated to produce a politics of
true universalism – an inclusive multicommunity 'multilogue', aimed as
standard-setting in ways that will reduce human wrongs, and balance
a tolerance of diversity with a diversity of tolerance.

The differences between pro- and anti- universalists are often less
than it appears – unless, of course, the anti- is a local regime using cultural relativist arguments as part of a 'Keep Out' campaign. Few people
would stand aside *in extremis* and say they are not willing to make universal judgements when some gross human wrong is being committed.
Similarly, there are limits on the numbers of those in the West who
would want to impose the Western way of life universally, though the
triumphalism of Western liberalism at the end of the Cold War, and
of global capitalism, might suggest otherwise. For the moment, true
universalism is best tested by listening to victims and trying not to offend
global civil society, the nearest we have to a conscience of world society.
The task is to work out a politics of true universalism, which obviously
cannot simply be a Western project. It is one aspect of false universalism
to believe that there is one answer, and a final answer.

To celebrate a world of difference, literally, is Utopian, totalitarian
and dangerous. James Der Derian has endorsed a Nietzschean perspective

on'the very necessity of difference', looking towards a 'practical strategy to celebrate, rather than exacerbate, the anxiety, insecurity and fear of a new world order where radical otherness is ubiquitous and indomitable'.[57] Celebrating anxiety, insecurity and fear, from the comfort of Western academe, on behalf of those anxious about being beaten up or worse, insecure about having any cash to feed their children, or fearing their total dependence on the next rainfall, strikes me as deeply patronising, immoral and unthinking. In the mid-1990s, on a visit to Britain, the new president of South Africa, Nelson Mandela, celebrated human solidarity (based on a politicised metanarrative against racism) in the cause of liberating his own country and other achievements. He said: 'One of the striking features of modern times is the number of men and women all over the globe, in all continents, who fight oppression of human rights'. In the case of South Africa the international process made an enormous difference. It created historical facts, as Mandela put it, 'in which the ordinary folk throughout the world have participated and shaped'.[58] If this is the choice which postmodern perspectives give us, then I have no doubt at all whose politics are best calculated to lead to human security, dignity and flourishing, and I have no doubt whose spirit I would prefer to have on my side if my back was pushed to the wall: it would not be the spirit and politics of Nietzsche, but of Mandela.

> *Universality in human rights is a flawed position because there are no universal values*

As mentioned earlier one of the most powerful criticisms of universal human rights is the argument that ideas about rights derive from, and must be embedded in, particular ethical communities; and since there is no universal ethical community, the idea of universal human rights must be an ethnocentric assertion, a drive to make the local into the global. The conclusion usually derived from this argument is either that the search for human dignity has to adopt a different route to that of rights, or that universalism must be conceived very thinly, allowing local cultures considerable space in which to interpret rights in their own ways. I want to make five arguments rebutting some of these points – and I especially want to reject the conclusion.

First, the critique of universality ignores the degree of actually existing universality in terms of human rights. Donnelly, for example, has argued persuasively that there are various sorts of universality – what he calls 'international normative universality'.[59] All states regularly proclaim their acceptance of and adherence to international human rights norms

– notably the 1948 Universal Declaration of Human Rights – and charges of human rights violations are among the strongest that can be made in international relations. Even abusers of human rights feel the need to defend themselves in the currency of the human rights discourse; they do not reject it.

Secondly, the critique of universality ignores the degree of value commensurability that exists between communities. Many writers – cultural anthropologists, psychologists, sociologists of religion, social scientists and philosophers – have argued, with increasing empirical support and epistemological confidence, that human beings, 'whatever their cultural contexts, tend to have many similar conceptions regarding rectitude, civility, right and wrong behaviour and duties and obligations towards other people'. What this tends to suggest, according to Donald Puchala, is that 'at a fundamental level, moral behaviour is not a cultural trait but a human predilection'.[60] It has come as a surprise to many that sociobiology, so long identified with the social spirit of the selfish gene, now has advocates who see 'the origins of virtue' in our biological characters.[61] It is less surprising that a neo-Aristotelian philosopher, Martha Nussbaum, argues that humans are entitled to be allowed to flourish in a human way, and to help one another to flourish equally.[62] Her requirements and entitlements for such flourishing closely match the Universal Declaration of Human Rights and the definition of 'human security' agreed upon by the UN Development Programme.[63] Whatever the origins of human moral behaviour – nature, god, right reason, or whatever – the important point is that actual social practices suggest a considerably higher degree of value commensurability across cultures than relativists would allow.

As a general rule, culture can indeed speak unto culture. There are exceptions, of course, and some of these might utterly reject some of the premises of human rights discourse – for example, the political agents and cultural value system which sustain the caste system in India. Sometimes regressive ideas have to be opposed, as were slavery and the burning of heretics. These ideas were once respectable, supported by their political communities and cultural value systems. It is a preposterous political position to argue that the idea of universal human rights is flawed because some groups cannot conceive the notion of rights. Are victims always to be left hostage to the selfish politics of the powerful? If we had to wait until everyone was persuaded before taking any step in life, we would still be in the Dark Ages. Progress in promoting liberty, equality and fraternity cannot be held hostage by those who support, for example, a caste system with a concept of 'untouchables'. Outsiders can best help by going with the grain of history, by helping those who want to resist to bring about reform rather than by imposing change. But *in extremis*, when gross abuse is taking place, and people are shouting for help, urgent choices have to be made, and sometimes the force of better argument has to be replaced by the argument of better force.

Thirdly, the critics of universality (and cosmopolitan perspectives) ignore a powerful alternative view of world politics, one that has thought in terms of a potential world community rather than particularisms. But history is written by the winners, and in this case the winners have been communitarians. This leads us inevitably back to history – the 'future of the human past' as Philip Allott has put it, in a different context.[64] It is only by looking at the human past, and rethinking it, that we can fully appreciate the potentiality for human becoming, rather than merely human being. This can be shown quite simply. Humans start learning about politics, including world politics, almost from the moment they are born. We are genderised, and then we are national-ised. We are taught, and learn, and discover politics from messages and images that are all around. (The implication of this is that what we learn we can also unlearn.) We are socialised by signs and stories telling us who is insider and who is outsider – the us and them. As a result of generations of nationalised upbringing, the great mass of people on earth believe that the national is natural, that we have tribal souls, that statist divisions are commonsensical and that concepts such as common humanity are naïvely utopian. But giving ultimate loyalty to nations and states, and accepting their ultimate decision-making power, is not a primordial condition. In reality, the international system in which we now live is a recent invention. The 350-year-old states system associated with Westphalia has been in existence for only about sixteen of the 5,000 generations of tool-making humans, while the nation-state iden-tified with the French Revolution has only been around for about eight generations. The point I am stressing is that the now powerful world political stories we have learned to live by – nations and states – are very recent inventions in historical time. They are neither natural nor primordial. This warns against drawing sweeping conclusions about what human rights 'are' or 'are not' from historical snapshots and culturalist stories.

Nationalism and state sovereignty are powerful universal ideas. One idea that has never been universally powerful, politically, but which has been influential for far longer than the modern idea of nations and states, is the story that our main identity should be common humanity rather than some part of it. Few children are cosmopolitanised as they grow up. Nevertheless, contemporary cosmopolitans can look back twenty-five centuries for intellectual and moral sustenance. The idea of a cosmic *polis* – the idea that we are all (potential) citizens of a universal city – can be traced in the Stoic philosophers of Greek times, the medieval idea of a united Christendom, the ideas of Dante and other writers about a worldwide empire, the Islamic vision of one *umma* or world community, the peace plans of the rationalist philosophers of the eighteenth and nineteenth centuries, the Enlightenment commitment to universal reason, the universalist ideals of *liberté, egalité* and *fraternité* released by the French Revolution, the schemes of World Federalists, imaginings of global Utopias and the rest.[65] However, some universalist ideas, those of a totalitarian nature, have not been inclusive or human-istic and I would reject these as false cosmopolitanism or universalism. Non-inclusive 'universalisms' privilege power over people. The rise and spread, particularly since the Second World War, of a universal human rights culture, feeds into the long tradition of ideas about a true politics of common humanity.

Fourthly, contrary to the argument that there is not a universal eth-ical community on which to base human rights universally, I would emphasise that there are indeed universal ethical communities; these derive from the fact that everyone on earth has multiple identities (de-riving from gender, work, family position, political status and so on). Why should 'culture' have primacy? If the best answer to this is not the geography of meaning – cultural geopolitics – then we have to weigh culture alongside other identities when asking the question: to whom or to what are ethical values to be relative in any given case? And this means, surely, that an individual has the right to refuse a cultural or ethnic (or gender or whatever) identity?[66] Should women in Afghan-istan, whose life-choices have been constrained by the Taliban, identify first with the views of the Taliban or with how they think and feel as women? Should 'untouchables' in India submit to the local elite or identify with oppressed groups elsewhere? Universal human rights are supposed to be invalid because there is no universal ethical community. But there is: the ethical community of oppressed women, the ethical community of under-classes; the ethical community of those suffering from racial prejudice; the ethical community of prisoners of conscience; the universal ethical community of the hungry . . . and on and on. Uni-versal human rights are solidly embedded in multiple networks of cross-cutting universal ethical communities. The fundamental weakness of the critics of universality is that they take too territorial a view of the idea of human community, human political solidarity and human social affinity. Their perspective is conservative, overdisciplined by constructed notions of states and cultures.

Finally, in addition to the social, philosophical and political arguments just levelled against the critics of universalism, there is a further one, this time powerfully made by a writer who is best known for adopting anti-foundationalist positions, Richard Rorty.[67] This is an argument that stresses the universality that derives from our common experiences as human beings. Rejecting foundationalist arguments on which to base human rights, Rorty writes that a 'better sort of answer is the sort of long, sad, sentimental story which begins "Because this is what it is like to be in her situation – to be far from home, among strangers," or "Because she might become your daughter-in-law" or "Because her mother would grieve for her." '[68] Such stories, he argues, are as good as it gets in terms of developing transcultural solidarities. There is indeed scope for 'sentimental education', what Annette Baier calls 'a progress of sentiments'.[69] Many people *can* understand the stories of faraway people in faraway places. Indeed, many regard such explorations not as an alien activity, but as a way of opening up their own mental landscapes, and so knowing themselves. It is important to recognise the universality of human sentiments, but it is hardly a strong enough position on which to base an entire theory and practice of world politics. It can only be a part. As Wilson has written, in criticising Rorty's position,

Yet one can only construct a very weak defence of actions by relying on emotions and courage alone, and eschewing all recourse to rational forms of argumentation. Rights without a metanarrative are like a car without seat-belts; on hitting the first moral bump with ontological implications, the passenger's safety is jeopardised.[70]

The conclusion of this defence of universality is that when faced by a human wrong, there is no sensible place to draw a line and say: 'This is no concern of mine.' The very multiplicity of identities that humans share destroys the assumption of black-boxed communities of value which the anti-universalist critique depends upon. We are connected, universally, to multiple networks of ethical communities. Against this, relativism asserts a single referent, constructed by traditional territorial power structures and a totalised conception of culture. Universality is therefore possible (ethical and other communities are universal), desirable (resistance to oppression requires universal ethics, and this position is more defensible than the alternatives) and logical (there is no other sensible place to draw lines). What finally binds all this together and gives a firm anchorage for universal human rights is the universality of human wrongs. Human wrongs are everywhere; all societies find it easier to recognise and agree upon what constitute wrongs elsewhere than they do rights; wrongs are universal in a way rights are not; and a concentration on wrongs shifts subjectivity to the victims by emphasising a bottom-up conception of world politics. This has the crucial effect of humanising the powerless. In the early 1990s Rorty was much troubled by the dehumanisation taking place in the Balkan wars. Some Serbs saw Muslims as uncircumcised dogs, and some Muslims made distinctions between humans (themselves) and blue-eyed devils (their enemies). When such dehumanisation occurs it becomes possible for groups simultaneously to believe in human rights but also carry out unspeakable atrocities, because they do not think *human* rights are being violated when what they target is an uncircumcised dog or a devil.[71] As ever, the relativist perspective concedes too much to local power, in this case that of the dehumanisers. A universalist perspective favouring the bottom-up perspective of human wrongs gets over this and allows the victim to assert and define his or her humanity, with the help of solidarist groups elsewhere. The invention of humanity and the definition of who is human cannot be allowed to be in the hands of particularist prejudices.

In the post-positivist phase of academic International Relations it is more common to contest the simple distinction between 'facts' and 'values' than was once the case. It has been more common in philosophy, and I want to endorse, with Mary Midgley, Geoffrey Warnock's argument: 'That it is a bad thing to be tortured and starved, humiliated or hurt is not an opinion: it is a fact. That it is better for people to be loved and attended to, rather than hated or neglected, is again a plain fact, not a matter of opinion.'[72] Expressing it differently, Wilson states that: 'Whereas human happiness is noted for its variety, human misery is relatively uniform, leading to a notion of human frailty as the universal feature of human existence.'[73] From these statements – which I believe represent universal social facts – I believe that universal human rights are possible, logical and desirable. They derive from our animal nature (the need for food and shelter) and from our social character and potentiality. The *is* of wrongs demands the *should* of emancipation.

We have therefore no firm grounds for saying, when confronted by gross human rights abuses – human wrongs – that 'This is no concern of mine.' On the contrary, our multiple identities give us grounds for involvement, whether one speaks as a parent, family member, neighbour, citizen, member of the human species or whatever category one can imagine. One might argue in a particular case that there is nothing one can do, or that one's priorities have to be with one's nearest and dearest, or that one's own nation must come first – or whatever – but the important point is that when faced with a human wrong – if one choose not to act – it is necessary to justify non-involvement. Kant is becoming right. He said that a 'transgression of rights in *one* place in the world is felt *everywhere*.[74] With the help of the media, to some degree, and global civil society, even more, people are increasingly confronted by concern, if only to the extent of having to justify non-intervention.

In sum, the argument for a universalist approach to human rights rests on the universality of human wrongs; the latter are universal social facts that derive from our animal nature and social character to date. This argument is then strengthened by two others: the existence of a universality of ethical communities – and especially those of victims – and the fact that when one is faced by a human wrong – be it a hungry child, a prisoner of conscience, a battered person in the street, a victim of torture, starvation, humiliation or hurt – there is no intelligible reason for saying 'this is not my concern'. Confronted by all our multiple identities, relativism, particularism, and forms of communitarianism are ultimately not coherent. Even if there are contingent reasons for not acting, there are none for feeling and being uninvolved.

Conclusion: 1948/1648

This chapter, long as it is, leaves many loose ends. But so it must, for there is a point in the human rights issue beyond which words cannot go. Philosophising can only go so far; the conclusion is in the doing; the outcome is in local struggles and individual efforts. For people wearing academic hats it might mean doing empirical studies of particular countries or particular human rights abuses, or investigating the workings of police and legal systems; for those with the role of activists, some of whom will also be academics, it means making choices and having the 'courage of their confusions'. This chapter has tried to give a comprehensive approach to taking such steps, based on the belief that human rights have a central role in the process of emancipation, which itself is central to human self-creation. Together, they speak to the predicament of living in the modern world, with all that this means: a situation in which human wrongs are universal, and a time when one of the great issues of the day is the task of mediating between the local and the global, when the meaning of each is in flux, as well as the relationship between them. Human rights is at the crux of all these matters, being concerned with what it is to be a human being, being human.

The Universal Declaration of Human Rights in 1948 can be seen as one of the steps towards the beginning of the end for a period of triumphant statism in world history, a period identified with the Westphalian system which had been formally inaugurated exactly 300 years earlier.

Westphalia, in its time, had represented a sort of anchorage, after the ravaging wars of religion. But the grammar of the system of state sovereignty and statism constructed from the seventeenth to the twentieth century led inexorably to the Holocaust and atomic warfare. These outcomes, evident to all in 1945, were not accidental factors in history, but the logical culminating points of an international system based on the idea that the sovereign state should represent the supreme locus of decision-making power and the highest focus of loyalty. Anarchy might be what states make of it, but humanity has not been. In the killing fields at the apogee of Westphalia – Dachau and Hiroshima – 'Hell was here.'[75]

In 1948, with the Universal Declaration of Human Rights, the individual was potentially brought back to the centre. A building block was constructed for the possible development of a cosmopolitan democracy in a world of post-sovereign states, in ways that promised – but certainly did not guarantee – to reconcile particular and universal conceptions of humanity in universally – if not totally – satisfying ways. 1948, and what the Universal Declaration symbolises, gives us cause for hope, though not optimism, that the next 300 years will offer more space for the creation of humanity on a global scale than the past 300 years, a period of limited emancipations and unlimited violences. If 1948 does not let us revise the grammar of 1648, so much the worse for the world – the human and the non-human. Successful revision of statist grammar requires many things, of which a culture of human rights is one. This in turn requires an escape from the three tyrannies discussed earlier, so that we can think, talk and act with respect to human rights free of the regressive grip of common sense, traditionalism and relativism. We have no better language at present to set us free, to mediate between the local and the global and to overcome territorial conservatism in the interests of the construction of true universalism. The development of a human rights culture is crucial, because it is one of the ways by which physical humans can try and invent social humans in ways appropriate for our dislocated, statist, industralised and globalising age. Each person on earth has several identities – chosen and/or ascribed. The truly emancipatory moment will be when the universal 'I' totally embraces the universal 'an other'. Human rights can educate here, because an individual's entitlement implies an other's duty, and because there is no more efficient way of learning how the world works than by identifying with the wrongs others suffer. If enough people can come to think and feel beyond their skins, we can continue the work begun in 1948. This is the hope of progressively leaving behind the politics of the concentration camp – the ultimate sovereign space – for a cosmopolitan democracy aimed at reinventing global human being – being human globally – based on the politics of the-I-that-is-an-other, and badged with common humanity.

Notes

1 Carol Rumens, *Thinking of Skins. New and Selected Poems* (Newcastle upon Tyne: Bloodaxe Books, 1993), pp. 87–90.
2 Jack Donnelly distinguishes between the Western conception of human rights and some non-Western traditions. Examples are Islamic *sharia* and Chinese traditional law which are concerned with ideas of dignity and limitations on arbitrary power rather than rights as such. They are rules constituted between rulers and divine authorities rather than entitlements deriving from being human. Jack Donnelly *Universal Human Rights in Theory and Practice* (Ithaca: Cornell University Press, 1989), esp. ch. 3.
3 For a critique of static conceptions of the so-called human condition, see Philip Allott, 'The future of the human past', in Ken Booth (ed.), *Security and Statecraft. The Cold War and After* (Cambridge University Press, 1998).
4 Michael Carrithers, *Why Humans Have Cultures. Explaining Anthropology and Social Diversity* (Oxford University Press, 1992), pp. 12–13.
5 In addition to stumbling across the poem by Carol Rumens, I was greatly encouraged by seeing the attack on what he called the 'ecstasy of is-sentences' in the 1995 British International Studies Association Plenary Lecture by Philip Allott. See Allott, 'Kant or won't: theory and moral responsibility', *Review of International Studies* 23 (1997): 339–57.
6 Carrithers, *Why Humans Have Cultures*, esp. pp. 4–11.
7 *Ibid.*, pp. 32–3.
8 *Ibid.*, p. 1.
9 *Ibid.*, p. 34.
10 *Ibid.*, p. 36.
11 C. Brown, *International Relations: New Normative Approaches* (Hemel Hempstead: Harvester Wheatsheaf, 1992), uses the communitarian/cosmopolitan distinction as the framework to discuss the whole history of normative thought about international relations.
12 See, for example, Derek Heater, *World Citizenship and Government. Cosmopolitan Ideas in the History of Western Political Thought* (Basingstoke: Macmillan, 1996).
13 Yehezkel Dror, *Crazy States. A Counter Conventional Strategic Problem* (Lexington, Mass.: Heath-Lexington Books, 1971), pp. 4–5. Dror's formulation started with 'was': 'Was Equals Is Equals Will Be'.
14 Richard A. Wilson, (ed.), *Human Rights, Culture and Context. Anthropological Perspectives* (London: Pluto, 1987), p. 1. Donnelly, *Universal Human Rights*, p. 109.
15 Carrithers, *Why Humans Have Cultures*, p. 8.
16 *Ibid.*, pp. 32–3.

17 The problem of authenticity is discussed in Ken Booth, 'Human wrongs and international relations', *International Affairs* 71 (1995): 112–17. Discussion of some of the cases in the rest of the paragraph can be found in the following: Jay Rayner, 'There is no such thing as Jewish sperm', *Guardian*, 29 January 1994. Ian Black, 'In the footsteps of the Ayatollah', *Guardian*, 9 October 1996 (the Taliban and the Shi'ites); Sin-Ming Shaw, 'Values true and false', *Time*, 15 December 1997 (the argument that Confucius would be a dissident); Herbert L. Bodman, and Nayereh E. Tohidi (eds.), *Women in Muslim Societies: Diversity Within Unity* (Boulder: Rienner, 1998); Shabbir Akhtar, 'Meaning in a silent universe', *Times Higher Education Supplement*, 21 March 1997; Geoffrey Wheatcroft, *The Controversy of Zion* (London: Sinclair-Stevenson, 1996); 'Egypt bans female genital mutilation', *Amnesty*, March/April 1998, p. 8; Douglas Jehl, 'A second wife to make a son: the film story all Iran is talking about', *The Observer*, 21 December 1997; Andrew Higgins, 'Free speech curbed at forum: Arafat and Muslim leader try to gag Palestinians', *Guardian*, 30 August 1995; Maggie O'Kane 'A holy betrayal', *Guardian Weekend*. 29 November 1997, 'The big story,' Granada TV, 27 July 1995 (the story of the meeting between British POWs and Japanese Officers); Marcus Mabry and David Hecht, 'Fighting for their rights. A local reaction to attacks on female circumcision', *Time*, 14 October 1996.

18 Eric Hobsbawm and Terence Ranger (eds.), *The Invention of Tradition* (Cambridge University Press, 1983).

19 Donnelly, *Universal Human Rights*, ch. 7 discusses caste in India.

20 Robert W. Cox, 'Social forces, states and world orders: beyond international relations theory', *Millennium* 10 (1981): 126–55.

21 Quoted in Alex Callinicos, *Theories and Narratives. Reflections on the Philosophy of History* (Cambridge: Polity Press, 1995), p. 190.

22 This is a similar argument to Aristotle's view that we become virtuous by practising virtue, the theme of Peter Singer, *How Are We To Live? Ethics in an Age of Self-Interest* (Oxford University Press, 1997).

23 This is discussed more fully in Ken Booth, 'Dare not to know: international relations theory versus the future', in Ken Booth and Steve Smith (eds.), *International Relations Theory Today* (Cambridge: Polity Press, 1995), pp. 347–8 and Booth, 'Security and anarchy: utopian realism in theory and practice', *International Affairs* 67(1991): 527–45.

24 Joseph Nye, 'The long-term future of deterrence', in Roman Kolkowicz (ed.), *The Logic of Nuclear Terror* (Boston: Allen & Unwin, 1987), pp. 245–7.

25 See Stanley Hoffmann, *Duties Beyond Borders: On the Limits of Possibilities of Ethical International Politics* (Syracuse University Press, 1981), p. 197.

26 Singer, *How Are We To Live?*, p. 265.

27 *Ibid.*, p. 263.

28 *Ibid.*, p. 265.

29 An account of praxis in Critical Theory is discussed in Richard Wyn Jones, 'Security, strategy, and Critical Theory', PhD thesis, University of Wales, Aberystwyth (1997), esp. pp. 52–8, 86–8, 163–83, 290–324. A shorter version will be published by Rienner (forthcoming).

30 The phrase 'World Order' is deliberately capitalised to indicate the association of the phrase with the ideas of the so-called World Order approach to

world politics. See, for example, Richard A. Falk, *A Study of Future Worlds* (New York: Free Press, 1975) and Falk, *The Promise of World Order* (Philadelphia: Temple University Press, 1987).

31 Quoted in Callinicos, *Theories and Narratives*, pp. 193–5.

32 Martin Hollis, 'The last post?', in Steve Smith *et al.* (eds.), *International Theory: Positivism and Beyond* (Cambridge University Press, 1996), pp. 301–8.

33 Booth, 'Human wrongs,' 105.

34 Quoted in Bernard McGrane, *Beyond Anthropology: Society and the Other* (New York: Columbia University Press, 1989), pp. ix, 113.

35 Steve Smith, 'Positivism and beyond', in Smith *et al.*, (eds.) International Theory: *Positivism and Beyond*, p. 38.

36 *Ibid.*, esp. pp. 11–13.

37 McGrane, *Beyond Anthropology*, pp. 4–5.

38 *Ibid.*, p. 117.

39 *Ibid.*, p. 113.

40 Quoted in Wilson (ed.), *Human Rights, Culture and Context*, p. 3. One sinister version of this romanticisation has been the defence of 'cultural weapons' by the Inkatha Freedom Party: sanctioned by Zulu tradition, *assegais* and *pangas* were used in ferocious attacks on political opponents. See Callinicos, *Theories and Narratives*, p. 198.

41 Smith, 'Positivism and beyond', p. 37.

42 William H. McNeill, 'Decline of the West?', *New York Review of Books*, 9 January 1997, p. 21.

43 Chris Stringer, 'The myth of race', *The Observer*, 27 April 1997; Kenan Malik, *The Meaning of Race: Race, History and Culture in Western Society* (London: Macmillan, 1996).

44 Wilson (ed.), *Human Rights, Culture and Context*, p. 8.

45 A. Robson, 'Torture not culture', *AIBS Journal* 63 (September/October 1993): 8–9.

46 Callinicos, *Theories and Narratives*, p. 198. A telling illustration is given of the way 'my culture' (Susan Sontag's phrase) obscures moral judgement and empirical reality.

47 Philip Allott, *Eunomia. New Order for a New World* (Oxford University Press, 1990).

48 Roberto Mangabeira Unger, *False Necessities: Anti-Necessitarian Social Theory in the Service of Radical Democracy* (Cambridge University Press, 1987).

49 On how so 'normal' an instrument of power, historically, became a 'scandal', see Michael Ignatieff, 'Torture's dead simplicity', *New Statesman*, 20 September 1985. On the fact that torture is not dead, see Antonio Cassese, *Inhuman States: Imprisonment, Detention and Torture in Europe Today* (Cambridge: Polity Press, 1996). On the problem of the meaning of torture, see Talal Asad, 'On torture, or cruel, inhuman and degrading treatment', in Wilson (ed.), *Human Rights, Culture and Context*, pp. 111–33.

50 Booth, 'Human wrongs', 114.

51 John Vincent, 'Modernity and universal human rights', in Anthony G. McGrew *et al.* (eds.), *Global Politics: Globalization and the Nation State* (Cambridge: Polity Press, 1992), pp. 269–92, at p. 271.

52 On rights as an aspect of power, see Wilson (ed.), *Human Rights, Culture and Context*, pp. 17–18.
53 Francis Fukuyama, *The End of History and the Last Man* (London: Hamish Hamilton, 1992).
54 Peter R. Baehr, 'The universality of human rights', paper presented at the Annual Conference of the International Studies Association, Chicago, 21–25 February 1995.
55 *Ibid.*, pp. 10–11. The practical engagement of the local with the global via the Internet in the rebellion in Chiapas in southern Mexico – the first 'cyberspace insurrection' – is a further development of this general point: see Wilson (ed.), *Human Rights, Culture and Context*, p. 11.
56 A preliminary contribution to this ambitious project is Danielle Archibugi and David Held (eds.), *Cosmopolitan Democracy. An Agenda for a New World Order* (Cambridge: Polity Press, 1995).
57 James Der Derian, 'The value of security: Hobbes, Marx, Nietzsche and Baudrillard', in Ronnie D. Lipschutz (ed.), *On Security* (New York: Columbia University Press, 1995), p. 42.
58 'Change the world', (Editorial), *Guardian*, 13 July 1996.
59 Donnelly, *Universal Human Rights*, pp. 1–5, 23–5. See also Baehr, 'Universality', p. 8, and Wilson (ed.), *Human Rights, Culture and Context*, p. 9.
60 Donald J. Puchala, 'The United Nations and the myth of unity of mankind', in Young Seek Choue and Jae Shik Sohn (eds.), *Peace Strategies for Global Community and the Role of the UN in the 21st Century* (Seoul: Institute of International Peace Studies, 1997), p. 175. This point is reinforced from a variety of different perspectives; for example: Singer, *How Are We To Live?*, p. 273 ('the golden rule'); Wilson (ed.), *Human Rights, Culture and Context*, p. 7 ('cross-cultural universals'); George Silberbouer, 'Ethics in small-scale communities', in Peter Singer (ed.), *A Companion to Ethics* (Oxford: Blackwell, 1994), pp. 14–28 ('characteristics common to all moralities').
61 Matt Ridley, *The Origins of Virtue* (London: Viking, 1996).
62 Martha Nussbaum, 'Human functioning and social justice: in defense of Aristotelian essentialism', *Political Theory* 20 (1992): 222.
63 Puchala, 'The United Nations', p. 177.
64 Allott, 'The future of the human past', *passim*.
65 Heater, 'World citizenship', *passim*; Booth, 'Human wrongs', 119.
66 See Thomas Hylland Erikson, 'Multiculturalism, individualism and human rights: Romanticism, the Enlightenment and lessons from Mauritius', in Wilson (ed.), *Human Rights, Culture and Context*, pp. 49–69. See also p. 19.
67 Richard Rorty, 'Human rights, rationality and sentimentality', in Stephen Shute and Susan Hurley (eds.), *On Human Rights: The Oxford Amnesty Lectures* (New York: Basic Books, 1993), pp. 111–34.
68 *Ibid.*, pp. 133–4.
69 Quoted in *ibid.*, p. 129.
70 Wilson (ed.), *Human Rights, Culture and Context*, p. 8.
71 Rorty, 'Human rights', pp. 112–14.
72 Geoffrey Warnock, *Contemporary Moral Philosophy* (London: Macmillan, 1967), p. 60; Mary Midgley, *Wisdom, Information and Wonder: What is Knowledge For?* (London: Routledge, 1989), pp. 154–63.

73 Wilson (ed.), *Human Rights, Culture and Context*, p. 5.
74 L. W. Beck (ed.), 'Perpetual peace', in *Kant Selections* (New York: Macmillan, 1988), p. 440.
75 Roy Bainton, 'Hell was here', *New Statesman & Society*, 28 April 1995. This is an account of a visit to Dachau, by an 'Englishman' with 'German' grandparents. At the end he concluded: 'Humanity should be stateless. The alternative leads here . . . To hell with "roots".'

2 The social construction of international human rights

Jack Donnelly

Human rights has been an established subject of international relations for only half a century. With minor exceptions – most notably, nineteenth-century efforts to end the slave trade and twentieth-century work on eradicating slavery and protecting the rights of workers and ethnic minorities – human rights simply were not a subject of international relations before World War II. Even genocidal massacres, such as Russian pogroms against the Jews or the Turkish slaughter of Armenians, were met by little more than polite statements of disapproval. Less egregious violations typically were not even considered a fit subject for diplomatic conversation.

This practice reflected a statist logic arising from the interaction of a realist notion of the national interest and a rigid legal positivist conception of sovereignty. To the realist, human rights are largely irrelevant to the national interest defined in terms of power. To the legal positivist, they present an archetypical example of actions solely within the domestic jurisdiction, and thus the sovereign prerogative, of states.

Although this radical statist logic has suffered some erosion, realist and legal positivist conceptions continue to shape dominant international human rights practices. This chapter seeks to chart the contours of contemporary international human rights norms and practices, with a special emphasis on the continuing centrality of the state.

The global human rights regime[1]

Despite the cautions and complaints of realists, states continue to pursue moral objectives in international relations. In this section I sketch the emergence of one particular set of moral concerns – human rights – as an institutionalised part of international politics. Although this story has been told before,[2] it sets a frame of reference for this volume. It is also a task assigned to me by the editors.

From Hitler to the Universal Declaration

World War II, beyond protecting material national interests and the statist ordering principles of sovereignty and territorial integrity, had significant moral overtones, especially on the American side. Beyond self-interested propaganda, there was a genuine belief that the war, particularly against Hitler's Germany, was a struggle not only against material danger but also against a moral evil that arose from the systematic violation of human rights. For example, Franklin Roosevelt's January 1942 'Four Freedoms' speech explicitly linked the war effort to protecting freedoms of speech and of worship and freedoms from want and from fear. By June 1943, planners in the US State Department had drafted a charter for a postwar international organisation that included an International Bill of Human Rights.

Human rights, however, remained a decidedly secondary concern in the wartime actions of the Allies. For example, the rail lines that kept the Nazi death camps functioning never were a major target of Allied bombing. Only as victory was being achieved, and the true horrors of the Holocaust became widely known and acknowledged, did human rights become a central concern.

Traditional international practice, however, lacked even the language with which to condemn the horrors of the Holocaust. Realist diplomacy could find no material national interest that was threatened. In fact, while German realists might have decried the diversion of strategic resources to the death camps, Allied realists could, with theoretical consistency, only see it as politically fortunate. Traditional international law was as much at a loss: massacring one's own citizens simply was not an established international offence. The German government may have been legally liable for their treatment of citizens in occupied territories, but in gassing German nationals it was simply exercising its sovereign rights.

The Nuremberg War Crimes Tribunal, despite the taint of *ex post facto* victors' justice, dramatically introduced the subject of gross violations of human rights into the mainstream of international relations. The charge of war crimes rested on a well-established body of positive international law, including the Hague and Geneva conventions. The charges of crimes against the peace and waging aggressive war, although more novel, still reflected a fundamentally statist logic. But the charge of crimes against humanity held German soldiers and officials liable for offences against individual citizens, not states, and individuals who often were nationals, not foreigners.

Of even greater long-run importance was the United Nations Charter. The exclusion of human rights from prewar international relations is perhaps best illustrated by the fact that even the notoriously idealist Covenant of the League of Nations does not mention human rights. In sharp contrast, the Preamble and Article 1 of the UN Charter include promotion of respect for human rights and fundamental freedoms among the principal purposes of the organisation.

The United Nations moved rapidly and vigorously to formulate international human rights norms. The Convention on the Prevention and Punishment of the Crime of Genocide, a direct response to the Holocaust, was adopted by the UN General Assembly on 9 December 1948. The following day the Assembly adopted the Universal Declaration of Human Rights. This was a decisive step in codifying the emerging view that the way in which states treat their own citizens is not only a legitimate international concern but subject to international standards.

The initial momentum of the immediate postwar years, however, was not sustained. Work on a covenant to give greater legal force and specificity to the rights enumerated in the Universal Declaration became bogged down, and had largely been abandoned by 1954. This reflected a more general return of human rights to the fringes of international relations. The rise of the Cold War, which decisively reshaped international relations in the 1950s, explains part of this recession. No less important, though, was the fact that most states were satisfied with an international human rights regime that included little more than a strong statement of norms.

For apparently genuine moral reasons, states were no longer willing to leave human rights entirely beyond international purview. But they were unwilling to allow multilateral monitoring of national human rights practices, let alone international implementation or enforcement. For example, at its first session, in early 1947, the UN Commission on Human Rights resolved that it had 'no power to take any action in regard to any complaints concerning human rights'.[3]

The International Human Rights Covenants

The early 1960s witnessed a new wave of UN human rights activity, led by the newly independent states of Africa and Asia. The International Convention on the Elimination of All Forms of Racial Discrimination, which addressed a topic of special concern to the Afro-Asian bloc, was adopted by the General Assembly in December 1965. Work also began anew on a comprehensive international human rights treaty. In December 1966, the International Covenant on Economic, Social and Cultural Rights and the International Covenant on Civil and Political Rights were opened for signature and ratification. Along with the Universal

Table 2. *Internationally recognised human rights*

The International Bill of Human Rights recognises the rights to:

Equality of rights without discrimination (D1, D2, E2 E3, C2, C3)
Life (D3, C6)
Liberty and security of person (D3, C9)
Protection against slavery (D4, C8)
Protection against torture and cruel and inhuman punishment (D5, C7)
Recognition as a person before the law (D6, C16)
Equal protection of the law (D7, C14, C26)
Access to legal remedies for rights violations (D8, C2)
Protection against arbitrary arrest or detention (D9, C9)
Hearing before an independent and impartial judiciary (D10, C14)
Presumption of innocence (D11, C14)
Protection against *ex post facto* Laws (D11, C15)
Protection of privacy, family and home (D12, C17)
Freedom of movement and residence (D13, C12)
Seek asylum from persecution (D14)
Nationality (D15)
Marry and found a family (D16, E10, C23)
Own property (D17)
Freedom of thought, conscience and religion (D18, C18)
Freedom of opinion, expression and the Press (D19, C19)
Freedom of assembly and association (D20, C21, C22)
Political participation (D21, C25)
Social security (D22, E9)
Work, under favourable conditions (D23, E6, E7)
Free trade unions (D23, E8, C22)
Rest and leisure (D24, E7)
Food, clothing and housing (D25, E11)
Healthcare and social services (D25, E12)
Special protections for children (D25, E10, C24)
Education (D26, E13, E14)
Participation in cultural life (D27, E15)
A social and international order needed to realise rights (D28)
Self-determination (E1, C1)
Humane treatment when detained or imprisoned (C10)
Protection against debtor's prison (C11)
Protection against arbitrary expulsion of aliens (C13)
Protection against advocacy of racial or religious hatred (C20)
Protection of minority culture (C27)

Note: This list includes all rights that are enumerated in two of the three documents of the International Bill of Human Rights or have a full article in one document. The source of each right is indicated in parentheses, by document and article number: D = Universal Declaration of Human Rights; E = International Covenant on Economic, Social and Cultural Rights; C = International Covenant on Civil and Political Rights.

Declaration they provided – and still provide[4] – an authoritative statement of internationally recognised human rights. Table 2 summarises the rights they recognise.

Further progress, however, was slow and erratic. The 1968 (Teheran) World Conference on Human Rights, held to mark the twentieth anniversary of the Universal Declaration, take stock of past achievements, and chart future priorities, was followed not by a new spurt of activity but by a decade-long lull. Part of this can be attributed, ironically, to the successful completion of the Covenants. While their comprehensiveness took much of the urgency out of additional normative work, it was to be nearly ten years before they received the necessary thirty-five ratifications to enter into force. The result was a frustrating delay in shifting from a near exclusive emphasis on standard-setting to an emphasis on international implementation.

The letdown of the early 1970s, however, also owed much to the persistence of a statist, sovereignty-respecting logic. This is most clear in the 'implementation' machinery of the Covenants and the Racial Discrimination Convention: periodic reports by states to a committee of independent experts. These supervisory committees were not authorised to find violations of the treaty, call for changes in state practice or seek remedy for victims.[5]

Human rights norms had become fully internationalised. Implementation and enforcement, however, remained almost completely national. States accepted an obligation to implement internationally recognised human rights. But they restricted international supervision of these obligations to non-intrusive international monitoring. The Covenants reaffirmed and helped to deepen the view that human rights were a fit subject for international discussion – but not for concrete, let alone coercive, international action.

This assessment of the decade following the adoption of the Covenants is perhaps a bit too harsh. Work on self-determination and apartheid intensified. In 1967, Economic and Social Council Resolution 1235 authorised the Commission on Human Rights to discuss human rights publicly (although with special emphasis on racial discrimination and colonial territories). And in 1970, Resolution 1503 gave the Commission the authority to conduct confidential investigations of communications 'which appear to reveal a consistent pattern of gross and reliably attested violations of human rights and fundamental freedoms'.

In practice, however, these new monitoring powers were little used during the 1970s. And even if they had been used in an aggressive, non-partisan fashion, they represented incremental procedural developments. Only persuasive verbal action against human rights violators was authorised. Additional talk rarely hurt. On occasion, it undoubtedly helped. But the limits of these procedures underscore the persistence of a strongly statist logic in the global human rights regime.

The Carter revival

The third wave of intensive international human rights activity came in the mid-1970s, triggered by three major events. Revulsion against the overthrow of the Allende government in Chile in September 1973 and the ensuing violent repression led to the creation of a UN working group on Chile. This was the first time that the practices of a gross human rights violator had been subjected to intensive, detailed investigation by the UN.[6] In 1976, the Covenants finally entered into force, providing a new, relatively non-partisan monitoring forum in the Human Rights Committee created under the Civil and Political Covenant. And in 1977, Jimmy Carter became President of the United States. Carter's embrace of human rights as a priority for American foreign policy at least partly disentangled international human rights from the East–West politics of the Cold War and the North–South struggles over a new international economic order. This gave new momentum and legitimacy to the work of human rights advocates throughout the world.

In the Commission on Human Rights[7] in particular, space opened for the emergence of a revitalised Western bloc, led by countries such as Canada and the Netherlands. Important new treaties were formulated, including the Convention on the Elimination of All Forms of Discrimination Against Women (1979), the Convention Against Torture and Other Cruel Inhuman or Degrading Treatment or Punishment (1984), and the Convention on the Rights of the Child (1989). Building on the precedent of Chile, special representatives and rapporteurs were appointed to study human rights situations in a growing and increasingly diverse range of countries, including Bolivia, El Salvador, Equatorial Guinea, Iran and Afghanistan.

The Commission on Human Rights also began to consider human rights violations on a 'global' or 'thematic' basis. Rather than examine abuses in individual countries, particular types of violations were addressed globally, wherever they occurred. Most prominent was the Working Group on Enforced or Involuntary Disappearances, created in 1980 to help families and friends determine the whereabouts of disappeared persons, which handled over 19,000 cases in its first decade of work. A Special Rapporteur on summary or arbitrary executions was appointed in 1982, followed in 1985 by a Special Rapporteur on torture.

No less important during the Carter era was the introduction of human rights into the mainstream of bilateral foreign policy. At the height of the Cold War, human rights were largely restricted to multilateral international arenas. The language of human rights was most striking for its absence in bilateral relations, even when dealing with central human rights issues. For example, the United States regularly used the language of freedom and democracy, not human rights, and the Soviets typically spoke of particular abuses, such as racism, colonialism and unemployment, rather than human rights in general.

In 1973, the US Congress explicitly linked foreign aid disbursements to the human rights performance of recipients. Tentative efforts in this direction were taken about the same time in the aid policies of the Nordic countries. The Jackson–Vanick Amendment to the Trade Act of 1974 linked liberalised US–Soviet trade to Soviet policies on Jewish emigration. And the Helsinki Final Act of 1975 introduced human rights into the mainstream of US–Soviet relations. The emerging trend represented by such initiatives received a major boost from Carter's prominent public human rights diplomacy.

Occasionally, this new bilateral emphasis on human rights was formally codified, as in the Dutch White Paper of 1979. More often, there was a less formal, yet surprisingly rapid and clear, change. By the mid-1980s, debate in most Western countries focused less on whether human rights should be an active concern of foreign policy than on which rights should be pursued where. Even the Reagan Administration, which in 1981 explicitly announced its intention to replace Carter's emphasis on human rights with an emphasis on combating international terrorism, increasingly came to justify its policies in human rights terms.

The mid-1970s also saw a major upsurge in international human rights activity by non-governmental organisations (NGOs), symbolised by the award of the Nobel Peace Prize to Amnesty International in 1977. These groups, in addition to their advocacy for victims of human rights abuses, have been important actors in changing bilateral and multilateral international human rights policies. For example, international campaigns against torture by Amnesty in the 1970s and 1980s played an important role in the drafting of the 1984 Convention Against Torture. At the national level, the Dutch section of Amnesty was involved in drafting the government's human rights White Paper. In the United States, several human rights NGOs were important players in the struggles over Central American policy in the 1980s.

Both the achievements and the limitations of the past half-century of international human rights activity deserve emphasis. By the end of the Cold War, human rights had become a regular and well-established part of international relations. And post-Cold War developments, discussed below, have produced further incremental deepening. States today, in sharp contrast to half a century ago, are subject to a considerable array of multilateral, bilateral and transnational monitoring procedures that aim to mobilise national and international public opinion and the normative force of the idea of human rights.[8] International attitudes and practices have over the past half-century been transformed, and the resources for national and international action are stronger than ever before.

States and their sovereign prerogatives, however, also remain strong. The global human rights regime continues to address only a partial (although very important) list of human rights and wrongs, as I will emphasise below. And institutionalised international mechanisms to address moral concerns outside the realm of human rights usually are even less well developed. Although we have in this one area of endeavour constructed a noticeably better world, the limits of the contemporary construction of international human rights should not be overlooked.

Right, wrong and international human rights

This global human rights regime rests on a distinctive moral and political vision. Internationally recognised human rights, I will argue, represent a distinctive strategy for responding to a relatively narrow yet very important set of human rights and wrongs. Were my inclinations more postmodern, I might describe this endeavour as an analysis of the discourse of human rights, or even a deconstruction of international human rights.

Right, rectitude and entitlement

To understand the particular character of human rights we must start with the fact that 'right' in English has two principal moral and political senses: rectitude and entitlement.[9] The sense of 'rectitude' is the more general. In this sense we speak of 'the right thing to do' and say of something that it *is* right (or wrong). The focus is on the righteousness of the required action, and the duty-bearer's obligation to do 'what is right'.

Entitlement is a narrower sense of 'right'. Rather than speaking of some*thing being* right, we typically talk of some*one having* a right. When one *has* a right, one is specially entitled to something, and therefore armed with claims that have a special force. The focus is on the relationship between right-holder and duty-bearer.

If Anne has a right to x with respect to Bob, it is not simply desirable, good or even merely right that Anne enjoy x. She is *entitled* to it. Should Bob fail to discharge his obligations, besides acting improperly and harming Anne, he violates her rights. This makes him subject to remedial claims and sanctions that she largely controls.

Anne is not merely a beneficiary of Bob's obligation. She may assert her right to x, in order to try to ensure that Bob discharges his obligation. If he fails to do so, she may press further claims against Bob (or excuse him), largely at her own discretion. She is actively in charge of the relationship, as suggested by the language of 'exercising' rights. Rights empower, in addition to benefiting, those who hold them.

Rights, in the sense of entitlement, are a special subclass of right. Rights, thus, are related only to a subset of human wrongs. Human rights – the rights one has simply because one is a human being – are a subset of rights. They thus deal with an even narrower range of human wrongs.

We do not have rights – let alone human rights – to all things that are good. We do not even have human rights to all *important* good things. Many notable rights (in the sense of rectitude) and wrongs – for example, charity, compassion and the support of loving family and friends – simply are not matters of 'human rights' (entitlement). Parents or partners that abuse the trust of children and partners wreak havoc with millions of lives every day. Not only do we not have human rights to compassionate, supportive and loving parents and partners, but to recognise such rights would radically transform these relationships (in a way that I think most people would find extremely destructive).

The emphasis on human rights in contemporary international relations thus implies selecting certain types of rights and wrongs for special attention, and thereby indirectly de-emphasizing or devaluing others. It also means selecting a particular mechanism – rights (entitlement) – for advancing those rights (in the sense of rectitude) and remedying those wrongs.

Human rights are not just abstract values, but a set of particular social practices to realise those values. Underlying values and aspirations, or the substantive object of any particular human right, should not be confused with that right itself, let alone with the broader idea or practice of human rights. Even where 'the same' values are pursued, their grounds and the means to realise them may differ dramatically.

For example, protection against arbitrary execution is internationally recognised today as a human right. But the fact that people are not executed arbitrarily may reflect nothing more than a government's lack of desire or capacity. Even if people are actively protected against arbitrary execution, that protection may have nothing to do with a right (title) not to be executed. For example, a divine injunction to rulers need not endow subjects with any rights. And even if one has a right not to be arbitrarily executed, that right need not be a human right. It might, for example, rest entirely on custom or statute.

Such distinctions are not mere scholastic niceties. When subjects lack a right (title), they are protected differently. There is an important difference between denying something to someone that it would *be* right for her to enjoy in a just world, and denying her something she is entitled (*has* a right) to enjoy. Violations of rights are a particular kind of injustice, with a distinctive force and remedial logic. Furthermore, whether the right is merely a legal right, contingently granted by the state, or a human right will dramatically alter the relationship between states and subjects, and the character of the injury suffered.

The historical particularity of human rights

Human rights are typically understood, following the manifest, literal sense of the term, as the rights that one has simply because one is human. They are universal rights: every human being has them. They are equal rights: one either is a human being (and thus has these rights equally) or not. And they are inalienable rights: one cannot stop being a human being, and thus cannot stop having these rights.

As I have argued in more detail elsewhere,[10] human rights, thus understood, rest on and seek to realise a particular conception of human nature, dignity, well-being, or flourishing. Human beings are seen as equal and autonomous individuals rather than bearers of ascriptively defined social roles. Individuals are also members of families and communities, workers, church-goers, citizens and occupants of numerous other social roles. A human rights conception, however, insists that essential to their dignity, and to a life worthy of a human being, is the simple fact that they are human beings. This gives them an irreducible worth that entitles them to equal concern and respect from the state and the opportunity to make fundamental choices about what constitutes the good life (for them), who they associate with, and how.

Although treaties and international declarations rarely point to their philosophical foundations, leading international human rights instruments do reflect something very much like this understanding. For example, the Universal Declaration of Human Rights begins by recognising 'the inherent dignity and the equal and inalienable rights of all members of the human family' and the International Human Rights Covenants explicitly claim that the rights they recognise 'derive from the inherent dignity of the human person'. Perhaps the clearest statement, however, comes in the second preambulatory paragraph of the Vienna Declaration and Programme of Action adopted in June 1993 at the (Second) World Conference on Human Rights.

Recognizing and affirming that all human rights derive from the dignity and worth inherent in the human person, and that the human person is the central subject of human rights and fundamental freedoms, and consequently should be the principal beneficiary and should participate actively in the realization of these rights and freedoms.

Such a conception of human dignity, well-being or flourishing is, in a broad cross-cultural and historical perspective, extremely unusual.[11] Many cultures and societies across time and space have shared values such as equity, fairness, compassion and respect for one's fellows. Very few, however, have sought to realise these values through equal and inalienable universal rights.

In most pre-modern societies, both Western and non-Western, persons were seen not as equal and autonomous individuals endowed with natural and inalienable rights but as differentiated occupants of traditional social roles defined by characteristics such as birth, sex, age and occupation. For example, ancient Greeks distinguished between Hellenes and barbarians (non-Greeks), who were seen as congenitally inferior. The Romans recognised rights based on birth, citizenship and achievement, not mere humanity. And Christians, despite a religious emphasis on the equality of all believers, often treated Jews, infidels and heretics as less than fully human. The idea that shared humanity provided all individuals with basic social and political rights simply cannot be found in the mainstream of classical or medieval Western political theory, let alone practice.

In pre-modern Western political thought, rulers were seen to have obligations to rule wisely and for the common good. These duties, however, arose from divine commandment, natural law, tradition or contingent political arrangements. They did not rest on the rights of all human beings to be ruled justly. In a well-ordered society, the people were to be beneficiaries of the political obligations of the rulers. But they had no (natural or human) rights that could be exercised against unjust rulers. The reigning idea was natural right (in the sense of rectitude) not natural rights (entitlements).[12]

Human rights – equal and inalienable rights, held by all human beings simply because they are human and exercisable against the state and society – are a distinctive, historically unusual set of social values and practices. The universality of human rights is a moral claim about the proper way to organise social and political relations in the contemporary world, not an historical or anthropological fact. Human rights are an eminently contestable basis for ordering social and political life. They are, however, as we saw above, the predominant model of social and political organization endorsed by contemporary international society.

A (very) brief history of human rights

The idea of natural or human rights permanently entered the mainstream of political theory and practice in seventeenth-century Europe, in response to the social disruptions and transformations of modernity. Political and economic centralisation and the growing penetration of the market created (relatively) autonomous individuals and families in place of members of traditional local communities occupying ascriptive roles. These new modern individuals and families were left (relatively) alone to face both the growing coercive powers of ever more intrusive states and the new indignities of free market capitalism. These same forces also supported the political rise of the middle classes, who found in natural rights a powerful argument against aristocratic privilege.

The substance of the human rights advanced by these newly emergent social actors was no less historically contingent. Consider, for example, John Locke's *Second Treatise on Government* (1688), which presented the first fully developed natural rights theory fundamentally consistent with later human rights ideas. Locke's list of natural rights to life, liberty and estates strikes most late-twentieth-century readers as far too narrow. Furthermore, despite the apparent universalism of the language of natural rights, Locke develops a theory for the protection of the rights of propertied European males. Women, along with 'savages', servants and wage labourers of either sex, were not recognised as right-holders.

The history of struggles for human rights in the following three centuries can be seen as leading to a gradual expansion of recognised subjects of human rights, towards the ideal of full and equal inclusion of all members of the species. Gender, race, property and religion have been formally eliminated as legitimate grounds for denying the enjoyment of natural or human rights in almost all realms of public life in almost all Western countries (and most other countries as well). In effect, racist, bourgeois, Christian patriarchs found the same natural rights arguments they had used against aristocratic privilege turned against them in a struggle to incorporate new social groups into the realm of equal citizens entitled to participate in public and private life as autonomous subjects and agents.

Property restrictions on the enjoyment of natural rights were often defended by arguing that those without property lacked the leisure required to develop their rational capacities sufficiently to be full participants in political society. The rise of mass literacy seriously undercut such arguments. Mass electoral politics, in which participation was conceived more as authorising and reviewing the actions of others than as direct political decision-making, also reduced the plausibility of such arguments. The common claim that the unpropertied lacked a sufficient 'stake' in society to be allowed full political participation fell to changing conceptions of political membership, beginning with the American and French revolutions, the rise of popular armies and growing nationalist sentiments. Legal discrimination based on an alleged lack of independence of the unpropertied gave way to social and economic changes associated with industrialisation, particularly the increasingly impersonal relations between workers and employers and the general depersonalisation of relations in urban settings. And the implicit assumption of the coincidence of wealth and virtue was eroded by general processes of social levelling and mobility.

Women and non-whites were until well into this century widely seen in the West as irreparably deficient in their rational or moral capabilities, and thus incapable of exercising human rights. But these racial and gender distinctions were, at least in principle, subject to principled and empirical counter-arguments. Movements against slavery, for women's suffrage and against discrimination based on race and sex had by the mid-twentieth century substantially transformed dominant Western political ideas and practices. A similar process led to the elimination of formal disabilities against Jews, some Christian sects, pagans, and atheists, which were the norm in eighteenth-century Europe. The logic was essentially the same: although different, adherents of different, even despised, religions were nonetheless fully human and thus entitled to the same rights as other human beings.

With an expanded range of subjects recognised to hold natural rights, the substance of those rights underwent parallel revisions. For example, the political left argued that existing private property rights were incompatible with true liberty, equality and security for working men (and later, women). Through intense and often violent political struggles, this led to the rise of social insurance schemes, regulations on working conditions and an extended range of recognised economic, social and cultural rights, culminating in the welfare state societies of late-twentieth-century Europe.

Our experience with modern states and markets has produced further changes in human rights ideas and practices. As the coercive capacity and penetration of the state grew, protecting space for autonomous public and private action became a growing priority. New legal rights have thus been recognised and a greater emphasis has been placed on an expanded understanding of such rights as freedom of religion, expression, association and assembly. As modern markets have transformed families and communities, new mechanisms for assuring subsistence and social welfare have been developed. Major changes in economic and social rights have also come from our growing understanding of the destructive unintended consequences of private property rights and a growing appreciation of alternative, rights-based means for realising economic security and participation in a world of industrial capitalism.

The International Human Rights Covenants can be seen as completing and codifying this expansion of the subjects of human rights by extending them globally. They also codify an evolved shared understanding of the principal systematic public threats to human dignity in the contemporary world and the practices necessary to counter them. To oversimplify only slightly, they set out as a hegemonic political model something very much like the liberal democratic welfare state of Western Europe, in which all adult nationals are incorporated as full legal and political equals able to claim by rights an extensive array of social welfare services, social and economic opportunities and civil and political liberties.[13]

Contemporary liberals may be tempted to see in this history a gradual unfolding of the inherent logic of natural rights. With the benefit of hindsight, it may even be illuminating to talk of a purification of practice to more closely approximate the underlying moral ideal of fully equal and autonomous human beings regulating their public lives through the mechanism of equal and inalienable natural rights. But we must be wary of Whiggish self-satisfaction and comfortable teleological views of moral progress.

There is nothing natural, let alone inevitable, about ordering social and political life around the idea of human rights. Furthermore, the particular list of rights that we take as authoritative today reflects a contingent response to historically specific conditions. For example, Article 11 of the International Covenant on Civil and Political Rights states that 'no one shall be imprisoned merely on the ground of inability to fulfill a contractual obligation', a clear response to the (historically very unusual) practice of debtor prisons. Contemporary conceptions of human rights reflect a long process of social and political struggle that might easily have turned out differently. And our list of authoritatively recognised human rights may change in response to changes in our understanding of human dignity, the emergence of new threats, and social learning concerning the institutions, practices and values necessary to realise that dignity.

The historical contingency of international human rights norms, however, does not make them any less authoritative. Neither arbitrary nor
capable of being changed merely through acts of the will, they are
deeply rooted social constructions that shape our lives. The vision of
human dignity they reflect and seek to implement is predominant in
contemporary international society, accepted by almost all states as
authoritative – whatever their deviations from these norms in practice.
Human rights have become a central, perhaps even defining, element of
the social and political reality of the late-twentieth-century world.

States and international human rights

If human rights are held universally – that is, equally and by all – one
might imagine that they hold universally against all other individuals
and groups. Such a conception is inherently plausible. It is in many
ways morally attractive. But it is not the dominant contemporary international understanding. Human rights, although held equally by all
human beings, are held with respect to, and exercised against, the
sovereign territorial state.

The Covenants and other international human rights treaties establish rights for all individuals. The obligations they create, however, are
only for states. And states have international human rights obligations
only to their own nationals (and foreign nationals in their territory or
otherwise subject to their jurisdiction or control). Contemporary international (and regional) human rights regimes are supervisory mechanisms that monitor relations between states and citizens. They are not
alternatives to a fundamentally statist conception of human rights. Even
in the strong European regional human rights regime, the supervisory
organs of the European Commission and Court of Human Rights regulate relations between states and their nationals or residents.

The centrality of states in the contemporary construction of international human rights is also clear in the substance of recognised rights.
Some, most notably rights of political participation, are typically restricted to citizens. Other rights apply only to residents. For example,
states have international human rights obligations to provide education
and social insurance only to residents. The remaining internationally
recognised human rights, such as freedom of speech and protection
against torture, apply to foreign nationals only while they are subject to
the jurisdiction of the state.

Foreign states simply have no internationally recognised human rights
obligation to protect foreign nationals abroad from, for example, torture. They are not even at liberty to use more than persuasive means on

behalf of torture victims. Current norms of state sovereignty still prohibit states from acting coercively abroad to remedy torture and most other violations of human rights.

This focus on state–citizen relations is also embedded in our ordinary language. A person beaten by the police has her human rights violated. But it is an ordinary crime, not a human rights violation, to receive an otherwise identical beating at the hands of a thief or an irascible neighbour. Internationally, we distinguish human rights violations from war crimes. Even when comparable suffering is inflicted on innocent civilians, we draw a sharp categorical distinction based on whether the perpetrator is (an agent of) one's own or a foreign government.

Although neither necessary nor inevitable, this state-centric conception of human rights has deep historical roots. The idea of human rights first appears in, and remains deeply enmeshed with, liberal social contract theory, the only major tradition of social and political theory that begins with individuals endowed with equal and inalienable rights. And the contractarian notion of the state as an instrument for the protection, implementation and effective realisation of natural rights is strikingly similar to the conception of the state in international human rights instruments. Both share the view that the legitimacy of the state is to be measured largely by its performance in implementing human rights.

The restriction of international human rights obligations to nationals, residents and visitors also reflects the central role of the sovereign state in modern politics. Since at least the sixteenth century, states (initially, dynastic ones and, later, territorial nation-states) have struggled, with considerable success, to consolidate their internal authority over competing local powers. Simultaneously, sovereign states in the early modern era struggled, with even greater success, to free themselves from imperial and papal authority. And their late modern successors have jealously, zealously and largely successfully fought attempts to reinstitute supranational authority.

With power and authority thus doubly concentrated, the modern state has emerged as both the principal threat to the enjoyment of human rights and the essential institution for their effective implementation and enforcement. Both sides of this relationship between the state and human rights require emphasis.

The immense power and reach of the modern state makes controlling it central to the realisation of any plausible conception of human dignity. The human rights strategy of control has had two principal dimensions. Negatively, it prohibits a wide range of state interferences in the personal, social and political lives of citizens, acting both individually and collectively. But beyond carving out zones of state exclusion, human rights place the people above and in positive control of their government. Political authority is vested in a free citizenry endowed with extensive rights of political participation (rights to vote, freedom of association, free speech, etc.).

The state, however, precisely because of its political dominance in the contemporary world, is the central institution available for effectively implementing internationally recognised human rights. 'Failed states', such as Somalia, suggest that one of the few things as frightening in the contemporary world as an efficiently repressive state is no state at all. Human rights are thus not only concerned with preventing state-based wrongs. They also require the state to provide certain goods, services and opportunities.

Although obvious for most economic and social rights, the essential positive role of the state is no less central to many civil and political rights. For example, the effective implementation of rights to non-discrimination often requires extensive positive actions to realise the underlying value of equality. Even procedural rights such as due process entail considerable positive endeavours with respect to police, courts and administrative procedures. And rights that guarantee political participation are not merely instrumentally valuable in controlling the state, but good in themselves. The state is thus required not merely to refrain from certain harmful actions, but to create a political environment that fosters the development of active, engaged, autonomous citizens.

Other strategies have been tried or proposed for controlling the destructive capacities of the state and harnessing its constructive powers for realising important human values and goods. For example, the virtue or wisdom of leaders, party members or clerics, the expertise of technocrats and the special skills and social position of the military have seemed to many to be attractive alternatives to human rights as bases of political order and legitimacy. But the human rights approach has proved more effective than any alternative yet tried – or at least that is how I read the remarkably consistent collapse of dictatorships of the left and right alike over the last dozen years in Latin America, Central and Eastern Europe, Africa and Asia.

These alternative strategies treat people largely as objects rather than as agents. They rest on an inegalitarian and paternalistic view of the average person as someone to be provided for, a passive recipient of benefits, rather than a creative agent with a right to shape his or her life. Thus, even if we overlook their naively benign view of power and the state, they grossly undervalue both autonomy and participation. By contrast, a human rights conception rests on a distinctive linkage of equality and autonomy, summarised in the notion of (individual and collective) self-determination, that has extremely deep contemporary resonance.

Nonetheless, it would be a limiting and potentially dangerous delusion to see current human rights ideas and practices as fixed, let alone the final and perfect unfolding of a comprehensive, timeless vision of human rights and wrongs. We must remain open to alternative strategies and practices for realising human dignity. One way to think about the subject of this volume is as an inquiry into the adequacy of singling out this particular class of human rights and wrongs in international relations. In what space remains to me, I will speculate on changes likely over the next couple of decades, again with special attention to the central role of the state in the contemporary international human rights regime.

Post-Cold War changes

The post-Cold War era has so far brought an incremental deepening of the global human rights regime. Existing multilateral procedures are being used more vigorously and with greater impartiality, and the UN High Commissioner for Human Rights, established at the end of 1993, has the potential to increase both the scope and depth of multilateral monitoring (although the activities of the High Commissioner have, to date, been modest). In bilateral relations, human rights in most countries continue to become a more deeply entrenched and less controversial foreign policy concern. In addition, non-governmental human rights organisations and advocates have become a significant part of the political landscape in a growing number of countries in the Third World and former Soviet bloc.

Perhaps the most dramatic progress in recent years has been in international responses to genocide. During the Cold War era, genocide and politicide, in places such as Burundi, East Pakistan, Cambodia and Uganda, were met by verbal expressions of concern, but little concrete action (except by neighbouring states – India, Vietnam and Tanzania – with a strong selfish interest in intervening). But the international tribunals for the former Yugoslavia and Rwanda, created in 1991 and 1994, have revived the long-dormant Nuremberg precedent. And the General Assembly's decision at the end of 1995 to create an international criminal tribunal suggests a deeper normative transformation. Genocide, it appears, has finally come to be considered truly intolerable by the international community.

A broader normative deepening was evidenced at the 1993 Vienna World Conference on Human Rights. Although much of the press coverage emphasised controversies over women's rights and cultural relativism, Vienna actually represented a dramatic decline in ideological conflict over human rights and a clear victory for advocates of the universality of international human rights obligations. For example, paragraph 1 of the Vienna Declaration and Programme of Action asserts that 'the universal nature of these rights and freedoms is beyond question'. Paragraph 5 in particular marked a decisive defeat for the advocates of strong cultural relativism:

All human rights are universal, indivisible and interdependent and interrelated. The international community must treat human rights globally in a fair and equal manner, on the same footing, and with the same emphasis. While the significance of national and regional particularities and various historical, cultural and religious backgrounds must be borne in mind, it is the duty of States, regardless of their political, economic and cultural systems, to promote and protect all human rights and fundamental freedoms.

This assertion of the interdependence and indivisibility of all human rights is stronger than in previous documents.[14] Furthermore, paragraph 10 asserts that 'the lack of development may not be invoked to justify the abridgment of internationally recognized human rights', thereby removing a standard defence of developmental dictatorships of the 1970s and 1980s. Although there are still huge gaps between principle and practice in most countries, the international normative consensus on human rights clearly has deepened in the past few years.

Normative deepening is also suggested by the growing penetration of human rights into other areas of international concern. Perhaps most striking is the explicit incorporation of human rights concerns into multilateral peace-keeping operations.

Until the late 1980s, peace-keeping operations were scrupulously organised and operated to avoid direct reference to human rights. This reflected the politicised nature of UN human rights discussions and the desire of most states to avoid creating any sort of precedent for direct UN multilateral action on behalf of internationally recognised human rights. In recent years, however, the link between human rights and international peace and security, which has been a central part of United Nations doctrine since the drafting of the Charter, has finally become a part of UN practice.[15]

UN peace-keeping operations in Namibia, El Salvador, Cambodia, Mozambique, Bosnia, Croatia and Guatemala have had explicit human rights responsibilities. UN operations in Haiti and Rwanda even had primarily human rights mandates. Operations in Somalia and northern Iraq also included a human rights dimension. The tasks of these peace-keeping forces have included monitoring the activities of the police and security forces, verifying the discharge of human rights undertakings in agreements ending civil wars, supervising elections, encouraging authorities to adopt international human rights instruments and comply with their international human rights obligations, and providing human rights education. Peace-keepers in El Salvador, Haiti, Guatemala and Rwanda even had explicit mandates to investigate human rights violations.

We should neither underestimate the reality and importance of the change represented by these operations nor overgeneralise from them. Because most of these cases arose in the context of ending internationalised civil wars, they do not provide an obvious precedent for UN action in the absence of a peace and security mandate. In addition, most rested on either the consent of the authorities of the state in question or the near complete collapse of civil authority. Only in Iraq, a very special case, and in Haiti, a questionable precedent because of American regional hegemony, was there a substantially coercive element directed against an established, functioning government.

But however special the circumstances or narrow the precedents, we for the first time have a clear and rather consistent stream of coercive multilateral actions on behalf of internationally recognised human rights. In earlier eras, the international community probably would have maintained the fiction of a functioning government in Somalia and Rwanda. And the willingness of new civilian governments in El Salvador and Guatemala to accept an active UN role in their internal political affairs reflects a major change in political attitudes. Furthermore, few of these cases are tainted by the crude self-interest that corrupted unilateral humanitarian interventions during the Cold War era.

Nonetheless, willingness to act in response to genocide, the collapse of civil order, or a brokered invitation does not obviously translate into willingness to take similar action in the face of human rights violations short of genocide, or even when a genocidal government maintains considerable control over much of its country. Sudan is instructive. Aid agencies have pressed the limits of sovereignty by providing humanitarian relief without government permission, and sometimes even when faced with opposition by the government in Khartoum. This suggests a further dimension of the weakening of sovereign prerogatives in the case of massive suffering. But Sudan's genocidal civil war, which has been fought on and off for four decades, still has not provoked coercive international intervention.[16]

In addition, cases such as China, Cuba, Zaire and Burma suggest that recalcitrant states can effectively assert their sovereign rights to engage in gross and persistent systematic violations of internationally recognised human rights if not indefinitely, then certainly for a very long time. Furthermore, more 'ordinary' or less spectacular patterns of systematic human rights violations still provoke remarkably modest international responses. In fact, the dramatic demise of many of the world's most brutal regimes seems to have at least partially obscured the public's awareness of or interest in the persisting serious human rights problems in numerous liberalised but by no means democratised regimes.

Furthermore, the penetration of international human rights norms into peace and security and humanitarian assistance issues has not been paralleled in other important areas. In fact, one could argue that there has been a growing contradiction between multilateral human rights initiatives and the activities of international financial institutions.[17] In the United Nations in particular, human rights have traditionally been rigidly segregated from political and especially economic (development) activities. This served the short-run political interests of Third World regimes in the 1970s and 1980s. Today, however, it leaves them without a well-established human rights argument against externally imposed structural adjustment programmes that require a reduction in the enjoyment of economic, social and cultural rights. And those in the international human rights community remain strangely reticent to press human rights arguments against structural adjustment.

Looking at these changes in the post-Cold War era from a broad, systemic perspective, the progress of recent years appears real but incremental and largely on the fringes. The international community has become willing to respond to gross human rights violations in a greater number of instances. A decision seems to have been reached that genocide will no longer be tolerated. But in situations of ordinary, even severe, violations short of genocide by governments with some capacity to rule, we still lack not only the authority for but even the rudimentary beginnings of a practice of coercive international action on behalf of internationally recognised human rights.[18]

The decline of the state?

A much more fundamental change in international human rights practices would involve reconceptualising the role of the state as the central provider of human rights. Article 28 of the Universal Declaration of Human Rights reads 'Everyone is entitled to a social and international order in which the rights and freedoms set forth in this Declaration can be fully realized.' Very little attention has been given to changes in the international order that would foster realisation of internationally recognised human rights.

Humanitarian assistance provides a possible start for change in this direction. One might want to read recent initiatives in Somalia, Bosnia and even Sudan as the first steps towards the development of a *right* to humanitarian assistance. The great lengths to which the UN has gone in Somalia and Iraq to deny that its operations have in any way infringed traditional notions of state sovereignty suggests to me at least that we are very far away from such a fundamental reconceptualisation. There are also serious practical questions about how such a right might be exercised. Nonetheless, a human right to humanitarian assistance might offer some sort of (very minimal) international safety-net in what would remain predominantly a system of national implementation.

More substantial changes in the central role of the state in the global human rights regime, however, seem to me even less likely. The centrality of the state as the bearer of duties correlative to internationally recognised human rights reflects not only its dominant place as an agent for delivering goods, services and opportunities but also its continuing role as the focal point of visions of political loyalty and community. Neither, in my view, is likely to change significantly over the next few decades.

Changing conceptions of political community

As noted above, the idea that the obligations of human rights are universal is inherently plausible and has considerable moral appeal. But without the development of a sense of cosmopolitan, or at least regional, moral community, state-centric conceptions of human rights obligations are likely to persist. And I see little evidence of such normative change.

Even some of the examples of 'progressive' change cited above have their dark side when considered from the perspective of changing conceptions of community. In Rwanda, Somalia and the former Yugoslavia, relatively cosmopolitan international responses were necessitated by the politicisation of narrow ethnic loyalties. More generally, the post-Cold War era has seen a major resurgence in nationalism. This at least partially counterbalances greater willingness to respond to certain kinds of suffering by foreigners.

Ethnic cleansing represents a vision of the nation-state in which peoples not territory define the central locus of political loyalty, obligation and organisation. Religious fundamentalism suggests replacing current territorial conceptions of community with an ecclesiastical rather than a global conception. 'Traditional community values', in their current Asian and North American incarnations alike, appeal to a community defined by a previous historical experience. At least some prominent competitors to secular territorial states are hardly attractive from a human rights perspective.

We must also note that few states are regularly willing to accept significant costs to pursue international human rights objectives. Consider, for example, the United States, which in recent years has been unwilling to impose economic sanctions on China for human rights violations, but made apparently credible threats to impose sanctions over CD pirating. A focus on narrowly defined national interests remains, and is likely to remain, predominant even as we witness the rise in salience of more cosmopolitan values.

We are witnessing a subtle, although important, transformation of the character of the state and its rights and responsibilities, rather than its demise or replacement by other actors in the field of human rights. Only in rare instances are states, separately or collectively, willing to intervene with force in response to even egregious human rights violations. But many states are no longer willing to stand by idly, even silently, in the face of systematic human rights violations and brutality. There thus are substantially greater political costs to human rights violations today than two or three decades ago.

Consider, for example, the surprisingly strong international reaction against Russian behaviour in Chechnya, which is almost universally recognised as part of their territory. International interest in and pressure on Burma, which is not significantly more repressive than ten or twenty years ago, is far greater today than in the past. And even China has been forced to change its tune, arguing for its practices as culturally appropriate implementations of international human rights standards, where during the Cold War era it rejected the very language of human rights, and even punished its domestic use.

In the contemporary world we are taking more seriously the idea that states can be held morally and politically liable at the international level for how they treat their own citizens on their own territory. But sovereign states remain the central mechanism by which contemporary international society seeks to implement internationally recognised human rights, as is underscored by the very modest incremental growth in the scope and powers of multilateral human rights institutions in recent years.

Verbal and persuasive policies have become both legitimate and common in contemporary international society. Coercive international implementation of human rights norms, however, remains illegitimate in most circumstances. The major treaties authorise multilateral implementation action that is, as we have seen, almost entirely verbal. Human

rights NGOs, by their very nature, can engage only in persuasive political action. Coercive bilateral intervention on behalf of internationally
recognised human rights remains impermissible. And few states are
willing to take more than symbolic foreign policy actions in the face of
most human rights violations short of genocide.

All of this, in my view, points to the persisting centrality of feelings of
national political loyalty and the continuing weakness of perceptions of
cosmopolitan political solidarity. And even where, as in Western Europe, some real sense of supranational political community does seem to
be emerging, states remain the central element in the mix of actors
with human rights obligations. We must not confuse the increasing
constraints under which states discharge their international human rights
obligations with a serious challenge to the state as the principal protec-
tor of internationally recognised human rights.

Global economic interdependence

If states are to be displaced as the central duty-bearers of internationally
recognised human rights, other social actors must emerge to perform
that role. International organisations are unlikely challengers, precisely
because these organisations are the creations of states, which continue
to manage them. Rather than look for direct threats from above, I
would suggest looking instead to the more insidious erosions rooted in
economic interdependence. Over the next few decades, however, the
human rights implications appear to me to be more troubling than
encouraging.

The globalisation of production is weakening state-centric schemes
for implementing economic, social and cultural rights, most dramatically in the wealthier countries of the Northern Hemisphere. It does
not, however, seem to be creating viable alternative mechanisms. Semi-
permanent unemployment, attributable in part to the development of increasingly global mechanisms of production and exchange, has already
led to a modest shrinking of the welfare state in many countries in
Western Europe. And in the United States, the loss of manufacturing
jobs, a dramatic decline in the real value of the minimum wage, and the
explosive growth of healthcare costs has made the coverage of the Western world's most inadequate welfare state even more incomplete and
inequitable.

One might argue that the new international division of labour has
simultaneously increased the enjoyment of many economic, social and
cultural rights in the newly industrialising countries. But we must be
careful not to confuse growth with economic and social rights, especially

in countries where the economic growth has been less dramatic and sustained. Human rights are about assuring minimum distributions of goods, services and opportunities to all, something that is by no means assured by economic growth (i.e. an increase in the aggregate sum of goods and services available within a society). Furthermore, we must not forget those countries, especially in Africa, that remain largely untouched by the new international division of labour.

Markets simply cannot do the job alone. The shortcomings of socialist command economies proved to be immense. But these failed experiments were efforts to overcome the undeniable inequities in market systems of distribution. And the real success stories of 'free markets' over the long run show the virtues of substantial redistributive interventions by liberal democratic and social democratic welfare states. Yet it is precisely such states that have been weakened by the globalisation of production. And economic interdependence does not seem to be spawning a plausible alternative provider of internationally recognised economic, social and cultural rights.

There is no logical reason that corporations, for example, could not be considered direct duty-bearers of obligations correlative to human rights. In some countries, such as Japan, South Korea and Singapore, the state has supported, encouraged and even mandated employment and labour practices that result in delivering through private firms many social welfare services that in the West are provided directly by the state. If the globalization of production continues apace, it is not implausible to imagine an attempt to extend such a strategy to the international level. But whatever the shortcomings of states in providing for economic and social rights, they pale before those of multinational corporations, which are shadowy, often distant, private entities over which individual citizens lack even the limited control provided by electoral participation.

We seem to be squeezed between persisting national loyalties and declining national capabilities. And to the extent that political loyalties in the age of the welfare state have come to rest on the ability of the state to deliver rising standards of living and high levels of performance in implementing economic, social and cultural rights, a very likely outcome is a rise in alienation, polarisation and disorder at all levels of politics – which brings us back to the discussion of the preceding subsection. A weakening of state loyalties *may* contribute to the development of stronger cosmopolitan sensibilities. But a no less plausible alternative, especially in the medium run, is the rise of nativist and nationalist sentiments that seek to blame others for our setbacks and for disturbing changes in general.

The shortcomings of state-centric systems of delivering internationally recognised human rights are manifest to those of us who have lived through them. But not all changes would seem to be progressive. States at least have devised relatively effective mechanisms to harness national economic actors and redistribute resources. Without the development of parallel mechanisms at the international level, the human rights implications of growing economic interdependence are not at all promising.

New conceptions of human dignity?

Perhaps the most profound transformations in currently dominant conceptions of human rights would arise from basic changes in underlying understandings of human nature, dignity, well-being or flourishing. I will argue, however, that the ideal of equal and autonomous individuals pursuing, within certain limits, their own conceptions of the good life, remains deeply entrenched as a regulative political ideal in contemporary international society. Controversy rages, and will continue, over the precise implications of these core values, but the basic contours of the contemporary construction of human rights seem firmly rooted and likely to persist for many decades.

As I noted above, a central achievement of the human rights movement has been to discredit moral or political doctrines based on fundamental inequalities between human beings. Social orders based on fixed status hierarchies have been largely replaced – in theory at least, and in most countries to a considerable degree in practice as well – by orders based on the fundamental equality of all citizens. Although many liberal advocates of human rights have emphasised individual liberties, it is the radical political egalitarianism of human rights that has had the most profound implications, both nationally and internationally.

One of the most troubling changes of the post-Cold War world is the resurgence of claims of group superiority. Genocidal violence in Bosnia, Croatia and Rwanda is just the most prominent example of a resurgence of politicised arguments of ethnic purity and superiority. Politically active religious fundamentalism, which has achieved its greatest success in several Muslim countries, not only imposes a narrow vision of the good life but also draws fundamental distinctions between citizens on the basis of their religion. The resurgence of nativist political movements and racist politics in North America and Europe raises similar concerns. And most of these movements are associated with a social vision committed to the subordination of women.

But the strong international reactions against contemporary manifestations of ethnic privilege, xenophobic nationalism and politicised religious fundamentalism – in Rwanda and Burundi, the former Yugoslavia, Sudan, Algeria, Israel and the former Soviet Union – suggest that such arguments have little appeal beyond those who see themselves as specially chosen. Unlike the status hierarchies of past eras, today it is rare for either those who are to be subordinated or those who look on from the outside to acquiesce in attempts to assert such claims of superiority. This, I would suggest, indicates the continuing, and even deepening, commitment to the basic moral equality of all human beings that provides the core of the vision of human dignity underlying internationally recognised human rights.

Arguments of irreducible qualitative differences between groups of human beings would also seem to be incompatible with the kind of (relatively) open, inclusive and tolerant international society to which we have been moving over the past century. Although cosmopolitan conceptions of world order have not penetrated very deeply, one of the great achievements of the spread of Western international society has been the entrenchment of doctrines of the equality of states and the self-determination of peoples. These doctrines rest on an at least grudging recognition that the differences between us and others do not justify their formal subordination. Taking them seriously radically reshaped the map of the world during the era of decolonisation. And it has subtly but significantly altered the character of international politics in our era.

This may reflect only a weak and negative notion of equality. It is, however, real and, I would argue, of immense importance. And the deepening penetration of international human rights into post-Cold War international politics suggests that we are at least beginning to take seriously the irreducible equality of individuals, even if it remains in practice subordinated to the equality of states.

The core human rights commitment to individual equality leads 'naturally' to an emphasis on individual autonomy. If one is equal to others, they have no right to force you to comply with their ideas of what is right and proper – or, more precisely, they may not force on you ideas of right that treat you as less than an equal moral agent. In fact, it is difficult to separate the 'natural' moral equality of individuals from the autonomy of these equal persons.

Without implying licence to act simply as one chooses, this suggests fundamental limits on what society may legitimately require or prohibit from its members. The nature of those limits, of course, is an appropriately central matter of moral and political conflict. The values of the Universal Declaration and Covenants, however, seem to continue to shape the range of arguments that receive considerable international endorsement.

Consider, for example, questions of sexual decency, a prominent issue in recent 'Asian values' critiques of the West and international human rights standards.[19] In most Western countries, freedom of speech is seen to permit the graphic depiction of virtually any sex act (so long as it does not involve and is not shown to children). Some Asian countries prohibit this and even severely punish those who produce or distribute such material. This dispute, however, is over the limits of autonomy, or the range of a particular right, rather than a fundamental rejection of human rights or the idea of personal autonomy.

Furthermore, this controversy rages within many countries at least as strongly. Every country criminalises some forms of pornography, and virtually every country permits some depictions of sexual behaviour that another country has within living memory banned as pornographic. Wherever one draws the line, it leaves intact both the basic internationally recognised human right to freedom of speech and the underlying value of personal autonomy.

Arguments about the allegedly excessive individualism of human rights have a similarly narrow scope. The basic moral equality of all human beings, once accepted, logically requires that each person be specially recognised as an individual. Some degree of individualism is inescapable when our moral and political starting point is the equality of each and every human being.

This, of course, leaves open the question of the relative weights to be assigned to the individual and the groups of which she is a member. For example, should traditional notions of 'family values' and gender roles be emphasised in the interest of children and society or should families be conceived in more individualistic and egalitarian terms? What is the proper balance between rewarding individual economic initiative and redistributive taxation in the interest of social harmony and support for disadvantaged individuals and groups? At what point should the words or behaviours of deviant or dissident individuals be forced to give way to the interests or desires of society?

Questions such as these are vital issues of political controversy in virtually all societies. Exactly where the lines are drawn differ considerably – although I would suggest that the differences are less than most authoritarian governments would have us believe. But the only answers that today receive widespread international endorsement – in fairly stark contrast to just twenty years ago – are those that leave a considerable space for the equal and autonomous individual.

Much the same is true of arguments over the use of (human) rights to protect individual equality and autonomy. Whatever the theoretical attractions of technocratic management, or some other system of rule by the enlightened, all our previous political experience suggests that the best mechanism is empowering these equal and autonomous individuals with human rights. Once again, this leaves us considerable space for political controversy. But for our purposes here, it is the bounded nature of that space that requires emphasis.

The common complaint that Westerners in general, and Americans in particular, have gone 'rights crazy' merits serious consideration. We must guard against what might be called the imperialism of rights, the view that all important human goods should be recognised as and implemented through the mechanism of (human) rights. As noted above, many important wrongs and harms do not now, and I would argue should not come to be seen to, involve violations of (human) rights. But the Universal Declaration of Human Rights, the normative core of the current international human rights regime, would seem largely immune from such arguments.

Few governments today repudiate rights to life, liberty, security of the person, equality before the law, a fair trial, political participation, social security, work, rest, leisure, education and an adequate standard of living; to freedom of thought, conscience, religion, opinion, expression, assembly, association and movement; and to protections against discrimination, slavery and torture. And when they do, as in, for example, Iran's persecution of Baha'is as apostates, these states receive little international support and considerable international criticism. There simply is not much international appeal today, as opposed to twenty years ago, to arguments that the list of internationally recognised human rights is either too long or systematically misguided.

This is not to deny that intense controversy continues to rage over the implications of the rather general rights specified in the Universal Declaration. For example, few countries in the world understand freedom of the press as broadly, and few developed countries construe the right to social security as narrowly, as the United States. But these are *relatively* modest variations in implementing internationally recognised human rights. And the general formulations of the principal international instruments set authoritative limits on the range of permissible variation.

There are few political issues more important than establishing the exact extent of the political space allowed to autonomous individuals in the exercise of their rights. Dominant understandings have changed over time, and will continue to change. My reading of current international political controversies over human rights, however, suggests that they continue to take place largely within a space delimited by a basic moral commitment to the idea that all human beings, simply because they are human, have the equal and inalienable individual rights recognised in the Universal Declaration and Covenants.

There is much of moral importance in international relations that falls outside the domain of human rights. Questions of international distributive justice, whether understood in cosmopolitan or statist terms, come most prominently to mind. Nonetheless, the increasing prominence of human rights in international relations over the past half-century, and the past two decades in particular, has given at least some questions of right and wrong an unprecedented place on international agendas. For all the shortcomings of this particular construction of right and wrong in international relations, I find the rise and persistence of human rights as a regulative international political ideal an unusually promising sign for the future.

Notes

1 My principal focus will be on multilateral instruments and institutions open to all states, with secondary attention to bilateral state policies. Regional human rights regimes – which are especially important in Europe – will not be discussed. For information on these institutions, see, for example, Burns H. Weston, Robin Ann Lukes and Kelly M. Hnatt, 'Regional human rights regimes: a comparison and appraisal', in Richard Pierre Claude and Burns H. Weston (eds.), *Human Rights in the World Community: Issues and Action* (Philadelphia: University of Pennsylvania Press, 1989); and Glenn A. Mower, Jr, *Regional Human Rights: A Comparative Study of the West European and Inter-American Systems* (Westport, Conn.: Greenwood Press, 1991).

2 See, for example, David P. Forsythe, 'The United Nations and human rights at fifty: an incremental but incomplete revolution', *Global Governance* 1 (1995): 297–318; Philip Alston, 'The UN's human rights record: from San Francisco to Vienna and beyond', *Human Rights Quarterly* 16 (1994): 375–90; and Jack Donnelly, *International Human Rights* (Boulder: Westview Press, 1993), ch. 1. For a thorough documentary history of the UN contribution, see United Nations, *The United Nations and Human Rights: 1945–1995* (New York: Department of Public Information, United Nations, 1995).

3 UN Document E/259, 1947, para. 22. This decision was ratified by the Commission's parent body, the Economic and Social Council, later that year in E/RES/75(V), which also severely restricted Commission access to the thousands of complaints being received by the United Nations.

4 See, for example, the eighth preambulatory paragraph of the Vienna Declaration and Programme of Action (A/CONF.157/24).

5 For a review of the strengths and weaknesses of reporting systems, see Donnelly, *International Human Rights*, pp. 79–81. For a detailed review of the procedures of the Human Rights Committee, see Dominic McGoldrick, *The Human Rights Committee: Its Role in the Development of the International Covenant on Civil and Political Rights* (Oxford: Clarendon Press, 1991),

ch. 3. These treaties also include optional provisions allowing individual petitions. Although these provisions have been of almost no interest in the context of the racial discrimination convention, the Human Rights Committee has handled a small number of significant individual cases. See McGoldrick, *Human Rights Committee*, ch. 4.

6 Work on apartheid, of course, predated these initiatives, but South Africa had always been an isolated exception. The Special Committee to Investigate Israeli Practices Affecting the Human Rights of the Population in the Occupied Territories, established in 1970, was also a very limited exception. Israeli practices were investigated only in the Occupied Territories. The Chile case was precedent-setting because it dealt entirely with internal human rights practices, without any significant connection to race or self-determination.

7 The standard study of the work of the Commission, which covers the period up to the mid-1980s, is Howard Tolley, Jr., *The U.N. Commission on Human Rights* (Boulder: Westview Press, 1987).

8 For a thorough review of the legal dimensions of interstate accountability for human rights, see Menno T. Kamminga, *Inter-State Accountability for Violations of Human Rights* (Philadelphia: University of Pennsylvania Press, 1992).

9 For more extended discussions of some of the conceptual issues raised in the following paragraphs, see Jack Donnelly, *Universal Human Rights in Theory and Practice* (Ithaca: Cornell University Press, 1989), ch. 2, and Donnelly, *International Human Rights*, pp. 19–28.

10 Donnelly, *Universal Human Rights*, ch. 3. See also Rhoda E. Howard, *Human Rights in Commonwealth Africa* (Totowa, N.J.: Rowman and Littlefield, 1986), ch. 2, and Rhoda E. Howard, *Human Rights and the Search for Community* (Boulder: Westview Press, 1995), ch. 4.

11 For extended and extensively illustrated arguments to this conclusion, focusing on non-Western societies, see Donnelly, *Universal Human Rights*, ch. 3. For ease of exposition, and to further emphasise the contingency of human rights ideas, the examples used below will be almost entirely Western.

12 For an extended argument to this conclusion in the case of Aquinas, see Jack Donnelly, 'Natural law and right in Aquinas' political thought', *Western Political Quarterly* 33 (1980): 520–35.

13 See Rhoda E. Howard and Jack Donnelly, 'Human dignity, human rights and political regimes', *American Political Science Review* 80 (1986): 801–17 for a detailed argument to this conclusion.

14 See, for example, Jack Donnelly, 'Recent trends in UN human rights activity: description and polemic', *International Organization* 35 (1981): 633–55, esp. pp. 643–6.

15 For a much more critical assessment of recent UN efforts, see Human Rights Watch, *The Lost Agenda: Human Rights and UN Field Operations* (New York: Human Rights Watch, 1993).

16 For a good general discussion, which makes considerable use of examples drawn from Sudan, see Larry Minear and Thomas Weiss, *Mercy Under Fire: War and the Global Humanitarian Community* (Boulder: Westview Press, 1995), chs. 2 and 3, esp. pp. 109–22.

17 For a considerably more positive assessment, see Katarina Tomasevski, 'International Development Finance Agencies', in Asbjorn Eide, Catarina Krause and Allan Rosas (eds.), *Economic, Social and Cultural Rights: A Textbook* (Dordrecht: Martinus Nijhoff, 1995).
18 One might argue that Haiti, and perhaps Liberia as well, suggests that collective coercive *regional* action against gross but not genocidal violators may be emerging as permitted. I am sceptical of such an argument, but practice over the next several years does seem to me to merit special attention.
19 For representative samples of such arguments, see Bilahari Kausikan, 'Asia's different standard', *Foreign Policy* 92 (1993): 24–41; Bin Mohamad Mahathir 'Rethinking human rights', keynote address at JUST International Conference, Kuala Lampur; and Fareed Zakaria, 'Culture is destiny: a conversation with Lee Kuan Yew', *Foreign Affairs* 73 (1994): 109–26.

3   Universal human rights: a critique

Chris Brown

Virtually everything encompassed by the notion of 'human rights' is the subject of controversy. The controversies of relevance here are not those associated with enforcing compliance to human rights law, or with the execution of foreign policy options allegedly dedicated to the protection of human rights – these are important topics but they are not the concern of this chapter. Instead its theme emerges from the fact that the idea that individuals have, or should have, 'rights' is itself contentious, and the idea that rights could be attached to individuals by virtue solely of their common humanity is particularly subject to penetrating criticism. That such criticisms exist is a commonplace, but what is less well established in the international relations discourse on human rights is the fact that virtually all the current arguments have a very long pedigree – indeed, are associated with positions that have been argued over for centuries within the canon of Western political theory. It is particularly important to stress that this is so, because so much of the current discourse on rights assumes that the conceptual problems thrown up by the notion are peculiarly the product of particular late-twentieth-century problems – the so-called problem of cultural relativism which, allegedly, has been generated by the globalisation of the international system.

This is a partial misapprehension: while it is indeed the case that the particular *forms* the contemporary dilemmas on human rights take are in part shaped by the problem of 'difference' and modern contextualist notions of ethics, there is a deeper sense in which the key elements of these dilemmas have been present since the beginnings of the discourse. It is a mistake, and moreover a mistake with serious political implications in terms of intercultural relations, to pass over this history in favour of a concentration on the present. Without a sense of the past of these dilemmas it would be easy to conclude, mistakenly, that the only serious difficulties associated with human rights thinking are generated by the unacceptable practices of alien Others.

The concern to dispel this notion dictates the shape of this chapter, which falls into two main parts. In the first part, the conceptual difficulties with the discourse of human rights will be examined; the conclusion will be that rights only make sense in the context of a particular kind of society – an 'ethical community', to use the language of contemporary communitarian thought – and what this entails will be briefly elaborated. The second, shorter part traces the implications of this position for the international protection of human rights and the characteristic agenda of late-twentieth-century thinking on the subject.

Before moving to this agenda, there is one important preliminary that must be addressed. This chapter is subtitled a 'critique', and this is a polite, academic, way of saying that in what follows the idea that there are universal human rights will be attacked, and attacked quite forcefully. Decent opinion – no irony intended – finds this distressing. Human rights activists are liable to respond in a pained way to this kind of discourse; they are in the firing line, sometimes literally, and, under-standably enough, they resent carping from academics who write of these matters from the safety of their studies in Western universities. This is a serious criticism but one that misses the point, and, ultimately, can lead to a counter-productive refusal to acknowledge important difficulties faced by human rights activists. Along, probably, with the majority of readers, the present writer would be glad to live in a world in which liberal, Western freedoms and rights were enjoyed by everyone, but one of the obstacles to the achievement of such a world is created by the unwillingness of some human rights activists to admit that the cause they espouse *is* liberal and Western. By adhering to the fiction of a universal grounding for rights independent of the particular kind of societies in which they are characteristically found, such advocates place themselves in a false position, and, perhaps paradoxically, weaken the credibility of their stand. In short, any violator of human dignity and decency who believes that this chapter provides a sanction for his or her activities is profoundly mistaken – and any rights activist who feels undermined has, equally, misunderstood the argument. These points will be readdressed in the conclusion to this chapter.

Thinking about rights

The liberal position

Since the late eighteenth century it has become a commonplace in liberal societies to assert that individuals possess rights to liberty, the secure possession of property, the exercise of freedom of speech and so on, that these rights are inalienable and unconditional, and that the primary function of government is to protect these rights – indeed that

political obligation rests on the extent to which governments at least try
to do this.[1] This position is the burden of such seminal documents as
the American Declaration of Independence of 1776 and the French
Declaration of the Rights of Man and of the Citizen of 1789, and
became the cornerstone of the political thinking of nineteenth- and
twentieth-century liberalism and progressivism. The language of rights
has facilitated the establishment of some of the freest, safest and most
civilised societies known to history;[2] on the basis of this record, the liberal
position, in the second half of the twentieth century, has been extracted
from its original association with particular kinds of societies and turned
into a template against which all regimes are to be judged. This universalism was, perhaps, always implicit; it is now explicit. The contemporary human rights regime is in general, and, for the most part, in detail,
simply a contemporary, internationalised and universalised, version of
the liberal position on rights.

The thesis argued here is that the liberal position on rights is now
and always has been incoherent and confused and that the undoubted
success of 'liberal' societies over the last two hundred years is not, at
root, traceable to their individualistic rights-oriented features. Before suggesting to what it *is* attributable, it is necessary to spend some time on
the philosophical and conceptual problems surrounding the discourse
of rights, because, as suggested above, these problems are particularly
pertinent when it comes to the international dimension of rights, and
it is important to stress that they are not generated by some new set of
circumstances, such as the problem of Other Cultures.

The philosophical background to rights thinking has been examined
at length in a number of very good recent studies.[3] One of the consistent themes of this work is the potential tension between legal and moral
conceptions of rights, or, perhaps better, between legal positivist and
naturalist accounts of rights. This tension emerges from both the history
of rights and the history of their conceptual validation and, as such, and
given the importance of this tension in the context of the modern debate,
it is worthwhile dwelling at some length on what is at stake here.

The American legal philosopher Wesley Hofeld produced the standard classification of rights in a work of 1919 in which he distinguished
among rights as claims, as liberties, as powers, and as immunities
(although in his view the only true rights were claim-rights, because
only here were correlative duties clearly identifiable).[4] The key point here
is that each of these categories makes sense only in the context of some
kind of legal *system*. Thus a contract which establishes specific claim-
rights and duties presupposes a context in which it is agreed that contracts ought to be observed. Likewise, liberties, powers and immunities

are ultimately notions which make sense only against the background of a system of law. However, this tells us nothing about the kind of law that is involved, and, historically, two quite different kinds of law have been invoked in rights discourse.

Positive law and natural law

On the one hand there is *positive law* – the kind of law enforced, we hope, by institutions such as the police and the judiciary.[5] On this count I, a citizen of the United Kingdom, can, in principle, enforce my claim-rights through the civil or, in some circumstances, the criminal courts; I am at liberty to dress as I please within the limits laid down by public order legislation; I am empowered to vote if over eighteen and not a peer of the realm or insane; and I am immune to criminal prosecution if under the age of ten. I possess these rights because such is the law of the land, whether the statute law enacted by Parliament, or the common-law heritage of the freeborn English (and Welsh but not Scottish) man (or woman). The history of these rights can be traced back to the alleged customs of our (notional) Saxon forebears and a long list of statutory instruments that conventionally begins with the Magna Carta of 1215. Whether or not these rights are adequate or easy to enforce is, of course, debatable; the key point is that they are the rights of a specific group of people. There is no sense in which they are, or could be, *universal* or *human* rights.

To establish human rights, a different kind of law is necessary; some version of *natural law*. The most developed version of natural law was established in the Middle Ages by Catholic Schoolmen, philosophers and jurists. One of their most distinguished modern successors has described the idea of natural law as being based on the existence of:

(i) A set of basic practical principles which indicate the basic forms of human flourishing as goods to be pursued and realised, and which are in one way or another used by everyone who considers what to do [and] (ii) a set of basic methodological requirements of practical reasonableness . . . which distinguish sound from unsound practical thinking, and which, when brought to bear provide the criteria [which enable us] to formulate (iii) a set of general moral standards.[6]

Rights – whether claims, liberties, powers or immunities – are based on these general moral standards, as are the duties which accompany these rights. Crucially, these standards are *general*, which is to say that they are not limited in application to the inhabitants of any particular jurisdiction or legal system, or to any race, creed or civilisation. There may be additional rights and duties associated with Christian acceptance

of Revelation but some general moral standards are common and bind-
ing on all people (and peoples).

The specific content of the natural law of the Schoolmen was challenged by social contract theorists such as Hobbes and Locke in the
seventeenth century, and many later versions of the idea are further
away from the substance of the original than that of Finnis – as is the
case, for example, with Alan Donagan's notion of common morality.[7]
Nonetheless, it seems that some idea of natural law must underlie all
genuinely universal approaches to human rights. If human beings have
rights by virtue of their common humanity it can only be because there
are some 'general moral standards' that are universal in application;
these standards must, in principle, be discernible by everyone, and, therefore, less obviously but still necessarily, must refer back to some kind
of common notion of human flourishing. These are the characteristics
of natural law thinking and thus natural law is the basic foundation
for rights discourse other than positive law.[8]

Natural law and positive law each have advantages and disadvantages
as foundations for rights. Rights associated with positive law are associated with particular jurisdictions and thus are not, as such, *human*
rights – but, on the other hand, their ontological status is secure. If I
am asked why I consider myself to have particular rights as a citizen of
the United Kingdom, I can, most of the time, point to specific pieces of
legislation or to common-law judgements to support my case. A citizen
of the United States can – probably with a greater chance of success –
point to the Bill of Rights and Supreme Court decisions, Germans to
the *Grundgesetz* of the Federal Republic, and so on. The problem here,
of course, is that the 'and so on' stands for a relatively short list of
countries where the rule of law applies and thus where the rights to be
found in constitutional documents have actual force. Those who live in
countries where this is not the case can find little solace in a view of
rights which makes them the product of positive law, and this is particularly unfortunate since it is clearly the case that it is in precisely
those countries where the rule of law is absent that individuals are most
likely to suffer the sort of oppressions that rights are designed to rectify.

The great merit of naturalist approaches is that they provide a basis
for a claim to possess rights which is not so unhelpfully restrictive. If
one has rights solely by virtue of one's humanity, the fact that one
happens to be the citizen of a tyrannical regime, while still deeply re-
grettable, no longer leaves one without intellectual resources, because
the heart of a natural law perspective is precisely the assertion of universal right against local custom. Potentially, natural law provides the
basis for a powerful critique of existing social institutions in a way that

positive law does not and cannot. Rights established by positive law may be critical in the sense that they may allow one to argue that a particular social institution is not working in the way that it ought to, but they are less useful when, as is too often the case, a social institution is working exactly as intended, but the intention is itself oppressive. Positive legal rights provide no basis for an argument that the whole way of life of the society in which they exist may be oppressive, because, by definition, they are based on that way of life. To exercise a critique at this level it is necessary to bring to bear the natural law position that general moral standards exist independently of the practices of any particular society.

But what are these 'general moral standards'? What is their ontological status? There are, broadly, two possibilities here, each of which is unsatisfactory.[9] On the one hand, these standards might be derived from actual practice, on the argument that all functioning societies need to have some kinds of rules which, for example, define property rights, or regulate sexual conduct, and that from these some kind of lowest common denominator can be discerned. There are two problems with this position. First, such a lowest common denominator is likely to be vacuous because customs vary considerably and any formula designed to cover all the possibilities is likely to end up devoid of real content.[10] Secondly, and more importantly, if general moral standards are defined in this way they lose their critical cutting edge – it ceases to be possible to use such standards to criticise existing practices if the former are defined in terms of the latter. The whole point of the exercise is to produce an account of rights which is discriminatory in a way that this kind of minimalist code cannot be; at best, the occasional, obviously deviant regime – Hitler's Germany, Pol Pot's Cambodia, Amin's Uganda – might be 'caught' by these criteria but, almost by definition, no long-standing system of injustice could be recognised as such by an argument that takes longevity as a sign of virtue. A common morality which is actually common to all societies is an uncritical notion.[11]

The alternative is that general standards might be derived without reference to any particular societies by the use of practical reason – reasoning from the basic forms of human flourishing by applying the standard requirements of sound reasoning. In principle, this restores a critical edge to the notion because there is no definitional reason why actual practices will always correspond to the demands of practical reason. But then a new problem emerges, namely that of explaining why local practices do vary, that is, why practical reason seems to produce different results in different places and at different times. To take an example much in the thoughts of contemporary Catholics who argue in this way, if practical reason tells us that abortion is contrary to natural law, why is it that so many societies now and in the past have sanctioned the practice? Finnis and his colleagues would clearly refuse to accept that contemporary American legal reasoning – and the widespread popular support for the product of this reasoning – meets the standards of practical reasonableness, but it is difficult to see why this denial should be convincing. Natural law theorists claim only to privilege the products of practical reason devoted to human flourishing but the claim that the operation of such reason leads always and everywhere to the same result seems to be contradicted by the fact of value-pluralism.[12]

The argument that 'we' (or at least those of us who are Catholic natural lawyers) are more intelligent or more moral than those who reach a different conclusion clearly will not do. The most plausible way out of this difficulty is not to suggest such a personal validation of the product of one's own thought, but to argue that practical reason is defective and likely to produce the wrong result unless situated within an authoritative tradition – such as, in this case, Thomism. In this way individuals are no longer reliant on their own resources; they can bring to bear the practical reasonableness of generations of thinkers as though it were their own. However, this clearly changes the nature of the argument and weakens the claim that general moral standards can be generated in this way. If it is the tradition itself that is the justification for a particular practice, the potential for universalist claims goes by the board, or at least is severely damaged.[13]

Thus far this discussion has centred on the universalist and particularist dimensions of rights discourse, but there is a further feature of this discourse that deserves, rather briefer, attention, namely the potential absolutism of the notion of rights. In Dworkin's famous formulation, rights are often seen as 'trumps' – cards which automatically win tricks – that is, as considerations overriding all other considerations.[14] It is easy to see how, on this account, rights could exist in opposition to the common good – indeed, the very point of having a right is precisely to be protected from someone else's notion of the common good. Rights absolutists may further reject the notion that there could be a 'common good' in the first place. This position is the origin of the inbuilt and necessary rivalry between utilitarians and rights theorists, a rivalry that dates back to Jeremy Bentham's fulminations against the idea that there are natural rights. It has become a commonplace of modern debate to suggest that the problem with utilitarianism is that it does not take seriously the fact that individuals are distinct from one another and have their own projects.[15] Conversely, one might argue that rights theorists take these distinctions *too* seriously. This is the position of a diverse range of modern thinkers from Brian Barry and Robert Goodin on the one hand, to Amitai Etzioni and Jean Bethke Elshtain on the other.[16] The absolutism of rights claims can be a menace to a civilised society, as the inability of the American public authorities to control the ownership of firearms in the United States illustrates quite vividly. Even in a less extreme case, it is not clear that the free-speech absolutists who defend all forms of expression in First Amendment terms are not acting against the public interest.

What is interesting about this critique is that it is particularly relevant to positive law accounts of rights. One of the important features of natural law thinking is that it relates rights to other features of the human condition, the requirements of human flourishing, and therefore is hospitable to a distinction between those rights which are absolute and those which may be overridden in the public interest or common good. Positive law approaches find it difficult to make such a distinction. Each item in the American Bill of Rights has the same legal status, whether pointing to a case where an absolute claim perhaps ought to be made, for example, barring cruel or unusual punishment, or where policy considerations might in some circumstances legitimate a restriction, perhaps regarding free speech, or where, as it happens, the right in question is positively harmful to the common good, most obviously the right to bear arms. It is not a necessary feature of positive law that it has to have this absolute quality – for example, the Canadian equivalent of the Bill of Rights has an override clause – but many supporters of rights would argue that absolutism is a desirable feature, and criticise Canada's law on exactly this point.[17]

Again, there is a genuine dilemma here. If rights are thought of as trumps, as absolutes to be defended in all circumstances, then it is very likely that some of these circumstances will involve the violation of an obvious public interest. However, if rights are thought of as less than absolute, as simply one set of considerations to take into account when deciding on the rightness or otherwise of action, then the protective power of rights simply withers away. The debates over 'hate speech' in the United States revolve exactly around this dilemma. On the face of it, defending speech that offends public standards of good behaviour and incites anti-social attitudes would seem perverse, and yet if free speech is a meaningful notion it must apply to 'offensive' speech, since no-one tries to ban any other kind.[18]

The liberal position re-examined

To summarise the story so far: 'rights' are tricky, slippery things, and rights discourse is a minefield, where each conceptual step risks a

detonation and self-destruction; moreover, this is so even without introducing complications allegedly generated by cultural relativism. And
yet, very little of all this comes through in the liberal position on rights
outlined at the start of this chapter. There is a clear disassociation
between, on the one hand, the conceptual failings and, on the other, the
rhetorical appeal of rights discourse. If it is indeed the case that societies built upon the liberal position on rights have been successful in
providing a context within which people can live civilised lives, ought
we to be concerned with the philosophical niceties?

It is now, perhaps belatedly, that the thesis of this chapter can be
stated more fully. It is that liberal societies of the last 150–200 years
have indeed been the freest and most generally congenial societies known
to history, but not because they have been constructed on the basis of
rights; their success has been based on features within them that pointed
towards a different, less individualist, context for political action. It was
because of the existence of this context, because these societies were, in
certain respects, ethical communities, that rights were widely honoured
and respected; a successful rights-based politics is parasitic on features
of the polity that have nothing to do with rights – indeed, which may
even be inimical to rights thinking. For this reason, the philosophical
niceties referred to above are important; it is implausible to think that
rights can be extracted from liberal polities, decontextualised and
applied as a package worldwide. This is not simply because of international value-pluralism; it is decontextualisation that is critical, whether
international or domestic. However, the international dimension of rights
will be the subject of the second section of this chapter, and the final
part of this section is devoted to an elaboration of the meaning of an
ethical community.

Community and rights

The term 'ethical community' rightly has strong Hegelian overtones
and the position in general is indeed characterised by a kind of coarse,
demythologised Hegelianism – coarse and demythologised because it is
usually presented without the reliance on *Geist* that Hegel himself would
have regarded as crucial. If we read the *Philosophy of Right* as a free-
standing text rather than as a work which is embedded in Hegel's system, it is not too difficult to extract the elements of a model of an ethical
community, elements which have been employed explicitly or implicitly
by later communitarians.[19] This community has three institutional
elements, or moments: the family, civil society and the state – the role
of these institutions being to 'constitute' individuality, that is to construct the kind of individual that liberal rights-based thought takes as

given.[20] Briefly, the role of the ethical family is to provide an environment within which the individual can develop a sense of self-esteem, where regard is unconditional, based on love rather than achievement.[21] Civil society provides a context where the individual differentiates him or herself from other individuals, making his or her way in the world, rubbing along with other people and acting in a context where law and government are seen as external forces; here we have the kind of atomised, self-interested individuals who are usually held to need rights to protect them from over-mighty rulers. Finally, we have the state, the location where these individuals come to see their competitors as fellow-citizens, and to realise that the laws that bind them are self-made. Here the 'rule of law' ceases to be an external phenomenon but comes to be seen as the product of one's own will.

This conception of a political community does provide a context within which rights can operate, but it is not a context which is always compatible with the *liberal* position on rights. The rights of the individual are of greatest significance in 'civil society'; it is in this realm that the power of the state appears to the individual as an externalised force from the operation of which they require the protection of rights. The state itself cannot be limited by rights in this way: the substantial unity represented by the state 'possesses the highest right in relation to individuals, whose *highest duty* is to be members of the state'.[22] Rights may exist but 'rights absolutism' cannot be a problem here. The idea that the rights of the individual are subject to the will of the collectivity is precisely what the liberal position is designed to avoid, but the reason that this need not be seen as a serious problem is that the communitarian position is not designed to work with *any* individual under *all* circumstances – on the contrary, what is being presented here is a package in which the kind of individuals who make up the community are not a more or less random collection of people who happen to inhabit a particular territory at a particular time, but rather a group of people who are simultaneously the creators of community and created by it. The 'rights' that they assign each other are not the manifestation of a general moral code or the product of universal practical reason – nor are they simply the product of a political bargain; rather, they are more like reminders that the community gives itself as to what it takes to be proper conduct. They are enforceable against the administration/government – the police and the corporation as Hegel would put it – but not against the state as such, that is the state in its role as the expression of a higher unity.

Only a strictly limited sense of universal or human rights can be drawn out of this. The approach is universalist in the sense that it is hostile to any kind of racial discrimination – 'A human being counts as such because he [sic] is a human being'[23] – but it is only particular kinds of community that are ethical, and it is only within such communities that rights are or can be situated. Cross-communal or intertemporal judgements on ethics miss the point. To criticise, say, Athenian slavery because it does not correspond to our understanding of the nature of human equality makes no sense because this understanding was not available to the Athenians. Slavery is incompatible with the modern, rational, ethical state but it was not incompatible with the Athenian *polis*. Any particular practice has to be contextualised. However, this does not mean that all contexts are morally equal. There is a role for moral absolutes in this schema, but the role is in terms of historical development – the unfolding of *Geist*.[24] The modern state represents a higher morality than the Greek *polis* – and, of course, than contemporary regimes that are not rational or ethical. But, notwithstanding this point, *Sitten* (ethics) are more important than *Moralität* (morality) in the actual life of the community.

Has all this any real purchase? That is to say, is an 'ethical community' simply an intellectual construct or has it any real-world reference point? It is very clear that there are not now, nor have there ever been, ethical communities in any full sense of the term. Indeed, it seems to me equally clear that for Hegel and many (most?) of his successors the model was intended to be critical.[25] His account of what an ethical, rational community would look like can be seen as providing an ideal against which existing societies can be measured, and found wanting. But there is also a teleological element here: the thrust of the argument is that the modern world, modernity if you like, has within it tendencies that make this kind of society desirable and, perhaps, approachable. The rational, ethical community is the answer to the question: 'How can we live rational, ethical lives in societies characterised by mass membership, an extended and complex division of labour and, if we are fortunate, some kind of representative and responsible government?' This is as important a question today as it has ever been, and the answer Hegel gave to it remains highly relevant.[26]

What is more, it is arguable that in so far as liberal societies have been successful over the last two centuries it has been because they have been constructed as approximations to the communitarian model rather than because of their dependence on rights-based individualism. This is the thesis of the communitarian movement in contemporary politics.[27] The United States functioned as a community when it had a strong family structure and an active civil society to go with its constitutional arrangements; in recent years, however, the former institutions have gone into decline and, as a partial response, the constitutional framework has grown in significance. Americans have more and more rights, but less and less of a society within which to exercise them. In the past, American individualism was embedded in a non-individualist structure; this is now fading, rights stand alone, and American society is in deep trouble. Similar sorts of stories could be told elsewhere. In Britain, for example, a deferential and traditional notion of community gave real meaning to the idea of rights, even though the rights themselves were poorly articulated within the legal system. As the old order fades away, attempts are made to situate rights within a new, more formal, context; unless the structures that might support such rights are rebuilt – on different foundations – this strategy is unlikely to succeed. Similarly, contemporary Russians and East-Central Europeans are learning that simply importing systems of rights without the institutions of civil society to support them is no recipe for a good polity.

Obviously there is much more that should be said about all this, but for the purpose of this chapter enough has been said to clarify the basic thesis. The next step is to relate these ideas to the international context, or, rather, to show that this step has already been taken, because all the resources that are needed to examine the international dimension are already present in the analysis.

The international dimension

The international human rights regime

International human rights legislation can be traced back to the nineteenth century but the modern regime really begins in the aftermath of the Second World War.[28] The Universal Declaration of Human Rights, adopted by the UN General Assembly in 1948, was a direct response to the atrocities of the war; it set an important precedent as the first attempt by the international community to set out what were, if taken seriously, quite strict limits on the range of variation of internal regimes that was to be tolerated.[29] It has been followed by a raft of legislation, regional and global, such that now, in the 1990s, it is no exaggeration to suggest that virtually all areas of the domestic structure of states are covered by some kind of international standard-setting. For the most part the standards in question are those of the liberal position set out at the start of the first section of this chapter. Although the Universal Declaration specifically recognised that the individual was entitled to 'the economic, social and cultural rights indispensable for his [*sic*] dignity and the free development of his personality' and this *aperçu* has become extended in later statements of so-called second-generation (economic and social) and third-generation (rights of peoples) rights, it remains the case that the first-generation (political, liberty) rights of the individual remain at the heart of the regime.[30]

It is clear that although the human rights regime is ever more elaborate in the demands it makes upon states, its actual influence on the conduct of states in their treatment of their own nationals is, if not minimal, at least not very extensive. It may be that the international protection of human rights has become a 'settled norm' of international society in the sense that states virtually never acknowledge that they are deliberately breaking internationally established standards, but this tribute that vice pays to virtue can be little comfort to those who would prefer actual compliance to verbal assent.[31] It is not too difficult to identify reasons for the failure of the regime, nor to see how these reasons relate to the difficulties with the notion of rights identified above.

There are obviously problems connected to compliance with and enforcement of international human rights which are related to the legal system within which these rights are embedded. International human rights legislation purports to create positive law in the same way that, say, the US Bill of Rights creates positive law, but it is clear that in practice this is not the case. The status of international law is a topic in jurisprudence that the wise avoid if they can, but it is reasonably uncontroversial that international legislation will not be effective unless the law-making parties make specific provisions for enforcement and compliance either by utilising existing institutions, such as the International Court of Justice at The Hague, or by creating new, treaty-specific bodies. With the exception of the 1950 European Convention for the Protection of Human Rights and Fundamental Freedoms, international human rights legislation has not involved the creation of effective enforcement machinery, for the obvious reason that not enough of the states involved wished to see human rights law enforced; indeed, even some states with a record of general respect for human rights have been unwilling to accept international supervision and have hedged around their ratifications of international agreements with extensive formal reservations – true of, for example, the United States and the United Kingdom.[32]

The result of these factors has been that enforcement of human rights by the international community is determined, in practice, by the foreign-policy imperatives of the major powers; on the whole, these imperatives give a relatively low priority to issues of human rights. During the Cold War, violations of human rights by the Enemy went unpunished because of its power, while violations by Friends were excused or justified on essentially strategic-diplomatic grounds.[33] Even now that the Cold War is over, commercial and financial considerations frequently get in the way of a high-priority, even-handed policy on human rights. That this is so may be deplorable, but it ought not to be surprising; the international legal system remains premised on the idea of sovereignty, international obligation remains dependent on particular sovereign wills, and within such a system it is implausible that states will actually allow their external policy to be guided consistently by an impartial concern for human rights – which is not to say that policy will always be determined by power and interest, rather that a systematic commitment to higher goals is always liable to be 'tainted with contingency'.[34]

One response to this might be to try to transcend these limits by moving beyond the 'anarchical society', beyond, that is, a legal system based on sovereignty. Apart from the obvious practical difficulties here (all it requires is 'the consent of Europe, and a few similar trifles' as Frederick the Great put it in another, not-dissimilar context)[35] this project runs up against the difficulties with 'universalist' accounts of rights outlined in the first section of this chapter. The present sovereignty-based international order allows for different and potentially competing accounts of the Good;[36] this contradicts the idea of universal human rights which, in the full package as developed since 1945, is based on one particular conception of the Good. If this contradiction is to be removed by the elimination of difference, then there had better be good reasons why rights-based individualism should be privileged in this way – and the burden of the first section of this chapter was that there is no such good reason, at least none that it would be unreasonable for those committed to another account of the Good to reject. It was argued there that the universal claims of natural law cannot be sustained, and that the argument from the consequences of rights individualism – namely, that societies where rights are established are more successful than those where they are not – misunderstands the nature of the success of 'liberal' societies.

It is important that the relationship between this chain of reasoning and the issue of international 'multiculturalism', relativism and contextualism be clearly understood. It clearly is the case that in the post-colonial late-twentieth-century world, different countries have different notions of what are the appropriate rights – if any – for their inhabitants. In parts of East Asia authoritarian regimes justify restrictions on individual liberty in the interests of economic development and, on their account, in accordance with local custom. Islamic regimes do not recognise certain rights regarded as crucial in Western liberal societies – the right to change one's religion being an obvious case in point.[37] It is difficult to see how notions of human equality could be consistent with a caste system, or with social arrangements that privilege the family rather than the individual. In many respects these differences are greater than those to be found within Western societies over the last two centuries; but the diversity that does exist within the West is such as to undermine naturalist accounts of what it is to be human without adding in these extra difficulties.[38] Moreover, on many issues, the relevant divide in the modern world is not between the West and the Rest; Catholic natural lawyers may well find they have more in common with their Islamic counterparts on many social (and especially sexual) issues than they have with secularists, Western or Eastern, while an issue such as the corporal punishment handed out to minor offenders in Singapore reveals a solid wedge of support in some Western quarters for the authoritarian capitalist mores of East Asia. The absence of consensus in the modern world is not simply the product of differences between the major world cultures – the fault lines run within as well as between cultures.

Contextualism and judgement

Does all this mean that we are committed to a relativist, contextualist approach which refuses to make judgements, which is obliged to accept that whatever practices exist and are long-standing are immune to criticism? Not necessarily; as is demonstrated by the presence of deep splits and arguments within our own culture(s), it is possible to criticise existing practices without reference to universal norms. What is important from this perspective is that social criticism should rest on conceptions of the good which relate to the contexts in which life is lived rather than that they should rest on 'general moral standards' applicable to all humanity. As Michael Walzer has demonstrated so capably, this kind of criticism is not an hypothetical possibility but an actuality; his 'company of critics' have engaged in critical interpretations of the shared moral understandings of their own societies without reference to transcendent norms or universal standards.[39] The key issue is whether this kind of social criticism can also be exercised beyond the community, in realms where, apparently, moral understandings are not shared.

Walzer's own account of this problem is attractive, but not, in the end, satisfactory. He argues for the notion that some kind of 'thin' moral code can be identified which is not in itself sufficiently rich to live by, but which has sufficient purchase to allow us to make some kinds of judgements.[40] Thus, when the citizens of Prague take to the streets waving placards with 'Truth' and 'Justice' written on them, we may not know exactly what they mean by these terms but we are still capable of catching their drift.[41] This seems to be right, but, as suggested above when examining lowest-common-denominator accounts of natural law, it is often the case that the devil is in the detail and broad-based categories may not get us very far. A thin moral code may enable us to identify a number of obvious evils, human wrongs on a large scale, but this is not necessarily where the most important debates are focused. Establishing that, say, genocide is to be condemned is highly desirable, but most international human rights issues involve rather less clear-cut cases.

Perhaps a better way into this issue could be found through the example of Athenian slavery alluded to above. The point made there was that it was not possible to criticise the Athenians for the practice of slavery because their form of life did not include the sort of concepts that would make sense of this criticism; social criticism must employ the material to hand, and the ideas of individual worth, autonomy and personhood that make slavery intolerable today were not part of the moral vocabulary – whether thick or thin – of classical Greece. So far the argument is potentially relativist, but where the Hegelian position moves beyond relativism is in its willingness to say that the mores of Athenian society have been superseded by the movement of *Geist.* Our moral vocabulary has become enlarged; we do have the means at hand to realise that slavery is wrong and it would be culpable of us not to act upon this. It becomes possible for us to assert with confidence both that the Athenians were not necessarily wrong in condoning slavery, and that our ways in this matter are better than theirs – history has moved on and moral development has taken place. Although values cannot be judged out of context, contexts themselves can be judged; contrary to Wittgenstein, forms of life do *not* have to be accepted.[42]

The Athenian example is intertemporal; Athens is separated from us by over two millennia. However, in Hegelian – and, perhaps, commonsense – terms it can be asserted that we are linked to classical Athens; it is part of our Western past. A key question is, how do these arguments play when what is at issue are cross-national, cross-cultural contexts where no such relationship is plausible? Put differently, can we find a way of recasting the discussion which does not rely on the Hegelian notion of absolute morality, of the movement of *Geist*? This is necessary because if *Geist* is taken as fact rather than as metaphor, cross-cultural judgements are as easy to make as intertemporal ones; the judgement that some cultures/societies are 'historyless', outside the scope of moral developmental schemes, and have nothing to offer the world except examples of prejudice and superstition, becomes a matter of fact rather than a judgement of value.[43] Perhaps fortunately, albeit inconveniently,

this kind of certainty is no longer available to our modern consciousness – it is not necessary to be postmodern to be sceptical about the
force of this particular metanarrative. Instead, if we want to use neo-
Hegelian notions in the way that they are used in this chapter we are
obliged to find a language that works without the reassurance that
underpinned Hegel's own work. Is such a language available?

Quite possibly not, but the writer who comes closest to providing
such a moral language is Richard Rorty, a 'postmodern' who explicitly
links his ideas to a demythologised Hegelianism.[44] Predictably, he is
opposed to any foundationalist accounts of rights. Rights act to 'summarise our culturally influenced intuitions about the right thing to do in
various situations'; such summarising generalisations increase 'the pre-
dictability, and thus the power and efficiency, of our institutions, thereby
heightening the sense of shared moral identity which brings us together
in a moral community'.[45] Since the Enlightenment, Americans and
Europeans have created a 'human rights culture' in opposition to prejudices of one kind or another – racial, religious, and, more recently,
misogynist and homophobic – and thereby extended the scope of this
shared moral identity. This is an achievement which is both based on
and reinforced by 'security' – 'conditions of life sufficiently risk-free as
to make one's difference from others inessential to one's self respect,
one's sense of worth'[46] – and 'sympathy', the ability to put one's self in
another's shoes, to perceive the Other as a fellow human-being. And, it
is worth stressing, it is also an achievement which is continually open to
question; our sense about 'the right thing to do in various situations' is
always corrigible; prejudice is never conquered once and for all, and
what counts as prejudice is never a closed issue. Nonetheless, Rorty's
suggestion that in the West the scope of shared moral identity has
expanded in this way seems to me to be broadly accurate, and a pretty
good way of putting what Hegel would have called the movement of
Geist into non-foundationalist, demythologised terms.

What does this tell us about societies where these extensions of shared
moral identity seem not to have taken place? What do we do, or could
we do, about, for example, Bosnian Serbs who kill Bosnian Muslims
because they cannot see them as fellow human beings, or, conversely,
Muslim extremists who think that the death penalty is an appropriate
response to apostasy (or writing a book that, allegedly, defames the
Prophet)? Rorty's point is that it is futile to suggest that these people
are *wrong* or *irrational*, that they have not understood that the nature of
human beings is such that these are not appropriate responses. There is
no such nature; there are no general moral standards that apply here.
UN Declarations, Covenants and the like cut no ice, because human

beings create themselves and if they have not created themselves in ways that are amenable to a human rights perspective nothing can get through to them. This does not mean we are unable to judge their conduct, but Rorty suggests that the best way to see such people is not as 'wrong' or 'irrational' but as 'deprived', deprived of the security and sympathy that has allowed us to create a culture in which rights make sense. They are in need of an environment in which they can reflect on these matters in relative safety; they are in need of a sentimental education – more accurately, it is quite likely too late to soften 'the self-satisfied hearts' of the killers and fanatics themselves; it is the next generation that is crucial to the 'progress of sentiments'.[47] In any event, he suggests, we need to argue for and promote the extension of the human rights culture as a *culture*, and not as a movement that could be grounded by some form of knock-down moral reasoning.

This perspective does not solve all the problems of relativism; indeed, critics will say that Rorty's redescriptions of our moral life simply conjure away all the important issues. What it does highlight, however, is a point made at length above, namely that rights are best seen as a by-product of a functioning ethical community and not as a phenomenon that can be taken out of this context and promoted as a universal solution to the political ills of an oppressive world. It may be that talk of a 'sentimental education' seems a woefully inadequate response to these human wrongs but it is difficult to see what other moral vocabulary is available to us once we reach the limits of an ethical community.

Conclusion

The argument of the first section of this chapter was that the standard liberal approach to universal human rights is based on a misunderstanding. Rights have no separate ontological status; they are a by-product of a particular kind of society, one in which the 'state' operates constitutionally under the rule of law, is separated from 'civil society' and the 'family', and in which private and public realms are, in principle, clearly demarcated. Societies in which human rights are respected are more civilised and secure than those in which they are not, but rights are a symptom of this civilisation and security, not a cause. To overemphasise rights in isolation from their social context is counter-productive, potentially undermining the very factors which create the context in which rights are respected. It follows from this analysis, as the second section of the chapter demonstrated, that the international regime which attempts on a global scale to promote decontextualised human rights is engaging in a near-impossible task. From the liberal perspective human rights are universals; from the perspective outlined above, they are associated with a particular kind of society, and to promote these rights is to promote this kind of society. Proponents of universal human rights are, in effect, proposing the delegitimation of all kinds of political regimes except those that fall within the broad category of 'liberal democracy'. Although such a delegitimation might be regarded as desirable, it is by no means clear that a majority of societies worldwide are actually capable of becoming liberal societies, at least in the medium run, and it is equally unclear on what moral authority those who require them to take this step can rely. Those who take these objections to universal human rights seriously either look to the promotion of a minimal, 'thin', moral code (Michael Walzer) or to the, admittedly nebulous, benefits of a sentimental education (Richard Rorty).

Many advocates of universal human rights will be untroubled by the critique made in this chapter. In so far as this is because they regard the ontological grounding of rights as an ivory tower issue of no relevance to real world problems – or, at worst, relevant only in that to raise such issues is to give aid and comfort to the enemies of human dignity – they are seriously mistaken. Even judged in its own terms, the international human rights regime has not been very effective, and this is at least partly because of the blithe unwillingness of some activists to recognise that there are philosophical and cultural problems associated with their position. There are, however, more serious and thoughtful critiques of the position outlined in the bulk of this chapter, critiques that will be addressed in this concluding section.

The basic argument of these critics can be presented in a composite form as follows:

of course, human rights are in some sense fictional, but they are *valuable* fictions; of course, in fact, human rights are associated with a particular way of life and cannot be taken in isolation, but this way of life is *actually* the way of life that most people would like to follow. The sort of objections you raise are those characteristically employed by power-holders who try to justify their privileges and bad behaviour in the name of culture and tradition. Ordinary people will have nothing to do with such arguments, the falsity of which activists in Indonesia and China, Saudi Arabia and Iran have exposed by putting their lives on the line. The international human rights regime may not be very effective but at least it gives those who would oppose tyranny some moral support and a standard to which they can appeal. We should be very careful about employing arguments which undermine this valuable work.

This is not a position to be dismissed lightly; one element can be accepted with no difficulty, but a second is quite crucial and gets to the heart of the matter. First, it can readily be accepted that not all of those national leaders who resist the demands of the international human rights regime do so from a genuine desire to protect 'difference' and a way of life; many, perhaps most, are simply concerned to protect their own position. There is a wider problem here. Normative work in international relations needs to be able to distinguish between those non-liberal regimes which are simply criminal conspiracies and those which genuinely incorporate what Walzer would call the 'shared understandings' of a society. John Rawls attempts this task in his recent essay on 'The Law of Peoples' in which he introduces the category of a 'well-ordered' but non-liberal society; unfortunately the example he gives of a well-ordered *hierarchical* society is designed on such peculiar lines that it is not much use in this context. However, there is clearly an issue here, and future work on this topic is called for.[48]

The more important point concerns the popular standing of the liberal position on universal human rights. One of the firmest of liberal beliefs is that liberal values are indeed universal, that we would all be liberals were it not for the distorting effects of ignorance on the one hand and privilege on the other. Deep-down, in our heart of hearts, we believe ourselves to be the autonomous individuals liberalism takes us to be, and thus the *real* wishes of the peoples of Indonesia or China, Saudi Arabia or Iran are represented by those relatively few free spirits who are active in the cause of freedom. Such is the liberal belief and the self-confident strength of this belief is one of liberalism's greatest political assets. However, in his last book, *Conditions of Liberty*, the great (liberal) scholar Ernest Gellner provides a sobering commentary on liberalism's self-confidence.[49] Without weakening his own commitment to liberty and civil society, he acknowledges its historicist foundation. Civil society is a profoundly unusual social formation in which political, coercive, power is concentrated but balanced by a separate set of independent institutions focused on the economy. This kind of society is associated with economic growth and scientific-industrial society generally, but in the late twentieth century limits to growth are emerging, and, in any event, industrial success is being experienced by societies which do not value an independent civil society. Most societies have valued order above either economic growth or political liberty and so have most people – civil societies are rare entities which will do well to preserve themselves from their internal and external enemies. It is an illusion to think that the truth that Gellner finds in liberal thought has, he argues, in itself any power, and the Enlightenment belief that a social order without coercion and falsehood is possible is equally illusory. As he puts it, any culture is a systematic prejudgement; the miracle of civil society is that, for once, and in exceptional circumstances, the prejudgement was made milder and flexible, and yet order was main-tained.[50] Repeating this miracle is always going to be difficult.

Gellner presents from within a liberal perspective an account of the achievement of civil society, and thus of individual human rights, that is in some ways rather more pessimistic about the possibility for general-ising the model than the neo-Hegelian account presented above. And so he is cited here not in support of the thesis argued in the bulk of the chapter, but as an antidote to the sometimes facile optimism of liberals less well versed than him in the history of human societies – and that means virtually all other liberals. Let his be the final words:

> But what point is there in vaunting our values, and condemning the commit-ment of others to absolutist transcendentalism or demanding communalism? They are what they are, and we are what we are: if we were them we would have their values, and if they were us, they would have ours. I am not a relativist – the existence of a culture-transcending truth seems to me the most important single fact about the human condition, and indeed one of the bases of Civil Society, for it made possible that cognitive growth and the denial of absolutism on which it is based. But all the same, preaching across cultural boundaries seems to me in most circumstances a fairly pointless exercise.[51]

Notes

An earlier version of this chapter was presented at the conference on 'Human Rights, Human Wrongs' at the University of Wales, Aberystwyth and appeared in *International Journal of Human Rights* 1 (1997): 41–65. I am grateful to the participants for their comments. Peter Calvert, Molly Cochran, Vivienne Jabri, Graham Smith and Susan Stephenson commented on still earlier versions of this and another, cognate, paper; again, I am grateful for their advice, and wish I had been able to take it more often.

1 In a recent defence of this position, George Kateb argues that the essential argument originates with the Levellers and other seventeenth-century Eng-lish religious radicals. See Kateb, *The Inner Ocean: Individualism and Demo-cratic Culture* (Ithaca: Cornell University Press, 1992), p. 9.
2 These are, of course, comparative terms; that injustices of many kinds have been perpetrated by and in these societies goes without saying.
3 Peter Jones, *Rights* (London: Macmillan, 1994) is the best single-volume survey, followed by the briefer, less substantial, but still useful, Michael Freeden, *Rights* (Minneapolis: University of Minnesota Press, 1991). John Finnis, *Natural Law and Natural Rights* (Oxford: Clarendon Press, 1980) is an important and authoritative restatement of natural law doctrine, while Hillel Steiner, *An Essay on Rights* (Oxford: Blackwell, 1994) is a fine re-working of a neo-Lockean position to the effect that all rights are essentially titles to property. The Oxford Amnesty Lectures series is proving an import-ant source of new thinking on rights; see, in particular, Stephen Shute and

Susan Hurley (eds.), *On Human Rights: The Oxford Amnesty Lectures* (New York: Basic Books, 1993). Jeremy Waldron (ed.), *Theories of Rights* (Oxford University Press, 1984) is a good collection of older essays.

4 Jones, *Rights*, ch. 1, gives a clear account of these categories and argues convincingly that Hofeld's categories are not simply applicable to legal analysis.

5 In legal philosophy 'positive law' is used in a rather more precise way than will be the case here; as with 'natural law' (see below) the term here is used to distinguish a broad approach rather than a precise doctrine.

6 Finnis, *Natural Law and Natural Rights*, p. 23.

7 Alan Donagan, *The Theory of Morality* (University of Chicago Press, 1977).

8 Freeden, *Rights*, writes of the 'natural-rights paradigm', on similar lines. It should be noted that this position does not endorse the Catholic, Thomist version of natural law as the only viable version.

9 The following discussion owes much to an excellent recent study, Samuel Fleischaker, *The Ethics of Culture* (Ithaca: Cornell University Press, 1994).

10 Thus, 'murder' is always and everywhere condemned, but what counts as murder (i.e. unlawful killing) varies so much from place to place that this is not very helpful.

11 This is a well-understood dilemma which will re-emerge at a later stage of this argument; one possible way out might be found in the neo-Aristotelian account of the virtues offered by Martha Nussbaum; see, for example, Nussbaum 'Non-relative virtues: an Aristotelian approach', in Martha Nussbaum and Amartya Sen (eds.), *The Quality of Life* (Oxford: Clarendon Press, 1993). However, to follow this up would be to move too far away from the rights-oriented focus of this chapter.

12 It is worth stressing again that this value-pluralism exists within as well as between societies, as the example of abortion illustrates.

13 The work of Alasdair MacIntyre revolves around these issues, and it is noteworthy that the emphasis of his work has recently shifted towards the nature of 'tradition'. See MacIntyre, *After Virtue* (Notre Dame, Ind.: University of Notre Dame Press, 1981); MacIntyre, *Whose Justice?, Which Rationality?* (London: Duckworth, 1988); and, especially, MacIntyre, *Three Rival Versions of Moral Enquiry: Encyclopaedia, Genealogy and Tradition* (Notre Dame, Ind.: University of Notre Dame Press, 1990), in which he uses 'tradition' to characterise what he previously described as Aristoteleanism, and later as Thomism.

14 Ronald Dworkin, 'Rights as trumps', in Waldron (ed.), *Theories of Rights*.

15 This is the burden of the critiques of utilitarianism by Bernard Williams and John Rawls. See J. J. C. Smart and Bernard Williams, *Utilitarianism: For and Against* (Cambridge University Press, 1973); John Rawls, *A Theory of Justice* (Oxford University Press, 1971).

16 See Brian Barry, 'And who is my neighbour?' in Barry, *Democracy, Power and Justice* (Oxford University Press, 1989); Robert E. Goodin, *Political Theory and Public Policy* (University of Chicago Press, 1982); Amitai Etzioni, *The Spirit of Community* (New York: Touchstone, 1993); and Jean Bethke Elshtain, *Democracy on Trial* (New York: Basic Books, 1995).

17 For an interesting discussion of the Canadian Charter of Rights and Freedoms of 1982, see Joseph Carens, 'Complex justice, cultural difference, and

political community', in David Miller and Michael Walzer (eds.), *Pluralism, Justice and Equality* (Oxford University Press, 1995), pp. 53ff.

18 The argument here can be followed in two excellent studies, whose titles are self-explanatory: Stanley Fish, *There's No Such Thing As Free Speech and It's a Good Thing Too* (New York: Oxford University Press, 1994); and Nat Hentoff, *Free Speech for Me – But Not for You: How the American Left and Right Relentlessly Censor Each Other* (New York: Aaron Asher Books, 1992).

19 G. W. F. Hegel, *Elements of the Philosophy of Right*, trans. H. B. Nisbet, ed. Allen B. Wood (Cambridge University Press, 1991). 'Communitarian' is a convenient portmanteau term to refer to writers from Green, Bradley and Bosanquet in nineteenth-century England to Sandel, Taylor and MacIntyre in the debates over Rawls in late-twentieth-century America. The term was actually coined by Michael Sandel (see Sandel, *Liberalism and the Limits of Justice* (Cambridge University Press, 1992)), but is now closely associated with a political movement whose most prominent supporter is Amitai Etzioni (see Etzioni, *Spirit of Community*). These latter communitarians play down or ignore the Hegelian origin of many of their ideas, probably because Hegel has had rather a bad press in the English-speaking world since 1914 and it takes too long to explain why this reputation is undeserved.

20 The idea that individuals are 'constituted' rather than 'pre-social' beings is the ontological side of the communitarian critique of liberal individualism; no great stress is placed on this argument here because there is no necessary connection between this ontology and the political argument presented.

21 Of these three moments – family, civil society and the state – the family used to be the least controversial; nowadays a positive account of the family is likely to be interpreted as support for patriarchy and right-wing 'family values'. This needs to be met head on; there is no reason why families need to be structured according to traditional gender roles, but there is good reason to believe that a stable home environment is a critical element in the making of functioning fellow-citizens. As Jean Bethke Elshtain points out, 'stemming the tide of family collapse is the best protection we can offer a child against becoming either the victim or the perpetrator of violence – or, as it turns out, poverty'. See Elshtain, *Democracy on Trial* (New York: Basic Books, 1995), p. 8, citing empirical evidence from Elshtain, William Galston, Enola Aird and Amitai Etzioni, 'A communitarian position on the family', *National Civic Review* 92 (Winter 1993): 25–35.

22 Hegel, *Philosophy of Right*, #258, p. 275, emphasis in original. It is this sort of sentence that frightens many, including modern communitarians, away from Hegel; read in context, it is less sinister than it seems to be.

23 Hegel, *Philosophy of Right*, #209, p. 240.

24 This point creates real difficulty for modern communitarians who want to present a demythologised version of Hegel, i.e. a version that refuses to treat *Geist* as more than a rather quaint metaphor. On this, see below.

25 This is, of course, controversial. The preface to the *Philosophy of Right*, with its famous couplet 'What is rational is actual; and what is actual is rational' and its reference to 'recognising reason as the rose in the cross of the present', clearly could be given a conservative reading, but this goes against the main argument of the text. *Ibid.*, pp. 20, 22.

26 It might be argued that 'globalisation' (whatever meaning one wishes to assign to this fashionable term) has undermined this position. Not so: globalisation throws up new challenges to the relationship between individuals and their communities, but it has not (yet?) created new contexts within which a meaningful life could be led.

27 Correct, that is, as a description of what has gone wrong and what needs to be done; communitarians are less successful in providing explanations. The movement has not yet developed an adequate account of the political economy of community – but this does not mean its diagnosis of our present ills can be disregarded.

28 For the texts of international legislation on human rights, see Ian Brownlie, *Basic Documents on Human Rights*, 3rd edn (Oxford: Clarendon Press, 1992). The secondary literature on the subject is extensive: any short list of particularly useful works would have to include R. J. Vincent, *Human Rights and International Relations* (Cambridge University Press, 1986); Jack Donnelly, *Universal Human Rights in Theory and Practice* (Ithaca: Cornell University Press, 1989); and Henry Shue, *Basic Rights: Subsistence, Affluence and United States Foreign Policy* (Princeton University Press, 1980).

29 Arguably the 'standards of civilisation' which were applied in the nineteenth and early twentieth century to non-European candidates for membership of the international system performed a similar role; see Gerritt Gong, *The Standard of Civilisation in International Society* (Oxford University Press, 1984).

30 Third-generation rights are, in effect, the subject of much of the following analysis; second-generation rights present real problems of analysis because it is not always clear against whom one is claiming, for example, a right to economic development – who it is that has the duty that corresponds to this right – unless, that is, it can be demonstrated that the poverty of some states is directly caused by the actions of others, in which case such agency problems disappear. Scholars such as Shue, *Basic Rights*, are clearly correct in stressing the importance of economic and social development; the question is whether it makes sense to talk about these issues in terms of rights.

31 On 'settled norms' see Mervyn Frost, *Towards a Normative Theory of International Relations* (Cambridge University Press, 1986), p. 121.

32 This is often seen as a fault on the part of the states involved; it could equally suggest a seriousness about the issue of human rights – and treaty obligations – not shown by those who are prepared to give formal assent to everything while actually implementing nothing.

33 As is the way of things, these strategic grounds were sometimes given ideological support, as in Ambassador Kirkpatrick's distinction between 'authoritarian' and 'totalitarian' regimes; Jeane Kirkpatrick, 'Dictatorships and double standards', *Commentary* 68 (1979): 34–45.

34 Cf. Hegel, *Philosophy of Right*, #333, pp. 336ff.

35 On Saint-Pierre's 'Project for a Perpetual Peace', cited in F. H. Hinsley, *Power and the Pursuit of Peace* (Cambridge University Press, 1963), p. 45.

36 See Terry Nardin, *Law, Morality and the Relations of States* (Princeton University Press, 1983).

37 It was on this issue that Saudi Arabia abstained from the vote on the Universal Declaration of 1948.

38 Of course, as Will Kymlicka points out in his recent work, virtually all modern states are, in one sense or another, multicultural – he instances Iceland and the Koreas as exceptions – and thus the problem of other cultures has been with the West all the time, even if only recently recognised as such; see Kymlicka, *Multicultural Citizenship* (Oxford University Press, 1995).

39 Michael Walzer, *Interpretation and Social Criticism* (Cambridge, Mass.: Harvard University Press, 1993); Walzer, *The Company of Critics* (New York: Basic Books, 1989).

40 The best account of this is in Michael Walzer, *Thick and Thin: Moral Argument at Home and Abroad* (Notre Dame, Ind.: University of Notre Dame Press, 1994).

41 *Ibid.*, p. 1.

42 'What has to be accepted, the given is – so one could say – *forms of life.*' Ludwig Wittgenstein, *Philosophical Investigations* (Oxford: Basil Blackwell, 1958), p. 226 (emphasis in the original).

43 Marx' notoriously embarrassing remarks about non-Western cultures have to be seen in this light; see S. Avineri (ed.), *Karl Marx on Colonialism and Modernization* (New York: Anchor, 1969).

44 Rorty's neo-Hegelianism is a major theme of R. Rorty, *Contingency, Irony and Solidarity* (Cambridge University Press, 1989) and the essays in Rorty, *Objectivity, Relativism and Truth* (Cambridge University Press, 1991). His mentors William James and John Dewey also saw themselves as heavily indebted to Hegel's historical account of the development of consciousness; this was before Hegel was sent to the Anglo-American 'sin bin' as an alleged defender of German militarism. Rorty's most explicit statement on human rights, 'Human rights, rationality and sentimentality' is in the Oxford Amnesty Lectures 1993, published as Shute and Hurley (eds.), *On Human Rights*, pp. 111–34.

45 Rorty, 'Human rights, rationality and sentimentality', p. 117.

46 *Ibid.*, p. 128.

47 *Ibid.*, pp. 130 and 129 respectively. Rorty takes 'a progress of sentiments' from the work of Annette Baier, and suggests there may be links here with some strands of feminist moral theory; see Baier, *A Progress of Sentiments: Reflections on Hume's Treatise* (Cambridge, Mass.: Harvard University Press, 1991); Baier, *Moral Prejudices* (Cambridge, Mass.: Harvard University Press, 1995); and Baier, 'Some thoughts on how we moral philosophers live now', *The Monist* 67 (1984): 490–7.

48 John Rawls, 'The law of peoples', in Shute and Hurley (eds.), *On Human Rights*, pp. 41–82. For a comment on the problems involved in his notion of a well-ordered hierarchy, see C. Brown, 'Theories on international justice', *British Journal of Political Science* 27 (1997): 273–97.

49 Ernest Gellner, *Conditions of Liberty: Civil Society and its Rivals* (London: Hamish Hamilton, 1994).

50 *Ibid.*, p. 32.

51 *Ibid.*, p. 214.

4   Non-ethnocentric universalism

Bhikhu Parekh

Responses to moral diversity

The obvious fact that different societies organise their moral lives differently and entertain different, even conflicting, conceptions of the good life has been noted and commented upon in almost all civilisations. In Western thought, reflections on the subject go back to the ancient Greeks, and have given rise to several responses, of which three have proved most influential. For convenience, I will call them relativism, monism and minimum universalism.

For the relativist, different societies throw up different systems of moral beliefs depending on such things as their history, traditions, geographical circumstances, and views of the world. We have no means of judging them for there are no objective and universal criteria available for the purpose, and even if there were, we would be too deeply conditioned by our own society to discover them. Unlike scientific inquiry, moral beliefs make no assertions about the world, and cannot be judged on the basis of an objectively ascertainable knowledge of the world. We cannot judge them on the basis of human nature either, because it does not exist or we are too profoundly shaped by our culture to acquire an unbiased knowledge of it.

For the relativist, members of a society grow up imbibing the prevailing system of beliefs and are not only entitled to, but can do no other than, live by them. The relativist admits that different systems of beliefs sometimes converge and agree on a body of values, but denies moral significance to such a consensus. It is a mere coincidence and does not imply that cross-culturally shared beliefs are rooted in and dictated by human nature, or true, or more true than those unique to each culture. Again, the relativist does not deny that members of a society can give reasons for their beliefs, but insists that these are internal to the system and hence ultimately circular. Furthermore, since the reasons are internal, they can only be given for specific beliefs and practices and never for the entire moral system, which cannot itself therefore be a subject of moral evaluation.

128

Sometimes the relativist goes further, and argues not only that different societies hold different moral beliefs but also that the beliefs are good for their members. Every society profoundly shapes the personality, self-understanding, temperament and aspirations of its members, and moulds them in a specific way. There is therefore a more or less perfect fit between the kind of persons they are and their beliefs. They are psychologically and morally equipped to live by these beliefs alone, and suffer a profound disorientation when required to live by others. Even if the beliefs are mistaken, which of course we have no means of knowing, they are *their* beliefs, tied up with *their* identity and moral constitution, and best suited to them.

In one form or another relativism has been a highly popular doctrine. Pindar expressed it well when he observed that 'custom was the king'. Since he used 'custom' to include much of what we today call culture and 'king' as a metaphor to describe someone who ruled over his subjects for their good, he said in effect that culture both determined the moral beliefs and defined and promoted the well-being of its adherents.[1] Some though not all Sophists shared his view, so did such writers as Pascal, Montaigne and Montesquieu in some of their moods, and so did Herder. In one form or another relativism also informs the thought of many contemporary communitarian and even some liberal writers, for whom we are 'constituted' by our societies, can only live by 'our' values, and have no means of defending them in a non-circular manner.

Moral monism takes a radically opposite view of moral diversity. For it, we cannot only judge other societies but also lay down what way of life is the highest or truly human. Morality is about how we ought to live as individuals and as a society. Since human beings ought to live and cannot ultimately avoid living in harmony with their nature (or the structure of the universe, or the will of God), morality has an objective basis. And since we have the capacity to discover the structure of human nature (or the universe, or to receive the divine self-revelation), we are able to arrive at the objective and universally valid knowledge required to decide what way of life is fully human and which ones are false or inferior.

In order to elucidate the inner constitution and *telos* of human nature, the monist needs to engage in double abstraction. Since human nature is culturally mediated, he needs to abstract away all cultural and other influences to discover it in its pristine form. He also needs correspondingly to abstract away his own culturally derived beliefs and prejudices and develop the faculty of pure or transcendental reason. The first reveals human nature; the second gives one the capacity to know it in an undistorted manner. Since these two complementary processes of abstraction are immensely demanding, the philosopher generally occupies a highly privileged position in monist thought.

The monist needs to explain the obvious fact of moral diversity. He does this in terms of such factors as moral ignorance, inertia, lack of intellectual rigour and unequal intellectual endowment. He appreciates that different societies have different histories, traditions and cultures, but assigns them no moral significance. They are ontologically inconsequential and do not in any way affect human nature, which is universally the same and entails a uniform conception of the good. At best they influence and regulate such morally indifferent areas of life as how one marries, disposes of the dead and brings up one's children, and the songs one sings and the stories one likes. While monism allows for cultural diversity, it has no space for moral diversity. Again, the monist acknowledges that not all human beings are able or willing to live up to the rigorous demands of the truly human way of life, but does not think that this poses any problem. The truly human way of life remains the norm by which to judge and grade such different ways of life as unequally endowed or enlightened individuals prefer to lead.

Like relativism monism has enjoyed great popularity throughout history. Indeed since they represent opposite points of view and feed off each other, they have tended to shadow each other. Plato was the first to articulate monism with great force and clarity, followed, no doubt with some reservations, by Aristotle, the Gnostics, Plotinus and Christian thinkers. Monism also informed the writings of several classical liberals, such as Locke, Tocqueville and J. S. Mill, for whom the truly human way of life was based on personal autonomy, rational self-reflection, a secular view of the world, material affluence and technological mastery of nature. Liberal writers judged and graded other societies by this standard and justified the imperial civilising mission. Monism also informed Marxist thought, for which only the world-conquering and wholly unconstrained life of the species being, towards which human history was moving anyway, was the highest.

Minimum universalism represents an intermediate position between relativism and monism. It agrees with relativism that moral life can be lived in several different ways, but insists that they can be judged on the basis of a universally valid body of values. While it thus far agrees with monism, it differs from it in arguing that the values can be combined in several equally valid ways and that the latter cannot be hierarchically graded. Since it rejects the monist ambition to show that one way of life is the best or truly human, it differs from the latter not just in degree but in its basic orientation, approach and assumptions. For the minimum universalist, the universal values constitute a kind of 'floor', an 'irreducible minimum', a moral threshold, which no way of life may transgress without forfeiting its claim to be considered good or even tolerated. Once a society meets these basic principles, it is free to organise its way of life as it considers proper.

Unlike relativism and monism, which were both developed in classical Greece, minimum universalism first emerged during the Roman Empire. The Empire extended over a large number of very different societies, each with its own moral beliefs and practices, thus raising the question as to how to regulate their relations in a just manner. Roman thinkers, especially the Stoics and the classical natural law theorists, concluded that universal principles were needed, but were divided about how to arrive at them. Some turned to human nature for a minimum and universally shareable conception of what it is to be human. Others thought that the universal or cross-cultural consensus was their only valid source, but disagreed about the scope and significance of the consensus. Some sought consensus among all societies, others only among the developed or civilised ones, considering the rest too primitive to matter or even to be considered human. Again, for some the consensus was sufficient and valid in its own right; for others it sprang from and derived its authority from the deeper truths of human nature. Whatever their preferred mode of arriving at and validating universal principles, the classical natural law writers called the universal principles natural laws or natural duties, and included such things as non-injury, keeping promises, and respect for human life and property.

Minimum universalism received further articulation during the period of colonial expansion, which brought European powers into close contact with non-European societies. A small minority of European thinkers stressed relativism, and urged that the latter be left alone to lead their traditional lives. The more influential among them advocated monism, and urged that 'backward' societies should be civilised and moulded in the image of Christian and later liberal ideas. Some were unhappy with both and urged minimum universalism. Grotius, Pufendorf, Suarez, Hobbes and other modern law writers belonged to this category.

Minimum universalism enjoys considerable popularity among contemporary writers. Moral monism is not absent, as is evident in the concern to reshape the rest of the world in the liberal-capitalist image of the West, nor is relativism, as is evident in some communitarian writings and in the kinds of reasons given for preserving the ways of life of native peoples and ethnic minorities. However, many writers feel deeply uneasy with both, and urge minimum universalism. H. L. A. Hart's minimum content of natural law, Michael Walzer's appeal for rights to life, liberty and the satisfaction of basic human needs, John Rawls'

primary goods, Stuart Hampshire's appeal to the principles of procedural justice, and Martha Nussbaum's Sen-inspired list of functional
capabilities are all examples of this.[2]

There is considerable disagreement among contemporary writers as
to how to arrive at universal principles. Some appeal to human nature
or what it is to be a human being, some to the nature of human agency,
some others to an empirically ascertainable cross-cultural consensus,
and yet others to a rationally grounded hypothetical consensus arrived
at behind the veil of ignorance, under ideal speech conditions, or something similar. Whatever their mode of arriving at universal principles,
these writers are all agreed that the principles specify the moral minimum
which all societies should satisfy. It is only when it has done this that a
society can enjoy what Hampshire calls a 'licence for distinctiveness'.

Before assessing the validity of these three responses to moral diversity, two general points need to be made. First, all three acknowledge
the two obvious facts that human beings belong to a common species
and share various attributes in common, as also that they are culturally
embedded and differ in significant respects. Their disagreement centres
on the importance they assign to the two and the manner in which they
relate them. For the relativist, culture is all important and the sole
source of moral beliefs. He does not deny that human beings share
various attributes in common and belong to a single species, but thinks
that this has no moral implications. The monist reverses the relationship. For him the shared human nature is all-important and the sole
source of morality. Culture regulates the morally indifferent areas of
social practices, customs and rituals, and determines not the content of
the good life but how it is to be realised in the context of particular
societies. For the minimum universalist the shared humanity and cultural differences are both important, but not equally so. She privileges
one or the other depending on how she arrives at universal principles.
When she derives them from human nature or the conception of what
it is to be human, she privileges the shared humanity and uses it to
determine the limits of cultural diversity. When she derives them from
a cross-cultural consensus, she privileges culture and uses it to determine the content and significance of shared humanity.

Secondly, although the three responses to moral diversity are logically distinct, their boundaries are often blurred in practice and a single
writer may display elements of two or more of them. A minimum
universalist might allow moral principles to be adjusted to local circumstances and come close to relativism. Conversely, a relativist might
stress the importance of cross-cultural consensus, and become indistin-
guishable from a minimum universalist. Again, however abstract they

might be, universal principles have a content. If a writer is not careful, the principles could easily become the vehicle of a strongly substantive conception of the good, and then minimum universalism would merge into monism. For example, Hobbes' 'precepts of right reason' have a minimum substantive content, and he is clearly a minimum universalist. Locke's laws of nature are thicker and make him a borderline case, which is why he justified English colonisation of America but not the dismantling of the Indian ways of life. J. S. Mill's principles of autonomy, rationality etc., were intended as regulative principles but in fact became substantive ideals, which is why he used them to grade all human societies and to justify the European, especially the British, civilising mission. The three responses to moral diversity should not therefore be seen as crude boxes into which to fit different writers, but rather as logical tendencies capable of sliding into and being brought into a creative interplay with each other.

Relativism

Relativism contains an important truth, and hence it has continuing appeal. It rightly insists that no way of life is objectively the best or suits all, that the good life cannot be defined independently of the character of the individuals involved, and that moral beliefs and practices cannot be detached from the wider way of life and abstractly judged and graded. While these are important insights, relativism exaggerates and offers a false account of them. As we have seen, it advances the following theses. First, individuals are determined, constituted or profoundly shaped by their culture or society, and as a result are unable to rise above its beliefs and modes of thought. Secondly, different societies entertain different bodies of beliefs and we have no means of judging these. Thirdly, the prevailing system of beliefs and practices best suits its members, who are therefore right to live by it. Each of these theses is wholly or partly false.

The first thesis makes sense under two assumptions. First, the agency determining or at least profoundly shaping moral beliefs, be it culture, society or something else, is self-contained, clearly bounded and not itself relative to or determined by something else. Secondly, human beings have no intellectual and moral resources other than those derived from their culture or society, and hence remain unable to take an independent and critical view of the prevailing beliefs.

The relativist is ambiguous about what the moral beliefs are relative to, sometimes pointing to culture and sometimes to society. Neither satisfies the first condition. Culture does not exist by itself. It is the way a society understands and organises human life, and both influences and is deeply influenced by the economy, the state of technological development and the political arrangements of the society at large. Being itself one of the several factors shaping the individual, and being additionally subject to the influences of others, culture lacks the independence and power to exercise the determining role. Furthermore, a culture is composed of beliefs and practices that tend to legitimise particular economic interests, forms of social relations, methods of social change, etc. As such it is a site of open or silent conflict, subject to different, even conflicting, interpretations, and lacks the cohesion and solidity required to determine or mould its members in a rigid and uniform manner.

What is true of culture is also true of society. Society is not a separate and self-contained entity but composed of interrelated institutions of various types, such as the economic, the religious, the political, the educational and the cultural. Although there is generally some harmony among these institutions, they have their own inner dynamics and momentum. The logic of economic power is different from that of political power, and both again are different from those of religion and education. Although those institutions are shaped by the general culture of society, each of them reflects, appropriates and in turn shapes it in its own distinct way. Every society, except perhaps the most primitive, is therefore internally differentiated. Its members are subject to diverse influences and never confronted by a solid and overwhelming social whole.

Even as neither culture nor society is a homogeneous and unified whole, individuals are not passive objects devoid of resources other than those derived from their society. They think, reflect, demand reasons, dream dreams of better conditions, ask critical questions, and are not always convinced by the prevailing system of justification. In spite of centuries of social conditioning both the Hindu untouchables and the African slaves in the West Indies and the United States retained a measure of scepticism about the dominant structure of beliefs, as is evident in their songs, proverbs, jokes and folklore. Although reflective and critical capacities are obviously developed in society, they have their own momentum and are never wholly controlled by society. Every society encourages its members to think critically about the beliefs and practices of outsiders as part of its self-reproductive mechanism. The critical faculty cannot, however, be quarantined and is often directed at their own beliefs and practices. Furthermore, by definition every culture has a history, and contains strands of thought, myths, stories of struggle and dreams of perfection inherited from the past, which provide a critical distance from the present and at least some resources to resist the prevailing beliefs.

As for the second relativist thesis, that we have no means of judging a society's moral beliefs and practices, it is clearly false. It rests on the view that there are no universally valid standards and that, even if there were, we lack a culturally unmediated access to them. As I show later, this view is deeply mistaken. Some values are embedded in and underpin all human societies, and a broad consensus on them either already exists or can be secured. To be sure, many relativists acknowledge this but dismiss the consensus as a mere coincidence. This is too lazy and superficial a response to be acceptable, especially when the consensus is deep and persistent.

Even if we agreed for the sake of argument that there are no universal values, the relativist conclusion that we cannot judge other societies would not follow. We can ask whether their beliefs are coherent and hang together, and whether their practices match their beliefs. Beliefs and practices also need justification, and we can ask if it is convincing. Again, since most moral beliefs presuppose empirical beliefs about man and the world, we can ask if the latter are correct. This is why many traditional moral systems felt threatened and were sometimes undermined by the development of modern science, technology and the spirit of rational inquiry.

The third relativist thesis, that the beliefs and practices of a society are good for its members, is a half-truth. When people grow up with a specific body of beliefs and practices, they generally get attached to and feel at home with it. A measure of congruence also develops between their beliefs and their psychological and moral constitution, and that gives them stability, the ability to find their way around in their society with ease, and even a sense of rootedness and existential security. However, this does not mean that the prevailing system of beliefs and practices is good for most of them or even for the society as a whole. It is clearly not in the interest of those it marginalises and oppresses, who often accept it only out of fear of consequences and circumvent it in all too familiar ways. The Hindu caste system was good for the upper castes but not the lower ones, many of whom deeply resented it and freely converted to Islam and later to Christianity which treated them better. The system was not good for Hindu society as a whole, including the upper castes. It fragmented the society, discouraged concerted action against external invaders, stifled talent, hindered entrepreneurial activity and the emergence of civil society, and arrested economic growth. As these and other consequences became obvious, a large body of Hindus including many from the upper castes began to campaign against the caste system. What is true of India is equally true of other Asian and African societies. When conquered and humiliated by European powers, they went through profound soul-searching and embarked on a fairly radical restructuring of their traditional beliefs and practices. A similar process occurred in Britain in the 1960s and 1970s, leading to a concerted campaign against the continuing legacy of the aristocratic and hierarchical culture. In short, culture is never self-validating and self-enclosed. It can be and is judged by its members in terms of such considerations as the kind of life it makes possible for them, and its ability to help them secure desired objectives and cope with external threats and changing circumstances.

Moral monism

Like relativism, moral monism contains important insights. It rightly argues that morality is a matter of rational reflection, that it presupposes some conception of human being, that at least some moral principles are universally valid and that ways of life can be critically evaluated. However, it misrepresents and draws wrong conclusions from these insights. Although morality involves rational reflection, it is too complex a system of beliefs and practices to be excogitated by reason alone. Since it regulates human conduct it must also take account of the traditions, temperament and moral and emotional resources of those involved, and these are not a matter of mere rational reflection. Again, although a moral system presupposes some conception of human being, the latter by itself is not enough. The fact that human beings have certain distinctive capacities does not by itself tell us why they should develop these or why only one of the several possible ways of developing and combining them is the best. Furthermore, human beings are culturally embedded, and each culture not only gives a distinct tone and structure to shared human capacities but also develops new ones of its own. Since cultures mediate and reconstitute human nature in their own different ways, a vision of the good life based on an abstract conception of human nature both misses out much that is relevant to the good life and fails to connect with lived reality. Even as the relativist cannot adequately explain significant overlaps between different moral systems, the monist cannot explain their differences. It would hardly do to say that they are all products of ignorance, unequal intellectual and moral endowments, lack of intellectual rigour or geographical circumstances. Since the monist does not acknowledge that the good can be plural and that human beings are creative enough to develop distinct visions of the good life, he neither takes moral diversity seriously enough to trace its deeper roots nor has the theoretical resources to appreciate its importance.

One can go further and argue that the very idea that one way of life is the highest or truly human is logically incoherent. It rests on the naïve assumption that valuable human capacities, desires, virtues and dispositions form a harmonious whole and can be combined without a loss. Human capacities conflict for at least three reasons, namely intrinsically and because of the limitations of the human condition and the constraints of social life: the first because they often call for different and contradictory skills, attitudes and dispositions so that the realisation of some of them renders the realisation of others difficult if not impossible; the second because human energies and resources are necessarily limited and one cannot develop all one's capacities; and the third because every social order has a specific structure which militates against the combination of certain sorts of capacities and values. Since human capacities conflict, the good they are capable of realising also conflicts. Like the human capacities, values too conflict for similar reasons. Justice and mercy, respect and pity, equality and excellence, love and impartiality, moral duties to humankind and to one's kith and kin, and moral claims of the contemplative life and those of the dying wife often point in different directions and are not easily reconciled. In short, every way of life, however good it might be, entails a loss. And since it is difficult to say which of these values is higher both in the abstract and in specific contexts, the loss involved cannot be measured and compared, rendering unintelligible the idea of a particular way of life representing the highest good.

The idea that different ways of life can be hierarchically graded is equally untenable. It presupposes that a way of life can be reduced to a single value or principle, that all such values or principles can in turn be reduced to and measured in terms of a single master value or principle, and that the good can be defined and determined independently of the agents involved. No way of life can be based on one value alone. It necessarily involves a plurality of values, which it balances and integrates in its own way and which cannot be reduced to just one of them. Furthermore, the values realised by different ways of life are of necessity too disparate and distinct to be translated into a common and culturally neutral moral language, let alone measured on a single scale. And since a way of life is meant to be lived, it cannot be abstracted from the capacities, traditions, dispositions and historical circumstances of its members, and called good or bad in the abstract and universally recommended (or condemned).

Minimum universalism

As for minimum universalism, it avoids many of the untenable claims of its rivals, and has much to commend itself. It is, however, open to three objections. First, its advocates generally derive universal principles from human nature or from universal or hypothetical consensus. Human nature is by itself too thin to offer principles with a meaningful moral content. And since it is differently defined and constituted in different societies, such principles as it generates are too abstract and culturally insensitive to make sense to and bind the latter.

As for universal consensus, either none may exist or it might be unacceptable. There is no universal consensus on the evils of cruelty, torture, inhuman punishment, and many of the other evils Walzer, Hampshire and other minimum universalists rightly condemn. The Hutus see nothing wrong in torturing and eliminating the Tutsis, and the Saudis think it right to stone adulterous women to death or publicly to behead drug dealers. When consensus exists, it is sometimes unacceptable. All religions take a low view of women, as do most premodern societies as well as a large body of conservative opinion in contemporary liberal societies. Indeed, inequality of the sexes is one principle on which there has been a universal consensus throughout recorded history. Racism, discriminatory treatment of outsiders, contempt for the poor, and social hierarchy too have long been cherished by most cultures.

Realising these and related difficulties, Rawls, Habermas, Hampshire and others appeal to a hypothetical consensus arrived at under ideal conditions, which they no doubt define and construct differently. Their approach runs into obvious difficulties. As we shall see later, it is difficult to imagine how a meaningful dialogue is possible in the moral and historical vacuum implicit in their ideal conditions of discourse. Besides since they abstract away deep cultural differences, they make the task of arriving at a moral consensus infinitely easier than it really is. And when such a consensus is applied to existing societies, it either breaks down or gets so attenuated as to lack a normative bite.

The second difficulty with minimum universalism has to do with the status of universal principles. Most writers see them as a kind of floor, an absolute moral minimum, and use them as mechanical yardsticks to judge all cultures. Since different societies are differently constituted and entertain different conceptions of the good life, they need to interpret, prioritise and incorporate universal principles into their ways of life in their own different ways. The principles cannot therefore be applied mechanically and treated as a set of passive and external constraints.

This raises difficult questions concerning what principles may not be traded off, how much leeway a society should have in reinterpreting them and how we can ensure that they do not interpret them out of existence, the questions minimum universalists do not even raise let alone answer adequately. A society does not enjoy a 'licence' to live as it pleases simply because it satisfies universal values, for we would want to know if the rest of its way of life is morally acceptable.

The third difficulty is that in much of the literature on the subject, universal principles are either defined so abstractly that they have no bite, or so substantively that they cannot be met or are open to the charge of ethnocentrism. To say that life should be respected and cruelty avoided falls within the first category. All societies value life in some form as otherwise they would not last a day, and they also generally seek to avoid cruelty as they define it. To say that all societies should follow principles of social justice as the early Rawls and Hampshire maintain, or that they should value private property and allow uncoerced choice of marriage partners as the United Nations Declaration of Human Rights prescribes, belongs to the second category. The Rawlsian requirement entails a distinctly social democratic view of society, and the UN Declaration an individualist view of life, and many cultures not only do not share these views but do not even see their point.

In the light of this brief discussion, monism and relativism are flawed responses to moral diversity. They neither adequately explain it nor, more importantly, deal with the normative problems it poses. Although minimum universalism has much to commend itself, it too is not free of difficulties. The outlines of an alternative approach are sketched below. It is tentative and inadequately worked out, but should give some idea of how one might more profitably proceed.

Towards a dialogue on universal values

If universal values are to enjoy widespread support and democratic validation and be free of ethnocentric biases, they should arise out of an open and uncoerced cross-cultural dialogue. Such a dialogue should include every culture with a point of view to express. In so doing we show respect for them, and give them a motive to comply with the principle of holding a cross-cultural dialogue. We also ensure that such values as we arrive at are born out of different historical experiences and cultural sensibilities, free of ethnocentric biases, and thus genuinely universal. The dialogue occurs both in large international gatherings of governmental and non-governmental representatives and in small groups of academics and intellectuals. The former gives it political authority derived from democratic validation and moral authority based on the consensus of world opinion; the latter gives it intellectual depth, provides forums for patient and probing exchanges of views, and helps generate a rational consensus that can be fed into international gatherings.

The point of a cross-cultural dialogue is to arrive at a body of values to which all the participants can be expected to agree. Our concern is not to discover values, for they have no objective basis, but to agree on them. This is not a matter of teasing out the lowest common denominator of different cultural traditions, for such commonality either might not exist or be morally unacceptable. Values are a matter of collective decision, and like any other decision it is based on reasons. Since moral values cannot be rationally demonstrated, our concern should be to build a consensus around those that can be shown to be rationally most defensible.

Given the nature of cross-cultural dialogue, the philosopher makes an important but rather modest contribution to it. His familiar professional abilities enable him to analyse the deep structures of different cultures, uncover common assumptions between conflicting points of view, and evaluate evidence and arguments. Just as his contribution is valuable, so also are those of cultural anthropologists, religious thinkers, literary writers and others, and hence the philosopher cannot exercise the kind of legislative role he has traditionally assigned himself. Furthermore, he has a persistent tendency, developed and encouraged by his discipline, to abstract away differences and concentrate on the general at the expense of the particular. In a cross-cultural dialogue, in which we need to think with and through differences, the philosopher can easily become an unreliable guide unless he learns to be sensitive to the depth and extent of cultural diversity. Such contribution as he makes is one voice among many and subject to the ultimate democratic approval of the international community.

Cross-cultural deliberation on moral values is an exceedingly complex activity. Participants do not share a common language, style of discourse, assumptions about the world, self-understanding, or even common values. It is tempting to appeal to the allegedly transcultural concept of human nature, but that does not help. Human nature is culturally mediated and we have no access to it save through its articulations in different cultures. After several millennia of acculturation and the consequent interplay between culture and nature, there is no raw human nature that we can hope to uncover by peeling off the cultural overlay or looking deep inside us. Human nature is not a datum but an inference, not a fact but a theory. Furthermore, since different cultures define and constitute human nature differently we cannot ask, let alone persuade, them to live by a conception of it that they neither recognise nor care for.

Richard Rorty is one of the few contemporary writers to appreciate the limitations of the concept of human nature, but his proposed alternative is flawed. He argues that rather than engage in sterile debates about what is man or human nature, we should build up human solidarity by getting people to appreciate that the differences between them are 'fewer and less important' than their similarities, and enlarging their sympathies by such means as story-telling and highlighting their shared vulnerabilities and needs. Rorty makes an important point. It is a rationalist fallacy to think that human beings are guided by reason alone and that reason operates within a cultural and psychological vacuum. If we detest a group of human beings or find no common bonds with them or if they mean nothing to us, no amount of argument will persuade us to take their interests seriously, and we will always find reasons and stress differences that justify us in putting them outside our moral concern.

Rorty's view, however, is open to two objections. First, it implies that human beings can be persuaded to care for each other only by emphasising their similarities. Such a view breeds intolerance of differences, and requires that unless others become like us we cannot share solidarity with them. Besides, since differences can never be eliminated, they can always be used at some stage to subvert such fragile solidarity as we might have managed to achieve. The relative ease with which erstwhile friends and neighbours were turned into strangers and almost a different species in Nazi Germany and more recently in Bosnia and Rwanda is a good example of this. If we can 'manipulate sentiments' in one direction, others can do so in another. We need to show which direction is better, and that requires argument.

Secondly, we cannot show that differences between humans are 'fewer and less important' merely by story-telling and stressing shared experiences. We need to show why some shared experiences are more significant to, and an integral part of, our humanity, than others, and that requires arguments based on some conception of human being. Although moral reasoning is never wholly in terms of arguments alone and involves appeals to emotions, shared sentiments, imagination and cultural values, as Rorty rightly argues, arguments are necessary to regulate the content of these appeals and to give the resulting sense of solidarity a relatively secure intellectual and moral basis.

Although we cannot appeal to a transcultural conception of human nature, we are not reduced to manipulating sentiments and story-telling either. We can appeal to those human capacities, desires, needs, etc.

that all cultures can be shown to presuppose and instantiate in their own different ways. For convenience I shall call them human universals or universal human constants.[3] In some cases they are relatively easy to identify; in others they require critical reflection on the beliefs and practices of different societies with a view to elucidating their deep structure in broadly the same way that linguists analyse the deep universal grammar of different languages. The human universals form the basis of our conception of what human beings are like, which is not the same as a conception of human nature. To talk of human nature is to imply that the universals are natural to human beings and not a product of human effort or history, that they propel them to act in certain ways and have a causal efficacy of a mechanical or teleological kind, that they can be at least conceptually detached from and contrasted with culturally acquired characteristics, that human beings could not have been (or become) otherwise, and so forth. We need not accept any of these problematic assumptions, and in any case it is enough for our purpose to say that the human universals underpin and are in one form or another evident in all cultures known to us. The universals constitute what I shall call human identity, a term free from the philosophical and historical baggage associated with such others as human nature, human essence and even the human condition.

The human universals constitute the context of cross-cultural moral deliberation. They indicate what is and is not currently possible, how human beings tend to behave in different situations, what they tend to desire and avoid, etc., and provide a background of relatively fixed points against which to decide what is good for them and how they should be treated. The universals do not entail values, for that is a matter for human decision, but they supply the indispensable raw material and context for that decision. Since moral values are meant for human beings not angels, and since they are intended to guide human conduct and not to be objects of contemplation, they can only be decided in the light of human universals.

Like all decisions, our decision as to what values to live by involves a choice between different values. While acknowledging the fact that human beings wish to live, we might either decide that they should do so and make human life a value, or conclude the opposite and decide that it is not. All moral reasoning is comparative in nature and involves showing why we should live by some values rather than others. Our reasons include assessment of our moral capacities, the likely consequences of pursuing different values, their compatibility, the ease with which they can be combined into a coherent way of life, past and present experiences of societies who live by them, and so forth. We decide in favour of some rather than other values not because the arguments for them are conclusive and irrefutable, for such certainty is rare in human affairs, but because they are stronger and more convincing than those for their alternatives. It is not therefore enough for the critic to say that our arguments are not wholly convincing, for that is a necessary feature of all moral reasoning; she needs to show that a much better or an equally good case can be made out for the opposite value. If she cannot, our decision stands. For example, although we can offer powerful even compelling arguments for the equality of the sexes and races, they are never conclusive and incontrovertible. However, if we can show, as indeed we can, that those for inequality are flimsy and much less convincing, we would have said enough to show that equality is a rationally defensible value and to be preferred over inequality.

Moral values have no foundations in the sense of an indisputable and objective basis, but they do have grounds in the form of well-considered reasons, and are therefore not arbitrary. And although our defence of them is never conclusive and beyond all conceivable objections, it is conclusive for all practical purposes if it withstands criticism and is stronger than the case that can be made out for opposite values. We can therefore legitimately expect others to agree to these values or show us why our defence of them is unconvincing. If they do neither, we can charge them with being unreasonable, for they reject the values without good reasons. Unreasonable people participate in a dialogue, demand reasons from others, but refuse to give or be guided by them when these do not warrant their preferred conclusions. Since we are all prone to the human frailty of assuming our values to be self-evident and defining reasons in an ethnocentric manner, we should be extremely wary about accusing others of unreasonableness. We should make every effort to enter into their world of thought and give them every opportunity to show why they hold the views they do. If they offer no reasons or ones that are flimsy, self-serving, based on crude prejudices or ignorance of relevant facts, they are clearly being unreasonable and have in effect opted out of the dialogue.

I have argued that universal values are best arrived at by means of a cross-cultural dialogue, and I sketch below the kinds of universal values we might arrive at by proceeding in this way. Since my concern is not to provide an exhaustive list of them, assuming that this is a logically coherent ambition, the list is only illustrative.

In all communities known to us, human beings display certain capacities, and only they seem to do so. These include the capacities to think, reason, use language, judge, dream dreams, form visions of the good life, acknowledge and discharge duties, and to enter into moral relationships with each other. They are not born with these capacities, for these can only be developed in society; rather they acquire them and society itself is a product of their exercise. The capacities define them as a specific kind of being and constitute their human identity. Thanks to them human beings are able to establish social, emotional and moral relationships with each other and enter into actual or potential fellowship. Human beings belong not only to a common species, as the animals and the plants do, but also to a potential universal community.

The common human identity is an interculturally instantiated and acknowledged fact. We have little difficulty recognising whether an unfamiliar outsider is a human being or a member of another species. Given their culturally derived ideas about how human beings appear and behave, we are sometimes perplexed by strange outsiders, but only a brief encounter is enough to allow us to decide whether or not they are human. The bewildered Indians in South America initially thought that the Spaniards had descended from the skies. For their part the latter too either genuinely thought that Indians were too strange to be human or refused to acknowledge them as such for self-interested reasons. It did not take long for both sides to discover their common human identity and to establish communicative, sexual, social and even moral relationship with each other. Every culture requires the concept of a human being, a being who can think, talk, relate to others and participate in social practices, and it expects of humans what it does not expect of animals and plants. And since it has a concept of human being, it is capable of imaginatively extending it to include others as well.[4]

Thanks to their unique and universally shared capacities, human beings are able to understand, control and humanise their natural environment, make sense of their lives, imaginatively explore experiences, and develop ideas of truth, goodness, beauty and love. They create aesthetic, moral, spiritual and other values, as well as a system of meanings in terms of which to assign different degrees of significance to different human activities and organise their lives. They are also able to enter into meaningful relations with each other and create a world of deep attachments and loyalties that gives their lives moral and emotional depth. In short, thanks to their unique capacities humans are meaning-creating and culture-building beings. Although different societies do this with different degrees of sophistication, each is a distinct human achievement.

Human beings possess not only certain common capacities but also certain desires and needs, and this again is evident in and affirmed by all cultures. As embodied beings they wish to live, desire food and physical wholeness, loathe disease and pain, require rest, need to remain active, and seek sexual satisfaction. Since they live in society, they also develop such socially derived desires as those for self-respect, the good opinion of others, friendship, love and forming relations with those they like (and avoiding those they do not like), and such fears as those of rejection and humiliation. As distinct centres of self-consciousness, they have an ineliminable inner life which is exclusively their own and forms the basis of their sense of subjectivity. They also have their moods, dreams, frustrations and unique experiences, which they need to integrate in their lives and come to terms with if they are to avoid the risk of disintegration. And they cannot do so without a relatively inviolable personal space and at least some measure of control over their lives. They require a long period of nurture and cannot grow into sane adults without a stable, loving and stimulating environment and a sense of belonging and rootedness. In order to feel secure, plan their lives and form stable relationships, they need a society free from an oppressive climate of terror and total unpredictability. They also need to acquire certain basic capabilities and skills in order to hold themselves together, make sense of their lives, adjust to changing circumstances, establish civil and moral relationships with others, find their way around in the wider society, take countless decisions doing the course of their lives, reflect on their actions, and so forth.

These and other constituents and conditions of human well-being characterise all cultures. There is nothing ontologically necessary about them, for human beings could have been different and might acquire radically different features in a currently unimaginable future; rather they characterise all societies known to us. In none of them are human beings six inches or six metres tall, asexual, endowed with unusual sense organs, immortal, free from physical vulnerability and decay, without emotions, able to grow up without adult help or lacking a sense of subjectivity.

In the light of our discussion the following features characterise human beings in all societies and form part of human identity. There are several others but these are some of the most important. First, all human beings are capable of entering into meaningful relations with others, and none is so alien and strange as to be unable to share a common life with others. Secondly, they have several capacities which are unique to them and privilege them over the non-human world. Thirdly, thanks to their unique capacities, they create a world of meaning and values and not only enrich the natural world but create a new one of their own. Fourthly, since human beings have common capacities, desires and needs, they need certain common conditions to survive and flourish.

These and related facts about us provide the basis and the context of our deliberation on which moral values are worthy of universal allegiance and should guide our relations with each other. Let us take each of them in turn. Since we are capable of fellowship in the sense defined earlier, we form a universal moral community. We can fall in love with, make love to, marry, have children with, make friends with, adopt the children of, understand the joys and sorrows of, and put ourselves in the shoes of our fellow humans from any part of the world. The fact that we can share a universal fellowship does not, of course, mean that we should. We might construct rigid walls between different races, nationalities and social groups and advocate and practise social exclusion, or we might instead build on the fact of potential human fellowship and seek to draw closer to each other in a spirit of human solidarity.

We need to decide which of the two is a better way of organising human relations. Briefly the exclusivist view has little to commend itself. It rests on the false assumption that some groups of human beings are so alien to others that they cannot share a common moral and social life. And since its underlying assumption is false, it can justify itself to its adherents only by means of further falsehoods, as is shown by even a cursory examination of racist and anti-Semitic doctrines. Such falsehoods can only be sustained by suppressing inner doubts, moral feelings and critical reflection, by encouraging morbid fears and irrational obsessions, etc., all of which take a heavy psychological and moral toll on those involved. As historical experience shows, the exclusivist view also breeds aggressiveness, hatred, intolerance and desire for domination, and leads to violence and bloodshed. What is more, it is difficult to sustain in practice. Since members of different groups cannot altogether avoid contacts with each other, they strike up friendships, moral bonds and sexual liaisons, and these generate contradictions between their profession and practice and the inevitable anxiety and hypocrisy. For these and other reasons we would be wiser to cherish and consolidate human fellowship and cultivate the value of human unity.

Human beings have several capacities which they know to be unique to them and make them superior to the animals. We might dismiss this as human hubris, or consider the capacities a source of human misery and advocate a primitivist way of life in the manner of Diogenes, or welcome and nurture it and use it for worthwhile purposes. Human capacities are a fact and cannot be wished out of existence. We can, of course, seek to reduce humans to zombies, but that is impossible, for those who do so will themselves escape the process, and also pointless. We therefore rightly recognise the fact of human uniqueness and superiority and embody it in the practice of 'human dignity' (or its analogues in other languages). Dignity is an aristocratic or hierarchical concept in the sense that it describes a status and only makes sense in relation to what is judged inferior. This is why every discussion of human dignity in one way or another compares humans to non-humans, and implies that they are not and may not be treated as if they were animals or inanimate objects. This does not mean that animals are human playthings and may be treated as we please, but rather that they are not our equals and that, although they should be loved and cared for, they have no dignity. Dignity is not an individual but a collective status, for the individual acquires it by virtue of possessing certain species-specific capacities and belonging to the human species. Human beings do not have dignity in the way that they have eyes and ears. It is a human *practice,* something they choose to confer on themselves and each other because of their mutual acknowledgement of their uniquely shared capacities. They have dignity because they have capacities which non-humans do not have and which they consider so significant as to make them the basis of an appropriate moral practice.

To say that human beings have dignity is to say that they ought to be viewed and treated in a certain manner, which is best expressed by the term respect (or its equivalent in other languages). Respect is a complex concept. Briefly it implies, negatively, that humans may not be treated as if they were inanimate things or insects, killed for food, hunted, used for target practice or dangerous medical experiments, humiliated, despised, or made to feel insignificant. Positively, respect implies such things as that we should help them develop and exercise their distinctive capacities, value their power of agency, invite their views on matters affecting them, understand them in their own terms, and justify what we do to them in terms of reasons they can appreciate.

The third human universal, or cross-culturally shared feature, relates to the human capacity to create a world of meanings and values as embodied in their aesthetic, social, intellectual, moral and other achievements. These achievements are worthy of admiration because they reflect creativity, energy, search for meaning and significance, depth of emotion, and capacity for co-operation and altruism, and add to the beauty of the world. Since human beings are capable of creating worthy things and leading worthy lives, they have worth and deserve to be cherished and valued. Like dignity, worth is not a natural human property but a moral practice based on a human decision. There are good reasons to value and encourage human achievements, and hence to confer worth on human beings. This is why we rightly confer value on such things as objects of art, cultural and religious communities, rare manuscripts and ancient buildings, and consider them worth preserving, sometimes even at the cost of human life.

It is, of course, true that some, such as idiots, imbeciles and mad people, lack some of the distinctively human capacities. However, they are rarely devoid of them altogether and are mad and imbecile in a way that only those possessed of these capacities can be. Besides, since idiocy and madness are not easy to define, once we go down this road we run the risk of encouraging others to draw the line differently and deny worth to others as well. Those afflicted with such infirmities are also the sons, daughters, brothers or friends of those who are free from them. They are thus deeply bonded to the latter, form an integral part of their moral and emotional world, and participate in their worth. Conferring dignity and worth on subnormal persons also tests, affirms and intensifies our general commitment to human worth for, if we are able to value them, we are even more likely to value and cherish our more fortunate fellow-humans.

To adopt the moral practice of conferring worth on human beings is to commit ourselves to treating them in certain ways. Negatively, we may not treat them as worthless or devoid of intrinsic value, and use them as a mere means to our ends, manipulate or brainwash them, sacrifice them for causes they do not share, violate the integrity of their intimate relationships, and treat with contempt what they deeply value. Positively, we should cherish their sense of self-respect and self-worth, value their individual and collective achievements, encourage them to develop and express their human capacities, and help create conditions in which they can lead worthy and meaningful lives.

Unlike the concept of dignity, which is based on a contrast between humans and monuments, the concept of worth has no such comparative reference. Human beings have worth because they can do worthwhile things and lead valuable lives. This is why they might not have dignity in the eyes of God, but they cannot be worthless. They might not be as worthy in God's view as they think, but it is difficult to imagine how any conceivable view of God could deny their worth altogether. And, similarly, if beings with infinitely superior capacities to ours were to descend upon the earth, we might not possess dignity in their eyes but our worth would remain largely unaffected.

Like the concept of human dignity, the closely related concept of human worth underpins and is affirmed by each culture. Culture is possible only because human beings possess certain unique capacities. Being a human creation, it cannot value and demand respect for its beliefs, practices and achievements without valuing both the capacities that made these possible and their human bearers. No cultural community can consider human beings devoid of all worth, for then it would itself have no worth either.

Human beings share common capacities, desires, needs etc., and require common conditions of growth. They also cannot develop their own sense of dignity and worth and appreciate that of others unless the conditions in which they live nurture, embody and publicly affirm both. These sets of conditions constitute their well-being and define the content of their fundamental human interests. Although different societies entertain different conceptions of the good life and differently define human well-being, the shared human capacities, desires, needs etc. imply that some constituents of human well-being are common to them all. These include such things as survival, means of sustenance, physical wholeness, good health, a stable, stimulating and loving environment, access to the cultural resources of their community, freedom from arbitrary exercise of power, a measure of privacy and control of their lives, and opportunities for self-expression. If we care for human dignity, worth and well-being, and we can give good reasons why we should, we have a duty to promote these and other fundamental human interests. Like dignity and worth, these interests are not given by nature but are a matter of human decision. We decide whether it is desirable that human beings should live rather than die, grow into intelligent adults or zombies, enjoy health or suffer from diseases etc., and how these values are best achieved. Promoting human well-being and defining it in a particular way is a moral practice.

Since all human beings have dignity and worth and need common conditions of growth, their claims to them deserve equal consideration and weight. The grounds on which one of them claims them commit him to respecting the similar claims of others. Equality is not a fact but a moral practice which we have good reasons to adopt, such as that it is required by considerations of moral consistency, ensures a sense of justice, reinforces the practices of human dignity and worth, and enables each individual to lead a rich personal life and to contribute towards a rich collective life. This does not mean that we might not admire some persons more, for that depends on their capacities and the way they use them, nor that all should enjoy equal income and wealth, for human capacities and efforts vary and the collective resources of the society might not allow such equality, nor that all should enjoy equal status and power, for that again is ruled out by inequalities of talents and the needs of wider society. Equality requires that all such inequalities should be compatible with and nurture and promote the dignity, worth and well-being of all.

In the light of our discussion, we arrive at a body of five universal moral values. They are human unity, human dignity, human worth,

promotion of human well-being or fundamental human interests, and equality. They are values because they deserve to be cherished and pursued, moral because they relate to how we should live and conduct our relations with others, and universal because they have claims to the allegiance of all human beings. The values are not *chosen* by us for that implies that they exist independently of our choice; rather we have decided for good reasons to live by them and confer on them the status of values. They are not specific to a particular culture or society, for they are grounded in an interculturally shared human identity and are capable of being defended by interculturally shareable good reasons. And they are not derived from a transcultural conception of human nature either, for we do not abstract away cultural differences but tease out the human capacities, desires, dispositions etc., that they presuppose and instantiate. Universal values form the basis of universal human rights, which are a subcategory of, and represent a particular manner of realising, these values.

Since the values can be shown to be worthy of universal allegiance and are in that sense universally valid, all societies can be expected to respect them both in their internal organisation and mutual relations. The values are unaffected by territorial boundaries, and it is self-contradictory to say that we should respect the dignity of our fellow-citizens but not that of outsiders. Every society needs to ensure that its way of life embodies these values and is not so constituted that it can flourish, or even survive, only by violating them elsewhere. It also has a duty to help others realise them within the limits of its resources and knowledge of their needs and subject to the basic respect for their decisions and ways of life. Since the dominant universalist discourse, both past and present, requires every society to respect certain values but does not impose positive or negative duties on others to give it such help as it needs and they can afford, it is partisan and morally incoherent. The universalist discourse makes sense only if mankind is conceived as a single moral community with all that this entails.

Reconciling universalism and cultural diversity

Although we can show, as I have tentatively tried to do, that some values are universally valid, they are by their very nature general and need to be interpreted, prioritised and applied to the particular circumstances of each society. Since different societies have different traditions and ways of understanding the world, they will naturally do so differently. For example, human life is a universal value, but different societies take different views on when it begins and ends and what respect for it entails. Respect for human dignity requires that we should not humiliate or degrade others or require them to do demeaning work. What constitutes humiliation, degradation or demeaning work, however, varies from society to society and cannot be universally legislated. In some societies an individual would rather be slapped on the face than coldly ignored or subjected to verbal abuse. In some, again, human dignity is deemed to be violated when parents interfere with their offspring's choice of a spouse; in others their intervention is a sign that they care enough for the latter's dignity and well-being to press their advice on them and save them from making a mess of their lives. Different societies might also articulate, defend and rely on different mechanisms to realise universal values. Some might prefer the language of claims and even rights, and maintain that human beings have rights to dignity and protection of their interests. Others might find this too formal, legalistic and impersonal and might prefer the language of duty, imposing stringent moral and social obligations on their members not to violate each other's dignity or damage their interests, and reinforcing these by social conditioning and collective pressure. Again, some might talk of the sacredness of human beings, whereas others might prefer the more neutral concept of worth.

Since universal values can be defined, prioritised and realised differently by different societies, we face a problem. We cannot expect a society to live by our views on the matter for that ignores its cultural differences, disrespects its capacity for self-determination, and requires it to live by norms it might neither understand nor be able to accommodate in its way of life. However, we cannot leave it free to define and practise universal values as it pleases, for it might interpret them out of existence, subvert their critical thrust, and even claim their authority to justify its unacceptable practices. This not only brings back relativism through the back door but allows it to masquerade as universalism.

The question of how to make space for the inescapable cultural mediation of universal values without depriving them of their normative and critical thrust has not received the attention it deserves. For their own different reasons monists and relativists have taken no interest in it. And since the minimum universalists do not allow for the cultural mediation of universal values, they too have largely ignored the question. I suggest that there are at least five ways in which we can both leave full scope for cultural mediation and ensure the integrity of universal values.

First, universal values can be understood in a variety of ways ranging from the minimalist to the maximalist. Respect for human dignity, for example, can be taken to mean minimally that no human being should be bought and sold, brutally tortured or subjected to genocidal policies, or maximally that they should be ensured all the desirable conditions of the good life. Although the maximalist interpretation has the advantages of pointing in the general direction in which we might need to move, preventing moral complacency and encouraging progress, it has its obvious limits. It is too open-ended and indeterminate to give political guidance or even set up moral guideposts and is often beyond the moral and material resources of most societies. The minimalist view has therefore much to be said for it, and we should in the light of our knowledge of human societies lay down the moral minimum that they must all respect. In some cases the moral minimum is best stated negatively as avoidance of certain evils, in others positively as guaranteeing certain goods. This is broadly what the United Nations Declaration of Human Rights does, and in so doing articulates what it calls the 'conscience' of mankind.

Secondly, since universal values are necessarily general and relatively indeterminate, they should as far as possible be articulated in the language of norms. Norms relate values to conduct, indicate how the values are to be interpreted, and give them a content. We should therefore not only say that human dignity is a value but also translate it into norms, and require that human beings should not be bought and sold, used as a mere means, killed at will, subjected to dangerous experiments etc. Although even these are open to interpretation, they are reasonably unambiguous and as specific as general statements can be.

Norms in turn can be articulated in either the language of rights or that of duties and obligations. We might say that every human being has a right not to be treated as a mere means, bought and sold, etc., or that human beings have a duty not to treat each other in these ways. The two languages are not mutually translatable, for they view general norms from different perspectives and highlight different aspects, and each is more appropriate to some areas of life than to others. Since different cultures are more at home in one language than in another, they should be free to use the one most suited to their moral culture provided that it ensures effective enforcement of the norms.

Thirdly, we should not confuse values with particular institutional mechanisms. Different societies are bound to devise different institutions to realise common values to suit their traditions, moral culture and historical experiences. Human dignity can be nurtured in an individualist as well as a communitarian society, and individual freedom can be secured in a liberal-democratic or capitalist system as well as in other types of political and economic systems. We might, of course, have good reasons to believe that values are more likely to be realised under one set of institutions than another, but we should neither be unduly dogmatic about our views nor so identify the institutions with the values that the latter cannot be discussed and defended separately.

Fourthly, since every society enjoys the moral freedom to interpret and prioritise the agreed body of universal values, we cannot condemn its practices simply because they are different from or offend against ours. The Zoroastrian practice of exposing the dead to the vultures might seem to us to violate human dignity, but reasons can be given for it and they are no better or worse than those behind the practice of leaving the dead to be devoured by worms. However, other practices might not be so easily explained and justified, and then we should ask the society concerned to explain itself. The resulting dialogue and the subsequent pressure of world opinion might seem a rather feeble way of upholding the offended values, but it is sometimes quite effective and often the only form of action possible in cross-cultural encounters.

Take the practice of stoning a convicted rapist to death in some Muslim societies. For most outsiders it is inhuman and degrading, but not in the eyes of those societies who think it fully justified. As they understand it the rapist has behaved like a beast and forfeited his dignity. Stoning him to death also publicly expresses the society's abhorrence of his crime and satisfies its sense of justice. It also has a morally regenerative and community-building dimension. It brings the members of the community together, forces each of them to take a stand on the crime, mobilises their collective moral energies, emotionally commits them not to engage in the crime themselves, and publicly reaffirms the authority of the values violated by the rapist. Unlike the discreet and impersonal administration of conventional forms of capital punishment which does not engage people's emotions, demand an individual response and regenerate the community, the Muslim form of punishment is praised for its democratic, participatory and transformative qualities.

Although the Muslim defence is not worthless, it is deeply flawed. It wrongly assumes that the criminal forfeits his dignity. His humanity is the basis of his dignity, and is not negated or undermined by an isolated deed. He retains his other human capacities, and can be reformed and reintegrated into the community or at least isolated and allowed to lead as worthwhile a life as he is capable of. Besides, stoning human beings to death implies that they may be so treated, and both weakens our commitment to the moral practice of respecting human dignity and brutalises us. Moreover, there is no empirical evidence that the practice has any of the desirable consequences claimed for it. Incidents of rape continue, victims are often bribed or blackmailed into silence, and judges feel reluctant to grant conviction. As for the stone-throwers, they are guided by all kinds of motives of which the sense of outrage is not always the most dominant, and are not known to be regenerated by their experience. For these and other reasons we can rightly argue that the practice is inhuman, has few if any compensating features and should be discontinued.

Finally, we might encourage regional arrangements for defining and enforcing universal values. The kind of cross-cultural dialogue I sketched earlier could be replicated at the regional level, and different regional communities could develop charters of rights and freedoms and evolve mechanisms for their impartial enforcement in the light of their cultural traditions. The resulting consensus would have the further advantages of carrying greater moral authority and guarding against both an overbearing and abstract universalism and a self-serving appeal to national values. In some sense this is already happening in several parts of the world. We could formalise the arrangement and find ways of integrating regional statements of universal values into a suitably differentiated global framework.

In the light of our discussion it would be useful to examine the much-debated question of Asian values. Leaders of almost all East Asian countries insist that some of the rights included in the United Nations and other Western-inspired declarations of human rights are incompatible with their values, traditions and self-understanding, and that Western governments should be more tolerant of their attempts to define and prioritise them differently. While agreeing that the rights are universally valid, the Bangkok Declaration of 1993 insisted that they must be defined and applied in the light of local 'history, culture and religious backgrounds'. The Singapore delegation to the 1995 Vienna conference challenged the very universality of some of these rights. Urging the West not to be 'so blinded by arrogance and certainties as to lose the capacity for imagination and sympathy', the delegation asked it to take a 'more modest approach' lest it should 'fracture the international consensus on human rights'. The widespread Western response is to reject appeals to Asian values as self-serving attempts to exempt these countries from the values embodied in the statements of universal human rights. In its view the so-called Asian values are neither unique nor common to all Asian countries, and cannot be allowed to subvert or limit human rights.[5]

The dispute between the two sides is far more complex than either appreciates. The appeal to national or regional values is not peculiar to East Asians. Americans insist that the European welfare state and the

Asian family structure, both of which embody important human values, are incompatible with and cannot be accommodated in their individualist way of life. The British would not follow the Singaporean ban on pornography and the French would not allow multiculturalism on the grounds that these sit ill at ease with their liberal values. If these societies are right to cherish their own or so-called Western values, there is no obvious reason why the East Asian should not. Again, it would not do to say that Asian values are not unique to Asian countries, for their leaders not only make no such claim but instead insist that the West too should, and once did, share them and is wrong to allow them to be overridden by liberal individualist values. Nor would it do to say that all Asians do not share these values, for there is no reason why they should. Racists, sexists and many conservative citizens of liberal society do not share the liberal value of equality, yet we consider it central to our vision of the good life and impose it on all without the slightest hesitation. In short we should not ask the abstract and misleading question as to whether East Asians have a right to live by their values, but rather what these values are and if and how they offend against the kinds of *individualist* universal values discussed earlier.

We can distinguish three different kinds of claims by East Asian leaders. First, many of them do not like the language of rights because it is individualist, legalistic, assertive and alien to their moral culture. They have no disagreement with the values stressed by the various declarations of rights, but prefer to articulate and defend them in the more communitarian, moral and accommodative language of duties, mutual concern or loyalty to the wider society, or in concepts that straddle and stress both rights and duties. Their claim is unobjectionable, for so long as the values are respected each society should be free to find the most effective way to popularise and realise them. We might feel that the communitarian language is vulnerable to collectivist dangers and that it does not generate the right cultural climate. However, the language of rights too has its obvious dangers, and so long as the East Asian practice does not violate the values, we should respect their differences.

Secondly, almost all East Asian leaders argue that the conventional declarations of human rights explicitly or implicitly prescribe the standard Western liberal-democratic form of government and brook no departures from it. In their view a good government should be just, accountable to its citizens, promote economic growth, hold the society together and reflect the basic values of its people. It does not have to be liberal in the sense of conceiving the political community as a contractual association between its members and having no other collective goals and values than to maintain their rights and promote their interests. Nor does it have to privilege the individual over the community, endorse state neutrality between different conceptions of the good, or share recent liberal hostility to paternalism, perfectionism and moral coercion. Unlike their Western counterparts, East Asian societies do share a broad moral consensus on the nature of the good life and see nothing wrong in enforcing it. They think they have a right and even a duty to respect democratic public opinion and ban pornography, protect religious beliefs and practices by restricting free speech, censure films and literary works that incite intercommunal hatred or mock established values, empower the police to test a person's urine for drugs if he or she behaves suspiciously, and require compulsory rehabilitation when the test proves positive.

As against the traditional disjunction between the state and society, East Asian spokesmen insist on their partnership, and argue that the state may legitimately make laws to protect the family, the neighbourhood and the environment by promoting the virtues of filial piety, good neighbourliness and respect for nature. Thus it may impose a fine on an individual for failing to report a theft or a fire in a neighbour's house or to save a drowning child, offer tax breaks to individuals who support their parents and siblings, and give parents over sixty a right to sue their children for maintenance. East Asian leaders also point to the problems involved in holding multi-ethnic societies together. Since some of their ethnic groups have no experience of living and working together, racial hostilities are easily aroused and require greater restrictions than usual on free speech. In many cases of racial unrest the process of trial itself inflames passions and increases tension, making it unwise to conduct it in the normal Western manner. Evidence may have to be gathered by covert operations and cannot be submitted to the open court or expected to meet the normal standards of criminal law.

This second East Asian claim does not reject universal values. It prioritises and relates them to local values differently to what is common in most Western societies, and seeks to develop somewhat different institutional mechanisms and follow different social policies. The East Asian leaders involved do not justify tortures, arbitrary arrests, tyranny, genocide, racial and other forms of discrimination and the denial of free elections and basic liberties. They are keen to pursue such goals as social harmony, moral and social consensus, the integrity of the family, the right to a decent life, and economic development. These goals involve greater restrictions on individual choice and free speech than is common in liberal societies. However, the latter have their own problems and cannot in any case be held up as universal models. So long as the East Asian countries are able to show that their goals are worthwhile, that these entail certain restrictions and that the latter enjoy broad popular support, their choices must be respected.

The third East Asian claim is quite different and is largely advanced by the bulk of Chinese and some Indonesian and Vietnamese leaders. Very briefly, they argue that the kinds of universal values that inspire declarations of human rights are essentially bourgeois and Western and inconsistent with their traditional values. For them, especially the Chinese, society is more important than the individual; social solidarity, a prosperous economy, and a strong and powerful state are the highest national goals; and the individual life has a meaning only in so far as it serves these goals. Accordingly, they reject all statements of human rights and virtually the entire democratic system of free elections, multiple political parties, political participation, free speech, peaceful protests, individual and organised dissent, and the rule of law.[6]

Although this claim is understandable in the context of Chinese history, and is far more complex and nuanced than my brief account implies, it is unsustainable. It sanctions terror, arbitrary arrests, gross violations of personal autonomy, destruction of the family, the worst forms of individual humiliation, disregard for human dignity and the use of individuals as a mere means to collective goals. One might accept some of these violations of basic values if the Chinese had convincing reasons to do so, such as the impending disintegration of the country as a result of civil war or foreign invasion or if this was the only way of eliminating acute poverty. None of these is the case. Economic development is certainly of great importance but it does not require and is positively hampered by such repressive measures. It also needs to be balanced against other equally important values. Economic development is meant to create the conditions of the good life, and defeats its very purpose if in the process it violates human dignity, self-respect and autonomy and renders its citizens incapable of leading such a life. The same is true of national unity and social solidarity, both of which are worthwhile goals but which are likely to be subverted by the methods the Chinese propose.

The Chinese leaders' claim that their traditional values are incompatible with human rights is equally unconvincing. It is, of course, true that the traditional Chinese view of the individual requires the concept of rights to be defined in less exclusivist, proprietary and absolutist terms than is common in all modern Western legal systems. Such a view of rights has something to be said for it. However, it can be easily reconciled with a suitably redefined conception of human rights. As their own human rights activists have pointed out, Chinese leaders misrepresent traditional values, for there is no evidence to show that the latter justify any of the practices mentioned above. And if they do, they need to be changed, for no values are sacrosanct simply because they are traditional. After all, neither the communist nor even the nationalist values which the Chinese have warmly embraced are traditionally Chinese. Again, it is true that, like its pre-modern European counterparts, traditional Chinese society relied on intricate social mechanisms to check political power and did not stress individual rights. However, their society today is quite different. The emergence of the centralised and bureaucratic state, urbanisation, increased mobility of labour and capital, social differentiation and industrialisation have undermined its traditional mechanisms of social self-discipline and required it to develop equally effective alternatives. The only ones that have worked reasonably well so far in most societies are the institutions of human rights, constitutionally limited power, a free press, etc. Since the Chinese leaders have not suggested a viable alternative, their rejection of human rights is self-serving and suspect.

Conclusion

I have argued the following in this chapter. It is both possible and necessary to develop a body of non-ethnocentric universal values. This is best done by means of an open-minded cross-cultural dialogue in which participants rationally decide what values are worthy of their allegiance and respect. I have briefly indicated how such a dialogue might proceed and what some of these values are. Given the differences in their history, traditions and moral culture, different societies interpret, prioritise and realise these values differently, and this is both inescapable and desirable. The values do not constitute a kind of floor or threshold subject to which different societies may organise themselves as they please, but represent a body of regulative principles that inform and structure all aspects of their moral lives. There is an inevitable dialectical interplay between the relatively thin universal values and the thick moral structures that characterise different societies. The universal values regulate the national structures even as the latter pluralise the values. If a philosophical label is needed, this position is best described as regulative or pluralist universalism.

Notes

I am most grateful to Steven Lukes, Seyla Benhabib, Joseph Carens, Jan Nederveen Pieterse, and the late Martin Hollis, for many helpful discussions on the subject of this chapter.

1 See Herodotus, *The Histories*, rev. edn (London: Penguin, 1972), book III, ch. 38. For useful references, see Steven Lukes, 'Moral diversity and relativism', *Journal of Philosophy of Education* 29 (1995): 173–9.
2 H. L. A. Hart, *The Concept of Law* (Oxford: Clarendon Press, 1961); Michael Walzer, 'Two kinds of universalism', in Grethe B. Peterson (ed.), *The Turner Lectures on Human Values*, vol. XI (Salt Lake City: University of Utah Press, 1991); Michael Walzer, *Thick and Thin: Moral Argument at Home and Abroad* (Notre Dame, Ind.: University of Notre Dame Press, 1994); John Rawls, *A Theory of Justice* (Cambridge, Mass.: Harvard University Press, 1971); Stuart Hampshire, *Morality in Conflict* (Oxford: Basil Blackwell, 1983); Martha Nussbaum, 'Non-relative virtues: an Aristotelian approach', in Martha Nussbaum and Amartya Sen (eds.), *The Quality of Life* (Oxford: Clarendon Press, 1993), pp. 242–69.
3 I borrow this expression from Nussbaum, 'Non-relative virtues', p. 252. As will become clear, I give human universals a different content and derive them differently.
4 See the excellent account in Tzvetan Todorov, *The Conquest of America: The Question of the Other* (New York: Harper and Row, 1981). Countless narratives of colonial encounters confirm this account.
5 For good accounts, see James T. H. Tang, (ed.), *Human Rights and International Relations in Asia Pacific* (London: Pinter, 1995); symposium, *Journal of Democracy* 8 (1997); and Roger T. Ames, 'Continuing the conversation on Chinese human rights', in *Ethics and International Affairs* 11 (1997): 177–205.
6 Even the Chinese do not always endorse such an extreme line and generally plead for a culturally sensitive definition and application of human rights. See the speech by Liu Huaqiu at the Vienna conference, in Tang (ed.), *Human Rights and International Relations*, pp. 213–17. In the Chinese arguments, but not in those of the East Asian countries, cultural differences are systematically confused with those based on political ideology.

5   Towards an ethic of global responsibility

Mary Midgley

It is striking how quickly the idea of human rights – only lately added to our moral vocabulary – has been accepted by the public as useful, indeed perhaps as indispensable for talking about the world that we live in. Throughout the West, and to some extent through the whole international community, people understand roughly what is meant by violation of human rights. And they use that phrase at times to say things that they find very important. It is the sense of our times that, whatever doubts there may be about minor moral questions and whatever respect each culture may owe to its neighbours, there are some things that should not be done to anybody anywhere. Against these things (people feel) every bystander can and ought to protest.

It is no wonder that academics are startled by this quick acceptance of the concept. They rightly point out uncertainties both about the central meaning of the term and about its borderlines. Yet in general the public is surely in the right to make use of the idea. This new conceptual tool is a powerful one and its power, like that of all such tools, is in some ways mysterious. Its full meaning is not easily explicated. It expresses rather more than we can yet put into our dictionaries. Those whose business it is to seek precision in these vast and ill-explored areas are therefore quite right to busy themselves in trying to work out its full implications and to point out the confusions which it may involve – as is done in this book. That critique is necessary because new moral insights always have to be checked for hitches and flaws. Without such checking they remain fanciful and cannot be realistically applied.

The checking, however, needs to be of a kind that is not predeterminedly destructive. The kind of reductive approach that rejects a new moral insight simply by pointing out that it cannot be expressed in the terms of its predecessors is guaranteed to miss the point. New insights are responses to changes in the world and our vocabulary always has to evolve to meet such changes. New wine always needs new bottles.

In this particular case, the change that confronts us is a very general and radical one which is troubling us on many fronts. It is simply the immense enlargement of our moral scene – partly by the sheer increase in the number of humans, partly by the wide diffusion of information about them, and partly by the dramatic increase in our own technological power – a power which now enables us in the dominant nations to damage radically both the human and the non-human world that we live in, or to refrain from such damage.

The problem about distant humans is, I think, more closely linked both to the environmental problem and to the problem about the way in which we treat animals than has sometimes been noticed. (Their linkage is often obscured by their being usually examined by different academic disciplines.) Technology has hugely multiplied both the range of matters that seem likely to concern us and our ability to affect those matters. And though that power often does not seem to be in our own individual hands, our civilisation as a whole clearly does bear some measure of responsibility for producing this whole situation. On this confusing scene, the idea of *human rights* is one of a number that have been evolved to help us select the most urgent points on which to concentrate our concern.

The problem of incredulity

We find it hard, however, to use it for this purpose simply because of the sheer difficulty of believing in the whole expansion. Can it really be true (we ask) that we have duties to people so distant from us, people belonging to quite other communities? Can we, still more strangely, have duties that concern the non-human world? Both these things seem implausible because the changes that have taken place are simply too large for us to take in imaginatively. We wander round the edges of these changes in bewilderment. Yet the changes are real. They demand some kind of adaptation from us, adaptation of a morality which was built for a quite different, much more manageable kind of world. We cannot go on acting as if we were still in that simpler world. On that path, we shall find no way through.

Here, of course, we are not alone. This is not the first time that people in our culture have faced such a radical conceptual emergency. During the decline of the Roman Empire, people lost a mighty framework which had seemed central to the whole meaning of their civilisation. Accordingly, when the Goths took Rome, St Augustine offered Christians the idea of the City of God as a better replacement – an ideal city much less local, much less corrupted, but also of course much more demanding. Other empires and cities too have fallen. People have repeatedly had to reshape their moral horizons. All such blows produce their own trauma and bewilderment, which has somehow to be met on each occasion by new moral thinking.

The flight to moral minimalism

What form, then, should that thinking now take? One possible way of meeting the crisis is to widen the scope of morality, as St Augustine did and as the insistence on human rights now does. But another, which is certainly just as natural, is to narrow that scope. When the world changes in a way that tends to remove social limits – to expose people to very wide demands – theorists may well restore those limits by contracting the social circle, by retreating into some kind of moral minimalism.

Since the Renaissance, this kind of contraction has in any case been happening in political philosophy in the West. Political thinkers of the Enlightenment systematically shrank morality by making it essentially a civic affair – a matter of mutual bargaining between prudent citizens within a limited society. Contract thinking sought to abolish the idea of duties towards anyone or anything outside that society. Of course the more subtle contract theorists, such as Kant and John Rawls, do not treat these duties simply as flowing from self-interested prudence, as Hobbes did. But the original point of the model was to limit the scope of the duties within a definite society, not to enlarge that scope.

That limitation had originally a most respectable aim. It was meant to debunk supposed duties towards the supernatural because those duties had been used to justify fearful religious wars and oppressions. The real target of contract thinking was a distorted notion of duties towards God, and towards earthly rulers who claimed to be God's regents. But this move had an unintended side-effect. It makes it quite hard for us now to make sense of our responsibility towards humans outside our own society, and almost impossible to explain our responsibilities towards non-human nature.

The wider horizon

Contract thinking, along with Utilitarianism, created a bog in which philosophers who try to do environmental ethics are now busily floundering, alongside the similar bog that traps theorists of human rights.[1] Our habitual, official legalistic-cum-philosophic language simply does not have suitable terms for either of these things. This minimalism has not, however, been the whole of our Enlightenment tradition on the matter. There was another, contrasting strand of thought which resisted it and which has in fact generated the current idea of human rights. This was an expansive, hospitable, universalising, humanitarian movement which worked to counter the narrow legalism of contract thinking. Kant always combined both strands in a constant dialectic, which is what makes him still one of our most interesting and fertile ancestors.

That humanitarian movement's first great project was the eighteenth-century's campaign for the rights of man. Campaigners for that extension attacked the meanness of limiting the idea of 'society' to certain privileged political units. They wanted to widen our duties so as to take in all the people excluded from those units, including foreigners and slaves. The language in which they expressed this proposal was, however, traditional. They used the existing idea of society though they widened its scope. They envisaged a super-society in which all rational beings (i.e. all humans – or at least all men) were Citizens of the World, which thus became a kind of super-city state. Kant expressed the point by talking of a Kingdom of Ends[2] – a realm of rational beings who, just because they were rational, must be viewed as existing as ends in themselves, not as mere means to the ends of others.

These reformers did not have to abandon the political language, because the idea of a wider city was already familiar. It has been pioneered by St Augustine's talk of the City of God and before that by the Stoics, who also spoke of a world-city, Cosmopolis. But the attempt to invoke this vast image outside a religious context conflicted with the pragmatic, reductive thrust of contract thinking, which insisted on pointing out that all states have limits and that all obligations must lie inside what is practical.

The Enlightenment's dialectic

These two elements in Enlightenment thought clashed at once in Rousseau's thinking and they have continued to clash ever since. For, in spite of much cheerful boasting by Nietzsche and the postmoderns, the Enlightenment is not something safely tucked away in the past, something obsolete that we can patronise. It is where we still live. Postmodern insights are themselves a recognisable part of it. That movement still sets our current moral scene simply because we have not yet managed to resolve the deep clashes that arise between the various elements that were jammed together in its message – clashes between order and freedom, between feeling and reason, between humanitarianism and the rule of law. Those clashes are the real source of our present problem.

Of course these clashes have not been merely destructive. They have often provided a fertile dialectic, a dialectic which makes possible the kind of development that a morality needs. Realistic reductivism has repeatedly done a real service to Utopian visionaries by forcing them to deal with nitty-gritty problems of detail. The effective reformers have been the people who have managed to operate on both sides of this divide, combining the two elements in their own thinking rather than fighting an external battle over them. They have been people who somehow contrived to fuse moral realism in this ordinary sense – not in the technical one which we will discuss presently – with bold aspiration, making practical thinking the instrument of their ideals rather than wasting effort in friction between the two. They have been able to interpret their long-term, demanding principles in terms of something immediately practicable without losing sight of the longer aim. This kind of twin vision is in fact the central thing that can make any kind of moral progress possible.

This feat is, however, extremely hard. The two strands of thought always tend to keep coming apart. Reforming movements, as they grow, perpetually find themselves, to their members' distress, splitting into extreme and moderate factions. Idealists dismiss those who concentrate on small, relatively practicable measures as mere compromisers while people who feel themselves to be practical accuse idealists of Utopian fantasy and humbug. Over our present topic – which is the scope of possible duties – this drama is usually still played out in the Enlightenment's terms as a conflict between legalistic reductivism and human sympathy, a conflict which is easily generalised into a wider war between reason and feeling.

These seductive formulations are, however, always misleading. Thought and feeling, law and sympathy are not – as the eighteenth century too often thought – separate imperialistic powers fighting a battle to take over the command of a country called morality. They are all complementary elements within it. The notion that they can be treated as belligerents or duellists is, however, still prevalent and it is the source of our present debates, as it is of current disputes about environmental ethics and about duties to animals. There, too, the argument surges mainly round attempts to find, somewhere within the conventional vocabulary, language which will give these matters the status that they now seem to us to need. And there, too, these attempts continually run up against the limits set by the tradition.

The notion that the environment in general – Nature as a whole – has value in itself, a notion which is expressed in terms such as 'deep ecology', is blocked by the more reductive idea that Nature cannot possibly matter except in so far as it contributes to human welfare. About animals, things are still more confused. The idea of dismissing them as mere disposable instruments now strikes many of us as immoral and repulsive. Yet the rationalist half of the tradition is deeply committed to claiming that only rational beings of a strictly human kind can have the kind of value or importance that would bring them within the scope of morality at all.

The persistent power of this view in government quarters can be seen in a recent move by the Charity Commissioners, who warned the RSPCA that it might lose its status as a charity if it went on campaigning against forms of animal abuse which were advantageous to humans. In a letter to the *Guardian* the Chief Charity Commissioner himself explained that campaigns for animal protection could only count as charitable in so far as they were aimed at 'raising public morality by repressing brutality and cruelty *and thereby elevating the human race by stimulating compassion*'.[3]

This principle – which seems not to be just his own opinion but the official remit of the Commission – rules that charities must confine themselves to doing good to the human race. They cannot attend to non-human sufferings. On this principle, cruel practices towards animals are not at all wrong in themselves.

They only become so if they make people less compassionate towards other humans. It would be uncommonly hard to establish this causal link and, indeed, some ill-tempered people, after all, might surely treat their families worse, not better, if they were forbidden to take out their bad moods on the dog. But this does not seem to settle the question whether they ought to be allowed to do so. The 'human advantage' which is held to justify these practices is evidently rather widely interpreted by the Commission to include simple profit, since the examples under discussion include not just medical research but the trade in the live export of calves from Britain, as well as hunting.

This bizarre piece of eighteenth-century rationalism is surely out of tune with our current moral insights. In fact, it has probably only been enabled to hold its place for so long because of the convenient twist which has so far allowed campaigning on behalf of animals to proceed under an indirect licence, nominally as a way of improving the human character. If the literal meaning of this remit continues to be pressed, public opinion will probably force it to be altered. On this point, as well as about the wider environment, the reductive, rationalist tradition no longer represents our current moral thinking. As quite often happens, the public is ahead of many academics morally and the conceptual scheme needs to be reshaped.

The point of exclusive humanism

This exclusive emphasis on human claims was not originally meant to work as a barrier against concern for other earthly beings. As just mentioned, it simply reflected a political campaign against the use of religion to justify oppression. It put forward a narrow, contractual view of political obligation as a defence against the exploitation of religiously motivated loyalty by self-interested rulers. And it was, of course, invented at a time when our understanding of the planet was quite different from what it now is. The possibility of real environmental disaster had not then come on the horizon at all. Its appearance there in the last half-century is surely one of the greatest changes that has ever happened to the human race. It would be surprising if it did not demand a change in everybody's conceptual scheme.

In the earlier history of the West, however, the narrow, contractual view of political obligation had become rather strongly entrenched. More generally, it had given rise to a tendentious, reductive notion of rationality itself as essentially the calculation of self-interest. This notion is still perpetuated in the language of economics and it surfaces whenever altruistic claims are brought forward in public debate. In particular, it furnishes a background which can make it seem flatly impossible for rational people to extend the notion of rights to remote humans or (still further) to animals, or to be directly concerned for the environment.

Is it just a verbal question?

There is a real difficulty here because the actual word 'rights' does have strong connections with the law-courts. It is by its nature forensic. It easily looks competitive and litigious. In law, 'rights' are always rights held by one person *against* another or others. They can also only be held by beings who are able in principle to appear and argue their case as litigants in court. Though these requirements are actually fudged for infants and other incapacitated humans by allowing others to be their representatives, many people still think that this makes it impossible that elephants or dogs should have rights. Right-bearers, they feel, need to be standard people directly involved in the political process even if they cannot actually stand up and speak in court. They should be fellow-citizens of some kind, a requirement which even the best elephants cannot meet. Still more clearly, the Antarctic and the rain-forest are not going to stand up and argue in court. And in the main tradition, each country has also viewed the inhabitants of foreign countries as standing outside the rights conferred by its own legal system.

The important question here is whether this is just a verbal restriction on the use of the word right or a substantial point about what we ought to do, a real limitation on the realm of what can rightly concern us. About animals, it is often possible simply to bypass the word rights and to talk instead of our duties or responsibilities towards them. This use of the word 'duty', however, has also been blacklisted by some moral theorists, who have insisted that 'rights and duties are correlative' – not just in the weak sense that if someone has a right someone else must have a duty to meet it, but in the much stronger sense that no-one can have a duty to anyone who cannot owe them duty in return.[4]

This idea is not very plausible in the case of incapable humans. Indeed it surely shows up the unreality of this whole contractual, rationalist approach. 'Responsibility', however, still remains as a less objectionable word for the claims that animals have on us. It is also quite a convenient one for cases like the Antarctic and the rain-forests, for which the word right is in any case less often invoked than value.[5] With this kind of rephrasing, many people find it possible to agree that there are real claims here – ones on which we must actually act – even though there is not, strictly speaking, a right.

Words are not just air

Will this sort of circumlocution help us to deal with the case of distant humans? I doubt it. People invoke the word right here for the same reason that led eighteenth-century reformers to talk about the rights of man – namely, its implacable force. Words like duty and responsibility can seem weaker in that they can be seen as reporting primarily facts about the person who is under obligation. You or I have a duty – perhaps we will perform it, perhaps not; who knows? This may look like our own affair, private between us and our own consciences. Besides, in many large-scale cases it is not at all clear to just whom the duty or responsibility belongs.

To talk of rights is, by contrast, to talk directly about the people who need relief. It aims to lay a burden publicly on anyone who stands in the way of relieving them – a burden which cannot be dodged by passing the can. The quasi-legal language invokes the broad impersonality of the law. It makes it much harder to say 'this is none of my business'.

So the inducement to use the word rights for these very wide, extra-legal purposes is strong, even though constant difficulties arise about specifying the details of its meaning when we have done so. The downside of that advantage is, of course, the drawback that always goes with employing stronger language. People who think this language inappropriate may simply label it as empty rhetoric and dismiss one's whole claim without even asking themselves about the substantial moral issue behind it – as if the mistakenness of the wording settled the matter. This has indeed happened to a considerable extent about 'animal rights', especially in Britain.

About human rights it is not happening at present to half the same extent, at least at the public level. Among academics, however, this confusion between the verbal and the substantial levels is surely rampant. There are some philosophers who seem to view the whole notion of 'moral rights' – i.e. non-legal ones – simply as a weed much like ground-elder, a nuisance that perpetually recurs because of public incompetence and must just be uprooted every time it does so.

In such cases, however, it is surely better to assume that people are trying to say something genuinely important, however faulty their language may be, and to work to improve that language. My own policy on such matters is always to try and take the pressure off the hotly debated word by looking around for near-synonyms by which to elucidate it rather than flatly taking sides for or against it. This is the line I have taken about the rights of animals, preferring always to talk about responsibility or duty.[6] In the United States, however, the Constitution has given the word rights a quite special importance which leads some people to think it indispensable for establishing the seriousness of any moral question. That is the view of Tom Regan, which he has argued in a number of books, notably in *The Case For Animal Rights*.[7]

What lies behind the law?

What, then, should we do about the case of humans? As just noted, when legal words like right are used outside the context of the law-courts the point of using them lies in their somewhat paradoxical force. The idea is to extend the authority of law, for overwhelming reasons, to areas that it currently fails to reach. On a good day, this language can work to bring these more distant cases fully and flatly into the same light as the ones that the laws of our own society literally require. The assumption behind the move is that we can appeal from law itself to some set of underlying principles that determine what is right and wrong, principles which always extend beyond existing law and are the source of that law's moral authority.

This assumption has often been expressed metaphorically by talk of a deeper, underlying law – natural law or the law of God or the moral law that Kant spoke of. These metaphors have considerable force but they also have well-known weaknesses. A great deal of ink has been spilt in discussing their faults and in trying to find ways of doing their work better. I cannot get involved in these disputes here. I want to suggest instead a rather simple approach to them which may be helpful for our present subject.

The problem of humbug

I suggest that, in practice, we all accept the idea of trying to reach consensus about deeper principles and using them to correct existing laws and customs. Everyone who takes moral questions seriously does this and thinks it right to do it. No reasonable person is really an extreme relativist of the kind that might suppose everything currently allowed to be equally right or 'valid'. Almost everyone at times finds existing law and customs utterly inadequate and suggests standards by which to change them.

The general standing of this kind of critical thinking is not itself in question. Nor ought the difficulty of clearly formulating these deeper principles stop us from keeping on trying to do so, any more than similar difficulties ought to stop us on any other troublesome intellectual quest. What does come in question – what does raise objections to the whole search for these deeper principles – is the apparently excessive nature of the demands they make once they are found.

These wider principles tend to ask for much more than the detailed laws that they claim to supplant. They tell us, for instance, to love our neighbours as ourselves, or to treat other people always as ends and not as means only, or to secure the human rights of people who are entirely out of our reach. The charge against people who make proposals like these is not just one of obscurity. It is a charge of unreality, of humbug, of indulging in fantasy. This is itself a moral accusation, which is why it is often somewhat virulently brought.

The issue of humbug needs close attention here because it raises big issues about the general relation between ideals and practice. On this topic a somewhat obvious point needs to be made. The mere fact that we recognise the importance of ideals that are better than our existing practice does not in itself mean that we are hypocrites or humbugs. It is normal. The whole point of having ideals at all is to criticise current practice. If there were a society whose ideals were no more than a description of its existing behaviour it would be almost inconceivably inert, far more so than any culture that we have actually heard of. Even systematically static cultures have to make an ideal of their staticness, actively resisting change and selecting certain issues as worthy of attention. A set of people who did not employ ideals even to this extent would have no mainspring for further action at all.

Ideals, then, do not become inert or unreal merely because they are far above us or ahead of us and are not likely to be reached in our time. That is their nature. They exercise their pull all the time by indicating a direction. Any existing situation, however bad, is still always the result of a struggle between prevailing ideals and the forces that resist them. The idea that it would be realistic to ignore or discount the force of those ideals is not sensible. Indeed it is itself a fantasy. It is an attempt to pretend that human life is far simpler than it is.[8]

It is quite true that this gap between ideals and practice does easily give rise to real humbug, and that it does so more readily when the ideals are specially demanding; hypocrisy is, as they say, the tribute that vice pays to virtue. We are therefore very prone to suspect that this is happening. It is also true that newly proposed ideals shock us particularly easily in this way. (Once they have grown more familiar, we get used to the discrepancy.) That suspicion works at present to make many people somewhat incredulous both about claims for human rights and about calls for environmental action.

It is surely important, however, not to attach too much importance to this chronic suspicion of humbug, because it so obviously arises about other kinds of claim too. Indeed it attends ethics generally. It tends to arise whenever we seem to be called on to do something new and inconvenient. Sometimes the suspicion of unreality turns out to be justified, sometimes not. In itself, however, this kind of suspicion is no more than a sort of warning-signal telling us to ask ourselves whether these particular duties are real or illusory ones.

The difficulty of real realism

By contrast, more reductive, debunking models get an easy hold on our imaginations because they are so familiar. That fact tends to make them seem more realistic and, when wider claims are advanced against them, there is always an initial sense of unreality, perhaps of humbug. But there does not seem to be much real force in this impression. What passes for a realistic attitude in morals commonly means little more than an addiction to current habits. That addiction is just as resistant to long-term prudence as it is to altruism. When new dangers appear, even very serious dangers (as has happened over the destruction of the environment), the *soi-disant* realist usually has great difficulty in believing that they may actually be real. Genuinely enlightened self-interest is rare and hard to come by – which is one reason why egoism cannot be relied on alone as the basis of morality.

This kind of 'realist' habitually dismisses all long-term views and unfamiliar projects on principle as Utopian and is (in particular) systematically convinced at present that all environmental protesters must have got their facts wrong. This kind of general, knee-jerk habit of suspicion is not, then, particularly important. Force of habit is extraordinarily strong, much stronger that the urge for self-preservation. It still produces this kind of incredulity even when the path that we are used to following is manifestly leading us towards the edge of a cliff.

What is a realist?

So far, I have (as I explained) been using the word 'realist' in its general, everyday sense. I must now move on from doing so to consider the special, technical sense that it bears at present in International Relations. I have to confess that I did not know of this special sense before I began, fairly recently, to look into questions about human rights. Before that time I knew of just two meanings for the word realism. I knew (first) the general moral one, which we have been considering so far, in which the word means honesty about unpleasant facts. Its opposite is then fantasy, Panglossism, sentimentality or humbug. I also knew the quite different scientific sense where realism means the belief that certain entities (such as quarks or electrons) are actual things in the world rather than merely convenient concepts which it is handy to use in calculation. The opposite of realism in this sense is operationalism.[9]

I was surprised, then, to discover that, in the field of International Relations, these two dissimilar senses had apparently been combined to yield the view that – to put it rather crudely – honesty calls on us to recognise the nation-state as a specially real entity, a peculiarly hard fact in the world, a unit so uniquely solid and objective that it can fix the limits of our moral obligations. In view of the changes that have continually taken place during history in the way the world is organised, this strikes me as a remarkably arbitrary proposition. I know of no good reason why the burden of proof should be put on anyone who proposes that people can have duties to other people outside their own nation-state rather than on someone who does not. The charge of fantasy, sentimentality or humbug, which the use of words like realism always suggests, is not in itself an argument for this restriction. It is just an all-purpose psychological weapon available against unwelcome demands of every kind.

The unit that we call the nation-state is, one would suppose, just a convenient division, in itself neither bad nor good. It is, as they say, a social construction – not only in the sense in which all our ideas are so, but in the much stronger sense in which our political and social arrangements are so and the sun and stars are not.[10] We in the West have invented nation-states during the last few centuries for whatever human purposes we have happened to have at the time. So it is up to us to attach to them today the kind of moral importance that we think they ought now to have.

Currently, financial practice and the general speeding-up of communication seem to be downgrading the role of nation-state relative to that of various other units and forces. Notoriously (for instance) the assets of some multinational firms exceed those of small countries which are members of the United Nations, so they may well have greater power. There is also at present a considerable worldwide surge of various 'nationalist' movements committed to redrawing the boundaries of existing states in a way that will better suit their 'nations' in the sense of ethnic or cultural groups. For some time, too, an uncomfortable discrepancy has been obvious between nation-states of varying sizes. Despite sharing the attribute of sovereignty, Monaco, Norway and China are not really units of the same kind. In the face of all these changing factors, political theories that give the nation-state a special, immutable moral importance surely need to defend their findings morally, by showing that this is the right way to treat it. There is no *a priori* reason why it should be seen as a general limit of duty.

We do meet here, of course, the problem of practicability which is set by all enlargements of duty. Even if the nation-state is not the ultimate moral boundary, this cannot mean that we actually have a duty to help everybody. Our powers are always limited. That perfectly sound point is what political 'realists' often have in mind, and so far as that *is* what they are saying, their claim to realism is justified. But the question how far our powers actually extend is not at all a simple one. Astonishing feats have often been performed by people who simply decided to view something as possible which others were saying was not so, as for instance the Athenians did when they decided to oppose Persia at the battles of Marathon and Salamis or as Florence Nightingale did when she invented nursing. We can often do enormously more than we are inclined to claim. And when we belong to powerful nations, our public opinion can undoubtedly sometimes influence the behaviour of foreign governments.

Epilogue

Is there any reason, then, why it should not make good sense to say that we can have a duty to help their ill-treated subjects? I should perhaps reminisce a little here to explain why I find it so hard to see how anyone could doubt this. I myself began to read the newspapers in the early 1930s, at the time when the Nazis were rising to power. Everyone who attended to this process saw, I think, that it was not just a local affair for the Germans but was the business of everyone in Europe. It altered the colour of the sky for everyone. And this was not just because the threat of another war might damage the local interests of people in other nations. It was because of the specific moral moves that the Nazis were making, moves which mattered to everybody.

The unbridled nationalism, the propaganda for racism, the justification of brutal methods of repression and the general cultivation of hatred were the direct concern of us all. These things did not strike us as merely the unavoidable eccentricities of bizarre foreigners but either as evils which we ought somehow to resist or – in the case of those who supported Nazism – as a creed to be welcomed. Nazi Germany, like Stalinist Russia, fell within our own moral universe. Hard though it might be to do so, we thought we ought to try and help the victims of both. And in the early days of both regimes we in the West could indeed have put on pressure to do so.

Thus, those of us who then noticed what was going on received at once the culture shock which only reached a much wider public after the war, the shock which later gave rise to the general endorsement of human rights. The *New Statesman* and similar papers were already telling us, at that time, quite enough about the concentration camps and about Stalin's treason trials to make us see that, whether we liked it or not, we were living in what the Stoics called Cosmopolis and the people to whom these things were happening were our fellow-citizens in it.

There was no way of isolating our country from them, no barrier that could make these things cease to be our business. Nor does anything that has happened since that time make me think that the view was mistaken. Indeed, since then the interdependence of distant nations has been steadily increasing. It surely seems quite as evident now that abuses in Nigeria or Tibet are our business as it then did that those in Russia or Germany were so. I think that the idea of 'human rights' is now an essential tool in making this point clear. Accordingly we must deal constructively with whatever difficulties may arise about it in a way that ensures we can continue to use it.

Notes

1 There is now an enormous literature on environmental ethics, largely stemming from Aldo Leopold, *A Sand County Almanack* (New York: Oxford University Press, 1949). Holmes Rolston III has defended the idea of the intrinsic value of nature in Rolston, *Environmental Ethics: Duties to and Values in the Natural World* (Philadelphia: Temple University Press, 1988). J. Baird Callicott has surveyed the case for and against this position with special reference to the value of biodiversity in Callicott, 'Conservation

values and ethics', in Gary K. Meffe and C. Ronald Carroll (eds.), *Principles of Conservation Biology* (Sunderland, Mass.: Sinaur Associates Inc., 1994). Callicott has also surveyed the views of various cultures on this matter in Callicott, *Earth's Insights: A Multicultural Survey of Ecological Ethics* (Berkeley: University of California Press). I have myself discussed the clashes that have arisen between the different principles invoked in environmental ethics and in the defence of animals in Midgley, 'Beasts versus the biosphere?', *Environmental Values* 1(1992): 113–22.

2 This is the well-known central doctrine of Immanuel Kant's *Grundlagen zur Metaphysik der Sitten*, trans. H. J. Paton under the title of *The Moral Law* (London: Hutchinson, 1948). Kant first establishes the status of rational beings as ends in themselves (*ibid.*, p. 90) and then that of the community which they (ideally) form (p. 95). This is the Kingdom of Ends.

3 See *Guardian* (26 March 1996), Letters to the Editor (emphasis mine).

4 It was Kant who spelt out this restriction with regard to animals. See Immanuel Kant, *Lectures on Ethics*, trans. Louis Infield (London: Methuen, 1930), p. 239. He was, however, ambivalent enough and worried enough about rejecting such duties to add the rather unconvincing rider that we must not, all the same, ill-treat animals, not because it is wrong but because doing so might make us ill-treat people. This piece of face-saving is the source of the Chief Charity Commissioner's doctrine just mentioned and of other similarly implausible stories that are still current. I have discussed it in Midgley, *Animals and Why They Matter* (Athens, Ga.: University of Georgia Press), pp. 51–2.

5 It has been very well used in John Passmore's admirable book, *Man's Responsibility for Nature* (London: Duckworth, 1974), which succeeds to a remarkable extent in avoiding pointless debates about words.

6 See Midgley, *Animals and Why They Matter*, ch. 5, esp. pp. 62–4 about rights. On this point Stephen Clark usually follows a similar policy, though he is careful to explain the substantial points which lead people to insist on the word rights – as indeed I am too. See Clark, *The Moral Status of Animals* (Oxford University Press, 1977), p. 34.

7 Tom Regan, *The Case for Animal Rights* (London: Routledge, 1983).

8 I have discussed these issues about the status of ideals in Midgley, *Utopias, Dolphins and Computers: Problems in Philosophical Plumbing* (London: Routledge, 1996).

9 Bishop George Berkeley seems to have invented operationalism; see Berkeley, *The Principles of Human Knowledge* [1710], ed. R. S. Woodhouse (London: Penguin, 1988), sects 58 and 107–16, where he criticises Newton. The idea, developed in the nineteenth century by Mach, has played an important part in many recent scientific controversies. It is quite intelligible in the context of Berkeley's radical idealism, but it plays a rather odd part today in the Copenhagen interpretation of quantum mechanics, and in the suggestion – put forward by some sociologists of science – that science as a whole is just a 'social construction'; see note 10.

10 To clarify this sense, see John Searle's very interesting book, *The Construction of Social Reality* (Harmondsworth: Penguin, 1995).

Part II

The practices of human wrongs

6 The challenge of genocide and genocidal politics in an era of globalisation

Richard Falk

Human wrongs as a world order challenge

Every phase in the history of international relations and world order can be identified by its distinctive achievements and failures. Almost as truly as Tolstoy observed with reference to families, each historical moment resembles all others with respect to its moral achievements, while defining its specific identity in relation to the particular form of its failures. Yet as Ken Booth observes in the essay that inspires this volume,[1] there has been a systemic refusal on the part of academic specialists and diplomats to acknowledge moral failure with respect to the organisation of international political life, that domain of political behaviour called international relations or world order.

World order has been analysed for centuries, with notable exceptions, as if human suffering was irrelevant, and that the only fate that mattered was either the destiny of a particular nation or state or the more general rise and fall of great powers, the latter being regarded as a virtually determined consequence of recurrent rivalry that is embedded in a world of self-regarding states competing for territory, wealth, influence and status.[2] Even such an egoistic moral aperture is generally misleadingly large, as it is rare indeed that the whole of a given people share in power and authority sufficiently to be regarded as effectively included in the self. The struggle in constitutional democracies to extend tolerance and suffrage to minorities and women reminds us that even in societies committed in principle to equality of rights, the representation of the self by the state is partial, at best, and by no means complete. In fact, arguably, one impact of globalisation has been to marginalise the participation of those victimised by the discipline of regional and global capital, as well as to undermine the capacity of the electoral process to serve the interests of society as a whole and of territorial interests in particular.

At most, international morality is reduced to lame 'realist' claims that peace is a public good achieved mainly through the rational calculations of the privileged, reflecting the dynamics of political will and relative power and given direction by a set of predatory assumptions about human nature. This realist mode of perceiving morality is rarely turned inwards, being quite comfortable with a hypocritical division between self and other, that demonises the latter if cast in the role of enemy, while portraying the innocent self as benevolent. This radical dichotomy between the general assessment of world order and the specific enactments of foreign policy has been particularly pronounced in this century, especially in the light of political myths associated with the United States' role as leading international actor that obscure its selfish motivations, insisting upon a recurrent innocence that claims on its behalf an invariable commitment to noble purposes.

This pattern of posturing allows that master practitioner of realist statecraft, Henry Kissinger, to contend that the United States has been captivated by Wilsonian moralism, to the effect of acting to make the world a better place for all peoples, to an extent that it has dangerously overlooked the protection of its own national interests.[3] Such a false rendering of American behaviour as world leader confuses, possibly deliberately, propaganda by leaders and compliant media with policy-making. It also is a message that is not credible elsewhere, even in Western Europe, where the American outlook is generally regarded, at best, as a compromise between moral pretensions and dangerous naïvety about how things 'really' work in international life. Indeed, it has been the role of the most influential realists to instruct the American people on how things really work, especially in view of the alleged failure of Wilson and the Wilsonian outlook to provide responsible world leadership after World War I, and the perceived success of a realist foreign policy throughout the Cold War era.[4]

In recent decades this realist way of conceiving the world has gained unchallenged ascendancy in policy-making circles and has been most prominently associated in this period with the ideas and practice of 'containment', 'deterrence', 'balance of power', 'credibility', and the like.[5] Such a self-satisfied orientation towards a bipolar image of world order was perversely captured by John Lewis Gaddis' encompassing 'the long peace', a phrase that resonated to the moral pretensions of Americans, while being monumentally insensitive to the bloody ordeal of many non-Western peoples during the last half-century, a 'peace' marred, and partially sustained, by more than 125 wars and upwards of 40 million war-related deaths.[6] The widespread acceptance of such a terminology in academic circles, especially in the United States, also exhibited the persisting Euro-centricism of mainstream intellectual approaches on matters of war and peace, of living and dying.[7]

Wars, especially those involving the leading states, are endlessly explicated as defining moments in international history with scant regard to the existential consequences for the peoples engaged and their societies.[8] The avoidance of war among the rich and powerful is premised on the distrust and countervailing destructive capacity and unlimited lethal will to destroy if challenged (unto omnicide given the arsenals of nuclear weapons held at the ready). Such violence-laden arrangements are, then, equated with peace. Even among allies, espionage is habitually practised and shifts of alignment are never ruled out in the inner circles of statecraft. Such a peace is never peaceful!

Aside from mounting an attack on the realists, and such mentoring forebears as Clausewitz and Machiavelli, Booth indicts as responsible for 'human wrongs' the Westphalian concept of world order that underpins contemporary diplomacy, including its internationalist embodiments in the United Nations and the European Union. As Booth vividly notes, 'the international system – in the guise of the society of states – has not been normatively successful for 350 years . . . In terms of spreading the good life, Westphalia is another of the West's failures.'[9] Although this is not the place to go over the strengths and weaknesses of the state system, I find it diversionary to associate the normative failures of world order predominantly with the Westphalian concept of a world of sovereign, territorial states. I would observe that any sweeping condemnation of Westphalia smooths out the ups and downs of history, and especially overlooks the extent to which the idea of the secular state was a significantly successful response to the torment of religious warfare in the seventeenth century, and indirectly fostered ideas of self-determination for colonial peoples and co-existence between ideological adversaries in the twentieth century. Plausibly, it would be the re-empowering of the state as associated with citizens and territory that provides the best hope in the near future for mitigating the current cruelties and inequities of economic globalisation. An aspect of this reluctance to pass negative judgement on the state arises from the absence in effective political space of any legitimating democratic or cultural mandate for alternative more beneficial arrangements of world order, either those leaning towards augmented global governance or those orientated towards a market-guided libertarian anarchism that promotes intergovernmental demilitarisation.[10] The constructivist outlook is also relevant, the state being not a real entity with particular features, but a social construction of the mind that reflects biases, perceptions, historical circumstances, aspirations and shifting priorities and values. In this respect, Westphalia as a construction of international reality retains a vast domain of unexplored normative potential, which will remain unexplored unless political forces with a moral vision of the possible and necessary obtain far greater access to policy-making, including the fashioning of hegemonic images of 'the real' in international life that challenge prevailing economistic and geopolitical world pictures.[11] The realist construction of world order should not be confused with the range of world order constructions that are possible within a Westphalian framework.

A sense of responsibility for human wrongs was weakened by two widely shared features of the Westphalian orientation as it evolved. First, the exclusion of religion from the affairs of state. This opened the way for political conceptions of community which were exclusivist, based on race, nation, civilisation, secular ideology, but which did not relate to humanity as a whole, to 'the human family' and sentiments of solidarity as primarily conceptualised for most people, if at all, through adherence to and participation in one of the main religious traditions.[12] Secondly, the impact of the Enlightenment, especially in the aftermath of the Industrial Revolution, gave rise to a civilisational consensus that modernity was synonymous with human material progress. Applying science and reason to social reality would produce an improving quality of life for all those who benefited from modernity, underpinning both a conception of happiness and a belief in progress. The most fundamental moral challenge for this Enlightenment project was to extend these benefits universally, helping those who were poor whether at home or abroad (although there was a strong racist strain in the Enlightenment that regarded non-Western peoples, especially those of Africa and of pre-Columbian societies in Western civilisation as 'barbarians', and not suited for the benefits of 'civilisation'). The political puzzle was to ensure that the spread of material benefits was consistent with other goals, either preserving domains of privilege for elites or encouraging revolutionary transformations through mass action, a split in the West that was precipitated by the French Revolution and its interpretation and generated the tension between conservatives and radicals, right and left. Liberalism in different forms emerged as a centrist compromise that offered enough to those currently disadvantaged to discourage recourse to revolution while providing essential stability for existing social and economic hierarchies.[13] As long as this belief in progress was shared there was an underlying conviction that evolutionary change would in time by its own natural dynamic overcome human wrongs, and that responsible political debate should concentrate upon the most appropriate means to achieve such results.

It is worth noticing that this focus on human wrongs is occurring in the West in a period when the project of progress and emancipation has virtually collapsed, which is part of the significance of the postmodern vogue. There is a confirming sense of despair in the popular culture, with its anger and obsession with violence, and its absence of hope about the future. This pattern is especially evident in current popular culture and is perhaps most vividly portrayed by the lyrics in the songs of the most widely acclaimed rock and rap groups.

Statism, like democracy, is in many respects a normative failure – unless it is compared with likely alternatives! Globalisation is weakening state structures, especially in relation to their capacity to promote global public goods, their traditional function of enhancing the quality of life within the boundaries of the state, and their most recent role of assisting and protecting the vulnerable within their borders. Such trends, in turn, encourage disruptive ethnic and exclusivist identities that subvert modernist secular and territorial commitments to tolerance and moderation. Globalisation is also unwittingly nurturing transnational social forces, and encouraging the reconceptualisation of democracy along cosmopolitan lines. However, the impact of these tendencies, here identified as globalisation-from-below to distinguish it from market/media forces, currently appears to be that of a rearguard tactic of minimal resistance which is only able to challenge globalisation-from-above at the local level, and then only on rare occasions in special situations.[14] To offset the harms being done by globalisation-from-above is exceedingly difficult at the present time, as the forces of resistance are too weak. The best hopes for the future seem to depend on the formation of new coalitions between grass-roots initiatives and selected governmental authorities, undoubtedly abetted by the uneven impacts of economic globalisation and the overall weakening of support for public goods, impacts which are likely to become manifest in the form of social and ecological disaster, as is already evident in some of the human catastrophes that are befalling sub-Saharan Africa in the 1990s.[15] Given such an analysis, the emergence of counter-politics in any serious form presupposes a reinvigorated and reconstructed, rather than a discredited, understanding of the Westphalian legacy.

A serious inquiry into the cause and cure of human wrongs must cast its net wider than Westphalia. It needs to consider the question of human evil with all of its biological, neurological, cultural, psychological and historical trappings, including the surprisingly robust re-emergence of religion as a political force.[16] A disturbing dimension of current human wrongs is the extent to which the generation of severe forms of human suffering enjoys populist and democratic backing, whether at a safe distance (Gulf War) or within the confines of intimate proximity (Bosnia, Rwanda). Put differently, if Gandhianism, not Machiavellianism, was defining the cultural frame within which influential inter- and intragovernmental narratives emerge, our normative appreciation of a Westphalian world would be different, and far more positive. Of course, Westphalia is cause as well as effect, and it is probably correct that sacralising national flags and territory contributes to hostile stereotypes of 'the other', encouraging violence and militarism, validating hierarchy, domination and inequality, and, overall, providing an ethical facade for the sort of patriotic sensibility that fosters an absence of moral scruples when confronted by the challenge of the other, and thereby facilitates the commission of human wrongs of unspeakable magnitude. But even nationalism is an ideology of choice within a spectrum of possibilities implicit in the Westphalian framework, and there exist a wide range of nationalist orientations, some of which are receptive to strangers and neighbours.

Against this overall background, I propose to consider two clusters of interrelated contemporary developments that are responsible for the most widespread and acute human suffering in the world: genocidal politics and economic globalisation. In both settings the fundamental ordering arrangements of international society and prevailing realist mentality seem unable and unwilling to protect vulnerable peoples. Human wrongs of horrifying magnitude result. Of course, the root cause of such abusive behaviour is often local or national, with deep historical roots, and the responsibility of international society is primarily associated with the failure to provide an effective, mitigating response.[17]

Genocidal politics

International society has exhibited little capacity to address the supreme moral challenge of genocidal behaviour. Despite decades of handwringing, the pattern of international response to Hitler's Germany unfortunately remains paradigmatic. As long as the Nazi persecution of the Jews (and others) was differentiated from an expansive German foreign policy, the leading governments and authority structures practised a diplomacy that was a compromise between denial and indifference, and included elements of accommodation. The 1936 Olympics were held in Berlin despite abundant evidence of severe human rights abuses taking place within Germany at the time, and there were no boycotting states. Only recently has it been confirmed that Swiss and other banks accepted deposits of gold and other assets that they knew had been confiscated from victims of Nazi persecution. The liberal democracies reinforced their indulgence with generally restrictive immigration policies that often made the life of Jewish refugees a second nightmare. Even when the war came, and the moral dimension was invoked to mobilise civic support, munitions were not 'wasted' in an effort to destroy the tracks that carried Jews and others to the death camps.

There were supposedly two 'lessons' drawn from the Nazi embrace of genocide: the first was the realisation that genocide, as such, does not engage the strategic sensibilities of most political leaders; the second was encapsulated in the Nuremberg trials and the pledge 'Never again!' which implied a geopolitical promise to impose criminal accountability on political leaders in the future for crimes of states, as well as to mount some sort of intervention in the face of future genocide, or its credible threat. As these two seemingly contradictory linkings of past and present evolved in the years after World War II, weak efforts to achieve reconciliation were fashioned. By widely ratifying the Genocide Convention, states seemed to acknowledge the strategic significance of genocide without making any specific commitment to take action in response.[18] At the same time the reluctance of governments, continuing to this day, to establish an international criminal court with jurisdiction over crimes of state, suggests the extent to which 'victors' justice' sets limits on the accountability of leaders. The identity of the victors can be blurred, as in the war in Bosnia, where the Serbs achieved most of their goals by recourse to ethnic cleansing, yet their primary leaders, Karadicz and Mladic, were made formally subject to arrest and prosecution; in a sense, the clearest victors in this end-game diplomacy were the geopolitical forces that dictated the terms of peace.

Ethnic cleansing in Bosnia provided the reality test for contemporary genocidal politics, exhibiting for many the abiding strength of the earlier evidence of strategic indifference and the weakness of the commitment by the organised international community to avoid a recurrence of genocide. But this geopolitical pattern had been revealed earlier by the manipulation of the diplomatic response to genocidal politics in Cambodia during the period of Khmer Rouge rule in the mid-1970s. The United Nations sustained for years the diplomatic credentials of the Khmer Rouge regime after it had been replaced in the aftermath of an essentially liberating intervention by neighbouring Vietnam, exhibiting far more concern about the extension of Vietnamese influence than about controlling the practice of genocide. The Vietnamese seem to have been primarily motivated by security concerns and secondarily by the desire to protect the Vietnamese minority in Cambodia, but the effects of their intervention were generally positive. Despite this, extensive aid to the Khmer Rouge from the Western alliance continued for years to flow through Thailand. In the background for the West was 'the China card', a means of increasing pressure on the Soviet Union, which meant supporting some of China's regional policies, among which was an intense anti-Vietnam posture. The fact that as many as one-third of the Cambodian population either died or endured traumatic deprivations was treated as an incidental feature of a geopolitically beneficial stance. Even the golden propaganda opportunity to emphasise the cruelty of a Communist elite during the Cold War was subordinated to the strategic assessment that 'containing' Vietnam and accommodating China took precedence over protecting the Cambodian people against genocide. If Western diplomacy had prevailed, Vietnam would never have invaded Cambodia in the first place, or if it had, its forces would have been withdrawn immediately, leaving Cambodia in all likelihood to be again governed by the Khmer Rouge. It was only through the dedicated initiatives of a small number of individuals in the human rights community and by Cambodians themselves that the genocidal pattern was fully exposed and documented. Cambodia made it clear that, whatever else, the pledge of 'Never again!' had not been meant for Asians.

What made Bosnia shocking was the revelation that the pledge was not even meant for Europeans. Of course, the principal victims in Bosnia were Muslim, and even if unacknowledged, this factor undoubtedly eroded the moral and political response to the evidence of massive ethnic cleansing. Although there were pretences of humanitarian concern expressed by leading European countries and by the United States, as well as in the main organs of the United Nations, the diplomatic responses fashioned exhibited an unwillingness to mount a credible challenge to the Serbian operations. Instead a series of marginal initiatives were taken with the objective of disguising the extent of strategic indifference: sanctions, medical and humanitarian assistance, food drops by air to beleaguered communities, pin-prick NATO bombing, ill-defended safe havens, and an underfunded war crimes tribunal. This marginality became fully manifest in the light of the responses to the Serb refusal to respect the safe havens established under UN auspices, especially the brutal attacks and civilian massacres carried out at Gorazde and Srebrenica. It was symbolised by the Security Council's imposition of an arms embargo that principally victimised the Bosnian government and by its mandate of impartiality as between the contending parties, an astonishing posture in view of the genocidal behaviour on display.[19] Only after the real stakes of the war had been resolved on the ground, did the diplomatic initiative of the United States succeed in imposing 'peace' in the form of the 1995 Dayton Agreement, which essentially ratified the main contours of genocidal politics. The strategic interest in the background was the containment of the conflict, avoiding a dangerous spillover to other parts of the Balkans and Greece, as well as stemming the tide of war-generated refugees that were causing serious problems in several European countries, especially Germany.

The events in Rwanda and Burundi are confirmatory of this pattern with only minimal efforts being made by the international community to protect the targets of genocide or to punish the main perpetrators.[20] No strategic interests were at stake. Even the normal concern with containment and refugee flows was not a big factor. There was a strong reluctance, above all, to get involved. The weakness of the UN response was partly a reflection of the earlier 1992–94 failure of humanitarian intervention in Somalia, and the consequent shift in outlook by the US government from an attitude of 'assertive multilateralism' to a posture of evasion and avoidance. This latter stance was highlighted by a directive within the Clinton Administration instructing officials to avoid characterising the events in Rwanda as genocidal because that would arouse public pressures to take some sort of action. Shashi Tharoor, a special assistant to Kofi Annan, currently the UN Secretary-General, has recently referred to 'that dreadful summer of 1994' when the Security Council wanted to send 5,500 soldiers to Rwanda with the hope of saving many civilians from the genocidal onslaught. All nineteen governments that had previously pledged a total of 31,000 troops for peace-keeping missions refused to take part on this occasion, and no strengthened UN response was forthcoming.[21]

The prevention of genocide is not, in the best of circumstances, a simple matter.[22] Often the passions of ethnic politics have been unleashed. Intervention would be vigorously resisted, with evocations of recent memories of colonial abuse, and might not succeed even if mounted in a serious manner. The logistics of interventionist diplomacy are difficult, at best, under contemporary circumstances, given the resolve and desperate tactics of indigenous opposition forces and the tangled perception of motives and deeds on all sides. But the focus of concern here is different: it is upon the low priority accorded to moral dimensions of foreign policy by the governments and elites of leading states as evidenced by the sort of commitments that have been made in response to genocidal politics. As such, it does support the view that the sort of human wrongs associated with genocidal politics continue to be insulated from effective international regulation by the predominant statist logic of existing world order arrangements, but not always. Human rights pressures on the Communist regimes in Eastern Europe, the anti-apartheid movement, and opposition to military government in the Western Hemisphere disclose that there exists a normative dimension of world order that can be politically effective under certain conditions, especially if linked to geopolitical projects (for example, opposition to strategic adversaries, or the containment of aggression) or to mobilised transnational ethnic forces (for example, the role of African-Americans in exerting pressure on the US government to impose sanctions on South Africa under apartheid).[23] There are two lines of interpretation that are unavoidably intertwined, and pose difficulties in relation to the assessment being made: humanitarian intervention, even if given strong support might fail for logistical reasons, and this could help explain the reluctance of potential intervenors to endorse such projects, but the reluctance might also be little more than a lame rationalisation. This latter line of interpretation seems more convincing in light of the absence of comparable reluctance when important geopolitical interests are perceived by leaders to be at stake.

Is this insulation of genocidal ordeals from interventionist reactions and procedures of accountability primarily to be understood as structural or ideological? If structural, it seems to be mainly a result of the weakness of relatively autonomous institutions of global governance with respect to the implementation of fundamental norms of human rights. If ideological, it is associated with the Machiavellian orientation towards political reality that dominates the policy-making domain of states, looking upon the self and the other in ways that do not encourage empathy, altruism or sacrifices for the sake of the afflicted stranger or foreigner. Undoubtedly, given the evolution of the state system over the past three and a half centuries, there is a tight interrelationship at this point between statist structure and realist ideology, an orientation reinforced by 'the reading' given to the outbreak of World War II and the avoidance of World War III, namely, the failure of appeasement and idealism in the former instance and the success of deterrence and containment in the latter instance. It is no wonder, then, that despite the end of the Cold War and the absence of strategic encounter, the states constituting international society are reluctant to contemplate serious demilitarisation and disarmament initiatives. And that even in countries with deep civic and democratic traditions, it has become indispensable for politicians, especially those suspected of anti-war sentiments, to demonstrate their credibility as military leaders disposed to rely on force to promote national interests. The behaviour of Bill Clinton, a most cunning political animal, has been revealing in this regard: trying his best to erase any societal memory of his adolescent opposition to the Vietnam War, boasting about his commitment to the development of new weapons systems, showing up at war memorials and events organised by war veterans, and making a point, even during the prior election campaign, of praising George Bush for his management of the Gulf War. Militarist credentials seem crucial as a qualification for political leadership in a leading constitutional democracy even during a time of international calm.

A further matter is whether this indulgence of genocidal politics inheres in world order, or can be overcome by a series of reformist steps: establishing an enforcement capability under a financially independent UN or under regional auspices, thereby weakening the ties to geopolitical calculations;[24] moving towards the creation of an international criminal court with competence to address genocide;[25] strengthening transnational civic capabilities to issue early warnings of incipient genocidal dangers; and increasing public revulsion and media concern. In other words, can reformist measures reorient geopolitical calculations, or better, establish capabilities for effective action independent of geopolitical endorsement? There is little basis for short-term optimism. What reformist steps seem politically feasible in the near future are almost certain to be subordinated to geopolitical control, by way of either a political or a financial veto. What is more, the ethos of neo-liberalism, as reinforced by 'third wave' technologies and a postmodern cultural outlook, and influenced by cyberpolitics, is likely, if anything, to weaken existing societal impulses towards compassionate politics on a global scale, especially as expressed under the control of governmental institutions.[26] This is a time of so-called 'compassion fatigue', the tightening of boundaries to stem refugee flows, a revival of capital punishment for serious criminals (and recourse to 'chemical castration' of sex offenders), and the denial of welfare benefits to illegal immigrants.

Additionally, as the next section argues, to the extent that geopolitics is being deterritorialised and the state internationalised in response to economic globalisation, the indulgence of genocidal politics is likely to persist unless particular instances of its occurrence are regarded by policy-makers as seriously detrimental to the interests of global market forces or to other strategic concerns, or unless countervailing political pressures emerge to challenge the economistic priorities of governing elites. A special consideration arises if the domestic constituencies of a leading state identify with the victims of genocidal policies, and are well enough organised to exert effective political pressure for an interventionist response.

Over time, the pressures towards integrated markets may possibly reorient geopolitical calculations in favour of maintaining conditions of moderation and stability throughout the world, thereby making the eruption of genocidal politics anywhere assume the character of a strategic threat, but the prospects for such a process seem remote with regard to the peoples currently most at risk, namely those in sub-Saharan Africa and the Balkans. But as matters now stand, genocidal activity has mostly occurred in settings (Cambodia, Bosnia, Rwanda, Tibet, and Burundi) that are not notable for market opportunities, and therefore not strong candidates for costly international efforts at prevention, mitigation and restoration.

Can non-Western influences in international life provide a new normative momentum? What of the emergence of the Asia/Pacific region as the epicentre of the global market? What of Buddhist, Confucian, Hindu and Islamic ethics? It is difficult to offer much speculation, but the prevailing tendencies involve protecting sovereign states from even minimal procedures of external accountability, encouraging regional zones of civilisational autonomy and resisting Western modalities of exploitation and genocidal abuse, but remaining relatively insensitive to internal patterns of abuse or indifferent in relation to those abuses situated outside their own orbit of sub-species identification, to borrow terminology relied upon by Erik Erikson. For instance, the Malaysian government is active in support of Muslim peoples whether their victimisation is in Kashmir, Chechnya or Bosnia, while being guilty of abuses of indigenous peoples located within its own boundaries.[27] Thus a world of plural civilisational identity does not seem likely to provide the foundations for the sort of effective world community needed to discourage genocidal politics, and, to the extent necessary, protect its targets. The best, and only hope, is the deepening and expansion of democratising tendencies, making leaders more consistently receptive to the constraints embedded in international law, and spelt out in the main human rights instruments. Whatever interrogation of such rights may proceed on the basis of cultural differences, there is a universal acceptance of norms of tolerance and of the criminalisation associated with genocidal practices. Establishing these normative attitudes is a challenge facing democratising tendencies in a variety of settings. The assumption here is that the human wrong of genocide needs to be addressed, to the greatest extent possible, by preventive modes, including education, and through the inclusion of tolerance as an integral element of democratic theory and practice. For the reasons argued earlier, reactive modes of response to genocide are likely to be ineffectual unless, as in the case of Cambodia in the late 1970s, it provokes a major response that reflects security priorities of strong neighbouring states (in this instance, Vietnam) or regional or global actors. In this regard, humanitarian intervention is a sham, either being cosmetic or a cover for a geopolitically motivated undertaking. To call it 'geopolitical' is not necessarily to condemn it for making evaluations depending on a mix of circumstances and effects. But such labelling at least discourages 'false advertising', and the tendency of politicians to exaggerate the strength of genuine humanitarian concerns.

Economic globalisation

Economic deprivation that results in the gross inability to satisfy basic human needs afflicts more than one billion persons on the planet. Such a condition is accentuated by the failure to devote the modest resources required to overcome a range of childhood diseases that take the lives of millions of children each year.[28] The international financial system continues to exert effective pressure on many governments of indebted poor countries to maintain fiscal austerity and abandon policies designed to subsidise those who are impoverished. There are many mutually reinforcing explanations of this turn away from the welfare-oriented consensus that had existed nationally and globally since the time of the Great Depression in the 1930s and World War II: the collapse of a socialist alternative; the weakening of organised labour as a progressive social force; the ideological hegemony of neo-liberalism and supply-side fiscal policies; the ineptitude of large, long-lasting governmental bureaucracies; the adverse fiscal consequences of a lengthening average period between retirement and death; citizen disillusionment with welfare approaches; societal greed that resists tax burdens associated with redistributive policies; the dynamics of international competitiveness that tend to penalise those societies that are most socially responsible and to reward those that are least responsive to the needs of victimised segments of their own citizenry or to claims made on behalf of domestic and global public goods; and a generalised postmodern malaise.[29] It is this pattern of developments that is associated with the uneven impacts of economic globalisation, making it reasonable to connect economic globalisation with an elusive set of concealed and distant mechanisms that produce human suffering in forms that are difficult to address through political action. Global market forces operate as an impersonal agency for the infliction of human wrongs, with territorial means of redress eroded.

Economic globalisation, leaving aside the vagueness and ambiguity of the term, has some positive normative effects. It has enabled a series of societies to make rapid economic progress, most spectacularly those on the Pacific Rim. For various reasons relating to land tenure and social structure, the benefits of rapid economic growth have reached a large proportion of the peoples living in these societies, greatly reducing the ranks of the impoverished and allowing the enjoyment of a more satisfying material existence for a significant proportion of society. In effect, the mobility of capital encourages a levelling up in certain settings and a levelling down in others, with the overall benefits and burdens of polarisation becoming more pronounced and reordered. Thus it is possible to report that while economic globalisation has had an homogenising effect on the relations of the North with certain parts of the South, it has also accentuated differences elsewhere, most notably in the contrast between the richest and poorest countries, and, in many settings, between the upper and lower classes. Further, globalisation, in conjunction with neo-liberalism, accentuates polarisation within the countries of the North as territorial interests are subordinated in the face of superior investment opportunities elsewhere. Similarly, the challenge of 'the dangerous classes' is being increasingly discounted or ignored, and addressed coercively, helping to explain the displacement of welfare concerns by a focus on prisons, police and punishment, and a weakening of commitment to ameliorative tactics.[30]

Despite the stress on territorial sovereignty, the Westphalian framework has facilitated the establishment of an elaborate normative architecture of human rights during the last half-century. The dynamics of economic globalisation are definitely undermining the will and capability of many states to fulfil their obligations, especially with respect to economic and social rights. Although the liberal democracies were always reluctant to encompass economic and social claims within the framework of human rights, preferring to limit the idea to political and civil rights, the *de facto* commitment of these governments to a welfare ethos assured high degrees of compliance. But with the reduction of 'social dividends' in capitalist countries of the North and the persistence of externally imposed fiscal austerity in the poorest countries of the South, the challenge of economic and social deprivations as violative of elementary human rights is mounting at an alarming rate.

Globalisation is relevant as it appears to inhibit efforts to devote resources to the alleviation of poverty and other forms of social distress. Of course, if those victimised were to be mobilised in forms effective in post-industrial settings, then one could imagine the possibility of a new global social contract that contained transnational class warfare. At present, the depoliticised ethos of cyberpolitics, combined with neo-liberalism and militarism, make it almost impossible to implement that portion of human rights concerned with economic and social issues. Governments take refuge in supply-side approaches that supposedly will spread the benefits of economic growth to all societal sectors, thereby deflecting what pressure exists to take direct action. Factors associated with competitiveness, especially a fiscal preoccupation with the reduction of trade and budgetary deficits, tax reductions, and the avoidance of inflationary pressures, add to the downward pressure on public goods. When large companies cut their employment rolls the price of their shares tends to rise in stock markets, while news of a drop in unemployment tends to arouse fears of interest rate increases, and sends stock prices reeling.

Such patterns are characteristic of an era of globalisation, with its logic being dictated by the well-being of capital rather than of people.[31]

Economic globalisation, then, weakens the overall capacity and will of governments to address human wrongs either within their own society or elsewhere. Further, by undercutting the basis for supporting most categories of global public goods, economic globalisation also weakens the resource base of international institutions with a mandate to alleviate human suffering. Such tendencies are currently abetted by an ideological climate that does not mount significant resistance on behalf of those being most acutely victimised by the discipline of global capital. For these reasons, it seems appropriate to link economic globalisation with a high threshold of tolerance for human wrongs, at least for now.

But what of later?

How can we envisage greater attentiveness to claims advanced to mitigate or eliminate human wrongs? There are several lines of response, each requiring patience and a realisation that the improbable is possible because so much of social and political reality is hidden, and obscured by the tenets of a conventional wisdom that has grown cynical about compassionate politics. One response is by way of reorienting inquiry into the character of world politics, injecting moral purpose at the centre of our evaluative procedures; international relations is a social construction, and its normative emptiness is not a necessity. Another response involves the emergence of global civil society through the efforts of transnational social forces to promote democratisation, globalisation-from-below, or what has been called elsewhere 'cosmopolitan democracy'.[32] Still another presupposes the emergence of geopolitical tensions and ecological crises generated by globalisation, giving rise to countervailing demands that will exert new social pressures to base governance on more inclusive and socially responsible conceptions of governance; in this sense, it should be recalled that during the Cold War, even sub-Saharan African countries counted in the geopolitical balance. One can discern the beginnings of such reactive patterns in the efforts to control the flows of economic migrants at their sources by improving social conditions. Another response could involve the re-empowerment of the state with respect to social issues as a result of a political climate that is less wedded to economistic goals that include fiscal austerity. Such a result could come about in a number of ways, but one promising avenue would be based on transnational agitation for the implementation of social, economic and cultural norms on a regional basis, and eventually interregionally as well.

Notes

1 Ken Booth, 'Human wrongs and international relations', *International Affairs* 71 (1995): 103–26.

2 See *ibid.*, esp. 118–19, for an enumeration of exceptions to his generalisation, that is, a listing of authors who do provide normative assessments of international relations. See also Roy Preiswerk, 'Could we study international relations as if people mattered?', in Richard Falk, Samuel S. Kim and Saul H. Mendlovitz (eds.), *Toward a Just World Order* (Boulder: Westview Press, 1982), pp. 175–97; Robert C. Johansen, *The National Interest and the Human Interest* (Princeton University Press, 1980).

3 Kissinger misleadingly conflates the triumph of Wilsonian rhetoric, relied upon by American political leaders to validate globalist projections of US power, with the actuating grounds of policy and the contours of behaviour, which conform closely to the dictates of realist geopolitics. For his argument see Henry Kissinger, *Diplomacy* (New York: Simon and Schuster, 1994), esp. pp. 804–35.

4 For example, see George F. Kennan, *American Diplomacy 1900–1950* (University of Chicago Press, 1951); Hans J. Morgenthau, *Politics Among Nations: The Struggle for Power and Peace*, 6th edn, ed. Kenneth Thompson (New York: Knopf, 1985).

5 For a clear delineation of the rationale for this conceptual framework in the setting of the Cold War, see John Lewis Gaddis, *Strategies of Containment: A Critical Appraisal of Postwar National Security Policy* (Oxford University Press, 1982); for a range of views that include realist adaptations to a post-Cold War global setting see Sean M. Lynn-Jones and Steven E. Miller (eds.), *The Cold War and After: Prospects for Peace* (Cambridge, Mass.: MIT Press, 1993).

6 The Gaddis article, 'The long peace: elements of stability in the postwar international system', was published as the leading piece in the influential anthology of Lynn-Jones and Miller (eds.), *The Cold War and After*, pp. 1–45.

7 In addition to the Lynn-Jones and Miller anthology, see Charles W. Kegley, Jr (ed.), *The Long Postwar Peace: Contending Explanations and Projections* (New York: Harper Collins, 1991). For an entirely different interpretation, see Samir Amin, *Re-Reading the Postwar Period: An Intellectual Itinerary* (New York: Monthly Review, 1994).

8 For a major study of warfare in this century that is admirably sensitive to overall human and societal consequences, see Gabriel Kolko, *Century of War: Politics, Conflict, and Society Since 1914* (New York: The New Press, 1994).

9 Booth, 'Human wrongs', 123.

10 For a generally well-intentioned, but rather confusing advocacy of 'global governance', see Report of the Commission on Global Governance, *Our Global Neighbourhood* (Oxford University Press, 1995), esp. pp. 1–7; see a more suggestive approach to governance in Johan Galtung, *There Are Alternatives! Four Roads to Peace and Security* (Nottingham: Spokesman, 1984); for earlier perspectives and proposals see Richard Falk, *A Study of Future Worlds* (New York: Free Press, 1975).

11 I think one of the strengths of Hedley Bull's work is to call sensitive attention to this unexplored normative potential. See Bull, *The Anarchical Society* (New York: Columbia University Press, 1977).

12 Of course, these world religions often operated on the basis of their own exclusivist ideas, but at least their worldview provided, and continues to provide, inspiration for inclusive perspectives. See, for example, the following rhetorical question put by Joe Nangle, 'A community of nations?', *Sojourners* 25 (October 1996): 42: 'For people of faith living in the United States, and dedicated to building up of human communities at every level, the question becomes: Are we citizens merely of this country, or do we strive to exercise our citizenship in the entire human family?' For a range of views on these matters of the orientation in an American setting of persons towards political responsibility, see Martha C. Nussbaum *et al.*, *For Love of Country: Debating the Limits of Patriotism* (Boston: Beacon Press, 1996); some of the same issues are explored in a European context in Bart von Steenbergen (ed.), *The Condition of Citizenship* (London: Sage, 1994).

13 This argument follows closely those of Immanuel Wallerstein, *After Liberalism* (New York: New Press, 1995); see also John Gerard Ruggie, 'At home abroad, abroad at home: international liberalization and domestic stability in the new world economy', *Millennium* 24 (1995): 507–26.

14 For a major effort at such a reconceptualisation see David Held, *Democracy and the Global Order: From the Modern State to Cosmopolitan Governance* (Cambridge: Polity Press, 1995), esp. pp. 219–86; see also Martha C. Nussbaum, 'Patriotism and cosmopolitanism', in Nussbaum *et al.* (eds.), *For Love of Country*, pp. 3–17.

15 In a vast literature, see I. William Zartman (ed.), *Collapsed States: The Disintegration and Restoration of Legitimate Authority* (Boulder: Rienner, 1995); Robert H. Jackson, *Quasi-states: Sovereignty, International Relations and the Third World* (Cambridge University Press, 1990).

16 For one important exploration, see Robert Jay Lifton and Eric Markusen, *The Genocidal Mentality* (New York: Basic Books, 1988).

17 See persuasive discussion of genocide in Rwanda as 'caused' by the disruption of pre-colonial ethnic accommodation as a result of British colonial policy. Mahmood Mamdani, 'From conquest to consent as the basis of state formation: reflections after a visit to Rwanda', unpublished paper (1996), esp. pp. 6–17.

18 *Convention on the Prevention and Punishment of the Crime of Genocide* (1951), esp. Articles IV–IX; text reprinted in *Human Rights: A Compilation of International Instruments* (New York: United Nations, 1988), pp. 143–7.

19 For expressive confirmation of this assessment, see David Rieff, *Slaughterhouse: Bosnia and the Failure of the West* (New York: Simon and Schuster, 1995).

20 See Mamdani, 'From conquest to consent'; see also Philip Gourevitch, 'Neighbourhood bully: how genocide revived President Mobutu', *The New Yorker* (9 September 1996), pp. 52–7.

21 See Paul Lewis, 'How UN keeps pace, with fewer troops to keep the peace', *New York Times*, 4 May 1997.

22 For discussion of this complexity see Richard Falk, 'Human rights, humanitarian assistance, and the sovereignty of states', in Kevin M. Cahill (ed.), *A Framework for Survival* (New York: Basic Books, 1993), pp. 27–40.

23 Such mobilisations of an exile community can be normatively oppressive as in the case of anti-Castro exiles in the United States.

24 For a careful proposal along these lines see Saul Mendlovitz and John Fousek, 'The prevention and punishment of the crime of genocide', in Charles B. Strozier and Michael Flynn (eds.), *Genocide, War, and Human Survival* (Lanham, Md.: Rowman and Littlefield, 1996), pp. 137–51.

25 Support for such an institutional innovation is contained in Report of the Commission on Global Governance, *Our Global Neighbourhood*, pp. 323–5.

26 See Mark Dery, *Escape Velocity: Cyberculture at the End of the Century* (London: Hodder and Stoughton, 1996), esp. pp. 1–18, 227–319; Alvin Toffler, *The Third Wave* (New York: William Morrow, 1980); also John Heilemann, 'The making of President 2000', *WIRED* 3 (December 1995): 152–5, 218–30; and Wallerstein, *After Liberalism*, esp. pp. 1–7, 126–61.

27 See discussion of species self in Lifton's *The Protean Self*.

28 See chapter in Richard Falk, *On Humane Governance: Towards a New Global Politics* (Cambridge: Polity Press, 1995) and UNICEF Yearbooks.

29 Why military expenditures, as a public good, remain an exception for powerful countries has to do with the greater willingness of elites to protect inequity than to correct it and with the social learning that supposedly validates a militarist foreign policy as the only true foundation of security in international society, especially given the predominantly non-territorial character of the most dynamic modes of wealth production.

30 Wallerstein in *After Liberalism* argues persuasively that social democracy and welfare ideas were primarily adopted as ways to contain the demands of the industrial workforce, but with the dilution of these demands, a less fiscally burdensome approach can be adopted.

31 For analysis along these lines, see Richard Falk, 'The making of global citizenship', in Jeremy Brecher, John Brown Childs and Jill Cutler (eds.), *Global Visions: Beyond the New World Order* (Boston: South End Press, 1993), pp. 39–50; and Falk, *On Humane Governance*.

32 Most comprehensively argued in Held, *Democracy and the Global Order*.

7   Transnational civil society

Mary Kaldor

In this chapter, I argue that the concept of transnational civil society is less a descriptive or analytical term and more a political project. Indeed, I go further and suggest that, in the post-Cold War period, the fundamental political cleavage, which could define the way in which we view contemporary society and the way in which we address a whole range of problems, is likely to be less the traditional left/right divide but rather the division between those who stand for internationalist, Europeanist, democratic values, including human rights, and those who remain wedded to national or exclusivist thinking. The terms 'civil society' or 'civic values' have become forms of political shorthand that characterise the first group.

It is generally assumed that the term 'civil society' has been reclaimed from an earlier period, that its meaning is drawn from debates about the origins of liberal democracy in the eighteenth and nineteenth centuries. In fact, the historically specific circumstances in which the term re-emerged in the 1980s and 1990s changed the way it is used and vested the concept with new content. In particular, the early modern conception of civil society was socially and territorially bounded. What is new about the contemporary use of civil society is both its transnational character and its emphasis on participation. In effect, it represents a demand for a radical extension of democracy across national and social boundaries.

In developing this argument, I will schematically trace the evolution of the concept of civil society in Europe, especially during the 1980s and 1990s, and finally try to relate the concept to the growing debate about globalisation.

The background[1]

The original meaning of civil society was linked to the concept of 'civility'.[2] It emerged during the seventeenth and eighteenth centuries at a time when earlier ties of blood, kinship and religion were breaking down.

With the development of what Giddens calls time-space distanciation[3] new more abstract forms of social interaction supplanted the personal face-to-face relations that characterised local communities. The growth of states and the establishment of a rule of law gradually eliminated private and often violent methods of settling disputes and created the conditions for these new forms of social interaction based on commonly accepted but impersonal means of communication, e.g. exchanges of money, newspapers, mail, etc.

Civil society meant respect for individual autonomy, based on security and trust among people who had perhaps never met. It required regularity of behaviour, rules of conduct, respect for law and control of violence. Hence, a civil society was synonymous with polite society, a society in which strangers act in a civilised way towards each other, treating each other with mutual respect, tolerance and confidence.

During this early period, no clear distinction was drawn between civil society and political society. Civil society required a state to guarantee the rule of law and the regulation of social behaviour. The boundaries of civil society were those of the state. Hence civil society was contrasted with the state of nature which was supposed to exist in the international arena, the jungle that was supposed to characterise relations between states, as well as societies without states and non-societies. The distinction between domestic and international or internal and external corresponded to the distinction between civil society and violent anarchy, between civility and barbarism. That is why, even today, wars between groups located within the territory of a state are referred to as 'civil wars' even though they are generally anything but civil.

A particular problem for theorists of civil society was how to reconcile individual autonomy with society, how to distinguish private concerns from the public realm. The answer for eighteenth-century thinkers was that society was held together by 'moral sentiments and natural affections'.[4] Civil society was an ethical arena, a realm of public morality, based on individual conscience. The early thinkers, strongly influenced by Calvinism, believed that this ethical arena was based on a divine underpinning, that knowledge of what was right and wrong was imprinted by God in the individual conscience. It was immanent in nature, whose author was God.[5] Later, as secular morality came to supplant religious injunction, this public realm was understood to be held together by nature, the natural tendency for affection, sympathy and friendship, and reason, the notion that natural behaviour is learned, and that through experience, men come to understand that altruistic behaviour sustains the public realm which is required for individual autonomy.

In the nineteenth century, as individuals became more atomised and as society became rationalised and functionalised (Weber), this answer came to be seen as less satisfactory. Utilitarian conceptions of individual behaviour, in which self-interest was more important than conscience, could explain the market but were less satisfactory in explaining the existence of a civil society which could provide the basis for a public realm. Some argued for the social extension of the concept of civil society; the early socialists called for solidarity and participation to be extended beyond the then narrow (male) political class. Others, e.g. Hegel, argued that civil society could only be realised through the existence of a strong state. Ernest Gellner stresses the importance of national identity as the glue of modern society. In his last book, he talks about what he calls the 'modularity of man' necessary for industrial and growth-oriented society. He argues that this 'modularity' has

two principal social corollaries: it makes *possible* Civil Society, the existence of countervailing and plural political associations and economic institutions, which at the same time are not stifling; and it also makes *mandatory* the strength of ethnic identity, arising from the fact that man is no longer tied to a specific social niche, but is instead deeply linked to a culturally defined pool.[6]

Thus for Gellner, civil society is, by no means, a necessary feature of the contemporary world, in contrast to national identity.

But if what holds modern society together is not morality but the state and/or ethnic identity, how can society remain 'civil'? What are the guarantees against abuse of power by the state? If the state is responsible for control of violence, how can the use of violence by the state be controlled? How can society ensure that the state itself respects the rule of law? To some extent these questions were anticipated by the early theorists of civil society, especially de Tocqueville and Adam Ferguson. A key component of the concept of civil society was the existence of a plurality of citizens' organisations through which the individual could express and make effective his own concerns and which constituted a countervailing pressure on the state. This is what Gellner refers to when he talks about the possibility of civil society. It should be stressed, however, that at that time, this was merely a component of the definition of civil society, a condition, according to some thinkers, for its realisation.

During the twentieth century, especially during and after the Second World War, the state grew and reached out to almost all aspects of social life. The potential for barbarism, the other side of the coin of civility, was expressed in unimaginable ways in the two World Wars and the totalitarian regimes of this century. The re-emergence of the concept of civil society was a reaction to state barbarity. Hence this latter meaning of civil society, as self-organised groups and individuals independent from the state and political society, came to have much greater salience. Indeed, today, this is generally what people mean when they refer to civil society.

The 1980s

In retrospect, the 1989 revolutions were about the opening up of Eastern Europe to the outside world. They demonstrated the impossibility of sustaining closed autarchic societies in a world of accelerated travel and communication and this was implicit in the evolution of the concept of transnational civil society, which was the outcome of an intense interaction between opposition movements on both sides of the East–West divide during the 1980s. The story of these exchanges, the ideas that were developed, and the way in which space was opened up in Eastern European societies has been largely absent from accounts of the 1980s.

It can be argued that a framework for the new movements of the 1980s was provided by the Helsinki Accord of 1975. This agreement, also known as the Final Act of the Conference on Security and Co-operation in Europe (CSCE), was the high point of the *détente* period between East and West. The agreement was a compromise which guaranteed the territorial status quo in Europe so as to satisfy Soviet security concerns and at the same time provided what appeared at the time to be only paper commitments to human rights to satisfy nominal Western concerns about Communism. The agreement also contained commitments for various forms of scientific and economic co-operation. Both the Western European peace movements and the new human rights groups can be viewed as progeny of that agreement.

On the one hand the explosion of the peace movement in Western Europe in the early 1980s was a reaction against Reagan's new generation of nuclear weapons, proposed so soon after the Helsinki Accord had appeared to remove the causes of war in Europe. The peace movement was probably the largest transnational movement in history. Some 5 million people demonstrated on the streets of different towns and cities in Europe in October 1981 and, again, in October 1983. While the immediate concern was the renewed threat of nuclear war, these movements also saw themselves as democracy movements. They were concerned about the extent of power wielded by the state, the fact that politicians literally had the power to decide, without any consultation, about the fate of millions of people. Nuclear war was the ultimate barbarity. Nuclear weapons symbolised the lack of individual control not only over the conditions in which individuals live but life itself. As E. P. Thompson pointed out in his pamphlet *Protest and Survive*, which was one of the inspirational documents of the movement, the power to decide about the very survival of humanity was not even in the hands of national politicians; ownership and control of nuclear weapons was in the hands of military personnel of a foreign military power. This 'new' and 'extraordinary' aspect of the contemporary situation, he argued, 'illuminates the degree to which the loss of our national sovereignty has become absolute, and democratic process has been deformed in ways scarcely conceivable twenty years ago'.[7] The new peace movements argued that, precisely because of this deformation, their concern was not to capture power but to change the relations between state and society to make the state more responsive to society.

On the other hand, dissident intellectuals found, in the Accord, an instrument they could use in their demands for human rights.[8] Groups like Charter 77 in Czechoslovakia, KOR in Poland or the Democratic Opposition in Hungary emerged in the late 1970s and broke definitively both with earlier traditions of revisionist opposition which remained within the Party and with the tactics of revolutionary overthrow. They developed ideas about creating autonomous spaces in society outside the purview of the totalitarian state and operating within the framework of democratic principles. In his path-breaking essay 'The New Evolutionism', Adam Michnik argued that the failure of opposition movements in Poland in the past, both the revisionist left and the 'neopositivist' Catholic left, was that they tried to create change 'from above'. What was needed now was to build opposition 'from below' which could occupy and expand whatever space existed within the framework of the 'Brezhnev Doctrine'.[9] Through 'self-limiting' behaviour a series of compromises could be made with the state, thus eroding the state's pervasive role. These ideas were to be put into practice by the movements that appeared in the late 1970s and early 1980s, most notably Solidarity in Poland but also Swords into Ploughshares, a mass movement that developed in East Germany under the umbrella of the churches, and the Dialogue group, a young people's peace movement that started in Hungary.

The dialogue between these movements was initiated by parts of the Western peace movement, most notably European Nuclear Disarmament (END) led by E. P. Thompson, the Inter-Church Peace Council in the Netherlands and the Greens in West Germany. Initially, the concern was partly tactical, to demonstrate in practice that concerns about nuclear war were genuine and not manipulated by the Kremlin. In the early stages, the dialogue was characterised by deep suspicions on both sides. On the Eastern side, peace activists were viewed as, at best, naive and misguided and, at worst, as fellow-travellers. The word 'peace', as Havel explained in a famous essay 'The Anatomy of Reticence' addressed to the Western peace movement, had, like the word 'socialism', lost all content and become merely an ideological label. For their part, many peace activists regarded the discourse of human rights as merely the rhetoric of the Cold Warriors, the hypocritical language of leaders like Thatcher and Reagan used to justify ever more armaments. Within the peace movement, an intense debate developed about the priority to be accorded to disarmament. Some parts of the British Campaign for Nuclear Disarmament or the West German Social Democrats argued that preventing nuclear war had precedence over democracy and human rights because the risk of nuclear war was so frightful and the latter would follow from a disarmament agreement. Some parts of the Eastern opposition argued the opposite: that totalitarianism was the cause of the nuclear arms race and democracy was the first priority, even at the risk of nuclear war. Gradually, however, the readiness of peace activists to share risks, the intense discussions, and the new ideas and language led to a coming together around new concepts, in which the inseparability of peace and democracy, disarmament and human rights, came to be mutually recognised.

For the peace movements, concepts like civil society (Michnik), anti-politics (Havel and Konrad), and 'living in truth' (Havel) seemed to express ideas and attitudes which were implicit in much peace movement thinking but which had never been clearly articulated.[10] The concepts of civil society and anti-politics were fundamentally about the need for self-organised groups and institutions outside the state and for political parties able to act and speak honestly without concern for the capture of power and able to act as a check or constraint on the power of the state. Such groups operated within a consensus about non-violence and within the framework of law so as to be able gradually to expand the arena for legitimate autonomous social activities. The concern with public morality, the idea of civil society as an independent ethical realm, had echoes of the Scottish Enlightenment.

For the opposition groups in Eastern Europe, the peace movements added a transnational and pan-European dimension to the concept of civil society. They argued that the creation of autonomous spaces was very difficult within the framework of the Cold War, which provided a tool for justifying oppression. Both at an intergovernmental level through such instruments as the Helsinki Accord and at the level of grass-roots groups, the opening up to the outside world helped to guarantee those autonomous spaces. *Détente* had, after all, provided an opening for

Solidarity. It was in the context of a new Cold War that the crackdown on Solidarity took place in 1981. And it was, of course, in the atmosphere of a new *détente* which followed the signing of the Intermediate Nuclear Forces Treaty in 1987 and the proposals for a range of arms control treaties that Gorbachev was able to enunciate his 'Sinatra Doctrine' – 'I did it my way' – for Eastern Europe. This marked the official death of the 'Brezhnev Doctrine' and provided the signal for the 1989 revolutions to begin.

This official *détente* was complemented by what became known as '*détente* from below' or 'citizens' *détente*'.[11] The exchange of ideas undoubtedly contributed to Gorbachev's New Thinking. More importantly, perhaps, the peace movements through constant pressure on officials and through publicising the activities of Eastern European movements were able to help expand the space for new movements in Eastern Europe.

The turning point came in 1985 when Charter 77 addressed the Prague Appeal to the European Nuclear Disarmament (END) Convention in Amsterdam. The Appeal called for a bloc-free democratic Europe including the removal of outside troops and of weapons of mass destruction. In the late 1980s, new movements, committed to both democracy and peace, developed in Eastern Europe directly out of the dialogue between East and West; these included Wolnosc i Pokoj (Freedom and Peace) in Poland, the Independent Peace Association in Czechoslovakia, and FIDESZ (the Young Democrats) in Hungary. The symbolic embrace between Jacek Kuron, one of the leading dissident intellectuals in Poland, and E. P. Thompson at the END Convention in Lund demonstrated how far the movements of the 1980s had travelled. As Adam Michnik put it, in an interview in 1988:

Just like in the West, new movements and new phenomena are being born here which no-one in their right mind can ignore. Whatever one might think about them – movements like the Greens in the German Federal Republic or the peace movements in Great Britain – one cannot deny their existence because they are an important new element in the the political map . . . One has to say that it is the Greens and those peace movements who are looking for allies here in movements such as Wolnosc i Pokoj and that is something invaluable. This is extremely significant particularly as it forms part of the peace-making process. It is typical of the Russians that they want to talk about reducing the number of missiles but they don't want to talk about the civil right to refuse to do military service as a way of guaranteeing peace. Why do they not want to talk about this? This is the great merit of these movements at least here in Poland (and, I think, also in the West) – that the problem of war and the army has been interpreted as a problem concerning human rights. Furthermore, when people ask me what I think about the Western peace movements, I always answer with another question: What do those movements think of Yalta? If those movements are for a unified democratic Europe, and if they are struggling for this unity without resorting to violence, then I am for them. I am for them because I believe that there lies the future.[12]

In other words, what emerged in the 1980s was a commitment to democratic peace, underpinned by the activities of what were then referred to as social movements acting across national boundaries. This was implied by the concept of transnational civil society. It was both a statement about certain civic internationalist values and a description of autonomous self-organised groups operating across borders.

The 1990s

The groups of the 1980s assumed the existence of an overbearing state and an inter-governmental state framework. Thus the term civil society was more or less synonymous with anti-politics; the emphasis was on the separateness of civil society from the state. In contrast to civil society which has a broader canvas of meaning, anti-politics referred to activities outside the state arena; it was a way of rejecting the Communist Party's monopoly of power, of coping with totalitarianism. In effect, it meant a withdrawal from the all-encompassing hold of official politics on society. As such, the term could easily be co-opted by neoliberal interpretations of politics in which civil society becomes a substitute for the state, taking over functions like welfare or humanitarian assistance – a kind of social or political *laissez-faire* doctrine. It was, for example, quite consistent with nineteenth-century ideas about charity. It could easily be depoliticised and used to refer to worthy non-political organisations ranging from the Boy Scouts to Women's Institutes to humanitarian organisations like Oxfam or Save the Children. Whereas in the 1980s the term used to refer to the agents of civil society (the groups in Eastern Europe, for example) was 'social movements', in the 1990s, it was replaced by the more anodyne 'non-governmental organisations' (NGOs).

This shift was more than just a change of name. The social movements of the 1980s received virtually no outside funding; they were dependent on voluntary contributions and the voluntary energies of their members. They were very political, in the sense that they were advocacy groups, challenging and checking state activities. The new NGOs of the 1990s receive funding from a variety of sources including governments, international organisations like the European Union, and private foundations such as Soros. The success of these organisations depends as much on their professionalism, their ability to manage budgets, public relations, fund-raising, etc. as on their public or social appeal. Undoubtedly, the growing respectability of these organisations has created a climate in which they can flourish, especially in Eastern Europe. On the other hand, it also helps to legitimise the withdrawal of the state from certain key functions.

In the aftermath of 1989, strategies of transition, guided by neo-liberal ideas, sought the privatisation and liberalisation of a range of social activities, especially but not only in the economic sphere. These strategies were quite similar to the strategies of structural adjustment which had been undertaken in many Third World countries during the previous decade. Although formal democratic procedures were intro-duced in all the Eastern European countries, e.g. elections, an inde-pendent judiciary, nominal freedom of the Press, etc., in practice, the emphasis on privatisation and liberalisation was much greater than the emphasis on democratisation. In other words, instead of forging a new more responsive relationship between state and society as the civil soci-ety theorists of the 1980s had anticipated, the state simply withdrew from large parts of society.

What was revealed underneath the layers of state control was not civil society but uncivility. The groups of the 1980s, as it turned out, represented a rather narrow stratum of society – well-educated young people who often spoke English, and, even if they were not allowed to travel, were cosmopolitan in outlook. Those who led the 1989 revolu-tions were quickly marginalised even in Poland where they had the largest mass following. The process of transition meant the breakdown of many established ways of doing things such as retail distribution or the provision of services; it meant the rise of new inequalities, and the loss of job security; and it also meant a struggle for power on the part of those who had not had the courage to participate in anti-politics. What emerged were new political currents based on the appeal to prejudice and fear, new criminal and mafia groups, new anti-cultures of guilt and insecurity which may have included deep and perhaps paradoxical re-sentment of the confident victors of 1989.

In Yugoslavia, and especially in Bosnia-Herzegovina, the state liter-ally disintegrated, as had happened earlier in several African countries. In the early stages of the war, there was in both Belgrade and Bosnia-Herzegovina, a very active civil society in the 1980s sense of the term. In Belgrade, students occupied the university; peace groups, like 'Women in Black' sprang up throughout Serbia; young men refused to be mobil-ised for the army. In Bosnia-Herzegovina, hundreds of thousands demon-strated for peace. In Mostar, people of different nationalities created a chain across every single bridge. In Sarajevo, together with European peace activists, a human chain linked the mosque, the Catholic church, the Orthodox church and the synagogue. The different faiths prayed together to prevent a war. In fact, the war began not as a scuffle between national groups. It began on 5 April 1992, when Serbian snipers fired on 200,000 young demonstrators in Sarajevo; the first person to die was a medical student from Dubrovnik. Thousands more people, from other towns in Bosnia-Herzegovina, were prevented from entering Sarajevo to join the demonstration by barricades erected by paramilitary groups. Civil society was ineffective because there was no rule of law; there was no public control of violence.[13]

A similar story can be told in Africa. Despite the growth of humanitarian and human rights organisations, nothing was done to stop the genocide in Rwanda or, indeed, other tragedies in Somalia, Sudan and Liberia. As one commentator wrote recently:

Rwanda had an exemplary 'human rights community'. Seven indigenous human rights NGOs collaborated closely with their foreign friends and patrons, providing unrivalled documentation of the ongoing massacres and assassinations . . . They predicted massive atrocities unless named perpetrators were called to account. But there was no 'primary movement' that could underpin the activists' agenda, no political establishment ready to listen to their critique and act on it, and no international organisations ready to take measures and risks necessary to protect them . . . On April 6 1994, the Hutu extremists called the bluff of the human rights community and launched their final solution. As well as eradicating all Tutsis, they embarked upon the systematic assassination of all critics. The UN ran away, while the US government thought up nice excuses for inaction . . .[14]

The war in Bosnia-Herzegovina can be interpreted not as a war between national groups but as a war *against* civil society. The victors of this war are nationalist extremists on all sides. During the war, most violence was perpetrated against civilians; as is the case with all recent wars, there has been a dramatic increase in the ratio of civilian to military casualties.[15] There were almost no battles and very little fighting between the warring factions except at certain key strategic points such as Brcko; rather the violence was mainly directed against the villages and besieged towns. The vast majority of educated young people, who represented the future hopes of civil society, left the country. Many of those who remained were killed. In the towns and villages that were ethnically cleansed, the 'intellectuals' were the first targets, slated for execution and not merely detention or rape. In Banja Luka, for example, only a few Serbian intellectuals remain. Above all, it was a war against the values of tolerance, mutual respect, and individual autonomy that were the centrepiece of the original eighteenth-century conception of civil society. The war was designed to instil fear, hate and insecurity.

The land of 'fear and hate' described by Ivo Andrić in 1929[16] had almost disappeared in the post-war period; the war was the instrument for restoring it. As one of the surviving intellectuals in Banja Luka put it: 'The war had to be so violent in order to make us hate each other.'[17]

What became evident in Bosnia-Herzegovina was that civil society cannot be a substitute for the state; civic values cannot survive without a rule of law. In the Bosnian war, the concept of civil society changed its meaning yet again. It no longer meant those groups independent of the state (although, of course, those who supported civil society were independent since there was no state); it meant those who support the values of civility. Thus, there was a lot of talk about independent media, since the media had played a horrendous role in mobilising fear and hate. What was actually meant by this term was media which represented other, non-nationalist, values; the word 'independent' was, in a sense, a remnant of 1980s thinking.

The one municipality which elected a non-nationalist coalition in the 1990 elections and which managed to sustain a civil society throughout the war was Tuzla. The town defended itself at the beginning of the war and although it was shelled continuously, managed to keep fighting out of the town and to keep crime rates low. The term used to describe the coalition of parties which controlled the municipality (Social Democrat, Reformist, and Liberal) was 'civic'. Likewise, the Tuzla Citizens Forum was a mass movement of citizens, with some 15,000 members, which promoted multicultural, multireligious, multinational *civic* values. In Tuzla, the argument was that democracy is an answer to nationalism. These people were not pacifist; on the contrary, they defended their town and called for outside help. They also extended the concept to the economic and social field, arguing that civil society has to demonstrate that it can meet people's needs. The municipality developed ideas about a localised, decentralised approach to economic development linked to international networks. Unlike other places in Bosnia-Herzegovina, it managed to maintain production throughout the war and introduced during the war an extensive e-mail network.

A similar division between civic and nationalist approaches characterised the outside response to the war. On the one hand, there were those governments anxious to find a quick solution who effectively aligned themselves to the nationalists. Although they expressed abhorrence at ethnic cleansing and genocide, they argued a 'pragmatic' case for negotiating between the warring factions in order to bring about a rapid end to the fighting. It took three-and-a-half years to negotiate this 'quick solution'. Agreement was only reached when ethnic cleansing was virtually complete and some two-thirds of the population had been displaced. In the aftermath of Dayton, none of the commitments to civic decency, such as return of refugees, prosecution of war criminals, freedom of the media, etc., have been honoured. Instead, the nationalists have tightened their authoritarian control over their fiefdoms, harassing and intimidating those who dare to stand for civic values. Arkan, thought to be the most notorious ethnic cleanser of them all, actually received funds from the international community for his political party to campaign in the elections.

On the other hand, there were those in both government and international organisations and among NGOs who called for measures to protect civilians and uphold international humanitarian principles. One example was Tadeusz Mazowiecki, formerly a Solidarity leader and Polish prime minister who became the United Nations' Special Rapporteur for Human Rights. Many of those who had put forward ideas about democratic peace in the 1980s were the most foremost advocates of military intervention or peace enforcement to control the violence. Pressure from transnational public opinion – the international media and many NGOs and campaigning groups active in Bosnia – did lead to a series of innovative Security Council resolutions for safe havens, humanitarian corridors, the prosecution of war criminals, a no-fly zone, etc. which had the potential through a step-by-step approach to restore order. But none of them were ever effectively implemented. When the so-called safe haven of Srebrenica fell, accompanied by some of the worst atrocities of war, no-one felt responsible. Mazowiecki was the only official to resign.

The violence of the 1980s and the impotence of the NGO community has thus led to an implicit reconceptualisation of civil society. The term civil society, at least as it is used in places like Bosnia-Herzegovina, has a much more political connotation. It means standing for the values of civil society, for democracy and non-violence, for multiculturalism and secularity. It means taking risks; it means something worth fighting for. Hence, the term civic resistance is increasingly used. It requires, of course, individuals and self-organised groups to mobilise around these values. But it also requires institutions, whether local, national or transnational, which can uphold these values, and which can maintain the peace and administer justice. In Tuzla, the concept also acquired the character of a forward-looking project that could offer hope for a better future in contrast to the backward-looking nostalgic projects of the nationalists who had no answers to individual or social problems.

As in the 1980s, the concept was also transnational in character. Those who stood for civic values expected 'Europe' or the 'international community' to help them. Often, the words 'European values' were used interchangeably with 'civic values'. There was no state. There were only expectations from international organisations. From the very beginning, the civic groups called for an international protectorate. Those governments which opposed this idea and which pinned their hopes on talks argued that the Bosnians had to solve their own problems. Indeed, they argued that if the war could not be solved, at least it could be 'contained'. But, without control of violence, there was no way that Bosnians could 'solve' their own problem. Moreover, the argument presupposed that this was a localised war. Just as in Africa, no wars are purely local any longer. The global presence ranges from foreign journalists, international peace-keepers and humanitarian NGOs to transnational criminal networks selling arms and drugs and diaspora nationalists coming to aid their romantic causes. Neither the causes of a war – the pressures of global trade and structural adjustment, for example – nor the consequences of a war – the waves of refugees, the spread of criminalisation – can be localised.

Globalisation and civil society

Giddens defines globalisation as a further 'stretching' of time-space distanciation. More and more aspects of the lives of individuals are influenced by events taking place further and further away in time and space. Some argue that the capitalist economy has always been global and that globalisation began with the so-called modern age.[18] I would argue, however, that what makes the last two decades or so qualitatively different has been the revolution in travel and communication, especially the processing and transmission of information.

As discussed in the first part, the notion of civil society originated in a period of time-space distanciation when abstract means of communication began to supplant face-to-face personal relations in everyday life. These means of communication were, by and large, territorially bounded. What Giddens calls the 'disembedding mechanisms' of modern society, the abstract symbols of social trust like money or professional qualifications, were largely national. The language of communication was national; civil society was bounded by an 'imagined community' constructed out of the spread of secular culture, through such instruments as novels and newspapers, in the vernacular language.[19] There were, of course, mechanisms for global communication – the gold standard, for example, or the diplomatic use of the French language – but these did not impinge deeply on everyday life. It is worth noting that when Immanuel Kant wrote *Perpetual Peace*, he thought that a sufficient condition for perpetual peace was that cosmopolitan right could be confined to the right of hospitality, i.e. the duty to treat foreigners with civility but not to treat them as fellow-nationals.

The revolution in travel and communication reflects and reinforces an intensification of globalised or transnationalised activity in a range of fields – political, economic, military and cultural – which give rise to new social and geographical divisions. It is possible to talk about a new global class of people who participate directly in these globalised activities. These are the people who travel in aeroplanes or on the Eurostar trains, who communicate by telephone, fax and e-mail, who use internationally recognised credit cards, who have access to satellite television, and who, for the most part, speak English. They are still a minority. The vast majority of people remain territorially, linguistically and culturally tied; nevertheless, their lives are profoundly influenced by the activities of the former group and, indeed, are largely dependent upon them.

The world is still divided into rich parts and poor parts and the rich parts are more globalised than the poor parts. Indeed, certain parts of the world such as large parts of Africa or Latin America are virtually excluded from globalised activities. But it is also the case that, unlike the postwar period, these new social divisions exist side by side in all parts of the world. Every big city contains its globalised enclaves serviced by deprived territorially tied dependent groups.

The concept of transnational civil society should not, however, be equated with this new global class. On the contrary, the emerging political cleavage between civic values and exclusivist claims cuts across both groupings. Of course, it is the case that those who are territorially tied are most vulnerable to nationalist and exclusivist philosophies. They may see these ideas as a way to reclaim control over their lives; they may seek scapegoats to explain the sweeping impersonal changes that have affected them; they may seek security in primary loyalties to clan, tribe or ethnic group; or they may simply be forced by economic circumstances to join a criminal gang or a paramilitary group or be attracted by the adventure of a romantic nationalist cause. But such people find allies and patrons within the global class. Many nationalist groups rely on diaspora support, especially in North America or Australasia, where ethnic immigrants have retained and indeed reinvented their identity; such are the Croatian Canadians, the Irish Americans, the Greek and Macedonian Australians who provide money, ideas and even volunteers. Likewise, transnational criminal networks are often crucial in funding and supplying 'uncivil' wars. And there are more respectable groupings within the global class who do not necessarily share exclusivist thinking but effectively align themselves for what they see as 'pragmatic' reasons. These include the 'realists' who still believe in the nation state as the centrepiece of international organisation and the main instrument for stability or the 'neo-liberals' who believe that order imposed, if necessary, by force is the necessary condition for a global market. These are the people who favour a partitioning of Bosnia-Herzegovina, who are ready to support Yeltsin whether or not he can win elections, who think Saddam Hussein should be kept in power to prevent a vacuum in the Middle East or chaos. They prefer the appearance of democracy but they believe in vertical hierarchies of power and are ready to align themselves with local bigots if they can convince themselves that this is the way to achieve stability.

It is also the case, of course, that those who support civic internationalist values are most likely to be found among those who have access to global communication: the cosmopolitan young people to be found in almost every city from Sarajevo to New York. They are the people who may be active in NGOs or they may work in international organisations or the international media. Or they may simply be cosmopolitan-minded; they may be the people who join organisations like Greenpeace or Amnesty International, who join protests about the war in Bosnia and the construction of motorways, who offer voluntary contributions to cosmopolitan causes, who read international journals. Equally, if not more importantly, however, are those courageous territorially tied people who attempt at a local level to combat racism or other forms of exclusivism, who engage in various solidaristic activities, who try to sustain civic values in schools, hospitals and other local institutions. These can be found in all war zones, especially, but not only, among women's groups, mothers of soldiers, refugees and displaced persons, families of missing persons, and so on.

Transnational civil society has to be viewed as a political project which crosses the global/local divide. Unlike the Cold War period, when Europe and North America were effectively insulated from poverty and violence in the rest of the world, and when it was possible to describe the world as peaceful because wars did not take place in advanced industrial countries, the new uncivility is globalised. Cosmopolitan ghettos cannot be effectively sealed off despite the array of new types of security apparatus to protect airports, homes, rich suburbs, public buildings, etc. Neither the wars in Bosnia and Northern Ireland, nor the crime in many inner cities can be spatially 'contained'. At the same time, those who are trying to exert a constructive influence over local life in a globalised world, can only succeed if they have outside support and access to those international organisations that can influence governments and global regulatory processes.

Conclusion

The lessons of the 1980s were that civil society has to be built from below through the efforts of self-organised groups of citizens working together across national boundaries. The lessons of the 1990s are that such groups cannot succeed in a globalised uncivil world without responsive institutions at both local and transnational levels. Thus the concept of transnational civil society not only has to cross the global/ local divide but also has to embrace both institutions and independent citizens groups. As a political project, it has to be relevant to individuals as power-holders as well as independent citizens. For independent-minded citizens, the concept implies that local activities and campaigns have to be linked into networks of support across national boundaries and have to have access to a range of institutions. For power-holders, the concept implies a responsibility (and self-interest) to provide enabling support for those struggling to uphold civic values at a local level – support which can range from moral and financial support to effective policing, the control of violence and the administration of justice in cases of extreme uncivility.

Civil society thus consists of groups, individuals and institutions which are independent of the state and of state boundaries, but which are, at the same time, preoccupied with public affairs. They are, in effect, the guarantors of civil behaviour both by official institutions (states and international institutions) and in the world at large. Defined in this way, civil society does not encompass all groups or associations independent of the state. It does not include groups which advocate violence. It does not include self-organised groups and associations which campaign for exclusivist communitarian concepts. Nor does it include self-interested private associations like those of criminals or capitalists. A bank or a corporation is only part of civil society to the extent that it views itself, as many do, as a public organisation with a responsibility to society that takes precedence over profit-making.

To be part of civil society implies a shared commitment to common human values and, in this sense, the concept of global civil society might be equated with the notion of a global human rights culture, as described by Dunne and Wheeler in the Introduction to this volume. Some would argue that civil society is broader since it encompasses issues such as peace, gender equality and the environment. But these can easily, and in some cases rather usefully, be reconceptualised as human rights issues. Hence, Russian human rights groups who campaign against the war in Chechnya argue that the war is a massive violation of human rights. Likewise, independent trade unionists in

Russia argue that they are human rights organisations concerned with workers' rights. The advantage of the human rights discourse is its globalist character and its emphasis on the individual – the 'last child' as Gandhi put it. But the advantage of the language of civil society is precisely its *political* content, its implications for participation and citizenship. It adds to the human rights discourse the notion of individual responsibility for respect of human rights through public action.

Advocates of transnational civil society share with the eighteenth-century theorists of civil society the notion of a public morality based on individual conscience. This is indeed the reason for retaining the term. The difference is that the ethical arena, the realm of public morality, is greatly extended. It is a plea for cosmopolitan rights that takes us well beyond the right to hospitality. Critics might argue that it is thus a modernist/universalist project on an even more ambitious scale than earlier modernist projects like liberalism or socialism and contains within it a totalitarian claim. Moreover, given the secular character of the concept and the explicit rejection of communitarianism, especially those forms based on ethnicity, it might be argued that the concept is open to more severe charges of utopianism and inconsistency than was the eighteenth-century concept.

Public morality is underpinned by universalist projects, although those projects are periodically changed by circumstances; they always produce unintended consequences and have to be revised. Thus, they can never be universalist in practice, even if they always appear to make universalist claims. Such projects, like liberalism or socialism, are validated by circumstances, at least for a time, or discredited. The eighteenth-century idea that reason is immanent in nature implied that rational (moral) behaviour could be learned through experience; there is a reality in which there are better or worse ways of living and that how to live in these different ways can be learned through experience, for example, the experience of happy or unhappy families or of war and peace. These lessons are never learned for ever because reality is so complicated and the exact set of circumstances in which a particular rationality seems to work cannot be reproduced.

The 1989 revolutions seemed to validate the concept of transnational civil society. But the concept was used in ways that were totally inadequate to deal with the uncivility of the 1990s even though many individuals sustained the ideals of 1989 through this period. From this vantage-point, the concept does indeed seem ridiculously utopian. On the other hand, the selfishness of the 1990s, the belief in utilitarian self-interest, the prevalence of exclusivist communitarian claims, the 'pragmatic' readiness to acquiesce in violations of public morality ranging from authoritarianism to genocide, the cosmopolitan myopia of many members of the new global class, all suggest that there is little alternative to such a ridiculously utopian project. The absence of such a project gives rise to circumstances that are almost unbearable to contemplate.

Notes

1 For discussion of the evolution of the modernist concept of civil society, see Adam B. Seligman, *The Idea of Civil Society* (Princeton University Press, 1992); Jean Cohen and Andrew Arato, *Civil Society and Political Theory* (Cambridge, Mass.: MIT Press, 1994); John Keane, 'Despotism and democracy', in John Keane (ed.), *Civil Society and the State: New European Perspectives* (London and New York: Verso, 1988).
2 For a discussion of 'civility', see John Keane, *Reflections on Violence* (London and New York: Verso, 1996).
3 See Anthony Giddens, *The Consequences of Modernity* (Cambridge: Polity Press, 1990).
4 Seligman, *The Idea of Civil Society*, p. 33.
5 According to Hugo Grotius, 'Just as even God, then, cannot cause that two times two should not make four, so He cannot cause that which is intrinsically evil be not evil.' Quoted in *ibid.*, p. 21.
6 Ernest Gellner, *Conditions of Liberty: Civil Society and Its Rivals* (London: Hamish Hamilton, 1994), p. 127.
7 E. P. Thompson and Dan Smith, *Protest and Survive* (London: Penguin, 1980), p. 45.
8 As Milan Šimečka, a Charter 77 spokesman was to say later:

> I remember how all those disarmament talks in the seventies – even Helsinki itself – looked very dubious dealing to us, or like a party at the expense of East European countries which we paid for in the currency of imprisonment, decline and stagnation. This was not entirely true, of course, and as it turned out, what seemed no more than agreements on paper about human rights were, amazingly enough, to prove instrumental in achieving certain improvements. The third basket at Helsinki was originally intended as the price the Soviet Union had to pay for recognition of the status quo in Europe. The Soviet Union was only too happy to pay it, since our political culture contained thousands of artfully contrived methods for skirting human rights obligations. Indeed, in Czechoslovakia, the immediate post-Helsinki period was a time of the worst persecutions. A deaf ear was turned to any reference to the Helsinki Final Act and, as I know from personal experience, any talk of Helsinki in those days would send police officers into fits of laughter. That all assumes a different aspect, however, if looked at in longer perspective. Over these past years . . . much has changed. Concepts have emerged which were previously unknown. These concepts undoubtedly penetrated the reform thinking then coming to fruition in the Soviet Union. If nothing else, by confirming the outcome of World War II Helsinki served to rid the Soviet Union of its old obsessions about external threats, and this subsequently had a positive effect on its attitude to detente.

'From class obsessions to dialogue: detente and the changing political culture of Eastern Europe', in M. Kaldor, G. Holden and R. Falk (eds.), *The*

New Detente: Rethinking East–West Relations (London and New York: Verso, 1989), p. 363.

9 See Adam Michnik, *Letters from Prison and Other Essays* (Berkeley and London: University of California Press, 1985).

10 See, for example, *ibid.*; Václav Havel, *The Power of the Powerless* (London: Hutchinson, 1985); George Konrad, *Anti-Politics* (London: Quartet Books, 1984).

11 The term '*détente* from below' was first used by Mient Jan Faber, the General Secretary of the Dutch Inter-Church Peace Council. 'Menschenrechte und Enspannung von unten', *Frankfurter Hefte*, Friedrich Ebert Stiftung 3 (1986).

12 Adam Michnik, 'On Detente', in Kaldor, Holden and Falk (eds.), *The New Detente*, p. 128.

13 For an account of this period, see Neven Andjelić, 'The rise and fall of civil society in Bosnia-Herzegovina', MA thesis, University of Sussex (1995).

14 See Alex de Waal, 'Becoming Shameless', *Times Literary Supplement*, 21 February 1997: 3–4.

15 See Mary Kaldor, 'Post-Clausewitzian Warfare', in Mary Kaldor, Basker Vashee and World Institute for Development Economics Research Staff, *Restructuring the Global Military Sector*, vol. I: *New Wars* (London: UNU/ WIDER, Cassell, 1997).

16 Ivo Andrić, 'Letter from 1929', in *The Damned Yard and Other Stories* (London and Boston: Forest Books, 1992).

17 Interview with Miodrag Žhivanović, Professor of Economics and Leader of the Liberal Party.

18 See, for example, Paul Hirst and Graham Thompson, *Globalisation in Question* (Cambridge: Polity Press, 1996).

19 See Benedict Anderson, *Imagined Communities* (London: Verso, 1983).

8   Global voices: civil society and the media in global crises

Martin Shaw

This chapter examines the conditions under which the voices of the most oppressed, struggling and victimised sections of human society are able to be heard in world politics. It does this first by elaborating a theoretical account of the development of 'global society', the globalisation of state power leading to what I call the 'global state', the novel processes involved in the constitution of contemporary 'global political crises' and the nature and role of 'global civil society'. Secondly, it looks more closely at the problem of 'global representation' in relation to Western civil society and state, and argues that we need to test the idea of global civil society by examining these problems within global crises.

The chapter then introduces a more specific discussion of different civil society institutions, based on my study of civil society in responses to the Iraqi wars of 1991 (I use this general term to indicate the importance of the Iraqi revolts compared to the Gulf War which has held the overwhelming attention of Western academics).[1] First, it examines the limitations of national civil societies and traditional representative institutions in the West, highlighting especially the routinised nature of debates about war within them. Secondly, it discusses the inadequacies of some new representative institutions of global civil society, such as transnational social movements, in representing those struggling in zones of crisis, arguing that their ideological agendas too are often geared to the pro- and anti-nation-state approach. Other new, globalist institutions, such as humanitarian agencies and campaigns (which are forms distinct from social movements), have been more effective.

The chapter argues, based on a study of the Kurdish refugee crisis of 1991, that global television has a unique capacity to represent 'global voices'. It examines how television news moved from managed medium (during the Gulf War) to active representation of victims of violence (in Kurdistan). However, I argue that even at best, television tends to do this indirectly, representing people as pure victims rather than as protagonists or combatants, and through the authoritative voices of Western reporters rather than in their own words. Television exerted great leverage

214

on Western leaders, leading them to change policy over the Kurds, but this depended on the nexus of responsibility which these leaders had themselves created. Televisual mediation has become a constitutive part of global crises, as other cases show, but rarely does it involve strong, direct leverage of the kind shown in the Kurdish crisis.

The chapter concludes by summarising the difference between the approach from global theory, on which the argument is based, and traditional approaches in International Relations, based on states. I argue that these different approaches entail different normative perspectives. Global theory does not just explain the limitations of representation, but looks to the development of global civil society and the global state to allow more voices to be heard – and to be effective.

Global society

As we enter the twenty-first century, the clear outlines of a global society can be discerned, and the boundaries of national societies are becoming ever more fluid.[2] Production is based to a considerable degree on a global division of labour and co-ordinated in many areas by globally active corporations. Global markets are the context within which regional, national and local markets are defined. Communication is developing on a global scale, through media of both mass communication (such as television) and individual communication (such as phones and computers). Global awareness of problems such as environmental degradation and disease is growing.

A global society exists in the sense that these global connections constitute a social framework to which individuals across the world refer, more or less consciously, in many of their interactions and exchanges. This is not to say that all social action is globally defined in a narrow sense – any more than all action was nationally defined in the era of nation-states. Networks of social action have boundaries of many kinds: familial, industrial, professional, lifestyle, as well as local, regional, national and international. Most of these boundaries are less than global, in the most obvious sense of that word. The boundaries are, however, more porous than ever before, and there is growing awareness of a global context, in which the relations between different fields of action are defined.

Global society possesses some of the attributes previously attributed to 'a society'. Elements of a global culture have been coming into existence for some centuries, although they coexist with elements of a more local and national character. Global institutions have proliferated in the economic, cultural and political spheres. Values like democracy and liberty, largely Western in origin, have been increasingly globalised. Nevertheless, while a society can be said to exist in the 'factual' sense – increasingly dense patterns of social interaction – in the 'normative' sense, value cohesion is still limited and problematic.

While these standard criteria for the existence of a society may be applied, it would be a mistake to think that we can seek a close correspondence between how societies have been understood in the past and how global society is to be understood today. The separateness of discrete societies was always 'relative' to larger social contexts: groups of hunter-gatherers to other such groups, territorially fixed tribes to other tribes, principalities and kingdoms to the wider realm of European Christendom, and latterly 'nation-states' to a European and ultimately worldwide system of states. A global society is a society in which the wider reference has ceased to be an external demarcation and is becoming constitutive of the framework of social life. It is necessarily different from all previous forms of society.

Global state

One way in which global society differs from many other societies, and from the conventional notion of a society as it has been understood in the era of nation-states, is that global society does not 'have' a state. Of course, societies have not always involved state institutions, and even within a world of states, many 'societies' have not 'had' states.[3] Within states, minority or oppressed communities often feel that state institutions belong to the majority or oppressor group. Within colonial and post-colonial states, state institutions have often been superimposed on tribal and other pre-colonial societies, to which they do not 'belong' in a more organic sense.

The fact that global society does not 'have' a state, in any simple or obvious sense, is not therefore an insuperable objection to its qualifying as a society. But it does raise the question of whether there is any sense in which state institutions correspond specifically to global society. One could argue that while nation-states correspond to national societies, the system of states corresponds to global society. This answer is not irrelevant: clearly there are links between the development of world society and the evolution of the state system in the last few centuries. The 'international society' of the English school of International Relations is best understood in terms of the development of a common culture and norms among state elites, which has reflected the growing integration of world society as a whole. However, this answer is insufficient, because it fails to capture the specific transformations of state

institutions on a global scale in recent times. The half-century since the
end of the World War II has seen not only the greatest acceleration of
globalising trends in society, but the most important changes in state
institutions. The years since 1989 have seen not only dramatic new
manifestations of globalisation, but also a new stage in the development
of global state organisation.

Within global society at the end of the twentieth century, there is a
globalisation of state power.[4] This process is indirectly acknowledged
by the discourse of global governance. This reflects the blurring of state
demarcations in the last fifty years, but it does not explicitly recognise
the key change which has taken place: the pooling of the monopoly of
violence among major states. The defining character of the system of
nation-states, the individual state's virtual monopoly of violence within
its territory and its resort to violence externally to assert its interests
against other states, has been fundamentally modified. The central states
of the international system have largely abandoned war as a means of
resolving disputes among themselves (if not with other states and groups).
They have created common institutions through which, to a crucial
extent, not only *their* means of violence, but those of the whole world,
are managed.

This means that global society at the end of the twentieth century is
not so far from having a global state, after all. After 1945 there emerged
a relatively coherent Western state, pooling the control of violence
among major states like the USA, the UK, France, and subordinately,
Germany and Japan, as well as a large number of lesser states in Western Europe, North America and Australasia. Until 1989, the development of the Western state was conditioned by the Cold War with the
Soviet state and its satellites, which also masked the West's effective
global dominance.

After 1945, the world also developed a set of legitimate interstate
institutions, the United Nations system, to which almost all nation-
states paid at least lip service. This system was largely neutralised by
the Cold War, but has played a new role since 1989. Although far from
being a world government, the UN has constituted a legitimation framework for the emergence of the Western state as the *de facto* centre of
global power. UN institutions have not been permitted to develop an
effective independent capacity, especially in the military sphere. But
they have remained the principal source of legitimate global authority
to which the Western state, and especially its organising centre (the
USA), have found it expedient to resort in all important cases.

The emerging global state of the late twentieth century is therefore the
Western state together with its legitimation framework, the UN system,

through which other states and – to a lesser extent – world society are drawn into political relationships with it. The Non-Western states and various sectors of global society are of course involved in all sorts of other relationships with the Western state and its components, in economic, political and military senses. The primacy of the Western state derives ultimately from the concentration of economic power within it. Economic connections draw many other states, in Asia, the Middle East, Latin America and Africa, into close relationships with Western power.

The global state – the globalisation and global legitimation of Western state power – is certainly a precarious and fragmentary arrangement. The unity of the Western state, the roles of nation-states within it, its legitimacy within the global system of states and even more within global society, the credibility of the legitimating institutions of the UN – all these are undoubtedly in question. Their viability is only established, and can only be understood, by examining how they are tested in practice, above all in what we can call global political crises.

Global political crises

Before 1945, global political crises were constituted by the political-military rivalries of the major nation-states; between 1945 and 1989, by the rivalries of the Western and Soviet states. During both of these periods, local wars between lesser states sometimes constituted global crises because of their linkages with the major rivalries.

Since 1989, the rivalries of major states have not disappeared. In a political-economic sense, rivalries within the West, between Western Europe, North America and Japan, as well as between the major European states, have actually become more apparent. But no-one – not even the most unreconstructed realist or Marxist – seriously expects these rivalries to degenerate into war, even in the medium to long term. In a similar sense, rivalries between major non-Western states (such as Russia, China and India) and the West have been largely political-economic rather than political-military. Clearly, it cannot be ruled out that these will still take military forms (as the 1996 Sino-American crisis over Taiwan revealed) although a more likely source of conflicts are the rivalries *between* these major non-Western powers, or between them and other significant states.

The major international crises of the post-Cold War years have arisen, moreover, from local wars involving second- or third-rank powers, and above all from state disintegration and civil war. It is worth asking by what token we can consider these conflicts as global political crises. In some cases it is clear that 'old' criteria have been operating: conflicts have been of global significance because they have touched the interests, if no longer so much the rivalries, of major powers. Thus the Iraqi invasion of Kuwait was of global significance because it threatened the control of major sources of oil, not only for the USA but even more for Japan, Western Europe and indeed many Third World states. More than this, it threatened the emergence of a totalitarian regional superpower in this key area. At the same time, it was the first time that a UN member had not only been invaded but had actually been annexed by another state. Other crises have been of global import because they have been within the spheres of interest of major powers: Haiti because it was within the USA's traditional regional sphere, Chechnya because it was actually within the Russian Federation, and above all Yugoslavia because it was on the borders of the European Community and had implications for the stability of Europe in the wider sense, in which both the USA and Russia retain an interest.

Nevertheless, it is arguable that all of these crises became global political crises in a fuller sense than that indicated by their simple significance for great power interests. In all cases, the crises were greatly magnified by their mediation by mass communications. While in the Gulf and Chechnya, the USA and Russia respectively decided on the basis of a calculation of interests that military intervention was necessary, in Haiti and especially in Yugoslavia, the USA and the European powers were reluctant to intervene. Television, above all, exposed the human costs of Clinton's unwillingness to halt Haiti's military violence, and repeatedly thrust the appalling murderousness of the wars in Croatia, Bosnia and Kosovo on to Western publics. Clearly, the mediation of these crises was a constitutive part of the process by which, in the end, the Western state and especially the USA intervened in both these situations.

Other conflicts became global political crises – in the sense that they evoked either globally legitimated interventions by major powers or at least a widespread demand for such intervention – even though they manifestly failed to impinge centrally on their interests as traditionally understood. Somalia was in a region, the Horn of Africa, where the end of the Cold War removed the superpower underpinnings of local states and conflicts. The disintegration of the Somali state was partly a symptom of the *withdrawal* of great-power interests from the region. Its human consequences touched humanitarian impulses through media coverage, without significant economic or strategic interest. Similarly, Rwanda was in a region, sub-Saharan Africa, which declined dramatically in geopolitical significance with the end of the Cold War. Even in larger states, such as Angola and Mozambique, the great powers were making strategic withdrawals. In tiny Rwanda, superpower interests had never been strong. It was only the televisual mediation of the terrible violence of the 1994 genocide that forced Rwanda on to the global political agenda.

In Somalia, the USA and the UN carried out a botched intervention; in Rwanda, they avoided intervention (although France intervened for its own particular interests) until it was too late. Neither episode represented a strong example of global political-military intervention for humanitarian goals. Nevertheless, it was clear that both cases constituted crises of global significance, to which the West and the UN were forced to make some response. It was equally clear that these global political crises were largely constituted, as those in Yugoslavia and elsewhere were partially constituted, by global media (largely television) coverage and the responses which this evoked in civil society. They were constituted, moreover, around definitions of crises which centred on the relief of human suffering rather than the realisation of strategic interests. The mediated social dimensions of wars came to constitute a major element of global crises.

What was striking, however, was that while these crises became of global significance partly or mainly through their mediation by television, scores of other crises remained localised and failed to secure similar mediation. These included long-term conflicts involving very great civilian suffering: in the former Soviet area, the civil wars in Tadjikistan, Georgia and the Armenian-Azerbaijani war, and in Africa the renewed Angolan civil war and the conflicts in Liberia and Sierra Leone. It is clear that the mediation effect of communications has been very selective. It is necessary to explore the nature of the mediation process and the means by which it becomes effective, through civil society and in the state.

Global civil society and media

Much critical literature in International Relations has centred on the concept of civil society and the putative emergence in recent times of a 'global civil society'.[5] Civil society has meant many different things in theoretical writing over the last two centuries, but the concept which is most relevant here is that which arises from the Gramscian debate in western Europe and the oppositional discourse of central Europe in the final stages of the Cold War.[6] In both these discourses, civil society is not 'society minus the state' in the classic sense of Smith, Hegel or Marx (i.e. centred on economic relations)[7] but a sphere of association *between* economy and state. Civil society is the arena in which groupings in society represent themselves, ideologically and institutionally, both in relation to other social groups, and in relation to the state. This is the sense in which civil society is used here.

Although some see civil society as a sphere of universal principles, and hence implicitly transnational, in recent history civil society can only be seen as largely national in character. During the era of nation-states, which is only now drawing, slowly and fitfully, to a close, civil institutions have largely been circumscribed by national boundaries. National societies and civil societies have corresponded to nation-states. Even clearly universalist institutions, such as Christian churches, have adopted largely national characters: Protestant churches have often been organised explicitly on national lines and even the 'one, universal' Roman Catholic Church has in practice adapted strongly to national state institutions. Social-democratic and communist parties, representatives of a different kind of universalist ideology, have also been heavily nationalised. During the era of nation-states, the universal aspect of civil society has only been able to take 'inter-national' forms.

Global civil society has been identified not so much in international linkages of these and other national civil institutions – although they are not without importance – as in the growth of new forms of action in civil society. 'New' social movements (as opposed to 'old' labour movements) have been seen as implicitly transnational and as tending to develop global reach. The principal 'new' movements (peace, student, women's, democracy, human rights and environmental) have been seen as spearheading globalism. The growth of explicitly globalist campaigning organisations, such as Greenpeace, has seemed to represent a new potential for global consciousness.

Although globalism is at the core of the development of global civil society, two related tensions can be identified within this tendency. First, the new forms of civil society, like the old, embody tensions between national and global ideas *of* civil society. This is evident in the West, where national civil societies are relatively well established, but even more in the former East and South, where the emergence of civil society is linked simultaneously to the recovery of national identity and to the sense of global (and in Europe especially, regional) participation.

Second, there is the problem of the representativeness of globalism. Globalist ideas may represent inclusive global interests in an ideological sense, but how far do they actually involve people across the globe? Virtually all the implicitly global social movements listed above have originated among Western social elites – the partial exception is the democracy movement which spread from the ex-communist to Third World states. Although they all have echoes in many parts of the world, like other sorts of transnational and multinational actors they still have strong affiliations to their countries, regions and social strata of origin.

These question-marks over the coherence of global civil society can be supplemented by other issues. Theorists of global civil society often fail to root their analyses in a comprehensive discussion of civil society. On the one hand, this means that they miss issues like the tension between the national and the global, which are in fact constitutive of civil society in our era. On the other hand, it means that they fail to analyse the full range of civil society institutions, focusing too much on social movements.[8]

A particular problem which is of great importance to this chapter is the role of communications media in civil society. Media are often treated apart, and indeed communications research tends to be a different kind of discourse, but in any systematic account it appears that media should be seen as central institutions of contemporary civil society in general and of its global forms in particular. And yet 'bringing media in' to civil society debate is likely to change some of its terms radically, as we shall see below.

Global representation, global voices

I have argued above that civil society is defined by the function of representation of society in general. Through civil society, groups in society represent themselves, both to the other members of society and to the state. This representative function is particularly problematic at the global level, in two related senses.

First, to whom does global civil society represent itself? On our analysis, global civil society is likely to represent itself to the emergent global state. Indeed, the global state context is extremely important to the coherence of global civil society, as a framework within and against which demands and ideas are formulated. And yet, as we have seen, the global state is the Western state writ large, surrounded by the wider legitimation framework of the UN in which non-Western states participate.

This leads to the second problem: how does society in non-Western states participate in global civil society and represent itself to global institutions? How do we create the 'cosmopolitan democracy' which Held and others have advocated?[9] This problem is compounded by other considerations. At best, many non-Western states are weak and have far less global leverage than Western states – so that simple representation within the local state guarantees little in the way of global representation. At worst, non-Western states are actually the problem faced by people within those states, and thus the reason why they might seek global representation. While few Western states are paragons of democracy, many non-Western states are sources of stark oppression and denial of democracy. The recourse to global representation and the need for global civil society is actually a way of mobilising against national states.

From the viewpoint of many groups in non-Western society (as well as of some in the West), being involved in global civil society is in fact a way of connecting to Western civil society and hence of securing some leverage with the Western state which is at the core of global power. From the point of view of many sectors of Western civil society, the purpose of global civil society is to facilitate the representation of the weak and powerless in the non-West.

The question that arises is whose voices are heard, and how? If Western civil society is the core of global civil society, just as the Western state is the core of the global state, how do non-Western voices become heard? How far do non-Western interests make themselves felt within Western-dominated world civil institutions? How far can non-Western voices make themselves heard directly? In what ways are they filtered by Western civil society, and how is their representation affected by the specific characteristics of Western civil institutions? How far are these Western institutions geared to the representation of global rather than national interests and voices?

This problem is most acute in the new global political crises discussed above, and where the issue of globally legitimate intervention by the Western state is raised. In such crises, groups within non-Western societies are often in the most desperate situations, most failed by local state institutions, and most likely to look to global state institutions to remedy their distress and assist in achieving their aims. Such situations are ones in which the capacity of Western civil society to assist global representation and the reality of global civil society are put severely to the test.

Testing global civil society in crises

In a recent study I have attempted to analyse the role of various civil society institutions in the seminal crisis of the post-Cold War world, the Iraqi wars of 1990–91. I refer to the 'Iraqi wars' rather than the '(Persian) Gulf War', because the Gulf War – the US-led coalition's assault on Iraq in January–February 1991 – was only one of a series of short wars involved in the crisis of the Iraqi state and society, beginning with the Iraqi invasion of Kuwait in August 1990 and ending with the Shia and Kurdish insurrections and their brutal suppression in March–April 1991. These wars in turn grew from the deep crisis of the Iraqi state in its relations with other states and with society, manifested in the long war with Iran and the genocide of the Kurds in the 1980s.

It is a major failure of academic research to transcend ideology and popular debate that most analyses of 1991, whether in International Politics, Strategic Studies or Communications Studies, have ignored the insurrectionary wars in favour of the interstate conflict. They have not been good examples of a new global analysis which recognises the importance of civil society. And yet only by examining the crisis as a whole, and specifically by putting the insurrectionary wars alongside the interstate war, can we obtain a rounded understanding of this crisis either as a political-military or, which is most relevant here, a socio-political crisis. Only by examining this crisis in its totality can we grasp the contours of post-Cold War politics which it defines.

The problem is that the rapid transformations within the Iraqi wars – from the fiscal and political crisis of the Iraqi state which impelled its Kuwaiti adventure, through the interstate crisis, back to the social and political crisis of the Iraqi state – confused academic analysts as much as they evidently wrong-footed George Bush and John Major. And yet such transformations are typical of the new global political crises, in which we move constantly between societal disasters such as the Bosnian and Rwandan genocides and the geopolitics and domestic politics of the major Western and non-Western powers.

Global politics today are characterised by the phenomenon of serial crystallisation, in which the same sets of forces are configured in radically different ways in rapid succession.[10] Not only do crises present themselves, first as economics and geopolitics, then as social revolt and humanitarian crisis, but actors rapidly change roles: in the case of states and militaries, from war-makers to agents of humanitarian relief in a matter of weeks. No wonder these *bouleversements* are confusing for those involved at all levels, from governments to civilian victims, guerrillas to aid agencies, and media to academics.

It is the argument of this chapter that, just as these crises have posed difficulties for academic analysis and for political leadership, so they have found Western civil society wanting. While the old institutions of civil society have been constrained by nationalist frameworks and assumptions, the newer transnationally oriented institutions have also demonstrated their limitations. And the role of mass media, not only in constituting global political crises in a wider societal sense, or in propagandising power, but also in representing social groups within them, has become ever more critical. In the remainder of this chapter I shall

attempt to explain and illustrate these theses, and finally draw together
the theoretical and political implications of my argument.

The limits of national civil society

I argued above that civil society has had, historically, a predominantly
national character. We may distinguish two main kinds of institution,
representative and functional. On the one hand, there are institutions
which represent particular groups and interests in both practical and
ideological senses; on the other, there are those which have functions in
organising general ideological diffusion, apparently on behalf of society
as a whole. Examples of the former are the traditional representative
institutions of civil society – churches, parties, trade unions, the press
and the intelligentsia. Major functional institutions include schools and
universities, television and radio.

Both sets of institutions have had strongly national forms. Indeed,
both can be seen as the 'organic' civil institutions, to use Gramsci's
language, not so much of modern, capitalist society in general, as he
believed, as of the modern nation-state. Representative institutions have
represented society above all in the context of the nation-state – I
discussed above how their most universalistic pretensions conceal adaptations to the nation-state and its ideology. Functional institutions have
educated and informed within and on behalf of nation-states, perform-
ing essential roles in national socialisation and mobilisation, although
often proclaiming universal notions of knowledge and truth.

In both kinds of institution, there have been tensions between the
universalistic values and norms around which their ideologies revolve,
and the national context in which they have been inserted. These tensions were often extremely acute in the 'high' period of the nation-state.
Some Christians, at least, agonised over the conflict between their
universalist, originally pacifist ideology and the killing imperatives of
nation-states – although many became ideological servants even of the
most extreme forms of nationalism. Some liberals agonised over the
inequities of imperialism, although others apologised for them. Some
socialists stood out for internationalism and against war, although
others (most notoriously in 1914) fell in line with their states. Some
communists upheld a genuinely international vision, while most equated
their ideals with the interests of Stalin's totalitarian empire. Only conservatives and, of course, fascists were relatively united in consistently
supporting nationalism and war.

These tensions and the debates in which they are expressed are now
highly routinised and traditional, even if they take slightly different

forms in each war. The major development since the early twentieth century is that issues of nation, empire and the morality of killing which arose in the First World War have been overlain with the larger ideological motifs of the Second World War and Cold War – democracy versus fascism and communism. With the major exception of 1939–45, in which few in the liberal democracies opposed war, these ideological shifts made remarkably little difference to the line-up in civil society. In virtually every war from 1914–18 to Algeria, Vietnam and the Falklands, institutions in Western civil societies have been divided around the axes of nationalism versus internationalism, imperialism versus anti-imperialism and militarism versus pacifism.

The Cold War and nuclear weapons gave these new twists, but they did not alter the fundamental tensions. This was partly because the conflicts of the international blocs were still mobilised as national issues, especially in the major states. It was also because the hot wars, like Algeria, Vietnam and the Falklands, were still national conflicts. So when the Gulf War came along, the traditional representative institutions of Western civil societies mobilised very much as they had in previous conflicts – pro- or anti-war, pro-nation or internationalist and imperialist or anti-imperialist. Across the churches and the left parties, especially, majorities – as in virtually all previous wars – supported the war against Iraq; minorities opposed it, or, more commonly, expressed agonised doubts. (Leaders of these institutions gave deliberately nuanced support – signalling participation in the 'national' consensus while placating the reservations of their members. They generally placed the management of their institutions' internal tensions ahead of a clear, principled attitude to the conflict.[11])

Because of the structures of these debates, few picked up on the novelty of the Gulf War – that whatever the proportionality of the means (and in *some* respects the US-led coalition did attempt to limit civilian harm), this was not a national war but an international war globally legitimated by the United Nations. Because of these structures, too, few were prepared for the radical transition from interstate war to civil war at the end of February 1991. As George Bush declared his ceasefire, people in southern Iraq took up the fight against Saddam. But the anti-war section of Western civil society was geared to opposing Bush, not to supporting the Shi'ites. The critics of war had tracked the Western states' campaign, with the sole objective of limiting it (to its stated, statist aim of liberating Kuwait) and halting the war. They were not geared to supporting new protagonists or stopping Saddam's new slaughter. The critical bishops and left politicians fell silent. The anti-war columnists failed to pick up the issues (and only a few of the pro-war liberals in the press were consistent enough to see that they had to demand Western support for the people the West had incited to fight). Even when the Kurdish refugees became a massive media *cause célèbre*, the anti-war section of the traditional representative institutions had little to offer. It simply did not fit their traditional paradigms.

New representative institutions of global civil society

The Kurdish crisis – when the 'new world order' turned inside out and the great 'triumph' of the Gulf was revealed in all its contradictions – was the defining moment of the new era. It set many of the terms which were to dominate in Bosnia, Somalia and Rwanda: above all, the primacy for the UN and the West of protection of civilians from local state and quasi-state violence and genocide. The 'international community' – the global state in caring guise – and 'humanitarian intervention' – that new but questionable paradigm of International Relations discourse – came into their own in Kurdistan. This was the moment when the old Westphalian principles of sovereignty and non-intervention were most strikingly breached: the critical precedent of the new era.

Western civil society was manifestly central to this transition. Bush, Major and Mitterand did not proclaim a 'safe haven' in Kurdistan because they wanted to. They had set their faces very solidly against any further intervention in Iraq. American troops had listened, a mere thirty miles away, to the sound of the Republican Guard destroying the opposition in Basra. Even after a month of revolt and repression, Major had made his most Majoresque pronouncement – 'I do not recall asking the Kurds to mount this particular insurrection' – as he turned his back yet again on the Kurds. Bush went fishing, golfing, anything to show that normality had returned, and with it his victorious troops. That this normality included the slaughter of those whom he had incited to rebel was the last thing he wanted to recognise.

The eventual Anglo-American-French intervention to save the Kurds, with its great policy 'U-turn', was a triumph of civil society. But not, as we have seen, of the traditional representative institutions of Western civil society. So was this the moment of the new 'global civil society', of which several writers have given general accounts? The archetypal institutions of the emergent global civil society, we saw above, are transnational social movements. There were two signs of such movements in the Iraqi wars of 1991. One, neglected probably because it hardly fits the globalist agenda, was the pan-Muslim support for Saddam Hussein, not only throughout the Arab world but also among the Arab population of France and even the Pakistani, Bangladeshi and other

Muslim populations in Britain. The other, perhaps more obvious to Western social science, was the anti-war movement which arose in most Western countries during the five months before the Gulf War, but declined once war had broken out.

The striking thing about both these transnational social movements is that they were largely, like the responses of traditional representative institutions in Western societies, reflex responses to international state intervention. Many Muslims assumed that because Saddam was taking on the West, he represented them in their grievances against local states and global power. My study of British Muslims, who emerged as a distinct political force partly because of the war, showed that their responses were partly generalised reactions to the West, partly mobilisation of local grievances.[12] The one thing that they did not do in any serious way was to respond to the fight of the opponents, or plight of the victims, of Saddam Hussein among the (Muslim) people of Iraq.

Similarly with the Western anti-war movements: they too were stuck with old, general ideas that hardly fitted the new situation and its particularities. Like the left in the traditional representative institutions, they responded to the Gulf War largely in terms of 'old' anti-war politics, based on pacifism and anti-imperialism. Although the more pacifist wing recognised the legitimacy of an international response to aggression, this recognition was uneasy, because of its rejection of the means of this response (once sanctions gave way to war). On the other hand, the Marxist and anti-imperialist wings rejected 'international' intervention in principle, seeking refuge in such platitudes as the call for 'an Arab solution' (the impossibility of which was recognised both in Arab states' support for Western intervention and, even more pertinently, in the Iraqi rebels' pleas for Western support). When the revolts in Iraq posed the dilemma of new Western intervention to support the rebels-turning-victims, both wings of the anti-war movement were debilitated by their ideological positions.[13] No more than the pan-Muslims were they capable of generating a response to the Kurds which might have represented 'global-civil-society-in-action'.

Such a response did not come, then, from social movements, the supposedly archetypal institutions of global civil society. In fact, it came more from humanitarian agencies and campaigns. Such institutions are often confused with social movements: but while social movements are characterised by relatively spontaneous mass mobilisation or participation, humanitarian agencies/campaigns are based in contrast on more continuous formal organisation and relatively passive mass support. Because humanitarian agencies and campaigns are more formal organisations, with clearly articulated goals and structures designed to achieve

them, they are more capable of articulating consistent globalist policies than are social movements. In the Iraqi wars, some humanitarian
organisations initially adopted a distancing response to protect their
own agendas (e.g. aid to Africa) but many quickly changed tack as the
Kurdish crisis developed. These institutions had a dual function: to
mobilise financial and political support for the Kurds within Western
states, and to provide practical support for the refugees on the ground
on the Iraqi borders. Both were carried out with great effect, but equally
both depended on a different sort of institution for their mobilising
power.

Television from propaganda to critical representation

The central agencies of global civil society in the Kurdish crisis, the
institutions which forced the changes in state policies which constituted
'humanitarian intervention', were, in fact, television news programmes.
Television – not newspapers, not social movements, certainly not the
traditional representative institutions – took up the plight of the Kurds
and in an unprecedented campaign successfully forced governments'
hands. I looked at British television news – BBC and ITN – during
March–April 1991, the two months after the Gulf War. It is clear that
the two channels not only showed massive amounts of graphic film of
the terrible circumstances in which the Kurds existed on the border
with Turkey. They overlaid this film with an unremitting commentary
pinning responsibility simply and directly on Western leaders, especially Bush and Major. Eventually, Major buckled and repositioned
himself as the saviour of the Kurds (if not of their unwanted insurrection). After this switch, Bush had eventually to fall in line and commit
American troops and planes to protect Kurds in northern Iraq.[14]

Television news' role in the Kurdish crisis is all the more surprising,
at first sight, since it contrasted so clearly with the managed medium
which they had represented during the Gulf War. Nevertheless, there is
an umbilical connection between the two roles. It was precisely because
the West had intervened in Iraq, and incited its people to revolt, that
television could expose the consequences of revolt and call for action to
save the victims of Saddam's repression. And who better to do this than
the media and journalists who had most fully mobilised support for the
original intervention? (Journalists' unease about their propaganda role
in the Gulf may also have contributed to their critical intervention in
the Kurdish crisis.)

Nevertheless, television's role as a representative of threatened sections of society in zones of crisis has definite limitations. First, television

can only fully represent people with film. The Shi'ite rebellion, earlier, probably larger and even more brutally repressed than the Kurds', remained for the most part a global non-event for the simple reason that Western television cameras and portable satellite dishes never made it to the centres of their revolt. Many global voices are never heard because of these simple lacks. Secondly, television represents people better as victims than as combatants or protagonists. The Kurds only became a *cause célèbre* after their insurrection failed and they became pure victims. Their political goals and tactics were lost in their simple human fate.

Thirdly, and relatedly, television mainly represents people indirectly. The Kurds rarely spoke for themselves: the campaign was built up, instead, by the authoritative voices of Western television reporters. Global voices, as such, are rarely heard. Finally, television generally depends on state policies to give it its cues. The Kurds were a uniquely successful television cause precisely because governments gave television its cue, by inciting the Iraqi people to revolt. In other cases, Western governments do not carry such direct responsibility for people's plight and television does not hold them responsible to the same extent. Only rarely does television expose a truly awful catastrophe, like the genocide in Rwanda, without such leads from Western governments. And then it cannot force their hands in the same way.

Conclusions – theoretical and political

This chapter has explored some of the contours of the new global politics of the era after the Cold War. Whereas international theorists have seen world politics as structured by relations between states, global theory of the kind argued for here makes three fundamental conceptual moves. First, global theory sees social relations, rather than interstate relations, as the largest defining context of world politics. World politics is constituted by an increasingly global society, and by its economic and cultural dynamics, and not just by states. Secondly, global theory sees states differently because of this. Starting from global society rather than from interstate relations, it is apparent that state institutions are also being globalised. Globalisation is not something which 'happens to' nation-states, reducing their economic and social leverage, but a set of processes in which changes of state power are very much constitutive as well as constituted. Global state structures are being formed, which are both cause and effect of global societal developments. The concept of global civil society needs to be understood in relation to the emergent, contradictory global state, not merely in relation to nation-states.[15] Thirdly, crises in world politics need to be seen

not primarily as interstate crises (in which some other 'actors' sometimes get involved) but as global crises, which are structured by the
interactions of state and society, and constituted by media and other
institutions in civil society as well as by states.

These fundamental movements of theoretical perspective have normative presuppositions and implications. Starting from the state system
prioritises the voices of state leaders, leaving the voices of individuals
and social groups secondary and marginal. Starting from global society
implies that the voices of the members of that society are important in
themselves. Global theory leads us to look, as this chapter has done, at
institutions of state and civil society in terms of how far they enable
people's voices to be represented. The normative implication is that we
seek to develop existing or new institutions to secure better representation. This entails a different vision of civil society – and the state – in
the global community of the twenty-first century.

Notes

1 Martin Shaw, *Civil Society and Media in Global Crises* (London: Pinter,
   1996).
2 This argument is based on Martin Shaw, *Global Society and International
   Relations* (Cambridge: Polity Press, 1994), ch. 1.
3 This relationship between 'a' state and 'a' society is theoretically difficult.
   I attempt to deal with it in other ongoing work.
4 I first developed the concept of the 'global state' in Shaw, *The Global State
   and the Politics of Intervention* (London: LSE Centre for the Study of Global
   Governance, 1994). I discuss the conceptual and historical issues more fully
   in my book, *The Unfinished Global Revolution* (Cambridge University Press,
   forthcoming).
5 See, for example, Michael Walzer (ed.), *Towards a Global Civil Society*
   (London: Berghahn, 1995); Richard Falk, *On Humane Governance: Toward
   a New Global Politics* (Cambridge: Polity Press, 1995).
6 Antonio Gramsci, *Selections from the Prison Notebooks* (London: Lawrence &
   Wishart, 1971); John Keane (ed.), *Civil Society* (London: Verso, 1988).
7 Some recent writers in International Relations use a more classical concept
   of civil society: for example, Justin Rosenberg, *The Empire of Civil Society*
   (London: Verso, 1994), which fails, however, to define 'civil society', and
   Mervyn Frost, *Ethics in International Relations: A Constitutive Theory* (Cambridge University Press, 1996). In neither case, however, does this concept
   lead to a substantive analysis of civil society such as that proposed here.
8 See Martin Shaw, 'Civil society and global politics: beyond a social movements approach', *Millennium* 23(1994): 647–68.
9 This is an extremely important agenda for change. For the most recent and
   fullest account of his position, see David Held, *Democracy and the Global
   Order* (Cambridge: Polity Press, 1995). In the world of the late twentieth

century, however, the formal institutional side of this debate still has little purchase outside elites. The development of cosmopolitan democracy in practice depends on the growth of global civil society – which may be the context in which the formal democratic debate must first be advanced.

10 I owe this idea to Michael Mann's study of nineteenth-century states in Mann, *The Sources of Social Power*, vol. II (Cambridge University Press, 1993).

11 I demonstrate this in the cases of the British churches and Labour Party in Shaw, *Civil Society and Media in Global Crises*, pp. 32–45.

12 *Ibid.*, pp. 65–9.

13 I demonstrate this in the case of the British anti-Gulf War movement in *ibid.*, pp. 60–3.

14 For the detailed analysis to support this discussion, see *ibid.*, pp. 79–95.

15 This argument about the globalisation of state power distinguishes my understanding of global politics from the looser discourse of 'global governance', advanced for example by Falk, *On Humane Governance*. See my review of the latter in *Millennium* 25 (1996): 183–4.

9 Refugees: a global human rights and security crisis

Gil Loescher

Genocide, politicide and internal conflicts generated by state disintegration, ethnic tensions and the crisis of development are triggering
new mass movements of people across the globe. In 1980 there were
about 6 million refugees and 2 million internally displaced persons
worldwide. By the end of 1995, the number of externally displaced had
increased to 13.2 million, and the number of internally displaced had
reached an estimated 30 million.

These figures do not tell the whole story, however, as many victims
of forced displacement do not feature in these statistics. These include
migrants who have been expelled *en masse* from their countries of residence and people who have been uprooted by development projects,
among other causes. While it is difficult to provide accurate figures,
there are probably more than 50 million people around the world who
might be legitimately described as 'displaced'. This figure means that
one out of every 130 people on earth has been forced into flight.

No continent is now immune from the problem of mass displacement. Regarded for many years as a Third World phenomenon, significant refugee movements have taken place in recent years in the Balkans
and throughout the former Soviet Union. At the end of 1995, refugee
populations in excess of 10,000 could be found in over seventy different countries around the world.[1]

The global refugee crisis has confronted the international community
with a range of urgent political challenges and ethical dilemmas for
which there are no easy answers. This chapter attempts to address the
following questions: what defines a refugee and what factors account
for the recent large and sudden movements of displaced people? What
international refugee mechanisms exist and how can intergovernmental
agencies, governments and non-governmental organisations respond more
effectively to refugee crises? What approaches and strategies are being
formed to address the root causes of refugee flows before they start and
to reduce or contain population movements which have already begun?

How effective are preventive measures and do they endanger the practice of asylum?

An appropriate refugee definition

At a time when the numbers of refugees, and particularly internally displaced, are growing rapidly and likely to grow still further, the question of precisely who is, and who is not, a refugee, is one of considerable controversy. International concern for refugees is centred around the concept of the protection of human rights. The principal international definition at present is the United Nations concept that was formulated in the immediate post-World War II period, largely in response to European refugee flows and in the context of the Cold War. According to the 1951 Convention Relating to the Status of Refugees, a refugee is:

any person who, owing to a well-founded fear of being persecuted for reasons of race, religion, nationality, membership of a particular social group or political opinion, is outside the country of his nationality and is unable or owing to such fear, is unwilling to avail himself of the protection of that country . . .[2]

Persecution often occurs in situations where there is conflict over political and economic power. Research indicates that these disputes are at their most intense during periods of rapid political change, typically 'in the midst of revolutionary upheaval, immediately following a regime transition or at the emergence of a new state'.[3]

According to international legal norms, a refugee is a person who has fled across the physical borders of his homeland to seek refuge in another place and who, upon being granted refugee status, receives certain rights not available to other international migrants, including the right of resettlement and legal protection from deportation or forcible return to his country of origin (the so-called *non-refoulement* protection). People requesting refugee status and seeking permanent settlement in a country of first asylum to which they have already fled are referred to as asylum-seekers. The international organisation mandated to oversee the implementation of the 1951 Convention and offer protection to the world's refugees is the Office of the United Nations High Commissioner for Refugees (UNHCR).

Apart from the narrow internationally agreed-upon definition, the term 'refugee' has been widened in practice to cover a variety of people in diverse situations who need assistance and protection. The most notable of these expansions is found in the Convention on Refugee Problems in Africa, a regional instrument adopted by the Organisation of African Unity in 1969, which includes people fleeing 'external aggression, internal civil strife, or events seriously disturbing public order' in African countries.[4] The Cartagena Declaration of 1984 covering Central American refugees also goes further than the 1951 UN Convention by including 'persons who have fled their country because their lives, safety or freedom have been threatened by generalized violence, foreign aggression, internal conflicts, massive violation of human rights or other circumstances which have seriously disturbed public order'.[5]

These regional legal norms are in fact much more inclusive and in keeping with the actual causes of flight in Africa and Central America and throughout the rest of the Third World than are those of the UN. They respond to the reality that many refugees were in fact fleeing generalised violence and severe human rights violations in which it was often impossible for asylum-seekers to generate documented evidence of individual persecution required by the 1951 Refugee Convention. Indeed, there is an emerging consensus among analysts of the causes of refugee movements that the majority of the world's refugees are fleeing from generalised political violence.[6] While causes of specific refugee movements may differ in terms of how they affect the direction, duration and size of population displacements, some political analysts argue that most contemporary mass exoduses occur when political violence is of a generalised nature rather than a direct individual threat. Two major forms of generalised violence lead to large-scale refugee migration: internal wars and severe repression, particularly genocide and politicide.[7]

Recognising these realities, the UNHCR has (in practice) interpreted its mandate over the past several decades to include those who have been forcibly displaced from their countries because of internal ethnic or religious upheavals or armed conflicts. However, in recent years there has been great resistance in the West to this pragmatic expansion of the refugee definition and of the UNHCR's mandate. In most industrialised nations the 1951 definition, with its focus on individuals and on persecution, is used for resettlement and asylum purposes, although groups of people at risk of death or grave harm from violence if returned home are often given temporary protection.

In addition to the variety of legal definitions of refugees, there are several other categories of uprooted people. For example, some 3.3 million Palestinians are registered with the UN Relief and Works Agency for Palestine Refugees in the Near East whose mandate is limited to Syria, Lebanon, Jordan and the Israeli-occupied territories. There are also large numbers of internally displaced people, namely people who are uprooted within their own countries because of armed conflict and ethnic strife, or because of forcible relocation by their governments or opposition movements, and who do not or cannot seek refuge across borders. Many displaced people are either victims of the same civil wars which formerly produced refugees out of Afghanistan, Angola, Cambodia or Guatemala, or are victims of ethnic strife which the cloak of statehood has failed to suppress or curtail, for example, in Liberia, Ethiopia, Somalia, Sudan or throughout the Balkans or the former Soviet Union. Indeed, because of their greater numbers and the seemingly intractable problems involved in intervening in the domestic affairs of a state in order to gain access to victims of conflict, internally displaced people have become and are likely to remain a central part of the global refugee crisis. The internally displaced pose particularly difficult problems. Because internally displaced persons remain within their own country and do not cross international boundaries, they cannot be protected as refugees. Unlike for refugees, no international organization has a mandate to protect and assist the internally displaced, and there are serious gaps in international law regarding their protection and assistance.

Another group in need of assistance are those who have been refugees who have repatriated to their countries of origin. Sometimes returnees go home under the auspices of UNHCR, from which they receive temporary assistance, but usually such people go back without international sponsorship because they do not want to be publicly known as former refugees. However, there are many constraints on providing protection and assistance to returnees, especially when the conditions in the countries of origin which generated the exodus continue to exist.

Finally, there are those who leave their countries because of economic factors and who are thus considered to be economic migrants. These people do not qualify for UNHCR protection or assistance. However, in many developing countries which have few resources and weak government structures, economic hardships are generally exacerbated by political violence. In many poor countries, economic hardship is the proximate cause of flight, but the root causes are political. Therefore, it has become increasingly difficult to make hard and fast distinctions between refugees and economic migrants.

The expansion of forcibly displaced persons in need of assistance today raises questions about the applicability of conventional concepts to current realities. For the purposes of this chapter, the term refugees refers to people who have been forcibly uprooted because of persecution or violence, regardless of whether they have left their country of origin or whether they are recognised as refugees by the governments of their host countries or by the UNHCR.

International refugee mechanisms

Although intergovernmental co-operation on refugee problems has existed for about three-quarters of a century, states have been traditionally ambivalent about international co-operation over refugee issues. On the one hand, states have a fundamental, self-serving interest in quickly resolving refugee crises. Refugee movements create domestic instability, generate interstate tension and threaten international security. Thus, states created an international refugee regime prompted not by purely altruistic motives, but by a desire to promote regional and international stability and to support functions which serve the interests of governments – namely, burden-sharing and co-ordinating policies regarding the treatment of refugees.

On the other hand, state independence is also an issue. States often are unwilling to yield authority to international refugee agencies and institutions and seek to limit their responsibilities to the forcibly displaced. Consequently, governments have imposed considerable financial and political limitations on the activities of international refugee organisations. For example, the first intergovernmental activities on behalf of refugees after World War I and during the interwar period were limited to specific groups of European refugees. The series of international organisations created to deal with situations of forced migration possessed limited mandates of short duration. Similarly, after World War II and in the early Cold War period, governments sought once again to limit the contemporary refugee regime's responsibilities in the context of the emerging global refugee problem. The Western powers were unwilling to commit themselves to indefinite financial costs and large resettlement programmes. Thus, the UNHCR was created as a temporary, small international agency that would pose no threat to state interests or national sovereignty, that imposed no financial obligations on states, and provided no open-ended commitment to refugees.

Nonetheless, despite state reservations, significant intergovernmental collaboration on the refugee issue has in fact occurred on a regular basis. Most significantly, since 1950, the international community has developed a complex network of institutions, norms and agreements specifically designed to respond to refugee problems. This international refugee regime is essentially led and co-ordinated by the UNHCR which has developed response strategies that permit some refugees to remain in their countries of first asylum, enable others to be resettled in third countries, and arrange for still others to be repatriated to their countries of origin.

Traditional approaches to refugee problems

Throughout the Cold War, the refugee regime approached the refugee problem in a manner which can be characterised as reactive, exile-oriented and refugee-centric.[8] The agency primarily worked with people after they had fled across borders to neighbouring countries where they required protection and assistance. UNHCR staff concentrated their activities on assisting refugees in camps and negotiating with host and donor governments for support. The agency focused exclusively on the consequences of refugee flows rather than on the causes and paid little or no attention to preventing or averting refugee movements. It placed primary responsibility for solving refugee problems on states that received refugees rather than on states that caused refugees to flee. Hence, the UNHCR emphasised local settlement and third country resettlement over repatriation.

The UNHCR also concentrated almost exclusively on people who were deemed to fall within the 1951 UN Refugee Convention definition or those in less developed countries who were forced into exile because of war or related causes. The international refugee regime expended little time or resources on internally displaced persons, returnees, or asylum-seekers whose claims for refugee status had been rejected. This approach was replicated at the UN level. Refugees were essentially a problem to be solved by the UNHCR, while other institutions in the UN system separately addressed closely related international problems such as underdevelopment, environmental degradation, human rights abuses and international peace and security.

Since the end of the Cold War, the traditionally favoured solutions of third country and local resettlement are no longer viewed by states as adequate. Since resettling the Indochinese refugees in the late 1970s and early 1980s, Western countries have largely refused to accept permanent resettlers. Overseas resettlement is generally viewed as too costly in terms of expenses and cultural adjustment on the part of host societies and refugees alike. Even traditional first asylum countries in Africa and Asia are increasingly reluctant to give asylum to people from neighbouring countries, much less to accept them as permanent citizens. In many less developed countries, refugees are perceived as a threat to the physical environment or security of the host state, especially when they include elements who are determined to use the asylum country as a base for political and military activities. In late 1996, for example, hundreds of thousands of Hutu refugees in Zaire and Tanzania were returned to their home countries in a repatriation which Amnesty International characterised as neither voluntary nor safe. Repatriation is thus becoming the most favoured solution of states, but the persistence of violence and economic devastation in countries of return frequently makes voluntary return under safe conditions difficult if not impossible.

In future years, the problem of forced displacement is likely to become larger, more complex and geographically more widespread. The largest growth of forced migrants will be internally displaced persons, who will be uprooted because of persecution or violence, but who will be compelled to remain in their own countries. Increasing attention will have to be given to the question of how to provide in-country protection and assistance to internally displaced populations, often in the context of intrastate conflicts.

A shift in focus to the prevention of refugee movements

There is growing recognition that as long as the global refugee crisis is driven by severe human rights violations and intrastate conflicts in the Third World and the former Eastern bloc countries the prospects for a resolution depend largely on the reduction of these conflicts. While these conflicts remain unresolved, not only does the immediate impetus for flight continue but the displaced are unable to return to their homelands. Since recent research[9] indicates that it is the incidence of increasing levels of violence in conflicts and the proliferation of arms that are generating more refugees and internally displaced today, international action should aim to reduce arms and to make aid and investment contingent on the reduction of arms and defence expenditures. It is also evident that if the international community seeks to curb refugee migration, its efforts should be directed towards preventing initial exodus, since it becomes very difficult to contain refugee migration once the outflow has begun and once family and friends have become established in exile countries. Thus, governments and international organisations must take action to try to influence countries whose internal conditions might put people to flight and to enable those who have already fled to return home.

In recent years, the international community has been placing a greater emphasis on addressing the underlying causes of the refugee problem in the countries of origin. The fundamental principle of this new orientation is that refugee movements can be averted or ameliorated if action is taken to reduce or remove the threats which force people to flee their own country and seek asylum elsewhere. Thus, states are attempting to develop a proactive policy which aims to address the root causes of refugee flows. Such a policy includes early warning, preventive diplomacy and ensuring respect for human rights. In an effort to halt conflicts and reduce refugee flows in the last few years, the international community has increasingly employed interventions in the form of aid, trade and investment conditionality, sanctions, coercive diplomacy and armed intervention.

Many of the recent attempts at prevention and intervention have proven to be problematic because governments remain reluctant to divert resources from conflict management to conflict prevention. Moreover, recent events in Bosnia, Rwanda, Zaire and elsewhere cast doubt on any assumption that human rights abuses and widespread loss of life, in and of themselves, now galvanise the international community to significantly more rapid and more effective preventive action than in the past.

Under certain conditions governments may permit humanitarian assistance by international agencies, but most governments and opposition movements engaged in persecution or ethnic cleansing are usually unwilling to permit outsiders to mediate their internal disputes or to examine their human rights record. The UN was created to deal with interstate disputes, not intrastate conflicts. While the international community has increasingly intervened to curb domestic disorder since the end of the Cold War, these intrusions have been accepted only reluctantly by many UN member states. As long as the international community is hindered from working within countries over the objections of governments, its capacity to prevent conditions from arising that lead people to become refugees will be limited.

The establishment of 'safe areas' or 'security zones' in conflict areas demonstrates better than anything else the restrictions under which international agencies operate. In Bosnia, for example, so-called safe areas were established without the consent of Bosnian Serbs, and used as military bases by the Bosnian government forces. These actions not only made a mockery of the humanitarian purpose of safe areas but actually provoked attacks on the residents and relief personnel they were intended to protect. In the wake of the massacres which followed the collapse of Srebrenica in July 1995, the credibility of these new mechanisms has been considerably undermined. In Zaire, the international community very late and only reluctantly intervened to rescue starving refugees who had barely survived massacres and intimidation at the hands of Kabila's forces.

UNHCR's new approaches and strategies

As the UN has undertaken new forms of collective and preventive action, the UNHCR has had to adapt by developing its own strategies and approaches intended to address the root causes of refugee flows before they start and to reduce or contain population movements which have already begun.[10] A preventive approach of averting crises is less costly in terms of financial outlays and human suffering than one of launching emergency relief operations once mass population displacements have taken place. For example, the international community spent some $2 billion in emergency relief aid in the first few weeks of the Rwandan refugee crisis in mid-1994. Preventive action to avert the crisis would have been much cheaper and would have saved many more lives.

UNHCR's shift to a preventive strategy, however, cannot be accomplished easily or quickly. Working in countries of origin differs substantially from working in countries of asylum. Unlike in countries of asylum, UNHCR must work with governments as well as opposition movements and guerrilla factions, often in the context of collapsing states and where population displacements are among the central objectives of war. UNHCR is ill equipped to respond to the needs of internally displaced people and returnees who live amid conditions of inter-communal violence and ongoing conflict. UNHCR staff are now engaged alongside UN peace-keeping forces in anarchic and unstable countries which lack viable local and national structures. Their activities include protecting civilians against reprisals and forced displacement, relocating and evacuating civilians from conflict areas and assisting besieged populations, such as that in Sarajevo, who choose not to move from their homes. Frequently, however, UNHCR lacks any firm institutional and legal basis for this work. Furthermore, most staff are neither recruited nor trained to work in the cross-fire of internal conflicts where soldiers and guerrillas view the internally displaced and returnees as the enemy and UN assistance as favouring one side to the disadvantage of the other. In situations like Bosnia, the Caucasus or Tajikistan, UNHCR uses humanitarian and legal interventions similar to those used by the International Committee of the Red Cross (ICRC), but its staff lacks the special training, skills and experience of ICRC staff members.

A major obstacle to taking a more active role in refugee protection in countries of origin derives from the international refugee regime itself. The UNHCR was designed to appear to be non-political and strictly humanitarian, a strategy employed to receive permission to work in host countries and to secure funding from donor governments. UNHCR, as it is presently structured, is not mandated to intervene politically against governments or opposition groups, even where there is clear evidence of human rights violations. In addition, UNHCR staff are often unfamiliar with human rights and humanitarian law and are uncertain of how governments and opposition groups will react to their interventions using these protection norms.

In many internal wars, relief assistance operations are also vulnerable to political manipulation by the warring parties who perceive humanitarian assistance as one of several weapons of warfare. For example, food assistance is very often used as political leverage. Adversaries sometimes divert assistance from proper recipients for military or political goals, and deny assistance to certain populations and geographical areas by blocking access to international agencies.

Long-standing institutional constraints

In addition to political factors, several long-standing institutional constraints inhibit UNHCR preventive action. In particular, the absence of an autonomous resource base and the limited mandates and competencies of international humanitarian agencies continue to limit the international community in its response to most post-Cold War refugee crises just as they have done for the past fifty years.

Inadequacy of existing resource base

The 1990s have presented UNHCR with several new emergencies and its overall expenditures have therefore grown significantly. The sum required for UNHCR operations has risen from around $550 million in 1990 to about $1.3 billion in 1996.

In addition to the huge costs incurred in responding to refugee crises, internal displacements and repatriations, humanitarian missions today are likely to be protracted affairs with no clear outcome. During the conflict in the former Yugoslavia, for example, UNHCR committed approximately one-quarter of its staff and one-third of its total resources worldwide to providing assistance and protection to nearly four million people.[11] UNHCR extended assistance to all the victims of former Yugoslavia's wars regardless of their physical location or legal standing. 'War-affected populations', that is people who had not been uprooted but needed humanitarian assistance and protection, comprised a substantial proportion of UNHCR's beneficiary population during the height of that conflict. Worldwide, refugees now constitute only 50 per cent of UNHCR's beneficiaries.

One of UNHCR's most significant weaknesses is its dependence on *voluntary* contributions to carry out existing and new programmes. Annual budget projections are based on existing and anticipated refugee case loads, while *ad hoc* appeals are issued to meet sudden emergencies. The flow of assistance from donor governments is neither reliable nor always in the most appropriate form. In addition, funding is frequently provided late and is often earmarked for particular uses with political or geostrategic overtones.

In the past, donor governments have often made funding contingent upon external political factors. Today, however, these governments are less influenced politically by refugee situations, which they view as local or regional problems of little if any direct foreign policy or security value. Without compelling strategic and ideological motivations, funding for refugee operations is being cut back in favour of the domestic priorities of the industrialised states. Indeed, the increasing number of humanitarian emergencies during the past five years has coincided with falling foreign aid budgets in many of the important donor states, particularly the United States and Britain. Too little funding has been invested in post-conflict rebuilding. The major powers are reluctant to provide funds for rebuilding war-torn societies when internal conflicts in aid-recipient countries continue unabated. Thus, despite the clear links among situations involving displacement and regional security, such as in the Caucasus, Central Asia, and the Great Lakes region of Africa, there is weak donor interest in funding a comprehensive strategy for dealing with refugees and internally displaced people. In 1992, for example, the UN was unable to raise $100 million for the reconstruction of Afghanistan from states that during the previous decade had spent over $10 billion on its destruction. In the Great Lakes, the international community has remained largely indifferent to the economic plight of the states in that region. Western donor interest in reconstructing Rwandan society is minimal and it is likely that the international community will remain indifferent to the desperate situation in Zaire after the collapse of Mobutu, despite the fact that this is a country the size of Europe and rich in diamonds, oil and other mineral resources.

Inadequacy of existing mandates and international humanitarian law

While there is a clear mandate for the protection of refugees and the provision of humanitarian assistance to them, existing political, diplomatic, economic and legal mechanisms are not sufficiently developed to cope with the increasingly complex and volatile population movements of the post-Cold War period. In particular, there are no specific international organisations mandated to protect and assist the internally displaced.[12] At the same time, the political issues involved, particularly state sovereignty and non-intervention in domestic affairs, make the issue of the internally displaced one of the most challenging problems confronting the international community in the 1990s.

Furthermore, existing human rights and humanitarian laws offer internally displaced persons inadequate protection. They also do not adequately cover forcible displacements and relocations, humanitarian assistance and access, the right to food, and the protection of relief workers.[13] In particular, situations of public emergency and internal violence fall outside the scope of the Geneva Convention of 1949 and Additional Protocol II of 1977. As a result, many human rights provisions are suspended when an emergency threatens the security of a state. It is precisely in these conditions that internal displacement often occurs.

The way forward: the need for new alliances and new actors

Hindered by both its dependence on voluntary contributions to carry out its programmes and its need to obtain the approval of host governments before intervening, UNHCR cannot resolve the problems of refugees, returnees and internally displaced people single-handedly. There is also increasing recognition that solutions to forced migration cannot proceed solely within the mandate of international humanitarian organisations and cannot be separated from other areas of international concern such as human rights, economic development, international security and migration.[14] Because refugee problems are multidimensional in nature, UNHCR needs to build bridges between itself and organisations dealing with issues such as human rights, sustainable development and peace-keeping and peace-making. This new approach to refugee problems involves an increase in the range of actors in the search for solutions, an increase in the range of issues the refugee regime seeks to address, and an increase in the range of people it is designed to benefit.

Human rights and the refugee regime

Human rights violations and refugee flows form a seamless web. As recent events in Albania, Bosnia, Haiti, Rwanda and elsewhere demonstrate, today's human rights abuses are tomorrow's refugee problems. Resolving refugee problems depends on a range of human rights activities, including establishing civil societies and pluralistic political systems, reinforcing legal and government structures, and empowering local grass-roots organisations. However, neither ensuring good governance nor respect for human rights falls within UNHCR's domain. The existing UN human rights machinery needs to be strengthened and applied more effectively to deal with refugees, returnees and the internally displaced.[15]

Despite the close connection between the refugee problem and the protection of human rights, the international community has until recently maintained a sharp distinction between the two issues. This division was a consequence of the reactive and exile-oriented approach to the problem of refugees which characterised the international refugee regime's activities during most of the Cold War.[16] UNHCR had almost no effect on human rights conditions in countries of origin, mainly because it dealt with refugees only after they had fled from a country where they were persecuted and sought asylum in another state. The causes of refugee flows were considered to be a separate concern, falling outside the organisation's humanitarian and non-political mandate.

Even in countries of asylum, the High Commissioner's activities on behalf of refugees have generally been limited to providing material assistance, citing violations of international law and uttering public condemnation for those violations. Although the Office has no power to force countries to provide refugees with even minimal humanitarian treatment, the High Commissioner's major weapon is diplomatic pressure to urge states to abide by international refugee law.

International refugee law provides a set of standards against which the actions of states can be measured and it places some pressure, especially on nations which have acceded to these international instruments, to meet the obligations they impose.[17] UNHCR's strategy is to measure state actions against these standards. The reality, however, is that the obligations international refugee law imposes lend themselves to a variety of interpretations. Therefore, considerable scope exists for governments to perceive their obligations in ways that suit their own national interests.

No supranational authority exists to enforce the rules of the international refugee regime. The system of international refugee protection differs from the UN human rights mechanisms.[18] There is no formal mechanism in international refugee law to receive individual or interstate petitions or complaints. States which are parties to the 1951 Refugee Convention have not given full effect to the requirement that they provide UNHCR with information and statistical data on the implementation of the Convention. There is no system of review of country practices through the examination of state party reports or other such information which can be used to formulate recommendations for government authorities. There are few if any safeguards built into the law itself to prevent abuse by states. It is not surprising, therefore, that many governments have in recent years circumvented several of the major provisions and have exploited areas left unregulated.

In the realm of asylum, states remain the final arbiters of refugees' fates. They retain the power to grant or to deny asylum. Furthermore, the international refugee instruments leave it up to governments to tailor refugee determination procedures to their administrative, judicial and constitutional provisions. States regard these procedures as part of their national sovereignty and have been unwilling to transfer this authority to UNHCR or any other intergovernmental body.

In recent years, this trend has been evident in the European Union where member states have greatly increased their co-operation on asylum matters. Meeting at a regional level, governments have drawn up a number of treaties and agreements regulating European refugee and asylum policies. Most of these intergovernmental discussions have been closed to outside observers, including the UNHCR, reflecting the close link between sovereignty and control of borders in Europe and the growing trend towards restrictionism in the region. In the United States, apart from the possibility of contacting government authorities to express its views, UNHCR has no role at all in the refugee determination process. For the past fifteen years, UNHCR pressure on the United States to make its policy towards asylum-seekers from Central America and the Caribbean accord with international standards has had little visible effect.

Traditionally, the UNHCR has been reluctant to become heavily involved in human rights monitoring in countries of asylum for fear of jeopardising the welfare of the refugees under its care. As noted earlier, in order to mount refugee relief operations, UNHCR must secure permission from countries of asylum to operate within their territories as well as raise money from donor governments to support these operations. As a result, the world's principal refugee protection agency is prevented from unduly criticising either host or donor governments' policies towards refugees. For these reasons, UNHCR took the position that it could not become active in monitoring the general human rights situation in countries where it had operations. UNHCR officials were therefore inclined to avoid raising delicate political questions when dealing with humanitarian issues for fear of overstepping their mandate or damaging relations with sensitive governments, most of whom would consider such intrusions to be interference in their internal affairs.

Refugees and the human rights regime

Until recently, the UN human rights machinery, likewise, has been reluctant to engage in human rights protection work for refugees. During the Cold War, the East–West conflict and the reluctance of authoritarian states to have their human rights monitored placed serious constraints on the Human Rights Commission and the UN Human

Rights Centre. Consequently, the UN human rights regime focused on developing international human rights norms and standards and promulgating a series of human rights covenants and treaties, but avoided developing serious enforcement measures. During the 1980s, the UN Human Rights Commission and the Human Rights Centre increased their range of interests and activities.[19] New mechanisms were created to monitor torture, disappearances, summary executions and imprisonment, and the Human Rights Commission became more open in reporting human rights situations in specific countries. Nevertheless, refugees and displaced people did not figure prominently in this expansion of activities.

Despite this long-standing neglect of refugee issues, the UN human rights regime has in recent years begun to demonstrate its potential capabilities to respond to both the causes and consequences of forced migration. Since 1992, the Commission has convened exceptional sessions to discuss urgent human rights situations in the former Yugoslavia and Rwanda, and since 1991 has regularly discussed the protection needs of internally displaced persons and the problems involving minorities.

At the same time, the UN Human Rights Centre, through its advisory services, has been associated with a number of UN peace-keeping or peace enforcement missions, providing significant technical assistance and co-operation to the UN human rights presence in the field, for example in Cambodia, El Salvador, Guatemala, Haiti, Somalia and Rwanda, under the leadership of the new High Commissioner for Human Rights. These actions underscore both the key potential role of the UN human rights machinery and the growing involvement of the Security Council in humanitarian matters, and the recognition that the promotion and protection of the human rights of refugees, returnees and the internally displaced are an integral part of UN peace-making.[20]

Despite growing recognition that the UN human rights machinery needs to become directly involved in refugee protection, many of the traditional constraints on the international human rights regime have not disappeared with the passing of the Cold War. At present, the UN human rights program is grossly understaffed and underfunded. At a time when billions of dollars have been poured into emergency relief programmes and peace-keeping operations, virtually no extra funds have been provided for the UN human rights regime, despite its potential to strengthen civil society, promote democratic and pluralistic institutions and procedures and, thereby, to prevent human rights abuses and mass displacements.

If the UN hopes to respond more effectively to the global problem of refugees, it must strengthen its capacity to monitor developments in human rights issues. A greater protection role in the field should be granted to UN human rights personnel. At present, the UN Human Rights Centre has country expertise but only very limited field presence. In the short term, the Human Rights Centre can strengthen its coverage in the field by the continued expansion of its advisory services and technical co-operation. In addition, by offering services such as training judges, strengthening electoral commissions, establishing ombudsmen, training prison staff and advising governments on constitutions and legislation regarding national minorities and human rights, the Centre is likely to be more successful in its activities and less threatening to governments than in more straightforward, field-oriented human rights monitoring.

In recent years, there has been much discussion about the creation of special human rights machinery for the internally displaced. At its 1995 session, the UN Human Rights Commission reappointed the Special Representative on internally displaced people to monitor developments and help to sustain a positive dialogue towards achieving solutions with governments. But the Special Representative must be given proper political support and funding to carry out his or her tasks effectively. A General Assembly resolution confirming the role and mandate of the Special Representative is now required to institutionalise this office further. A significant first step towards trying to deal with the problem would be to designate a permanent Representative for the internally displaced. This Representative could undertake fact-finding missions, intercede with governments, publish reports and bring violations to the attention of human rights bodies and the Security Council.

Recently, there have been attempts to create closer links between the UN refugee and human rights organs. UNHCR and the Centre for Human Rights have agreed to co-operate on information-sharing and training of personnel and are planning joint action with regard to the problem of stateless people. Despite these improvements, there is still an urgent need to develop a coherent and integrated approach to the defence of human rights, the protection of the forcibly displaced, and the resolution of the global refugee problem. Unfortunately, this continues to be an uphill struggle as long as states continue to guard their sovereignty and remain fundamentally opposed to international human rights monitoring and intervention.

NGOs and human rights protection of refugees

Responding to conflicts and humanitarian crises before they escalate has become a policy imperative not only for international organisations and governments but also for non-governmental organisations (NGOs). Ironically, as the number of humanitarian emergencies that combine civil war and severe human rights abuses has increased, public support in much of the industrialised world for foreign aid has diminished. For the United States and many other donor states, expensive and inconclusive operations in Somalia, Bosnia and Rwanda have chastened enthusiasm for the United Nations. The United States, in particular, perceives the cost of relying on the UN to manage conflict situations (UN peace-keepers cost \$3.7 billion at the height of UN peace-keeping missions in 1994) as too great. Yet, it is not possible to simply ignore these conflicts, because the international community inevitably responds with massive humanitarian operations to contain the subsequent refugee flows that threaten regional security. Responding to this situation, governments in many of the leading donor states have turned towards NGOs. The US government, in particular, is co-operating more closely with NGOs, not only in traditional areas of humanitarian relief and development, but also in the 'new diplomacy' of human rights, early warning and conflict prevention.[21] This emerging partnership between NGOs and donor governments rests on the common objective they have of sharing information for early warning of conflicts and refugee crises and of co-operating operationally to prevent or resolve conflicts.

NGOs have long been active in conflicts but their role in humanitarian emergencies in recent years has been changing. Traditionally, agencies like the International Committee of the Red Cross (ICRC) and other NGOs have worked with the permission of governments. But in recent decades, many NGOs have become impatient with these constraints and have begun to operate more independently. As a series of wars and natural disasters exposed millions of people to hunger and starvation during the 1980s, NGOs also assumed progressively greater responsibilities. Many of the UN agencies, hampered by their mandates and by the political interests of the Superpowers during the Cold War, were unable to offer an adequate response. Consequently, donor governments channelled more official funds through NGOs to high-profile emergency relief programmes.

NGOs now play important operational roles in internal conflicts.[22] In 1994, NGOs delivered an estimated 10–14 per cent of total international aid, more than the entire UN system (excluding the World Bank and the International Monetary Fund). Twenty per cent of US aid is now directed through NGOs, and the Clinton Administration intends to increase the NGO share to 50 per cent of the total US aid budget by the year 2000 and eventually to channel aid out of bilateral programmes to NGOs.

NGOs in general have made an enormous contribution in responding to the humanitarian needs of millions of refugees and displaced persons caught up in civil conflicts. Yet the effect of NGO relief programmes has not always been beneficial, and in some instances NGOs have worsened the situation by undermining the efforts of governments to become self-reliant and to provide their own services. Some NGOs have prolonged armed conflicts by providing aid that sustains a war economy. In some cases, NGOs have even remained silent about human rights abuses, fearing that such comments would jeopardise their relief work or their access to their client populations.

Post-Cold War humanitarianism has overwhelmingly emphasised the delivery of relief assistance over protecting human rights. Human rights have been perceived as the preserve of human rights NGOs, such as Amnesty International or Human Rights Watch. Apart from the ICRC, however, human rights monitoring and protection in armed conflict has been ignored by traditional human rights NGOs. Likewise, NGOs involved in relief activities during armed conflicts have regarded many human rights concerns as dangerously political and beyond their mandates. Consequently, NGO resources and programmes have consistently valued assistance over protection.

Recent events in Bosnia and the Great Lakes region indicate that the dynamics of internal armed conflict make emergency assistance and human rights protection inseparable. Human rights NGOs need to establish a continuous presence in regions experiencing conflict. 'Refugee Watch' organisations should be established within each refugee-producing region to monitor the protection needs of refugees, asylum-seekers and the internally displaced. Creating such organisations could provide a basis for consciousness-raising regarding humanitarian norms and democratic principles within regions, and it could enable local organisations to assume responsibility for monitoring, intervening, and managing humanitarian programmes without major external involvement or infringements of concepts of national sovereignty. Relief NGOs, likewise, have an essential protection role to play.[23] Their presence in most civil war situations makes them important sources of information on human rights abuses, refugee movements and emergency food needs. This information is crucial for human rights monitoring, early warning of conflicts and refugee crises and preventive diplomacy. Because NGOs also have a central role in securing humanitarian access to the civilian victims of conflicts and are often in close contact with both governments and opposition movements they can play a significant role in conflict resolution, mediation and reconciliation. NGOs' presence within communities at war and their ability to move among civilian populations and armed forces are characteristics not shared by UN agencies and donor governments. NGOs are well placed to engage in a new comprehensive form of humanitarian action, encompassing assistance and protection, mediation and conflict resolution.

Reintegration of refugees and rebuilding war-torn societies

Human rights monitoring and institution-building alone are not enough to create safe conditions in countries of origin for potential and returning refugees. The international community needs to take adequate account of the relationship between underdevelopment and displacement. Relief and development are now viewed as ends of a continuum rather than as separate and discrete activities.[24] Humanitarian aid activities should be conducted in ways that not only provide relief from life-threatening suffering but also reduce local vulnerability to recurring disasters, enhance indigenous resources and mechanisms, empower local leadership and institutions, reduce dependence on outside assistance and improve prospects for long-term development. Experts believe that relief and development activities that involve local participation generally prove more successful than those that do not.[25]

Despite a virtually universal consensus that peace agreements must be consolidated by investments which improve the security and economic well-being of the former adversaries and victims of conflict, too little funding has been invested in post-conflict rebuilding. International funding invariably declines soon after ceasefires are in place and elections are held. Moreover, the assistance given to countries emerging from war is conditioned in ways that emergency relief funds are not, with major impacts on humanitarian and social initiatives. In the future, greater resources must be devoted over longer periods of time to catalyse sustainable forms of development and to create conditions which will prevent refugee movements from re-occurring.[26]

Closer co-ordination between UN development and refugee agencies is also required in situations involving refugees, returnees and the internally displaced. Co-operation between UNHCR and the UN Development Program (UNDP) already takes place in quick impact projects (QIPs) that are aimed at assisting a variety of displaced groups in Central America, Mozambique and Cambodia. In addition, in recent years, in the Horn of Africa, the two agencies have established joint management structures to create preventive zones and cross-mandate programs to stabilise and prevent displacement in border areas.

Although there have been greater efforts at co-ordination between UNHCR and development and financial institutions like the UNDP and the World Bank, far more effective interagency planning, consultation and implementation are required. The roles and responsibilities of refugee and development agencies in such efforts continue to be determined on an *ad hoc*, situation-by-situation basis. In most countries, emergency relief aid is administratively and programmatically divorced from development concerns. Unlike refugee and relief-oriented organisations, development agencies usually work on the basis of long-term plans and programmes, making it difficult to respond to unexpected events such as refugee movements or repatriation programmes.[27] Thus, a 'development gap' exists between short-term humanitarian relief assistance and long-term development. UNHCR is not a development agency, and the task of the overall rehabilitation of these communities has to be carried out by UNDP, the World Bank, or by other agencies in the UN system which can more appropriately deal with reconstruction and development. This requires a full transfer of responsibility from UNHCR to the development agencies after the immediate emergency relief phase is over, but this is something which UNDP, in particular, consistently resists because it views itself as having a development, not an emergency, focus. Interagency co-ordination is especially important in the large-scale repatriations which UNHCR is planning for the late 1990s. Internal conflicts have been highly destructive of physical infrastructures and human capital. Ceasefires and repatriations usually require new financial and political commitments on the part of the international community. In countries such as Afghanistan, Angola, Ethiopia, Cambodia and Mozambique, a pre-condition for successful returns is development aid and reintegration assistance aimed at alleviating extreme poverty in countries of origin.[28] Recent experience in many of these countries has demonstrated that the governments of many war-torn societies are simply not in a position to assume full responsibility for the reintegration of returning refugees and other displaced populations. Without improved economic prospects for returnees and for foreign aid and investment for rebuilding the physical infrastructure in these countries, political instability and new displacements are likely to occur, resulting in a renewed need for humanitarian relief. A focus on safety of return and successful reintegration will involve a number of elements: rethinking the roles and mandates of international organisations and NGOs; shifting their operational priorities from receiving countries to countries of return; training agency staff to work in conditions involving development as well as relief assistance; and closer co-operation and co-ordination between development and refugee agencies on the one hand, and human rights and refugee agencies on the other.

In countries where central government itself is weak or non-existent and therefore unable to protect its citizens, the key issue will be not only how to bring together contending groups but how to build institutions of governance. In such situations, economic development and social stability are inseparable. Rehabilitative relief and development activities must be accompanied by support for civil society in order to be effective. Sustainable progress can only be achieved if built on a strong civil foundation that allows the gains made to be consolidated throughout society. Without this foundation, relief and development activities will constitute a one-time consumption of resources which will result in little long-term change. The development of civil society is also related to the avoidance of violence. Violent political conflict can generally be avoided only in a context in which the citizenry is able to participate meaningfully in the political decisions that affect their lives, can hold the persons and institutions that exercise power over them accountable for their actions, and is equipped to negotiate a change in a peaceful and effective manner.

International organisations need to adopt programmes and policies to strengthen civil society and local institutions. With the growth and strengthening of institutions, citizens and citizens' groups will be able to influence the behaviour of their leaders through pressure group activities, elections and other democratic mechanisms. Advocacy programmes that promote the cause of refugees and asylum-seekers at the local level and mobilise public support for these groups can have a very immediate impact on the world's displaced. The strengthening of democratic institutions and civil society are among the major preventive actions against future conflict and refugee migration.

Refugees, UN peace-keeping and outside military forces

The emergencies of the post-Cold War era have also highlighted the need for a more effective interface between humanitarian relief and political and security considerations. As part of the international community's increasing focus on preventive action, there is now greater emphasis on dealing with the problem of displacement in the country of origin. UN agencies and UN peace-keeping forces help to provide assistance to victims of ethnic conflict as close to their homes as possible, create havens or secure areas where displaced persons can get help in relative safety, deploy troops to prevent the expulsions of civilians in some areas, and protect relief workers who are caught in the cross-fire between opposing sides. In addition to greater pressures to provide in-country assistance and protection, there is greater emphasis on repatriation which involves organising the return moves, providing logistical assistance for the actual move, setting up on-site reception centres at the resettlement locations, and furnishing help in reintegrating refugees. Many refugees are returning home before all the problems that caused them to flee, including violence and persecution, have been resolved. There is the danger that premature returns will result in considerable human rights violations.

Under these circumstances, UN and outside military forces frequently work alongside relief agencies to meet humanitarian exigencies in conflict zones. The military brings logistics skills and resources that can meet the immediate needs of civilian populations at risk in humanitarian emergencies, including such activities as protecting relief shipments, creating safety zones, pre-positioning supplies and relocating or evacuating civilians.[29] While recent experiences have demonstrated that the military has unrivalled access to a range of material and logistical resources in transportation, communications and medical services which are simply not available to UNHCR and other humanitarian organisations, relief operations in Iraq, Somalia, Bosnia and Rwanda have also underscored some of the difficulties of military–civilian co-operation in providing relief in situations of continuing conflict. The objectives and working methods of the two groups of actors are different, and, in some cases, contradictory. Military staff are often unfamiliar with the mandates and priorities of relief organisations, lack knowledge of human rights norms and international humanitarian law, and demonstrate little appreciation or understanding of local customs and institutions. Military forces rarely, if ever, have a purely humanitarian agenda, and they are generally unwilling to work under external direction, even in operations conducted under UN auspices.

Recent experiences in Bosnia also demonstrate that the provision of military security for relief operations can compromise the neutrality of humanitarian aid agencies, and can even threaten the delivery of humanitarian assistance. In the former Yugoslavia, UNHCR has had difficulty in carrying out its mandate as a result of its close association both with the UN military forces on the ground and more generally with the punitive and economic actions taken by the UN Security Council. UN troops, mandated to ensure humanitarian access to civilian populations, were not given sufficient means and political backing to carry out their tasks. As a consequence, not only UNPROFOR, but also UNHCR, were criticised both for not providing adequate protection to civilians in their own communities and for not being able to rescue them when their lives were threatened.[30] In addition, sanctions imposed by the UN Security Council on the Federal Republic of Yugoslavia caused great hardship on civilians and undermined the credibility of UNHCR to act impartially in a civil war context.

Military and humanitarian intervention can also sometimes have an adverse impact on the resolution of conflicts. In the struggle to provide aid to the displaced and other war victims, the resolution of the root causes of the conflict can easily become increasingly peripheral. In Bosnia, inadequate humanitarian and military action, combined with selective sanctions and ineffective diplomatic initiatives, impeded more robust political and military pressures for most of the conflict. Thus, in future relief operations, it is likely that if humanitarian action is not accompanied by the necessary political will or action to resolve interethnic conflicts, military forces and relief agencies will become bogged down in long-standing, protracted humanitarian operations.

Dangers of the new approach

The new and more comprehensive approach to the global refugee problem poses a number of difficulties and dangers. As UNHCR has noted, while prevention can be used constructively to avert refugee movements and to meet the needs of uprooted populations once they have been able to return to their homes, the concept can also mean erecting barriers to stop the victims of persecution from entering another country, containing displaced people within their national borders, and sending refugees back to their homeland as quickly as possible, even if conditions there have not fundamentally changed.[31]

In recent years, many states have viewed refugees and asylum-seekers as an unwanted burden and as an unnecessary inconvenience. The post-Cold War period has witnessed a declining commitment of many states to the principle of refugee protection and a growing readiness to ignore long-established humanitarian principles. Some governments have seized the central concepts of the new preventive approach to legitimise restrictive measures which oblige displaced people to remain in or return to their homeland and effectively deny people their right to seek and enjoy asylum in another country.

The danger exists, therefore, that a new approach to the refugee problem is emerging, based not on the traditional notion of asylum, but on the concepts of prevention, containment and rapid repatriation.[32] An increasing number of countries have closed their borders when confronted with a refugee influx from neighbouring states. The emphasis of post-Cold War humanitarianism has been to pour relief aid into civil wars in order to contain the outpouring of refugees and to stabilise regions. In a number of instances, such actions have been accompanied by the creation of internationally supported safe areas or security zones within the country of origin. On several recent occasions, states have admitted refugees on a temporary basis while at the same time making clear their determination to repatriate the new arrivals as quickly as possible, sometimes without due regard to established international protection principles, including the refugees' own wishes and the conditions prevailing within their homeland. For example, in 1996 and 1997, Tanzania, host to huge numbers of refugees from neighbouring countries, expelled and refused entry to thousands of asylum-seekers and refugees fleeing violence in Burundi and Rwanda, and the Tanzanian army forcibly repatriated over 200,000 Hutu refugees to Rwanda. Restrictive policies are also present in the industrialised states where asylum-seekers have been intercepted while making their way to a potential country of refuge and sometimes returned home. Consequently, there exist parallel asylum crises in both the North and South.

The current inclination on the part of states across the globe to erect new barriers to deter population movements will not make the refugee problem go away, nor will it ensure a stable political base for international relations. Much as we may prefer to focus our attention closer to home, the persistence of refugee problems makes it impossible for states to ignore conditions which create forced migration. In the longer term, states must recognise that lasting solutions to the problem of displaced people will only be found if a concerted effort is made to defuse ethnic and religious tensions, resolve armed conflicts, protect human rights and promote equitable and sustainable development.

Generating support for new international initiatives will be difficult. Nevertheless, in the realms of human rights and forced displacement, international and regional stability and idealism often coincide. Policy-makers need to build on this coincidence of factors to achieve political will both to address these problems and to develop the institutional capacity to respond more effectively to future refugee crises.

Notes

1 UNHCR, *The State of the World's Refugees: In Search of Solutions* (Oxford University Press, 1995).
2 United Nations Treaty, 28 July 1958. 'The 1951 United Nations Convention Relating to the Status of Refugees', vol. 189, no. 2545, p.137.
3 J. Craig Jenkins and Susanne Schmeidl, 'Flight from violence: the origins and prospects of the Third World refugee crisis', paper presented at a meeting of the International Studies Association Chicago, March 1995. See also Aristide R. Zolberg, Astri Suhrke and Sergio Aguayo, *Escape From Violence: Conflict and the Refugee Crisis in the Developing World* (New York: Oxford University Press, 1989).

4 Organisation of African Unity, 'The Organisation of African Unity Convention Governing the Specific Aspects of Refugee Problems in Africa' OAU Document CM/267/Rev.1 (10 September 1969).
5 UNHCR, *The Cartagena Declaration of 1984* (Geneva: UNHCR, 1985).
6 There are at least three major approaches to the study of the causes of refugee movements. These are: (a) historically based analysis (Zolberg *et al.*, *Escape From Violence*; G. Loescher, *Refugee Movements and International Security*, Adelphi Paper 268 (London: International Institute for Strategic Studies, 1992); Sadruddin Aga Kahn, 'Study on human rights and massive exoduses', ECOSOC Document E/CN4/1503 (1981)); (b) sociological and theoretical model-building studies (E. Kunz, 'The refugee in flight: kinetic models and forms of displacement', *International Migration Review* 7 (1973): 125–46; A. Richmond, 'Reactive migration: sociological perspectives on refugee movements', *Journal of Refugee Studies* 6(1993): 7–24); and (c) aggregate data analysis (T. R. Gurr, *Minorities at Risk* (Washington, D.C.: US Institute of Peace, 1993); H. Hakovirta, 'Third World conflicts and refugeeism: dimensions, dynamics and trends of world refugee problems', *Commentationes Scientarium Socialum* 32 (The Finnish Society of Sciences and Letters, 1986); A. Onishi, 'Global early warning system for displaced persons: interlinkages of environment, peace and human rights', *Technological Forecasting and Social Change* 31(1991): 269–99). A useful survey of macro-level theorising of causes of forced migration movements is contained in Astri Suhrke, *Analyzing the Causes of Contemporary Refugee Flows* (Brussels: NIDI and Eurostat, 1995).
7 Susanne Schmeidl, with Astri Suhrke, 'Political turmoil and forced migration', Pew Project on *International Migration in Global Perspective* (New York: Center for Migration, Ethnicity and Citizenship, New School for Social Research, 1995).
8 UNHCR, *The State of the World's Refugees*.
9 Myron Weiner, 'Bad neighbors, bad neighborhoods: an enquiry into the conditions for refugee flows', paper for the German-American Migration and Refugee Policies Project, American Academy of Arts and Sciences, Cambridge, Mass. (March 1995).
10 Office of the United Nations High Commissioner for Refugees, 'The Report of the UNHCR Working Group on International Protection', Inter-Office Memorandum No. 78/92, UNHCR, Geneva (31 July 1992).
11 Author's interviews with UNHCR staff in Geneva, May 1994.
12 Francis Deng, *Protecting the Dispossessed: A Challenge for the International Community* (Washington, D.C.: The Brookings Institution, 1993).
13 Norwegian Refugee Council and Refugee Policy Group, *Human Rights Protection for Internally Displaced Persons* (Washington, D.C.: Refugee Policy Group, 1993).
14 For a more detailed discussion of both the short-term and long-term policies for dealing with the global refugee problem, see Gil Loescher, *Beyond Charity: International Cooperation and the Global Refugee Crisis* (New York: Oxford University Press, 1993).
15 Roberta Cohen, *Introducing Refugee Issues in the United Nations Human Rights Agenda* (Washington, D.C.: Refugee Policy Group, 1990); Roberta Cohen,

United Nations Human Rights Bodies: An Agenda for Humanitarian Action (Washington, D.C.: Refugee Policy Group, 1992).

16 UNHCR, *The State of the World's Refugees*.

17 Guy Goodwin-Gill, *The Refugee in International Law* (Oxford: Clarendon Press, 1995); Atle Grahl-Madsen, *The Status of Refugees in International Law* (Leiden: Sijthoff, 1966); and James Hathaway, *The Law of Refugee Status* (Toronto: Butterworth, 1991).

18 See UNHCR, 'UNHCR and human rights', UNHCR Discussion Paper, Geneva (1996).

19 David Forsythe, 'The UN and human rights at fifty: an incremental but incomplete revolution', *Global Governance* 1 (1995): 297–318.

20 Alice Henkin (ed.), *Honoring Human Rights and Keeping the Peace: Lessons from El Salvador, Cambodia and Haiti* (Washington, D.C.: Aspen Insitute, 1995).

21 William DeMars makes these points in DeMars 'Mercy without illusion: humanitarian action in conflict', *Mershon International Studies Review* 40 (1996), Supplement 7: 81–90.

22 'Non-governmental organizations, United Nations and global governance', Special Issue of *Third World Quarterly*, 16 (1995).

23 I am indebted to William DeMars for drawing my attention to the important human rights roles that relief NGOs could play in internal conflicts.

24 Larry Minear and Thomas Weiss, *Mercy Under Fire: War and the Global Humanitarian Community* (Boulder: Westview Press, 1995).

25 Mary Anderson and Peter Woodrow, *Rising from the Ashes: Development Strategies at Times of Disasters* (Boulder: Westview Press, 1989).

26 Patricia Weiss-Fagen, *Peace Making as Rebuilding War Torn Societies* (Geneva: UNRISD, 1996).

27 Leon Gordenker, *Refugees and International Politics* (New York: Columbia University Press, 1987).

28 A study which examined some of the possibilities and problems of repatriation and reconstruction in the early 1990s is Anthony Lake with other contributors, *After the Wars: Reconstruction in Afghanistan, Indochina, Central America, Southern Africa and the Horn of Africa* (New Brunswick, N.J.: Transaction Publishers, 1991).

29 Leon Gordenker and Thomas Weiss (eds.), *Soldiers, Peacekeepers and Disasters* (Basingstoke: Macmillan, 1991).

30 Larry Minear and associates, 'Humanitarian action in the former Yugoslavia: the UN's role 1991–1993', Occasional Paper 18, Thomas Watson Institute for International Studies, Brown University.

31 UNHCR, *The State of the World's Refugees*.

32 Bill Frelick, 'Preventing refugee flows: protection or peril?', in *World Refugee Survey 1993* (Washington, D.C.: US Committee for Refugees, 1993); Andrew Shacknove, 'From asylum to containment', *International Journal of Refugee Law* 5 (1993): 516–33.

10   The silencing of women

Georgina Ashworth

'Human rights are gender neutral.' This view dominated human rights thinking in theory, in law, in practice and in popular opinion, until the last few years, when it has been increasingly contested by feminist advocates in their writings and participation at international conferences. In fact, the belief in neutrality disguised trenchant masculine bias in the selective promotion and protection of human rights. This in turn contributed to the hierarchy between men and women, their legal capacities, and their approved behaviours.

The focal point of this chapter is the response by activists in the women's human rights movement to the built-in selectivity of the regime. The chapter charts their attempt to modify the regime in the period before the world conference in Vienna and afterwards. Given my vantage point, watching history being made from the front row, I am able to pose important general questions about the relationship between theory and practice. How has new thinking on women's human rights shaped the work of intergovernmental human rights agencies and non-governmental organisations? Specifically, the four parts of the chapter deal with key aspects of the feminist advocacy of women's human rights, drawing on illustrations of the tactics employed, surveying the changes wrought, and concluding with some thoughts on the prospects for the Universal Declaration fifty years on.

The hinterland

Until the late 1980s few authors, academics and human rights experts within the United Nations or regional bodies addressed the question whether women were enjoying the human rights guaranteed to them in the Universal Declaration and the two Covenants on 'civil and political rights' and 'economic, social and cultural rights'.[1] Some academic journals published sporadic commentaries[2] but there was no visible response – in submissions, interventions or reporting guidelines – from 'practitioners' (governmental or non-governmental delegates to the UN

Commission on Human Rights, the Subcommission on the Elimination of Discrimination and Protection of Minorities, and the treaty-monitoring bodies).[3] When women were discussed at all, it was as biological child-bearers through the issue of abortion. Even in UK parliamentary debate 'the essence of women' was described in terms of 'their fertility' not their humanity, harking back to the restricted reference to women solely in biological terms, as child-bearers.[4]

When, in the course of the UN Decade for Women (1976–85), the International Convention on the Elimination of All Forms of Discrimination Against Women (hereafter, the 'Women's Convention') was adopted in 1979, its preamble remarked that despite the existence of numerous covenants and conventions developed over a long period of time, discrimination against women was endemic. The Decade for Women had come about in response to the overwhelming evidence that post-colonial 'development' was not benefiting women when measured in terms of political participation, wealth, health and education.[5] As an instrument invoked by women's groups and interpreted by its monitoring committee (Committee for the Elimination of Discrimination Against Women or CEDAW), the Women's Convention had considerable effect[6] – but this could have been far greater if states had not entered so many reservations[7] and if mainstream human rights jurists had paid it the attention it merited.[8]

Before the adoption of the Women's Convention in 1979, I formed CHANGE as the first contemporary organisation with the objective of raising awareness of the 'human rights and human dignity of women', as distinct from 'women's rights', and alerting public opinion to their violation 'whether by state, individual or commercial interest'. The strategy of the non-governmental organisation (NGO) sector is to use the human rights Covenants as a standard by which to measure the quality of women's lives. It could be said to be a strategy which calls the bluff of human rights organisations by comparing the documentary evidence of horrendous daily realities experienced by women with the standards laid down in the human rights regime.

In 1979, there were no like-minded NGOs, and both human rights organisations and women's organisations regarded these initiatives with puzzlement and occasional ridicule. There were particular struggles to acquire funding; US and European foundations known to fund research for campaigns on the persecution of ethnic or religious minorities could not see their way to fund research to identify and resolve the different forms of denigration, subordination or persecution of women.

There were, however, other like-minded individuals from different disciplines and standpoints, and over the ensuing decade these gradually found each other through publications, conferences and thematic networks. Sociologists writing on domestic violence came to perceive the connection between the occurrence of fear in private and in public, and the basic right to freedom from fear and to security of the person; similarly, in the case of acts of torture in the home and those by agents of the state,[9] female torture victims themselves analysed the gendered features of their experience.[10] Feminist anthropologists contributed their analysis of economic and political power within the household,[11] and its relationship to public power. Feminist political scientists questioned the patriarchal origins of citizenship and its continuing legacy in state–citizen relations; among the most influential was the work of the Australian Carole Pateman.[12] Feminist lawyers, and more recently international lawyers, added their weight to the arguments expressed by those within feminist groups and NGOs.[13] Health professionals, including reproductive health advocates, also turned to the language of rights during this period, either to express anger over the continuation of such practices as female genital mutilation and non-consensual adolescent marriage or to protest against the absence of reproductive choice, or indeed against forced abortion, sterilisation and medical experimentation, practices which continue even in well-known hospitals.[14] Since inequalities between women and men are most quantifiable in economic terms, feminist economists have made an important contribution to this unfolding conversation among women from different disciplines and professional backgrounds.[15]

The common denominator of analyses from all these disciplines is that women have been silenced, both as subject and object, and made invisible, while simultaneously being present in society in so far as the reproduction of the species is concerned and also in terms of their function to help men perform their conventional public roles. In the silencing, the fact and acts of silencing also become invisible: without a visible victim, there is no crime, and without a crime there is no perpetrator. And so the history of rights and citizenship examines those who fought for and were successful in obtaining citizenship and rights, rather than the actor and the acts of exclusion and the destiny of the excluded, who form the majority. These 'minority' studies are not generally considered to be deficient, except by feminist analysts. Thus, as an example, many historians and political scientists fail to remark that the French Revolution literally developed *les droits de l'homme*, to the exclusion of all women, with tremendous consequences for French society (and French colonies) for the ensuing 200 years. These authors also fail to observe that there were champions of women's right to rights, notably Olympe de Gouges who was silenced, literally by execution, and has had to wait those 200 years for her vindication.

The 1688 revolution in Britain had the same effect. In English law, as expounded by Blackstone, women were subsumed into the name and the legal personality of their husbands; they had no rights of their own but had many moral responsibilities. This also codified men's rights over their women, including the rights to marital rape, to force child-bearing on a wife and non-consensual marriage on daughters, to beat and impose punishment for behaviour whose acceptability was determined by the husband, to assume and control any income or property, to control women's time, and to take custody of children. Today, there are still remnants of this in the drafting of legislation, where masculine terminology is used, in court practices and in gendered judicial attitudes to victim, crime and criminal.

State formation and reconstruction from Westphalia onwards were based on male citizenship, male leadership, male nationality, male military service, and male sacrifice. Even with the suffrage extended to women in different countries from 1893 onwards, no constitutional guarantees of equal citizenship were given in any country until the independence of Namibia and later the 1994 constitution of South Africa. However, it has required recent feminist scholarship to demonstrate the significance of this to women themselves, to the men with power over their wives and dependants, and to the structure and behaviour of society in general. All but a few exceptional women, mainly queens (and concubines), have been written out of history,[16] and also excluded from the theory and practices of democracy and governance.[17] These are now being challenged, particularly on the issue of consent to acts carried out by governments without consulting the majority.

In 1986, my *Of Violence and Violation: Women and Human Rights* was published by CHANGE; it became a catalytic document for those struggling within traditional human rights organisations to put across their interpretation of women's human rights, and was copied by teachers and students and translated into several languages. The basic question I raised was, if Roosevelt's four freedoms were guaranteed to all human beings without exception, regardless of race, sex, religion and ethnic or social origin, why are women the world over living in fear, hunger, silence and imposed conformity? Some answers included the fact that women are not constructed as fully human, fully able and capacitated; indeed they are often regarded as alien, disabled, and incapable. Other answers concerned the wider issue of Western failure to promote any economic and social rights, which are as critical for women as civil and political rights. The principle of national self-determination meant the prevalence of men's interests, and brought no guaranteed political representation, justice or freedom for women; in many cases, the opposite.

A double standard prevailed; some 'champions of liberty' even justified the subjugation of women, or beat their wives (and did not see that their behaviour could be construed as violating another's freedom) while the 'watchdogs of freedom', the media, often savaged the female victim – misrepresenting, ridiculing, denigrating, and inciting sexual hatred (even where racial hatred is not tolerated). 'Non-discrimination', I argued, is insufficient to prevent the daily violence and abuse that women experience, abuses which are tolerated, condoned or even exonerated by the very political institutions which should be condemning them. If such a scale of violations were experienced by men there would be a well-funded worldwide campaign, but since the abuse is experienced by women, it is part of the norm. Both fear and hunger – from which human rights are intended to deliver us all – are experienced by the person, and they do not stop at the door of the household. Whether caused by the state, greedy entrepreneurs or husbands and sons, violations of these fundamental freedoms within the private domain are violations. Fear is a great silencer.

Masculine language reinforces the socialised lack of self-esteem that many women grow up with, obliterating their presence and their needs, rights and priorities, while also implicitly reinforcing male rights. Thus, the Universal Declaration of Human Rights was rewritten, replacing 'he' and 'his' with 'she' and 'her'. This simple device, adopted in the Women's Convention, has the effect of appropriating for women each one of those 'rights denied' to them throughout the postwar era. Thus, the Preamble asserts:

Whereas it is essential if woman is not to be compelled to have course, as a last resort, to rebellion against tyranny and oppression, their human rights should be protected by the rule of law.

This meaning was taken up by others and explored and expanded in teaching courses, within women's groups and NGOs, and by experts at the UN human rights bodies. Notably, the South American Women's Law Network published an alternative Universal Declaration on the same basis; and the Central American Law Group began its campaigns stimulated by these arguments, as did Amnesty-USA. These Latin American groups have since disputed the issue of the impunity of perpetrators of private acts of violence, monitoring violations by the state police, paramilitaries and other agents. The Global Center for Women's Leadership at Rutgers University, New Jersey, now seen as one of the prime movers in this cause, launched its annual anti-violence campaigns using the same text. It was used in teaching in the Philippines, Turkey and France by various political and legal networks. In the aftermath of the publication of *Violence and Violation*, I was commissioned by the OECD's Development Assistance Committee to prepare a policy paper and an up-to-date resource paper, citing both current literature and active organisations, for their use and adoption.[18] The arguments in these have gone on to be used by, *inter alios*, the UNDP Human Development Report, which in 1995 seriously began to measure the inequalities between girls and boys and between women and men, and to develop a monitoring system of gender empowerment measures.[19]

Research into these inequalities, and the evidence of wrongs committed against women and girl children, has grown in recent years as a result of a number of trends: increased female poverty; limited political representation with which to defend economic rights against globalisation; and cuts in education and health provision. Many examples of human wrongs against women can be given. In some countries one in six girls are sexually abused before the age of sixteen. Millions are married and have children by the age of twelve before they are physically (let alone emotionally) mature. Hundreds of thousands are engaged in child prostitution in East and South Asia having been sold from Cambodia to Vietnam, or from Nepal to India, and many do not even reach adulthood because they have contracted AIDS or died from botched abortions or in childbirth. In India, nine out of ten husbands beat their wives, and 'Eve-teasing' (sexual harassment and molestation) is a daily feature of public travel for those women unable to afford taxis. In Africa, 80–100 million girls and women have been mutilated to control their sexuality. In Saudi Arabia, no public office may be held by women, and they may not drive cars. In Pakistan, looking at an unrelated man (or *zena*) is punishable by stoning. In China and many other Asian countries, girls are deprived, neglected and killed in favour of sons even by their own mothers who bow to the traditional values of male superiority. Where there is illiteracy and limited education, two-thirds of those affected will be girls, who are then as adults unable to compete with men in the skilled labour market and are forced into low-pay, low-skilled jobs – or prostitution. Food taboos, and customary preferences to feed men and boys, restrict health security in many communities. Widows, if not burned, in some communities are ostracised and starved, in others obliged to marry their brother-in-law. Rape by military 'protectors' in refugee camps and settlements for internally displaced people is commonplace;[20] and, of course, every six minutes a gang or individual rapes a woman in the United States. Without the exercise of property rights, destitution is more common among women than men, and a vulnerability to other violations is structured into daily life. Destitution combined with family responsibilities obliges women to accept minimal wages, contributing to what neo-liberal economists would describe as a 'lean' and 'fit' business environment, one which competes in the world system on the basis of violating human rights.

This acute summary shows that whilst the problems start at a young age they are chronic throughout the lives of many women. It also demonstrates the linkage of the inability to exercise one right with the incapacity to exercise others. Moreover, certain customs and cultural norms tolerate and even approve of such violations, thereby creating a long and conflictual agenda for the future. It also shows that, were the quantity and quality of these violations used in the evaluation of countries' human rights records, quite different situations would be described.

Not all the groups and organisations engaged in researching these practices or campaigning against them originally saw themselves as part of the human rights movement, in part because human rights have been projected as 'elsewhere' and the subject of foreign policy rather than rooted in indigenous culture or domestic policy, and in part because interdisciplinary study of women's human rights has been considered to be lacking in academic rigour. The gradual identification of such groups with the universality, interdependence and inalienability of human rights enforceable at home was to become a major feature of the 1990s, while the conventional human rights organisations, such as the International Human Rights Law Group, Human Rights Watch and Anti-Slavery International, also began to work on areas of women's human rights.

The un-silencing of (a few) women

Feminist advocates of the reacknowledgement of the human rights and dignity of women gathered together on a number of occasions in 1992 and 1993[21] to prepare sections as well as intermittent phrases for inclusion in the draft Declaration and Programme of Action to be adopted at the Vienna World Conference on Human Rights. The objectives were:

- to demonstrate how the recognition of women's right to enjoy human rights had been suppressed;
- to highlight some of the forces acting against women's equal enjoyment and exercise of human rights;
- to propose some lines of countervailing action.

These were introduced at the final Preparatory Committee in April 1993, held after earlier drafting processes had broken down over the 'right to development', which the West opposes and developing-country governments use as an argument for economic sovereignty.[22]

United Nations events today are almost always accompanied by a 'forum' of non-governmental activities. In this instance, events such as a 'tribunal' on the different forms of violence against women were held. It drew intense media attention, shocking spectators into considering the detail and scale of man's inhumanity to woman. Other strategies were to ensure that the 'mainstream' issue-based non-governmental seminars included women as speakers and gender experts so that the other 4,000 or so participants would be introduced to elementary gender dimensions of the subjects in hand – democracy, indigenous peoples' rights, and so on. The cumulative effect was to prevent women's human rights from being confined to an intellectual ghetto.

Another characteristic of world conferences in the past five years has been the increasing effectiveness of the interest-cum-lobby group system, with women's lobbying being amongst the most successful – as indicated both by results, and by equal measures of compliments and envy on the part of others. In Vienna, it was the concern of the lobbying group to ensure that the sections introduced at the final Preparatory Committee be strengthened or maintained, but certainly not weakened. Vigilance was vital in view of the gathering forces of religious and economic fundamentalism, on top of the lethargy of the previous forty-five years.

The lobby group was led, *faute de mieux*, by this author; those from the wider women's caucus interested in lobbying identified themselves by wearing a purple ribbon, and found themselves committed to weekend and late-night drafting as well as to tugging the sleeves of selected delegates. This new form of diplomacy from below, drawing on activist groups in civil society, is increasingly welcomed by government delegations and UN officials, who need the substance and expertise that many NGOs have, or who find NGOs' freedom of expression greater than their own.

In retrospect, the output from the World Conference does not look very great, especially when compared to the input. However, the volume of ingenuity, time and resources that was necessary is also an indicator of the size of the problem. An entire world conference of some 175 delegations needed to be made aware that the imposed silence of women about their human rights and the built-in privileges of men over women was coming to an end, and persuaded to adopt measures to bring about effective change. It is also having a longer-term impact as its recommendations were, and are still, being articulated into resolutions for the Commission on Human Rights, the Subcommission on the Prevention of Discrimination and Protection of Minorities, and supposedly all the Working Groups and Treaty Monitoring Committees, thereby setting off a longer-term process of consciousness-raising about the language used about, and meanings given to, women's human rights.

What, then, did the World Conference achieve? Let us first examine the text of the Vienna Declaration itself. Paragraph 18 in the Preamble reaffirmed the human rights of women and girl children as an 'inalienable, integral and indivisible part of universal human rights', and notes that it is 'deeply concerned at the discrimination and violence to which women continue to be exposed'. A substantial section (3: paragraphs 36–44) in the Programme of Action again asserted the priority of women's human rights and suggested lines of action for the UN system, and the world in general:

[The] importance of working towards the elimination of violence against women in public and private life, all forms of sexual harassment, exploitation and trafficking in women, the elimination of gender bias in the administration of justice and the eradication of any conflicts which may arise between the rights of women and the harmful effects of certain traditional or customary practices, cultural prejudices and religious extremism . . .

It also recommended that the draft Declaration on the Elimination of Violence Against Women should be adopted by the UN General Assembly in its ensuing session, which indeed took place. This Declaration is firmly based in human rights language, citing the Convention on Torture and the International Covenants rather than 'women's rights'. Its definition of the term 'violence against women' is:

any act of gender-based violence that results in, or is likely to result in, physical, sexual or psychological harm or suffering to women, including threats of such acts, coercion or arbitrary deprivation of liberty, whether occurring in public or in private life.

Unlike the 1994 Inter-American Convention on the Elimination of Violence Against Women, the Declaration has no full legal force, but adds to the body of soft law lining up behind the varied issues of women's human rights. However, it does contain some practical measures including a plan of action for national governments, and it recommends re-education of the male population rather than simply the provision of measures to 'patch up' the victims; for example, providing shelters, though necessary, does not modify actual behaviour. This re-education has yet to be implemented by governments. If it were to be specifically included in human rights education, it would have long-term beneficial effects for all societies.

Since the Vienna World Conference, the UN system has had to respond to vast and visible crises, most notably those in Bosnia and Rwanda, where in each tragic case, human rights violations against women have been documented and proven,[23] and have even caught the attention of the media. At a broader level, there is also the context of the hegemonic grip of conservative ideas which aim to restrain, contain, and even destroy the gains made by women, as came to be demonstrated at the International Conference on Population and Development (ICPD) in 1994 and the fourth World Conference on Women in 1995. In the preparatory processes and at the events themselves, which took place in Cairo and Beijing respectively, women's groups worked energetically to ensure their concerns were fully integrated, despite these pressures. In the case of the ICPD, this work was on reproductive rights including consent to sex and to pregnancy, which had never been mooted before in this series of primarily demographic population conferences. Men's responsibility for their own socio-sexual behaviour was also emphasised. In these and other measures concerning the 'empowerment' of women, they had the full support of the Secretariat and the official conference Secretary-General, Nafis Sadik, head of the UNFPA, but not the Holy See (along with one or two largely Roman Catholic countries and one or two Islamic states). This conflict between religious institutions and women's groups was carried forward to the World Conference on Women itself. There, those on the religious right from the United States, Iran and Sudan, together with the Holy See, were to take many common positions, particularly over certain clauses such as the one on sexual orientation. The Holy See had also lobbied the Women's Conference Secretary-General, Gertrude Mongella (a Roman Catholic), on several occasions in the hope of reducing the emphasis placed on reproductive rights. Nevertheless, certain gains were made in Beijing over the ICPD, chiefly in the adoption of 'sexual rights', which are encoded in the health section of the Platform for Action. This maintains that

[t]he human rights of women include their right to have control over and decide freely and responsibly on matters related to their sexuality, including sexual and reproductive health, free of coercion, discrimination and violence. Equal relationships between women and men in matters of sexual relations and reproduction, including full respect for the integrity of the person, require mutual respect, consent and shared responsibility for sexual behaviour and its consequences.[24]

The health section linked to human rights the following issues: marital rape, involuntary multiple pregnancies, and the coercive practices emerging from laws such as China's one-child policy. (In the interests of reducing population growth, this policy prohibits urban women from having more than one child at all, and rural women from having more than one if the first is a boy, which has had the effect of forced abortions, wife-battering and divorce for women, and informal female infanticide through the abandonment of girls to the 'dying rooms' of orphanages.) Education was reaffirmed as a human right, and the unequal exercise of that right was condemned. This is important in the context of women's health because education, has been shown over decades – by scholars as well as governments and NGOs – to be an effective method of empowering women to gain control over their own fertility.

The 'full realization of the human rights of all women migrants . . . and their protection against violence and exploitation' were endorsed and expanded after solid lobbying from the caucus representing migrants, refugees and internally displaced women. To return from the conference in Beijing and read about the execution of Sara Balagapan, a Filipina domestic servant who killed her rapist employer-attacker in self-defence, made these phrases yet more poignant. The masses of refugees and displaced women in Somalia, who are attacked by their 'protectors', the border guards and Kenyan police, and then cast out as bringing shame on their clans and families, also demonstrate the need for particular protection against violence. The issue of persecution on grounds of gender, pioneered in Canadian and French law, was acknowledged but not expanded.[25] The potential of this issue is enormous and it can be expected that courts will find more and more individual cases before them.

The section on violence, which was distinct from those on both human rights and conflict, nevertheless correlated with them. It was uncontroversial, since the Declaration on the Elimination of Violence Against Women was still new, and it is not respectable even for hard-nosed diplomats to be in favour of violence against women – although in private conversation some men justify 'correcting' their wives or using violence to 'clear the air'.[26] However, there was some controversy over female foeticide, which arises from the deadly combination of advances in diagnosis and the low social value attributed to girl children, particularly in Asia among educated classes able to afford the tests. It has subsequently been outlawed in India.

The background provided by Bosnia and Rwanda and the nuclear tests by China and France both contributed to the length of the section on 'peace, conflict resolution and the impact of armed or other conflict on women', which required substantial negotiation. The section did not restrict itself simply to rape and forced pregnancies in war, but emphasised the broader connection between women's lack of decision-making power and political representation in 'normal' circumstances, which makes them unable to participate in attempts at conflict prevention. It also commented on the deprivation of resources which resulted from spending on armaments – 'toys for the boys'– without corresponding resources being invested in post-conflict reconstruction. It also argued that equal numbers of women and men should be nominated to war crimes tribunals, and that prosecutors, judges and other officials should be appropriately trained to handle rape, indecent assault, forced pregnancies and other forms of torture which women suffer in times of armed conflict. Even the achievements of women's peace movements, so often the butt of media and politicians' hate-speak, were officially commended.

The weakest sections in the World Conference on Women Platform for Action were those on women's poverty, women and the economy, and women and the environment, none of which referred to poverty violating rights or to state responsibilities for income distribution. The section on the girl child, keen to outlaw child labour, early marriage and exploitation of unpaid work within the family, was perhaps sharper in its arguments, using the 1989 Convention on the Rights of the Child as a foundation. Negotiation about equal property rights and inheritance, and their relationship with economic independence, was difficult in the face of Islamic pressure (for Islam prescribes a one-third inheritance for girls) but was pushed forward by progressive African delegates, who were keen to see international law override tribal customary ownership. This section should have implications for the inheritance of titles and land in the UK, and therefore for the structure of the House of Lords, if any lobby group were to pursue it. The section on human rights themselves, while relatively straightforward throughout, did refer to the discrimination against women in the allocation of economic and social resources as directly violating their human rights and fundamental freedoms.

Conclusions and future activities

The several world conferences discussed above have set short time-frames for implementing their decisions. It is government, and the UN system itself, which must implement these documents to which they have given their agreement. Alert NGOs and women's groups need to set about monitoring UN member-state compliance to these documents as well as working out ways to be more effective in their advocacy of areas like economic rights.

What grounds are there to be optimistic about future developments? There has been a continuing expansion of activity outside the formal UN human rights mechanisms since 1993. The International Labour Office continues to develop labour protection for women, adopting in

1996 the International Convention on Homeworking (or sub-contracted outwork). This document affects millions of informal sector workers hitherto untouched by labour legislation despite forming the majority of workers worldwide (of whom a majority are women). However, effort still needs to be put into asserting the basic 'right to life' as rights to both food and shelter, assertions which were articulated at the World Food Summit and the Habitat (urban settlements) conferences, respectively, in the teeth of opposition from the US delegations.

The Council of Europe was inspired by the commitment of Mary Robinson, when President of Ireland, to women's human rights. In addition to its already good reputation for working to eliminate sexist and masculine language, and lobbying against the trafficking of women, the Council has become more sensitive to the link between human rights and democracy. Few intergovernmental agencies have yet to grasp the issue of women's right to political representation as a social group which the Council of Europe also espouses through its principle of 'parity democracy', and on which there has been considerable campaigning in France. Similar initiatives, questioning the validity of democracy which excludes half the population from decision-taking, have been started by the Inter-Parliamentary Union.[27] However, the otherwise innovatory Democracy Audit in the UK missed the opportunity to assess the quality of democracy in terms of women's full participation.[28]

Women themselves have begun to use the 'mainstream' human rights systems more effectively. While not abandoning the Women's Convention, they aspire to see the equality promises in the major covenants and conventions become real for themselves and their sisters. Activist women are now teaching engagement with regional regimes. For example, the Inter-American Commission on Human Rights, based in Costa Rica, has a vigorous history of contact with feminist groups, having drafted and adopted the Convention on the Elimination of Violence Against Women in 1994. An increasing number of women's groups are writing alternative or shadow reports when their governments submit their periodic accounts to the UN Human Rights Committee, or to the Committee on the Elimination of Racial Discrimination. Successful 'exposure' and training programmes have been mounted in Geneva to coincide with the UN Human Rights Commission and Subcommission. The objective of these is to empower women to use these bodies, while also enabling the officials to recognise what they would normally term 'women's issues' as human rights issues.[29] The response is still very uneven: with the exception of Francis Deng, the Special Rapporteur on displaced persons, and Linda Chavez, on violence in conflict, there is little use of gender analysis or reference to women in the thematic or country reports to the UN. Experts in poverty as a violation of human rights, presenting to the Subcommission in 1996, the Year of Poverty Eradication, did not direct their attention to the measurements of women's poverty and related powerlessness issued by the UNDP and others.

The question of trafficking in women, and the possibility of a new convention, have been given a higher profile in debate, and controversy between those who oppose all prostitution and those, perhaps more realistic, opponents of coerced prostitution who favour the implementation of the existing Convention. Coercion, it should be understood, has many faces: pimps *and* poverty both contribute to the exploitation and lack of choice faced by girls and women sold or tricked into prostitution, false marriage and bogus employment contracts – which were all identified by the Special Rapporteur on violence against women. However, coercion is also a feature of daily life for many girls and young women forced into marriage, and of many more coerced daily into unremitting domestic servitude, including non-consensual sex, by violence or the threat of destitution or purely that of social sanction. Violations within marriage are a major issue which has yet to be addressed by any human rights agency.[30]

It is important to set these reasons to be optimistic alongside new and old dilemmas. In the area of economic and social rights – where NGOs and women's groups are working out ways to be more effective – the mobilisation of enormous resources will be required to overcome human wrongs such as the illiteracy of several hundred million girls and women. The political will to allocate these resources for transformation will be the real deciding factor in this global struggle for human rights. There also remain familiar problems concerning the implementation of decisions about women's human rights on a national basis. There is the old resistance to feminism (or even to reading books and assessing data on gender differences) by those who consider themselves scholars and by conventional opinion-formers – in political parties, academia and the media. There is also the particular resistance in Western countries like the UK, France and Germany to adopting international directives on policy and structural change, even when their own governments have been party to negotiations. Developing countries are comparatively more used to the invasion of their sovereignty by external agencies like UNDP, UNICEF and the World Bank, although they are often resistant to human rights for the reason that they see such legislation as ideological in character. There are additional general problems with translating the 'soft law' of the world conferences into government policy or into 'black-letter law'; some of the political and intellectual reasons for this resistance have already been interwoven throughout this chapter but to these must be added the male-oriented focus of legal systems. Put simply, as most men perceive that they would lose status and control by conforming to new norms of equality and shared responsibilities, they are bound to resist.

There remain the threats of religious fundamentalists who, whether in the United States or the Islamic and Hindu worlds, now constitute enormous political forces ranged against women's enjoyment of their human rights, especially their reproductive rights. Not only do they persecute and make outcasts of proponents of toleration, they also threaten the livelihoods and even the security of anyone courageous enough to stand up for women's self-determination. The combined claim of unique righteousness in the interpretation and fulfilment of their faiths and the 'right' to exterminate 'heretics' makes them 'sainted' perpetrators of human rights violations, who deny their human accountability by calling on metaphysical support.

Developments in the scientific area pose new challenges. It is generally agreed that social mechanisms for debate and control are far behind technological developments. Many of these concern reproduction and genetic engineering, essentially 'women's issues', but in which women are denied a voice. Internet pornography, denigrating and violating women as well as girls (and some boys), has now joined the unresolved debate about conventional pornography which many feminists regard as an affront to human dignity, even though it is protected by many states in the interests of freedom of speech. Sooner, rather than later, these issues will have to be brought into the human rights regime, exempting no government, no individual and no commercial interest.

Those who remain sceptical of the need to take women's human rights seriously should reflect on the ways in which the gender of the victim matters to the perpetrator. The masses of refugees and displaced women of Somalia, who are attacked while going to collect firewood in the fulfilment of their gendered social reproductive role, raped by their 'protectors' (the border guards and Kenyan police) and then cast out as bringing shame on their clans and families, give part of the answer. In the face of these tragic stories of human wrongs perpetrated against women, a heavy burden of responsibility falls on the shoulders of women's human rights activists. They will need to draw heavily on their ability to build progressive coalitions to mobilise theoreticians, politicians and other NGOs alike to fulfil their commitments to generating a human rights culture for all in the future.

Notes

1 Indeed, it had not been a foregone conclusion that the Universal Declaration would include the right to the equal enjoyment and exercise of rights

by women as well as men; Latin American women leaders, such as Bertha Lutz, struggled alongside Eleanor Roosevelt to ensure women were written in, rather than out, from the beginning of the post-1945 human rights regime.

2 Rebecca Cook, 'Human rights and world public order: the outlawing of sex-based discrimination', *American Journal of International Law* 69 (1975): 497–533; Rebecca Cook, 'Women and international human rights', *Human Rights Quarterly* 3 (1981): 1–155; Margaret E. Galey, 'International enforcement of women's human rights', *Human Rights Quarterly* 6 (1984): 463–90; Helene Kaufmann, 'An analysis of gender-based treaty law drawn in historical perspective', *Human Rights Quarterly* 8 (1986): 70–88.

3 I first attended the UN Subcommission as an NGO Observer in 1975, and have had occasion to follow most of the UN Human Rights Centre publications aimed both at the general public and at those responsible for periodic reports to the Human Rights Committee, the Economic and Social Rights Committee, the Committee on the Elimination of Racial Discrimination, etc.

4 Michael Meacher MP in the debate on surrogate motherhood, *c*.1990.

5 There are innumerable titles from this period, but the chief stimulus was Ester Boserup, *Woman's Role in Economic Development* (New York: St Martin's Press, 1970).

6 The main non-governmental body monitoring the Convention is the International Women's Rights Action Watch (IWRAW), which publishes a monthly bulletin outlining case law on developments worldwide.

7 According to the annual review of its status published by Andrew Byrnes, the Women's Convention is subject to more reservations than any other, and the UK has entered more than any other country. CEDAW annually repeats the urgent necessity for governments to lift these reservations to ensure that its spirit and function are respected.

8 Human rights jurisprudence developed through the Commonwealth, for example, failed to make more than a footnote reference to the Convention.

9 The first International Tribunal on Crimes Against Women was held in 1976 in Brussels, beginning an era of feminist demands for public policy on private acts of violence. The International Conference on Violence, Abuse and Women's Citizenship in 1996 reviewed progress since 1976.

10 Ximena Bunster B. was the first to publish a description and analysis of the torture of women in Chilean jails, which involved watching the torture of family members, the use of dogs and rats to assault women sexually, rape by guards and the use of electric prods, beatings etc. Later evidence has been collected in the Netherlands and at the Danish Centre for Victims of Torture. The rape of women in prisons and police stations in many countries, whether the women are political prisoners, accused, condemned, or even just making a complaint, has unfortunately not been taken up by the leading human rights international NGOs.

11 Henrietta Moore, *Feminism and Anthropology* (Cambridge: Polity Press, 1988).

12 Carole Pateman, *The Sexual Contract* (Cambridge: Polity Press, 1990). In addition, see the proceedings of the Conference on Women's Citizenship at Greenwich University, London in 1996 in *Feminist Review* 57 (1997).

13 For example, see Andrew Byrnes, 'Women, feminism and international human rights law: methodological myopia, fundamental flaws or meaningful marginalisation?', *Australian Yearbook of International Law* 12 (1992): 205–15; Hilary Charlesworth, Christine Chinkin and Shelley Wright, 'Feminist approaches to international law', *American Journal of International Law* 85 (1991): 613–45; Rebecca Cook, *Women's International Human Rights: A Bibliography.*; Celina Romany, 'Women as *aliens*: a critique of the public/private distinction in international human rights law', *Harvard Human Rights Journal* 6 (1993): 78–91; Jane Connors, 'NGOs and the human rights of women at the UN', in Peter Willetts (ed.), *The Conscience of the World* (Washington, D.C.: Brookings Institution; London: Institute of International Studies, 1995).

14 Among these, one of the most eminent is Rebecca Cook, now better known as an international lawyer and bibliographer of women's human rights. Another is Ros Petechesky; see Petechesky, *Global Feminist Perspectives on Reproductive Rights and Reproductive Health* (New York: Hunter College, 1990).

15 While Bina Agarwal, Diane Elson, Nancy Folbre, Ruth Pearson and others were among the founding members of the International Association of Feminist Economists, the work of the interdisciplinary Third World Network, DAWN and similar collectives, has also given stimulus in questioning 'development', for which most models and practices have continued to impoverish and marginalise those with low social entitlements, or enforced rights. A. K. Sen's examination of the causes of famine, in which he identified the social scale of entitlements which result in women and girl children being the last to receive food and therefore the first to die, has also been extremely important in promoting gender awareness in developmental economics.

16 Sheila Rowbotham, *Hidden from History, 300 Years of Women's Oppression and the Fight Against It* (London: Pluto, 1973); Bonnie S. Anderson and Judith P. Zinsser (eds.), *A History of Their Own: Women in Europe from Prehistory to the Present*, 2 vols. (New York: Harper and Row, 1990).

17 Anne Phillips, *Engendering Democracy* (Cambridge: Polity Press, 1992); Georgina Ashworth, *When Will Democracy Include Women?* (London: CHANGE, 1992); UNDP, *An Agenda for Change: Gender and Governance* (London, 1996).

18 Georgina Ashworth, *Women and Human Rights – A Resource Paper* (Paris OECD-DAC, 1992); Georgina Ashworth, *Women and Human Rights: A Policy Paper* (Paris, 1992).

19 UNDP, *Human Development Report* (New York: Oxford University Press, 1995).

20 While this was generally known from emergency relief workers, Fawzia Musse consolidated evidence in Kenya in a paper for the Conference on Women and War in Africa, Oxford, 1993; the Women's International League for Peace and Freedom is now compiling evidence of this more systematically.

21 The North–South Center in Ottawa, Canada, the Global Leadership Center at Rutgers University, New Jersey, Women in Development Europe,

Madrid, Hom-Vrouwenberaad in The Hague, were all major hosts to these funded events. CHANGE in London held a series of open seminars to make best use of the limited resources available in the UK to women's interests; some 200 people attended overall, more than at the other events put together.

22 The timing was most apt, and the persuasion of the delegates successful, largely through the help of the Canadian government. Canada's persistent support for women and for gender perspectives throughout the UN has been beneficial for all women, although it has been described as a middle power using its comparative advantage. Alger F. Chadwick, Gene M. Lyons and John E. Trent (eds.), *The United Nations System: The Policies of Member States* (Tokyo: United Nations University, 1995). It has also, at times, upstaged the United States, which has a much more erratic record.

23 The European Commission and the UN Division for the Advancement of Women both sent all-women investigative teams into Bosnia (but not Rwanda), thereby providing a precedent for implementing the feminist principle in the approach to violence of believing the victim, and not allowing intermediaries to interpret the case.

24 Fourth World Conference on Women, Platform for Action, Article 97, A/CONF.177/L.5/Add.7 (number refers to pre-publication version and may have been amended), Beijing, 1995.

25 Recommended in *Shaming the World: The Needs of Women Refugees* (London: CHANGE, 1985), a publication which was used by women's groups in Canada to influence Canadian government policy.

26 Remarks made to the author by male diplomats at the Commonwealth Ministers for Women's Affairs Conference in 1993.

27 Inter-Parliamentary Union, *Women and Men In Politics: Democracy Still in the Making. A World Comparative Survey: Series and Reports* 28 (Geneva, 1997) was presented to a major conference in New Delhi in February 1997 to develop the concept of male–female partnership in politics, rather than the one-sided politics of the present. Unusually for a conference covering the 'woman question', there were more men – two – than women among the 400 participants, who included people in the highest echelons of the 'world's largest democracy' and representatives of a handful of NGOs, including CHANGE.

28 Published as F. Klug, K. Starmer and S. Weir (eds.), *The Three Pillars of Liberty* (London: Routledge, 1996).

29 The first two of these, in 1996 and 1997, were conducted by the Women's International League for Peace and Freedom and CHANGE, respectively.

30 With the exception of Anti-Slavery International which has had a tentative programme on early and 'servile' marriage, and will be working with the International Planned Parenthood Federation on research in this area, which will be taken to the United Nations by CHANGE.

11 Power, principles and prudence: protecting human rights in a deeply divided world

Andrew Hurrell

The model of international society that developed in Europe and became global in the course of European expansion provided a political framework that was fundamentally inhospitable to the promotion by states of both human rights and political democracy. It was a society whose normative structure gave only an indirect and secondary role to both individuals and non-state groups. Its normative foundations lay in the mutual recognition by states of each other's sovereignty and their acceptance of the duty of non-intervention. This conception has changed markedly over the past forty years and, for some, still more dramatically with the end of the Cold War. The normative ambitions of international society continue to expand as co-operation has come increasingly to involve the creation of rules that affect very deeply the domestic structures and organisation of states, that invest individuals and groups within states with rights and duties, and that seek to embody some notion of a common good (human rights, democratisation, the environment, the construction of more elaborate and intrusive interstate security orders).

The hugely increased normative ambitions of international society are nowhere more visible than in the field of human rights and democracy – in the idea that the relationship between ruler and ruled, state and citizen, should be a subject of legitimate international concern; that the ill-treatment of citizens and the absence of democratic governance should trigger international action; and that the external legitimacy of a state should depend increasingly on how domestic societies are ordered politically.

This chapter examines five dilemmas that lie at the heart of contemporary debates about the place of human rights in international society. They arise from the expansion of the human rights agenda; from the move towards greater coercive enforcement of human rights norms; from the disintegration of states and weakening of state structures; from the limits to non-state actors; and from regionalist and particularist challenges that are power-political as well as cultural or civilisational.

All of these dilemmas highlight the immense difficulty of reaching a stable and sustained consensus on human rights in a world of cultural and religious diversity. But, to a much greater extent than is reflected in the literature on human rights, they are also intimately connected to questions of political practice, to patterns of unequal power, to the coherence of states and state structures and to the legitimacy of international norms and institutions. Indeed, it is a central argument of this chapter that the most pressing and intractable ethical dilemmas in the field of human rights are as much about practice, power and process as they are about philosophical foundations, and as such lie very much in the world of non-ideal theory.

The expansion of the human rights agenda

The human rights agenda evolved and expanded considerably through the postwar period, a process that has gathered pace in the post-Cold War period. This involved international agreements encompassing both civil and political rights and social and economic rights, as well as more recent claims to third-generation or solidarity rights (rights to development, peace, a clean environment, and a cultural identity). Other developments have included the attempt to apply the laws of war and humanitarian law to 'internal' conflicts and civil wars, and the revival of ideas of internationally recognised and protected minority rights regimes – as in the recognition process in the former Yugoslavia or the creation of a Commissioner on National Minorities within the Organisation for Security and Cooperation in Europe (OSCE).

One set of pressures for this expansion comes from *within* the human rights system. Although its origins were intimately bound up with the power, interests and values of the US and other Western states in the immediate postwar period, once created, the human rights regime provided both institutional platforms and normative handholds for weaker actors (both states and non-state groups) to press their interests. The programmatic use of 'soft law', the space provided for experts and working groups and the broader role of NGOs helped to open up the process of norm creation and development. State control over this process has been diluted and a degree of political space has been created for the elaboration and promotion of a new range of rights (for example, rights of future generations, rights related to the status of women, rights to cultural identity, rights to development and a clean environment).[1]

Expansion has also been closely bound up with arguments concerning the interdependency and indivisibility of rights. At one level this has been driven by politics: no bargain would have been possible, given the divergences between East and West and North and South, that did not accept international recognition of both civil and political and eco-nomic and social rights. Moreover, precisely because rights involve legal and moral entitlements, there are considerable political advantages to seeking to express claims and preferences in terms of rights. Yet indivisibility works also at a deeper and more substantive level. On closer analysis, distinctions between civil and political and economic and social rights, or between rights that demand state abstention rather than positive action and significant resources break down and become untenable.[2]

But the expansion of the normative agenda has also been driven by pressures and developments from *outside* the human rights system. In the first place there has been increasingly powerful political pressure to link human rights to the promotion of democracy. Thus, in marked contrast to the 1970s, US policy has come to lay ever greater stress on the holy trinity of political democracy, human rights and 'good governance' (transparency, accountability and participation). The reasons are mostly political. Although there are references to 'democratic' rights in the UN Declaration, the conditions of the Cold War meant that formal incorporation of political democracy into the human rights system was politically impossible. Yet this constraint was weakened by the wave of transitions from authoritarian rule in southern Europe and the developing world in the late 1970s and 1980s and by the fall of communism in Eastern Europe and the Soviet Union. As a consequence, the idea of a legal right to democratic governance has begun to gain some ground.[3] But again there is a more substantive side to the story. Surely, if we want to protect human rights on a sustainable long-term basis, we should also work to foster systems of government which are most conducive to that end? Equally, if we now know that democracies that respect the rights of their citizens are inherently more peaceful, then should we not promote democracy abroad in the interests of national security?

The final element in this process of expansion has been the return of arguments stressing the links between political liberalisation and market-based economic development. Western liberal thought has long stressed the deep theoretical interrelationship between these two processes. Yet attempts to bring them together at the level of foreign policy and within the institutional frameworks of the IFIs (international financial institutions) are a relatively recent development reflecting the renewed dominance of market liberal orthodoxy and Western confidence engendered by the end of the Cold War. Indeed, it is important to remember that the postwar period witnessed a long line of commentators, politicians and academics arguing that repressive governments were 'necessary' in order to implement liberal economic policies and to create the conditions for what was hoped would eventually become a self-sustaining process of development and modernisation. It is also important to note the reappearance of such a view, as in the debates on the 'sequencing' of economic reforms.

The expansion of the human rights agenda reflects, therefore, both the changing political context and substantive and important arguments about the linkages between different classes of human rights and between human rights, political democracy and the operation of markets. Those who press in this direction argue that there can be no neutral definition of human rights and that human rights cannot be logically disengaged from comprehensive notions of what constitutes a good society. Cut-off points between different clusters of rights will inevitably be arbitrary. On what basis (other than an unargued-for judgement as to what his well-ordered non-liberal societies will in practice accept) does Rawls include the right to life and the prohibition of slavery in his list of actionable international human rights but exclude freedom of the press or of association or the right to education?[4] In addition, the expansionists argue that we should keep pushing out the normative boat and keep asserting important sets of rights even if the chances of effective or consistent implementation remain slim – that is, after all, what having a normative agenda is all about.

Yet it is evident that this expansion of the human rights agenda and the concurrent attempt to promote other liberal goals raises very serious difficulties. First, it becomes very important to face up squarely to the tensions between the different elements of this agenda. Even in theory all good things do not necessarily go together. Thus, as debates on the Asian model have shown, the relationship between successful economic development and political democracy/human rights turns out to be far more complex and ambiguous than Western liberal rhetoric would suggest. There are also real tensions in the relationship between political democracy and the promotion of human rights. Writers such as Berlin and Elster have underlined the extent to which formal political democracy can entrench murderous majorities of all kinds – but most dangerously, perhaps, murderous ethnic majorities.[5] Many of the most serious abuses of human rights are visited on those who are deemed to be non-members of a particular state or political community; or on those who fall between the cracks of the state system, as with refugees (an area, incidently, where the record of Western states is far from self-evidently more impressive than, for example, states in Africa, the Middle East or parts of Asia).

Such problems are perhaps even more apparent in practice. Thus, for example, in the Americas the period that has seen the retreat of authoritarian rule and the gradual consolidation of democratic government throughout the region has also witnessed continuing serious violations of human rights and a weakening of the regional human rights system.[6] As José Miguel Vivanco puts it: 'the tendency to equate civilian government with respect for human rights has rendered the human rights machinery of the OAS less likely to condemn states for wholesale violations of human rights than during the period of military rule'.[7] Thus, despite its extensive investigatory powers, the Inter-American Commission has become more reluctant to undertake on-site investigations and issue critical reports, and not a single comprehensive report on the human rights situation of a member state with an elected government has been issued.

Secondly, the broadening of the agenda plays into the question of universality and the legitimate scope for states to make important decisions on the character of their domestic political, economic and social arrangements. Although the precise line may be very hard to draw, there has to be a moral difference in a world of cultural, religious and social diversity between proscribing and preventing manifest violations of human rights and externally seeking to dictate the ways in which societies organise themselves and determine their priorities and values. The international community has a legitimate role in ensuring that governmental power is not abused, in setting human rights standards and in reviewing compliance with those standards. But if external involvement is extended beyond this into the detailed ways in which policies are chosen and implemented, then central liberal principles of representation, of accountability, of pluralism and the respect for diversity will be undermined.

The arguments for the indivisibility of rights and especially for the deep linkages between civil and political rights and economic and social rights remain powerful and valid. Nevertheless, distinctions do have to be drawn between absolute insistence on the protection of fundamental human rights and a more flexible approach to both other rights and broader liberal goals. As Alston puts it:

Once we move beyond the core, physical integrity rights, the nature of the society, its traditions and culture, and other such factors become highly pertinent to any efforts to promote and protect respect for the rights concerned. We must recognize that the reflexive, often dogmatic, admonitory, and homogeneous approach that is appropriate to such core violations will simply be less productive, and achieve far less enduring results than a more sensitive, open, and flexible approach which situates the goals sought within the society in question.[8]

The promotion of universally proclaimed values does not preclude sensitivity to context but it does involve distinguishing between upholding particularly important core norms and attempting to export complete ways of life or conceptions of the good. This in turn means that international efforts to promote and protect human rights should be disentangled from notions of democracy or economic liberalisation and that the pursuit of human rights should be given priority. Why? Because such a move reduces the danger of cross-cutting political interests undermining both the effectiveness and legitimacy of international action; because human rights agreements provide a clearer and far better specified set of understandings of what domestic developments should trigger international actions (cf. difficulties of agreeing on meaning of democracy and on nature of democratic backsliding); and, finally, because such a course offers a better prospect of striking an acceptable balance between protecting basic human rights on the one hand and granting space for legitimate variation and diversity on the other.

Coercive enforcement

A second important issue of the post-Cold War period has been a revival of the question of stronger enforcement, of giving more effective 'teeth' to the norms of international society. In the area of human rights, as one moves beyond standard-setting, promotion and education, there are, broadly speaking, two roads.

Soft systems of implementation

The implementation of human rights standards under existing international human rights regimes is based largely on inquiry and exposure. These involve the creation of supervision bodies under major global and regional treaties, the submission of reports by states and the establishment of working groups and of theme and country rapporteurs and finding missions. Civil and political rights are generally the most strongly protected, with the 1966 UN Covenant establishing a body of experts, the Human Rights Committee, to receive and examine periodic reports from states, with an optional procedure allowing the investigation of complaints brought by states alleging a violation, and to investigate complaints by or on behalf of individual victims. The Latin American and European systems have dual structures of commissions of independent experts and regional human rights courts.

It is, of course, very clear that governments have sought to preserve their dominant position, to maintain control over the implementation procedures and to restrict the scope for individual action. It is equally clear just how difficult it has been to insulate the system from cross-cutting foreign policy goals and the ability of major powers to exempt themselves from scrutiny. Yet it is also important to note a number of positive developments: (1) the gradual increase in the range of states subjected to external monitoring and in the intrusiveness of the procedures; (2) the achievement of a greater degree of distance from direct political pressures, even within the UN system; (3) the enormous expansion in the availability of information on human rights conditions (produced and disseminated by national governments, by the NGO community, and by international institutions); (4) the extent to which state-based regimes have provided the political platform for ever greater NGO involvement.

On one level, the system seeks to protect human rights through the mobilisation of shame and by increasing the costs to a state's reputation (the extent to which China has recently been prepared to buy and cajole votes in support of no-action motions at the UN Commission on Human Rights provides some indication that reputational concerns do have some political impact). At another, and probably more important level, there is the role of international norms in strengthening and empowering groups struggling domestically – both legally and politically, and in creating both material incentives and normative pressures for the internalisation of such norms into domestic legal and political systems.[9]

Harder and more coercive enforcement measures

The first, and most familiar, category concerns unilateral actions by powerful states employing a range of positive and negative sanctions.[10] In the case of the United States the general issue of human rights has become relatively firmly established in both the foreign policy process and in political consciousness, with significant elements of continuity in the period since the mid-1970s and with a rhetorical reassertion of the importance of human rights and democracy in the Clinton Administration's talk of the politics of democratic enlargement.

Yet, aside from the vicissitudes of unilateral action, two other important developments need to be noted. First, we have seen an ascending scale of multilateral actions on the part of both the UN and regional bodies: from non-recognition (as with OAS and Haiti); to the application of economic sanctions; to conflict resolution and political reconstruction (as in Cambodia or El Salvador); to peace-keeping/peace-making with a strong humanitarian component (as in Somalia, Rwanda or Bosnia);

to military intervention to restore an overthrown government (Haiti). The most important elements of these developments have been the shrinking of understandings of non-intervention; the increasing tendency of the Security Council to act in response to breaches of legal obligations (as opposed to a strict concern with peace and security); and the inclusion of violations of human rights and of humanitarian law as problems justifying enforcement action under Chapter VII of the United Nations Charter.

Secondly, there has been the growth of human rights and democratic conditionalities – that is the institutionalised application of human rights or pro-democracy conditionality to interstate flows of economic resources as a means of inducing domestic policy change. Here it is important to note, first, the critical move away from conditionality as forming part of a specific economic bargain or contract (as was at least arguably the case with IMF economic conditionality) and towards using conditionality to promote objectives that are wholly unrelated to a specific flow of resources; and secondly, the entrenchment of political conditionality in the policies of the IFIs, and of the OECD Development Committee. A further important category of conditionality arises from the formalised establishment of criteria for admission to a particular economic or political grouping: the notion that membership of an alliance, economic bloc or international institution depends on the form of government or respect for human rights (visible in the increasingly explicit democratic membership criteria for admission to the EU or Mercosur and also in the OAS Santiago Declaration).

Each of these enforcement mechanisms raises particular issues, and generalisations are hazardous. Nevertheless a number of points can be made. Most familiar, but still most important, are the perils of unilateralism or of multilateralism that depends on, or can be manipulated by, major states. It would be politically and morally naïve to argue that unilateralism can never be justified or effective. Yet the problems of double-standards, of self-serving behaviour cloaked in idealistic clothes, of picking only those cases that serve other political or economic interests, remain all too evident and run the risk of undermining any claim that the system might have to normative coherence. This would matter less if the end of the Cold War had allowed for a broader definition of 'national interests' and greater room for the promotion of genuinely liberal goals. But, certainly in the case of the United States, there is no sign whatsoever that the tensions between human rights and 'harder' security or economic interests have altered in any significant way. Whilst action has indeed been taken in a number of cases where the costs were relatively low (e.g. Kenya and Malawi), the rhetoric of democratic enlargement is increasingly at odds with the direction of actual policy (the scaling-back of US human rights policy in Asia; major cross-cutting interests blocking any action or criticism in such cases as Russia, China, Saudi Arabia or Turkey; and the emergence in the United States of ever-stronger domestic opposition to multilateral involvement).

Secondly, there is the tension between the possibility of success via the imposition of coercion and the long-term process of regime-building. Attempts to move too rapidly towards the enforcement of international norms or agreements may well undermine the importance of consensus and of self-enforcement on which most international legal regulation continues to be based. Too strong an emphasis on enforcement may both hinder the hardening of existing human rights institutions and make states unwilling even to sign up to loose agreements or sets of principles for fear that they might be used to legitimise coercive intervention. Recent multilateral interventions provide good illustrations of the trade-off between short-term effectiveness and a long-term erosion of legitimacy.[11]

Thirdly, it has been extremely difficult to devise and maintain coherent and consistent systems of institutionalised conditionalities: political interests dictate when a particular conditionality will be upheld or dropped; non-trade conditionalities arise only for certain groups of states that are recipients of official aid, are in need of assistance from international institutions, or are applying to join regional bodies; powerful target states have been able to fend off inclusion (as with China) or to impose 'reverse' conditionalities (as with Malaysia in relation to Australia and Britain). There are also deep tensions between democratic/ human rights conditionality and the economic objectives that still dominate the relevant institutions; between the use of conditionality and the goal of promoting accountability (how can governments be held accountable for policies and priorities over which they have only limited control or authority?); and between the promotion of economic and political liberalisation *within* states and the maintenance of a manifestly unequal and undemocratic order *among* states and within the global economic system.

Finally, it is important to be realistic as to the limits of what can be achieved by external pressure and to evaluate empirically the role of different categories of external factors. Too often, judgements about the failings of the international human rights regime point simply to the absence of 'enforcement'. There is a powerful assumption, shared both by many liberals and by realist writers in international relations, that if only states and their governments had the will to enforce international norms, then human rights would improve.

International regimes for human rights are designed to encourage some states to adopt policies that they would not otherwise pursue. The question of whether states adhere to such regimes is not a function of the extent to which a regime enhances information or discourages cheating; rather it is a function of the extent to which more powerful states in the system are willing to enforce the principles and norms of the regime.[12]

Comparisons are frequently made with the abolition of the slave trade and with the willingness of the British government to deploy its navy over a protracted period. Yet whilst the political will to take strong measures up to and including military intervention may well in certain circumstances be both justified and effective, such a view lays too much weight on the role of external power and grossly overstates the impact and importance of external factors, especially in helping to sustain the conditions necessary for the protection of human rights and the maintenance of democratic systems of governance. It is not simply that the costs to major states of enforcing human rights norms may often outweigh the benefits to the would-be enforcers and distract them from other foreign policy objectives and concerns. It is rather that the viability of external coercive power to promote democracy and human rights over the long term is likely to be extremely limited.

As recent UN interventions have made all too clear, it is critical to think about both the possibilities and the limits of military intervention, about the trade-offs between conflicting goals during such interventions (delivering humanitarian relief vs promoting a political settlement vs punishing those guilty of war crimes), and about what might constitute an acceptable exit strategy (cf. the tendency to use elections as the cover for getting out). Moreover, whilst the category of 'democracy via invasion' does include some successes (e.g. Japan and Germany), success in these cases was due to a long list of very specific domestic and international factors. The empirical literature on international aspects of democratisation has tended to underscore the centrality of domestic political processes. Early writing in this field tended to allow only a very limited role for international factors. As one study noted: 'Without exception, each of our authors attributes the course of political development and regime change primarily to internal structures and actions, while acknowledging the way structures have been shaped historically by international factors . . .'[13] More recently, greater significance has been attached to the external context, but chiefly in terms of shaping the domestic context within which liberalisation and democratisation take place and of setting limits to the range of available policy options.[14] Empirical studies have certainly demonstrated that specific points of pressure (such as on human rights) can indeed make a difference.[15] Yet the idea that there are simple channels of external influence or effective 'levers' waiting to be pulled is wholly illusory.

State coherence

In the post-Cold War world the old dichotomy between domestic order and international anarchy has been recast in many parts of the world, with a number of states unable to secure even the most minimal conditions of social order and beset by ethnic and communal strife. Particularly when such breakdowns occur in parts of the world that lack either geopolitical or economic importance, the prospects for effective sustained action to prevent humanitarian disasters remain slim. Such problems are certainly not new. Consider the contemporary resonance of the following nineteenth-century commentary:

All men are not in fact completely free, nor are all states completely sovereign. There may be States in name, which are not such in reality – Governments which labour under an incurable incapacity to govern, and which a makeshift policy keeps alive under an irregular and capricious tutelage, in order to avoid, on the one hand, the embarrassments which be occasioned by their fall, and to prevent, on the other, as far as possible, (for such efforts often come too late) atrocious barbarities and gross oppressions. To such cases the principle [of non-intervention] does not apply, and the hopeless infirmity which makes interference necessary is an evil that we have to deal with in the best way we can.[16]

This category of problem is, however, by no means confined to cases of societal collapse, civil war and the total breakdown of central authority. Thus, for example, 'traditional' human rights violations by high-level agents of the state have undoubtedly declined in Latin America with the move away from military government. Yet sustained and 'structural' human rights violations still occur on a large scale: low-level police brutality, the murder of street children, rural violence, attacks on indigenous peoples. In many cases the role of state authorities may be difficult to demonstrate, or may indeed be wholly absent. And the capacity of weak and inefficient state apparatuses to correct these abuses may be extremely limited. The shift away from human rights abuses that are clearly the result of state action poses very major challenges for an international human rights system that is built around the protection of individuals against actions of the state; that is built around legal notions of state responsibility; and that assumes, politically, that pressure can be exerted on states which possess the levers to improve the situation – in other words that states which are part of the problem can also be part of the solution.

Finally, one of the major reasons for state breakdown has been the severity of conflicts between different and contradictory conceptions of a people. It is here that we encounter the problematic relationship between self-determination, democratisation and human rights. International law has sought to ring-fence the right of self-determination, to see it as a right enjoyed by individuals and groups within states. It has tended to deny any right to secession and to see the emergence of new states in such circumstances as an extra-legal fact to which it will respond as and when necessary but which is not subject to legal judgement. Major states have sought to welcome the idea of self-determination in theory but to restrict its application in practice, giving priority to the stability of frontiers and responding to secession crises in the light of shifting political interests.

States and other actors

One of the most important changes in the international context of human rights protection has been the expanding role of NGOs. This in turn has formed part of the broader emergence of what some have called 'international civil society', or, better, 'global civil society': the 'emergence of a parallel arrangement of political interaction . . . focused on the self-conscious construction of networks of knowledge and action, by decentred, local actors'.[17] The infrastructure of increased economic interdependence (new systems of communication and transportation) and the extent to which new technologies (satellites, computer networks etc.) have increased the costs and difficulty of governments controlling flows of information, facilitated the diffusion of values, knowledge and ideas, and enhanced the ability of like-minded groups to organise across national boundaries. From a liberal perspective, the strength of such groups rests on their ability to articulate a powerful set of human values, to harness the growing sense of a cosmopolitan moral awareness, and to respond to the multiple failures of the state system, both locally and globally. Influence does not derive from narrow economic incentives nor from power-political interests, but rather from ideas and values that are felt directly, if still unevenly, by individual human beings.

NGOs have carved out very important roles, four of which may be briefly noted:[18] (1) information-gathering and facilitating the flow of information from those directly affected to international human rights groups and monitoring bodies. This has been critical in opening up knowledge of human rights abuses in remote areas where national media might be uninterested in the assessment and evaluations of individual countries' records given the failings of formal implementing bodies to do this; (2) the 'hue and cry' function of such groups in using that information both to mobilise shame and to pressure specific cases and to extract from governments the need for new areas of rights; (3) NGOs and community organisations as a vital conduit for external assistance on human rights and for creating social structures within which external assistance can be effectively used, especially when state structures have been weakened or destroyed; (4) as a transmission belt for changes in attitudes and values where the focus of attention is not direct influence on governments, but rather broader social changes (although this kind of political role has more often been asserted than empirically demonstrated).

The multiple failings of the human rights system and the degree to which the state is so often a central part of the problem have led some to look beyond these activities, viewing NGOs and social movements as the most appropriate vehicle for fostering a transnational moral community, as the only way of driving states towards radical reform of human rights procedures, and, in the long run, as holding out the best hope of diluting the statist focus of the human rights system. As we have seen, that system is statist, not just in the extent to which it is so dominated by the political interests of states, but in its very foundations. To quote Henkin:

> In our international system of nation-states, human rights are to be enjoyed in national societies as rights under national law. The purpose of international law is to influence states to recognize and accept human rights, to reflect these rights in their national constitutions and laws, to respect and ensure their enjoyment through national institutions, and to incorporate them into national ways of life.[19]

The most ambitious alternative to this traditional conception is to strive towards a system in which human rights and democracy form part of the law of a transnational civil society, in which the state loses its place as an autonomous institution and instead becomes one of many actors and one participant in a broader and more complex social process.

Yet, whilst this alternative is superficially attractive, many obstacles emerge. First, it is important to note the enormous diversity of voices within the NGO movement and the lack of apparent means of mediating between them or evaluating their representational authority. Civil society represents an arena for political action, with many NGOs little more than self-appointed and self-created lobbies, despite their pervasive rhetoric of authenticity. Secondly, it is not clear that NGOs are best suited to long-term institutional action or involvement and there are deep divisions within and between human rights NGOs over the dangers of co-option and loss of autonomy. Moreover, particularly in cases of widespread violence and social conflict, NGOs cannot replicate the functions of the state, especially in the provision of security. Thirdly, whilst liberal ideas of transnational civil society claim to open spaces, it is equally possible that the dominant logic of that civil society will work to further processes of cultural homogenisation – witness the alacrity with which many NGOs have picked up calls for increased conditionality and intervention. And finally, there is the question of power. On the one hand, there is the problem of power relations within transnational civil society itself which are not necessarily any more equitable than those within the state system. On the other, the workings of transnational civil society may work to reinforce disparities of power between states and to open up new kinds of inequalities, again unmediated by the (albeit fragile) norms that have developed within international society.

The expansion of the human rights agenda, the move towards more coercive enforcement and the problems of state breakdown raise a further, and more general, problem in that the expansion of the human rights agenda and the concurrent attempt to promote liberal values reinforces divisions within international society into different categories of states. The creation of international society and, especially, the successful consolidation of an increasingly dense international society in particular parts of the world, leads naturally to divisions between insiders and outsiders. If there is an international society, what are its limits? Does it incorporate the entire human race or is it limited to a particular area? If it is limited, what are the principles of inclusion and exclusion? To what extent is such a division a source of instability and insecurity? On one side, there is a long Western tradition of doctrines and ideas that rested on principles of exclusiveness, based on being Christian, being European or being 'civilised'; on the other side, there is the powerful counter-current in Western thought that has maintained the existence of a universal community of mankind and that has drawn its primary inspiration from the long tradition of natural law.

A further question concerns patterns of interaction 'across the divide'. At one extreme, realist doctrines have often denied all legal and moral rights to those without the power to force respect for their independence. At the other extreme, revolutionist doctrines have insisted on an absolute equality of rights, both as individuals and as communities, and on a duty to assist their liberation. In between, liberals have been (and remain) deeply divided. One strand has argued for a strong (if never quite absolute) respect for pluralism and equality between communities and cultures and has laid great emphasis on the norms of sovereignty and non-intervention. The other (far more powerful) strand has accorded only conditional or secondary rights to those outside the inner core and has argued for intervention (or imperialism) to promote the intrinsically superior values of the inner core.

The dominant trend in the twentieth century has been to move against this exclusivism and exclusion – as exemplified in the struggle for equal sovereignty, for decolonisation, for racial equality and for economic justice. Moreover, the dominant norms of international society (non-intervention, constraints on the use of force, sovereignty equality) have offered a degree of protection – for good and ill – to many extremely fragile political entities ('quasi-states' to use Robert Jackson's phrase). Yet the promotion of 'universal' values and moves towards linking domestic and international legitimacy threaten to re-establish these older patterns of hierarchy and differentiation. Indeed, it is not entirely fanciful to see old nineteenth-century categories reappearing in the emerging late-twentieth-century distinctions between a core zone of liberal states, well-ordered non-liberal societies and states that have either 'failed' or should be classed as pariahs or outlaws.

There can be no doubt that many states have been extremely ill-deserving of any international protection and their claims to represent the interest of their citizens and embody a sense of national community have been tenuous, if not wholly deceitful. Yet there are problems of acting too directly on this fact. First, it runs the risk of reinforcing the power and values of the most powerful states in the system and of cementing international hierarchy. The paradox of universalism is that the successful promotion of 'universal' or 'global' values will often depend on the willingness of particularly powerful states to promote them and that their successful promotion can all too easily work to reinforce the already marked inequality of power and status. Many Asian states view the rhetoric of global values as a thin veneer covering the reassertion of Western hegemony. Secondly, adapting international institutions and diplomatic practices to new patterns of both formal and substantive inequality is likely to be extremely difficult.

Universality

To what extent can democracy and human rights be understood as universal values? Is there today a solid consensus on the model of political development most likely to be protective of human rights? For most people human rights are inherently universal, concerned with protecting and furthering the dignity and worth of all human beings. We are unavoidably dealing with rights that are enjoyed simply by virtue of being human. Yet the universality of both the notion of human rights and the nature of human rights has been, and remains, highly contested.

On one side, universalists of an optimistic frame of mind can point to a number of positive developments. In the first place, they note the hardening of an impressive normative structure and agreed standards built around a commitment to universality. The human rights regime that has emerged in the period since the Second World War is global in at least two senses: first, that the individual and collective rights defined in the increasing number of international legal instruments are indeed held to apply to all human beings; and secondly, that the UN has played a central role in the process of standard-setting, promotion, and (to a clearly far less satisfactory extent) protection of human rights. Moreover, on most core rights the scope for governments to exempt themselves or to raise the old claim of unlimited sovereignty has gone, or been very heavily constrained.

Secondly, they note the end of old divisions that marked the debates on human rights in the 1960s and 1970s: between East and West and between North and South.[20] These involved clashes about the nature of rights but were of course embedded in bitter political rivalries and reflected a very wide-ranging desire to defend absolutist conceptions of sovereignty from encroaching international institutions and regimes.

Thirdly, and even without accepting the more extreme forms of Western triumphalism, it is possible to argue that the position of Western values has undergone dramatic change – in relation to say the late 1970s at the height of the Third World challenge and at a time of re-emerging Superpower confrontation. In the political field, one can note the wave of democratisations of the 1980s and the extent to which many previous opponents of democracy have come to view political democracy as an intrinsic rather than an instrumental value. In the economic domain, this argument stresses the undermining of the challenges to liberal capitalism with the collapse of the socialist regime in the former Soviet Union. There is the widespread move away from statist, developmentalist thinking in very large parts of the developing world. One can observe the increasing power of the global economic system to homogenise the practical range of economic policies and, in effect, to make any notion of 'opting out' of the global capitalist system all but impossible.[21] And, finally, in the environmental field, the optimist can point to a gathering international consensus around the need for concerted international efforts to protect the environment and to the crystallisation in institutions and international agreements of new normative principles that have important implications for the human rights agenda – for example, the importance of transnational equity, of the rights of future generations, of the stewardship of biodiversity and the protection of indigenous cultures.

The optimistic Western universalist is also likely to underscore the impact of 'progressive enmeshment', developing the Kantian notion of a gradual but progressive diffusion of liberal values, partly as a result of liberal economics and increased economic interdependence, partly as a liberal legal order comes to sustain the autonomy of a global civil society, and partly as a result of the successful example set by the multifaceted liberal capitalist system of states. At one extreme, this has involved a strident reassertion of modernisation theories that stress both the convergence between societies and the links between economic and political liberalisation. But it is worth highlighting the extent to which weak versions of cultural relativism often accept these same assumptions – that the ideas of democracy and human rights are essentially a product of modernity and bound up with the development of the state and market; that allowances need to be made given the diversity of societies and levels of development; but that we can be reasonably hopeful that, in the long run, development and modernisation will work towards the diffusion of liberal values.

Finally, and again without necessarily buying into more extreme forms of liberal globalisation, the univeralist questions the essentialist vision of rigid and incommunicable cultures and stresses instead the fluidity and malleability of cultures and societies. On this view, it is highly doubtful that the world consists of a limited number of cultures each with its own indestructible and immutable core. If this is indeed not the case and if cultures develop and change over time, then values can be diffused and there is no reason in principle why European or Western human rights norms cannot be transferred effectively to other cultures. Given that all cultures are amalgams of various cultural components and influences, it is far from clear why Western ideas on human rights should remain permanently outside the experience of other cultures. After all, human rights were not some natural and inevitable product of Western culture but had to be consciously created, developed and extended – note the extent to which Western understandings of human rights have changed enormously in the course of the past two centuries.

Yet this rather rosy picture omits a number of important features and challenges. The rhetoric of universalism is all too often contradicted by the very different constructions placed upon international agreements, by deep-rooted philosophical and cultural divergences over the meaning and significance of human rights, and by the widespread denial in practice of the very same rights that are so widely applauded in theory.

Two classes of challenges are especially important and problematic. First are those that arise from the power of nationalist ideologies and the force of communitarian commitments. Human rights will always remain marginal for the nationalists who view the nation or the ethnic group as an objective phenomenon standing above the individual; who believe the character of all individuals to be shaped by, and only intelligible in the context of, the national group; who argue that loyalty to the nation overrides all other loyalties; and who preach an ethic of loyalty, belonging and sacrifice to the group or community. Global human rights will also remain insecure and uncertain for those, often liberal, communitarian theorists who believe that the survival and freedom of separate political communities represent the highest values of international society.

Secondly, there are the regionalist challenges, most notably in the Islamic world and in Asia. Regionalism was built into the human rights system, but principally in terms of implementation – 'the local carriers of a global message' to use John Vincent's apt phrase.[22] The rights themselves are universal, but their practical implementation would be more effective if devolved to the regional level. Thus we have seen a variety of regional human rights regimes in Europe, the Americas, Africa and the Arab world with differing degrees of institutionalisation (especially in terms of implementation) and, within the limits of global standards, some acknowledgement of cultural differences. As with co-operation more generally, so it is argued that greater social, political and economic homogeneity will make it easier to implement human rights at the regional level and make the inevitably increased intrusion into domestic affairs politically easier to accept. Thus, as in the areas of economics and security, there is a recurrent liberal vision of a productive partnership between the regional and the global and of the neat interlocking of regional political, security or economic co-operation within an overarching global order – a kind of interregional globalism.

Yet the line between global promulgation and regional implementation has always been a problematic one and it is hardly surprising that regional human rights frameworks (tied to the broader resurgence of regionalism) have re-emerged as vehicles for the promotion of conflicting conceptions of human rights and conflicting views as to how those rights should be promoted. Thus, far from slotting nicely into a neat pattern of global subsidiarity, regionalism and regional co-operation may form the political framework for conflict over the definition of human rights and over the means by which they should be enforced internationally.

Asia is the region in which the challenge to Western conceptions of human rights has been most systematically developed, in which political clashes have been most evident, and in which the 'regionalist' focus has been most dominant. Here it is extremely important to unpack and disentangle the various elements which together make up the 'Asian challenge'. Conflict over human rights is often presented by both sides (e.g. Huntington for the West and Kausikan for Asia) in essentialist terms.[23] On the critical side, there is the official Asian rejection of Western claims that effective and open markets, restrictions on state power and the strengthening of civil society work naturally to promote both economic success and Western-style political liberalism. On the more constructive side, there is the idea of a distinctive Asian approach to human rights built around the idea of 'shared values': a different conception of the relationship between the individual and the state; respect for the community; the central importance of the duties that individuals owe towards the group; and the particular differences that follow from these values in terms of freedom of speech and freedom of association.[24] 'Nation before community and society before self', as the 1991 Singapore White Paper expressed it. Or, as Kishore Mabhubani put it in 1995, drawing out the relationship between human rights and power: 'All human rights covenants were created when the West was in power. In the future, these agreements will assert the rights of society over the rights of individuals.'[25]

Yet it is far from clear just how much of the conflict concerns divergences over the meaning of human rights that are rooted in cultural or civilisational distinctiveness. In the first place, it is important to note the diversity of voices within this allegedly coherent regionalist construction: the diversity of cultures and cultural traditions; the equally wide range of economic and political systems; the tremendous pace of social and economic change that is transforming societies and remoulding traditions; the fact that several major states (most notably Japan) have kept their distance from the discussion of Asian values. Thus, even at the official level, notions of a unified and coherent set of Asian values need to be taken with a large pinch of salt. Beyond the level of governments, NGOs have propounded a very different message on human rights, upholding strong conceptions of universality, and arguing both for greater weight for civil and political rights and for social justice and grass-roots empowerment. Finally, as noted above, cultures are not best understood as closed and impermeable systems, and it is not clear that the substantive differences are as deep as often suggested. For example, the communitarian and social values of the Catholic and Christian Democratic tradition of human rights are just as much as part of the West as Anglo-American individualist liberalism.

In addition, a great deal of the conflict over human rights in Asia has to do with traditional and straightforwardly political factors. In the first place, we are dealing with a very clear 'statist' challenge that reflects a shift in relative political and economic power. These are mostly strong and economically successful states whose governments perceived in the aftermath of the Cold War and the Gulf War a unipolar moment in which the United States had emerged as the dominant power and which seemed to provide the basis for expanded Western hegemony. Thus the Clinton Administration's talk of 'democratic enlargement' and the notion of giving 'teeth' to the enforcement of human rights were widely perceived in the region as attempts to reassert US power and frustrate the reshuffling of the international hierarchy. On the economic side, this was expressed in the fear that the West was using human rights concerns as a cover for economic protectionism (e.g. developing new norms on workers' rights). Such concerns have been most clearly embodied in Mahathir's claim that the North is using human rights to counter the economic advantages and success of Asian newly industrialising countries.

The overtly political character of the clash is also visible in the specific terms of the human rights debate. As the Bangkok Declaration made clear, official Asian resentment is as much about how human rights are to be implemented as it is over the content of the rights themselves. Hence the central defence of state sovereignty (widely shared across the region), the attacks on double-standards and conditionalities, and the calls for greater democratisation in international institutions. On one side, then, this has been a defensive response to an external challenge and, as in many other parts of the world, the external challenge has fed into debates about greater regional awareness: what it is to be part of Europe, the Americas or Asia? How it is that 'we' are to be differentiated from 'them'? But on the other side (and this is what makes Asia distinctive, certainly in comparison with other parts of the developing world) we find a strident and spirited assertion by increasingly self-confident Asian states (whose development owed very little to either democracy or the protection of human rights) that there are alternative frameworks for human rights and democracy. As Huntington's critics have argued, the clash between different cultural conceptions of human rights is maintained and manipulated by states as part of rather traditional power-political and mercantilist rivalry. These are strong states, not seeking to opt out, but rather to draw the line between integration and national autonomy in a different place to where many Western states would draw it.

Secondly, there is the internal political dimension. This involves the narrow denial of human rights by regimes determined to consolidate their power domestically and prepared, if necessary, to trample on human rights in the process; the building-up of the discourse of Asian values and of a 'threat' to those values as a means to increase political legitimacy; and the broader claim that ethnic and social tensions must not be allowed to undermine social cohesion and that the rampant individualism allegedly central to Western conceptions of human rights would lead precisely to this end.

Thirdly, there is the developmentalist claim and the revival of the idea that economic development trumps Western liberal notions of civil and political rights. At one extreme (and still visible in Chinese official statements) there is the Marxist notion that bourgeois rights can mean nothing without an end to feudal and capitalist exploitation. But, more commonly, there is the argument, beloved of developmentalist states in the 1970s, that the Western emphasis on civil and political rights is 'premature' and that economic and social rights must be upheld, and indeed strengthened by a right to development. As the critics rightly note, this kind of developmentalism provides an all-encompassing cloak for political repression. 'Through the Declaration [of the Right to Development], Asian governments seek to promote the ideology of developmentalism, which justifies repression at home and the evasion of sovereignty abroad.'[26] But it is still important to note that this kind of argument does not necessarily imply that the eventual end-point is in-compatible with Western conceptions of human rights and democracy.

One basic point, then, is that there are many different things going on in the polemics on Asian values and that the exact extent to which these clashes actually reflect cultural and civilisational claims is both very hard to discern and almost certainly varies from case to case. Yet to recognise the multilayered character of the debate does not do away with the problem. Even if the challenge is political rather than cultural or civilisational, it is still powerful, with serious implications for both the international human rights regime and international efforts to promote democracy. In addition, even if manipulated and abused by governments, the Asian debate does highlight real and genuine conflicts over the nature of human rights, above all in terms of the value to be attached to community and the balance between individual rights and social duties.

Conclusion

The five factors discussed above all underline the immense difficulties of translating the idea of universal human rights into effective political practice. World society is indeed characterised by power-political con-flict and by profound and abiding human difference. Disagreement about moral values is a natural and inevitable feature of life. For both prudential and moral reasons, international society must be sensitive to the claims of difference and diversity and, as postmodernism warns us, must guard against the temptations of 'essentialising' or 'universalising' discourses. It is not simply that, as both E. H. Carr and Marx remind us, there are likely to be good grounds for questioning and unmasking the motives of all those who set themselves up as 'agents of the general good' – nor that, even when genuinely held, the promotion of global values can work to entrench the special interests of particular states and to exacerbate inequality. It is rather that even if Locke's 'great and natural community' of humankind does indeed exist, it is, to use John Dunn's words, 'an extravagantly variegated natural community'. Or, as Stuart Hampshire has put it:

The clash of moral and religious loyalties has come to seem, in the light of recent history, much more than a temporary accident of human development, to be dispelled by the spreading of the natural sciences and by healthy enlightenment. Rather the deep-seated spiritual antagonisms have come to seem the essence of humanity, and it is an accident of history if, in some regions and for some period of time, a relative harmony of shared values prevails within a modern society.[27]

Faced by this situation, there are two kinds of choices. The first is to maintain a clear faith in the universal truth of certain human rights, but to recognise the difficulty of making progress in the real world. This has the advantage of not confusing what is right with what is acceptable and of providing a clear external point of reference and judgement. Yet such a course risks casting many of most critical issues in the human rights field into the realm of un- or semi-principled prudence. The universalist might, for example, argue: 'We know what universal human rights are all about. The problem is merely one of application. We will press on whenever and wherever it is feasible and productive to do so.' Yet, as this chapter has sought to argue, the process of application and implementation is fraught with political, legal and moral hazards. What precisely should be the scope of the human rights agenda? How far should human rights norms be enforced by the use of physical coercion? Who is the 'we' who decide how and when this universal agenda will be pursued and when deviations should be permitted in the interests of practicality? Given the manifest weakness of international institutions, will not this 'we' inevitably become the most powerful state or group of states?[28] Perhaps most importantly, what moral meaning can be attached to even the purist and most serene universalist voice (whether of the Kantian liberal or of the religious believer) echoing down from the mountain if those to whom it is addressed do not believe themselves to be part of even the thinnest and most fragile shared community?

A better answer is to eschew or at least downplay concern with foundations, to accept that values and conceptions of rights will remain imperfectly grounded, but to build on and develop the human rights culture and community that has evolved in practice – the element of consensus visible in the actual practice of states. Although its philosophical foundations will remain contested, this practical consensus is politically powerful and morally meaningful. Three elements are critical.

First, this consensus reflects a shared and widespread apprehension in the face of cruelty, barbarism and oppression and a shared awareness of the reality of human suffering. Suffering is a brute fact of social life whose significance is widely shared across cultures and religions and which is trivialised by postmodern suggestions of sentimental story-telling.[29] Of course, such apprehension does not stand wholly outside historical circumstances. Nor is it universal. It is not shared by the torturers nor by all of those who justify cruelty and oppression in the name of some overriding political, economic or religious cause. But it remains the most resilient bridge between the objective position of impartiality and detachment that is central to all moral judgement and the subjective commitment to particular affections, local circumstances and individual histories that is central to all moral passion and purpose.[30] As Carlos Santiago Niño has argued so powerfully, the project of human rights is above all a conscious and artificial construction designed to uphold human dignity and to prevent suffering in the face of persistent human bestiality.[31]

Secondly, the international and transnational culture of human rights involves a widely shared common language, an inclusive moral vocabulary and an authoritative and well-developed normative structure from which very few groups are prepared to try and exempt themselves. This shared discourse implies a general acceptance of certain general principles and processes and of a particular kind of rationality and argumentation. It limits the range of permissible justifications and motivations; it empowers particular groups and particular institutions; and it helps create incentives for socialisation and internalisation. It is, of course, shaped by its historical origins within a particular culture; but it is open, dynamic and resistant to permanent capture by a particular interest or power-political grouping. However varied the philosophical, political or cultural backgrounds from which it is approached, the emergence and spread of this transnational moral and legal discourse represents a major historical development.

The third element of the evolving practical consensus concerns the extent to which this transnational discourse and this shared moral consciousness have become embedded in concrete political practices and specific institutional structures. This chapter has sought to give a sense of just how far these structures and practices have developed but also of how far they remain fragile and riven by political conflict and moral dispute. Precisely for this reason the first commitment needs to be to forging and upholding a *procedural consensus*: an agreement between states over the framework of international rules and institutions by means of which clashes of interests and conflicting values can be mediated and through which accommodation might be possible. Only on this basis might international society be able to move in a sustainable fashion towards a *substantive value consensus* and towards convergence around a shared set of moral values and justice principles.[32]

The risk is that such a course may lose all sense of moral direction and foster despair of ever finding a clear point outside the evolving consensus on shared values that can serve as a focus of independent judgement and evaluation. The line between simple acceptability and political expedience on the one hand and the gradual nurturing of a shared political and moral community is likely to be extremely thin.[33] But, if we are concerned with both what is just and what is possible, with making connections between the worlds of ideal and non-ideal theory, then it is the line around which the debate needs to be concentrated. It is, of course, not the case that the system of states represents the only framework by which these tensions can be mediated. But, whilst global markets and the operations of many groups within transnational civil society are indeed central elements of the world political system, it is around the normative structures and institutions of international society and around the significant degree of existing consensus that future tensions between the universal and the particular will have to be resolved.

Notes

1 For a discussion and critique of the expansion of rights, see Philip Alston, 'Conjuring up new human rights: a proposal for quality control', *American Journal of International Law* 78 (1984): 607–21.
2 See especially Henry Shue, *Basic Rights: Subsistence, Affluence and US Foreign Policy* (Princeton University Press, 1980).
3 For a strong argument that democratic entitlement is moving from being a moral prescription to an international legal obligation, see Thomas Franck, 'The emerging right to democratic governance', *American Journal of International Law* 86 (1992): 46–91.
4 John Rawls, 'The law of peoples', in Stephen Shute and Susan Hurley (eds.), *On Human Rights* (New York: Basic Books, 1993).
5 Isaiah Berlin, 'Two concepts of liberty', in *Four Essays on Liberty* (Oxford University Press, 1969), esp. pp. 165–9; Jon Elster, 'Majority rule and individual

rights', in Stephen Shute and Susan Hurley (eds.), *On Human Rights: The Oxford Amnesty Lectures* (New York: Basic Books, 1993), pp. 111–34.

6 See Francisco Panizza, 'Human rights in the processes of transition and consolidation of democracy in Latin America', *Political Studies* 43 (1995): 168–88.

7 José Miguel Vivanco, 'International human rights litigation in Latin America: The OAS Human Rights System', in Carl Kaysen *et al.* (eds.), *Collective Responses to Regional Problems: The Case of Latin America and the Caribbean* (Cambridge, Mass.: American Academy of Arts and Sciences, 1994).

8 Philip Alston, 'The UN's human rights record: from San Francisco to Vienna and beyond', *Human Rights Quarterly* 16 (1994): 375–90.

9 On such processes of internalisation see Harold Hongju Koh, 'Why do nations obey international law?', *Yale Law Journal* 106 (1997): 2599–2659.

10 Between 1993 and 1996 the US Administration and Congress imposed or threatened sanctions to promote foreign policy goals sixty times against thirty-five countries.

11 See David Caron's discussion of legitimacy and international governance, 'The legitimacy of the collective authority of the Security Council', *American Journal of International Law* 87 (1993): 552–88.

12 Stephen D. Krasner, 'Sovereignty, regimes and human rights', in Volker Rittberger (ed.), *Regime Theory and International Relations* (Oxford University Press, 1993), pp. 140–1.

13 Larry Diamond and Juan J. Linz, 'Introduction: politics, society, and democracy in Latin America', in Larry Diamond, Juan J. Linz and Seymour Martin Lipset (eds.), *Democracy in Developing Countries* (Boulder: Rienner, 1989), p. 47.

14 See, for example, Laurence Whitehead (ed.), *International Dimensions of Democratization* (Oxford University Press, 1996); Tom Farer, *Beyond Sovereignty: Collectively Defending in the Americas* (Baltimore: Johns Hopkins University Press, 1996).

15 See, for example, Kathryn Sikking, 'Human rights issue-networks in Latin America', *International Organization* 47 (1993): 411–41; Carlos Escudé, 'Argentina: the costs of contradiction', in Abraham Lowenthal (ed.), *Exporting Democracy. The United States and Latin America* (Baltimore: Johns Hopkins University Press, 1991).

16 Montague Bernard, 'On the principle of non-intervention', p. 8. Quoted in James Lin, 'Humanitarianism and military force: humanitarian intervention and international society', D.Phil. thesis, University of Oxford (1995), pp. 100–1.

17 Ronnie D. Lipshultz, 'Reconstructing world politics: the emergence of global civil society', *Millennium* 21 (1992): 389–429, at 390.

18 For a recent survey see Rachel Brett, 'The role and limits of human rights NGOs at the United Nations', *Political Studies* 43 (1995): 96–110.

19 Louis Henkin, 'International human rights and rights in the United States', in Theodor Meron (ed.), *Human Rights in International Law: Legal and Policy Issues* (Oxford University Press, 1989), p. 25.

20 These and other difficulties are examined in John Vincent, *Human Rights and International Relations* (Cambridge University Press, 1986), esp. chs 4, 5

and 6; and Jack Donnelly, *Universal Human Rights in Theory and Practice* (Ithaca, Cornell University Press), esp. ch. 3.

21 The greater apparent stability of the international rights discourse has also been facilitated by the more general retreat into the background of economic and social rights, influenced by the market liberal orthodoxy on markets and the retreat of the state and on the need to scale down the services which the state seeks to provide. If this path does not bring all its promises, then there is good reason to expect that the demand for greater attention to welfare rights will return, both within the industrialised world and internationally.

22 Vincent, *Human Rights and International Relations*, p. 101.

23 Samuel P. Huntington, *The Clash of Civilizations and the Remaking of World Order* (London: Simon and Schuster, 1997). For Asian government perspectives, see Bilahari Kausikan, 'Asia's different standard', *Foreign Policy*, 92 (1993): 24–41; and Robert Bartley *et al.*, *Democracy and Capitalism. Asian and American Perspectives* (Singapore: Institute of Southeast Asian Studies, 1993).

24 For an excellent elaboration of the debate, see Yash Ghai, 'Asian perspectives on human rights', in James Tang (ed.), *Human Rights and International Relations in the Asia Pacific* (London: Pinter, 1993), pp. 54–67.

25 Quoted in Michael Leifer, 'Tigers, tigers spurning rights', *Times Higher Education Supplement*, 21 April 1995, p. 16.

26 Ghai, 'Asian perspectives on human rights', p. 59.

27 Stuart Hampshire, 'Liberalism: the new twist', *New York Review of Books* 12 August 1993, p. 43.

28 The disturbing lack of self-doubt about the process by which these prudential decisions are to be made is very evident in Tesón's stridently cosmopolitan critique of John Rawls: Fernando R. Tesón, 'The Rawlsian theory of international law', *Ethics and International Affairs* 9 (1995): 79–99, esp. 97–8.

29 For such suggestions, see Richard Rorty, 'Human rights, rationality and sentimentality', in Shute and Hurley (eds.), *On Human Rights*.

30 See Thomas Nagel, *The View from Nowhere* (Oxford University Press, 1986).

31 Carlos Santiago Niño, *The Ethics of Human Rights* (Oxford: Clarendon Press, 1991).

32 On the centrality of process to international legitimacy, see Thomas Franck, *The Power of Legitimacy Among Nations* (New York: Oxford University Press, 1990).

33 See Jack Donnelly's discussion of the idea of consensus and the distinction between a practical consensus and a theoretical consensus: Donnelly, *Universal Human Rights in Theory and Practice*, pp. 41–5.

Ken Booth and Tim Dunne

Students have traditionally played a prominent role in calling for political change. Student groups – then small – were on the barricades of nineteenth-century Europe in opposition to authoritarian regimes. They took to the streets in much larger groups in the 1960s to attack the US war in Vietnam and the racist regime in South Africa. Since the end of the Cold War their political prominence has been greatest in the area of human rights and – surprisingly so to some – in tough regimes in Asia rather than in the liberal West. Student protests have been seen in South Korea, Indonesia and Burma, and most dramatically in Tiananmen Square in Beijing in 1989, resulting in the infamous massacre.

The particular role of students as agents of progressive change was stressed by Daw Aung San Suu Kyi in an address to the American University in Washington in January 1997. The address was delivered by her husband; not because – as is widely believed – she is unable to leave Burma but because she foregoes this freedom in order to continue the struggle against tyranny with other pro-democracy campaigners. In the address, she drew attention to the tradition in modern Burmese history of student opposition to authoritarianism. Her speech also contained important universalist references: to the 'human predilection for fair play and compassion'; to the belief that the 'cause of liberty and justice finds sympathetic responses around the world'; to the certainty that '[t]hinking and feeling people everywhere' understand 'the deeply rooted human need for a meaningful existence that goes beyond the mere gratification of material desires'. She then called upon those with an interest in expanding their capacity for promoting intellectual freedom and humanitarian ideals to oppose the Burmese military regime, by, for example, taking a stand against companies that do business with the regime. She ended with words that fittingly bring together most of the key themes in human rights – the universal and the local, the emancipatory and the immanent, and theory and practice: 'Please use your liberty to promote ours.'[1]

As a number of chapters have argued, the post-1945 world has witnessed the emergence of a 'global human rights culture'. Liberty, emancipation, education and universalism are integral to that culture; these are also ideals of the university – perhaps more usually expressed in terms of freedom of speech, overcoming ignorance, expanding knowledge, and searching for truth. Together, the ideals of the university and the spread of a human rights culture constitute learning beyond frontiers.

At the interstate level, the existence of a global human rights culture is evident from the growing body of human rights standards and conventions which the vast majority of states have signed. Over the past fifty years, the commitments articulated in the Universal Declaration have been embedded in the legal structure of international society to the extent that individuals are now subjects of international law. In Louis Henkin's words, 'Ours is the age of rights.'[2] This developing global human rights culture has been given a significant boost by the spread of democratic ideas and values in countries which previously rejected them. The transnational spread of – and problems with – these values has received considerable attention in International Relations in recent times.[3] But what has often been neglected in academic analyses of this subject (but not by Richard Falk and Mary Kaldor earlier in this book) has been a consideration of the way in which the emergent global human rights culture can be strengthened from below. One central aspect of this process, and the subject of this concluding chapter, is the role that education can play in promoting human rights values.

Thinking about the relationship between education and human rights draws directly from a cluster of themes addressed in both parts of this volume. The first part of our argument will make a case for a cosmopolitan education. Here we are implicitly building upon many of the contributions to Part I, which argue for a more expansive understanding of our obligations to others whilst remaining sensitive to cultural difference. In particular, we will be defending the justifications made by philosophers and moralists who have argued for an education which transmits certain core 'liberal' values. The next step in the argument provides a brief empirical discussion about the nature of the 'right' to an education. A crucial question here is the extent to which this right has been met. Although there has been significant progress in the overall access to and participation in education worldwide – over 1 billion young people are now in formal education as compared with around 300 million in 1953 – the proportion of those who are illiterate is alarmingly high and unevenly spread (51.2 per cent in the least developed countries as against 1.3 per cent in the developed world).[4]

The level of educational provision is largely an empirical question, as the previous statistic about literacy rates suggests. Below, we explicitly bring together the right to an education with the normative claim that this right should include an education in human rights. Being literate is not enough if 'elementary' education is informed by xenophobia, intolerance, militarism, class or caste elitism, or hyper-masculinity. For this reason, we argue that education *as* a right should be integrated with an education *about* human rights. Although we would argue that human rights can be integrated into education at all levels, the discussion here will be restricted to the role that universities can play. This obviously raises a number of fundamental questions about the appropriate relationship between values and pedagogy in the context of university education.

Part II of the book explores a number of issues in the human rights field, including the key question of 'agency'; or, to put the point another way, what can different actors do to increase awareness of and compliance with human rights agreements? We felt that the most appropriate conclusion to a book which is guided by the negative dialectic – 'there are all these rights, yet the bodies keep piling up' – would be to reflect on the issues affecting those with a responsibility to educate university students. For this reason, this concluding chapter ends with a discussion of the kinds of values education should cultivate in students. In short, what does it mean to be teaching and researching human rights in the final years of a paradoxical century that has been described as both *The Age of Rights* (Louis Henkin) and *The Age of Extremes* (Eric Hobsbawm)?[5]

Inventing humanity

Richard Rorty deploys the phrase 'global human rights culture' (coined by the Argentinian jurist and philosopher Eduardo Rabossi) in order to defend a liberal account of human rights which does not commit what he regards as the twin errors of epistemological foundationalism and ontological universalism. By taking rights out of metaphysics, he succeeds in part in opening up a philosophical space for thinking about different practices and the ways in which these may sustain or undermine political communities. In place of moral philosophy, Rorty wishes to develop a social theory of solidarity, grounded in no more than the physiological claim that all human beings have a capacity for feeling 'pain and suffering'. It is only through a 'sentimental' liberal education that individuals learn to extend their sympathy to strangers.[6] (Whether educating the sentiments is a strong enough basis on which to attempt to deal with a world of human wrongs was challenged in chapters 1 and 4.)

Of course, Rorty's emphasis upon the centrality of education in promoting a civic culture is only the most recent example of a history of thought about education that reaches back centuries. Indeed, Rorty's injunction, to imagine ourselves in the 'shoes of the despised', is exactly the sentiment that Shakespeare stirs in *The Merchant of Venice*. Shylock begins his defence with the claim that Jews have eyes, organs and passions just like any other human beings. The climax of his speech is reached when he universalises his pain and suffering in terms of common humanity: 'If you prick us,' Shylock pleads to his accusers, 'do we not bleed?'

It is to Plato that we traditionally turn in order to find a discussion of the need for a positive link between education and the health of the political community. Plato prescribed a particular kind of pedagogy in which moral learning proceeds dialogically. As he argued in the *Republic*, education is not about imparting 'true knowledge into a soul that does not possess it'. Instead, Plato advocates what has come to be known as the Socratic method which sees education 'as leading or drawing vision out of the student rather than putting it in'.[7] In contemporary debates about higher education (particularly in the United States) it is possible to discern a liberal arts pedagogic culture which views learning as a process of 'drawing out', strongly opposed by traditionalists who hold fast to the idea that education consists of 'imparting' knowledge about a particular 'canon'. Our view is that knowledge has to be imparted – we can see further by standing on the shoulders of great thinkers, as the old adage has it – but the traditional canon is not enough. It should be expanded and problematised, and the main aim is to help students think for themselves. Kant's motto for the Enlightenment – 'dare to know' – still stands.[8]

Whilst the Enlightenment resurrected the belief that citizens needed to be educated in order to realise the 'good life', this ideal remained deeply gendered in its application. This can be seen clearly in Rousseau's *Emile*, who required a different education from Sophie for the reason that girls were 'unlike' boys 'in constitution and temperament'. This patriarchal argument in favour of single-sex education was dismissed by Mary Wollstonecraft, who noted how this emphasis upon sexual differences could 'taint the mind'. Where the contemporary debate differs markedly from the eighteenth century is that educationalists and policymakers today recognise the fundamental right of women and men to have the same access to education – except, that is, for regressive polities such as Afghanistan and Algeria. What this illustrates is the way in which the right to education – like all other rights – has been contested historically. The idea of education being a *right* is a relatively recent invention – but it is a crucial one in the process of humanity's self-invention.

Assumptions about gendered differences are one example of exclusionary practices which have prevailed historically in the thinking of most societies about education. The greatest exclusionary practices, however, developed in parallel with the processes of state formation. Across the world, education became intimately enmeshed into the nation-building process.[9] And it remains so, and not only in 'new' nations. Learning became nationalised, with the result that education failed to live up to the Stoic belief that we are all citizens of the world.[10] As the dialectic of nationalism and Westphalia led to the ideal of the sovereign nation-state, so did the norm of learning within frontiers. The United Kingdom is a good example of a state whose educational provision has been determined overwhelmingly by 'national' needs. Although today education in Britain generally complies with the standards laid down by the human rights regime, this is not because successive governments have believed that a right to education (and the right to a human rights education) is *universal*, but because liberal education is consonant with 'our' particular legal traditions and civic habits (an argument made by Chris Brown in chapter 3). Rights talk, after all, has traditionally been alien to British public life, hence we should not be surprised by the fact that international human rights treaties are referred to neither in British legislation nor in the judiciary.[11]

The prospects for cosmopolitan education – learning beyond frontiers and taking a global perspective on the human future – is in practice heavily circumscribed by cultural particularity and by statism. Even in the realm of ideal theory, the idea of cosmopolitan education is only faintly apparent in the writings of contemporary philosophers and educationalists. One of its most articulate recent exponents is Martha Nussbaum. She has mounted a powerful case against communitarian liberals who believe that education should, first and foremost, promote national values. In place of a pedagogic politics which emphasises differences between communities, Nussbaum advocates a 'cosmopolitan education' which teaches children and young adults how to draw the outer circle of obligation (common humanity) in towards the centre (family, community). Learning beyond national boundaries is central to realising the cosmopolitan ideal that all individuals are of equal moral value and should be part of 'our community of dialogue and concern'.[12] In other words, a cosmopolitan education must be at the heart of the invention of an other-regarding global community.

There is no guarantee that the sort of argument favoured by Nussbaum and ourselves will produce a world characterised by individual and group peace and security. It would be naïve to equate formal education with humane behaviour: it helps, but it is far from sufficient. As A. C. Grayling reminds us, 'no doubt there were SS officers who read Goethe and listened to Beethoven, then went to work in the gas chambers'. A liberal education does not automatically produce better people, though we agree with Grayling that 'it does so far more often than the ignorance and selfishness which arise from lack of knowledge and impoverishment of insight'.[13] When she was Prime Minister, Margaret Thatcher asked rhetorically of one of her ministers: 'What have educated people ever done for this country?'[14] 'What did ignorant people ever do?' we would reply, and here we are not talking of lack of education in the narrow sense, of literacy and numeracy, but in terms of sensibility, and of ethics.

Like Nussbaum, Grayling writes in the tradition of those who have argued for an escape from the narrow confines of 'morality' into the broader conception of 'ethics', as conceived by the Ancient Greeks.[15] For the latter, the whole of life is to be conceived as an ethical encounter ('one lives and does well as a whole person, and both one's flourishing and one's effect on others flows from the fact that one has a certain total character'). This, for Grayling, is what should underpin a liberal education. In its content such an education should include a knowledge of literature, history and the arts, in order to help us to live 'more reflectively and knowledgeably, especially about the range of human experience and sentiment, as it exists now and here, and in the past and elsewhere'. A person who has approached study in this way is better equipped to understand the 'interests, needs and desires' of others, so that they can be treated with respect and sympathy, 'however different their choices or the experiences that have shaped them'. When respect and sympathy became mutual, the prospects for social and political friction diminish – the latter, we would add, is always a matter of interest for students of International Relations.

In recent years a great deal of criticism has been directed at the condition of the Western university. Edward Shils, for example, has attacked the way universities have been deflected from their essential commitments by pressures from governments, the demand for immediate 'pay-offs', and attempts to be all things to all people. For Shils the essential commitment of the university must consist of research – the pursuit of truth – and the education of students – in what they should know, not necessarily what they want to know.[16] On a similar theme Robert A. Nisbet has complained about how American universities have had to concentrate on the immediate usefulness of their work, and have abandoned the idea that a university's greatness and a scholar's stature should be measured not by corporate criteria but rather by the extent to which universities and scholars contribute to the search for understanding and truth about humanity and nature.[17] Such dissatisfaction at the state of the contemporary university is shared by Grayling. He writes:

Education is mainly restricted to the young, and it is no longer education as such but, or rather, training, which is what best produces economic cannon fodder. This is a loss; for the aim of liberal education is to produce people who go on learning, who think and question. Moral dilemmas will always occur, and will always have to be negotiated afresh every time; so we need to be such people.[18]

Nowhere are such people needed more in our opinion than in the area of human rights, for here the subject matter is no less than applied ethics on a universal scale – the inventing of humanity.

Education as a human right

Without a right to education, there can be no comprehensive education in human rights. The previous discussion noted the significance of education because it serves to inculcate and disseminate a particular set of social values. According to a different view, education has (increasingly) become identified with the need to supply intellectually able and motivated individuals who can contribute positively to economic development. Together, their viewpoints explain in part why some have argued that education belongs to the category of 'fundamental' or 'basic' human rights, since the enjoyment of other rights (such as civil and political rights) is conditional upon an appropriate education.[19]

Within the UN system, the commitment to education is contained in a number of key documents. Article 26 of the 1948 Universal Declaration of Human Rights proclaims a right to education. It was included in the Declaration as part of a new category of economic and social rights which were grafted onto the civil and political rights found in the constitutions of liberal states like France and the United States. The radical dimension to the Declaration should not be underestimated. For example, it maintained that primary education should be both free and compulsory. Technical and higher (or tertiary) education was to be made 'generally available' and 'equally accessible to all on the basis of merit'.[20] These commitments were restated in more detail in the 1966 International Covenant on Economic, Social and Cultural Rights (ICESCR), and can be found in an array of subsequent UN and UNESCO documents.[21]

When we compare these standards with the actual access to education in different parts of the world, a disparate picture emerges. There are currently 900 million illiterate people in the developing world,[22] women outnumbering men by two to one.[23] Whilst the education 'gap' in the industrial countries is at the tertiary level, where around 60 per cent of the population do not have any 'upper-secondary' education,[24] in the developing world the priority is to increase the proportion of children receiving elementary education. Enrolment in primary education among children in these states increased from 48 per cent in 1960 to 77 per cent in 1991; however, 130 million children remain outside the school system, rising to 275 million at the secondary level.[25]

Although UN-sponsored research highlights unequal access to education for men and women, a much greater determinant of literacy and educational participation is income. It is the world's poor who are the world's illiterate. As UNESCO puts it, 'illiteracy and poverty not only go hand in hand, but shoulder to shoulder, each supporting the other'.[26] For this reason, it is crucial that the right to education is not seen to be autonomous from the broader context of economic and social development.

In a mid-1990s report by the World University Service (an INGO), the link between poverty and underachievement in education was made abundantly clear. Take by way of example the status of education in Malawi.[27] One of the poorest countries in the world with a per-capita average income of $160, the infant mortality rate is 153 per 1000 live births and life-expectancy is 46 years. Enrolment in primary schools is barely over 50 per cent, in secondary 4 per cent and at university, only 1 per cent. One of the main reasons for the low enrolment in schools is the high level of fees (up to as much as four-fifths of the per-capita average income). From 1993 onwards, Malawi has been moving slowly towards a more democratic system of governance. In part because of pressure from the Clinton Administration and major Western aid institutions, the Banda government permitted a referendum on democratic reform. A clear majority voted in favour of democratisation, leading to a greater freedom of the press and a lifting of the ban on opposition parties. Although such reforms are crucially important, they are not in themselves enough to ensure that children and young adults in Malawi receive a decent education. Before the right to education in Malawi and in numerous states throughout the world can be realised, the chains of poverty must be broken. Only then can attention be given to the issue of chronic overcrowding in schools and universities, inadequate teacher–pupil ratios, and poor enrolment levels.

The link between poverty and underachievement which manifests itself on a global (North/South) scale, is also evident within countries

– even rich ones in global terms. In Britain, for example, the Assistant Director-General of UNESCO told university teachers in 1997 that if an inability to pay was shown to affect access to higher education, it could be in contravention of the Universal Declaration of Human Rights.[28] The fact seems to be that in education, as in health, there is a direct relationship between wealth and access, money and flourishing. It is far beyond the scope of this chapter to explore these matters, as it is to speculate about the stress facing educational systems everywhere, for a mixture of political and philosophical reasons.[29] It is necessary, however, to mention them in order to underline the difficulties confronting the spread of a human rights education.

Although the standard set by the international human rights regime for educational provision is not high, in practice few countries comply with their obligations in full. This is in part due to the lack of clarity about what constitutes the standard. Is attendance at school sufficient, or does the obligation to provide universal primary education entail specific standards in relation to literacy or numeracy? Does the right to education imply the right to free books and materials? Although the ambiguities in the International Covenant on Economic, Social and Cultural Rights represent a genuine problem, they are not an excuse for the way in which governments consistently draft their five-yearly educational reports (mandated by the Covenant) in such a way as to conceal their inadequate provision rather than admitting to difficulties they are encountering in meeting the standard.[30]

But overcoming these problems in supplying basic education is only a start, as we argued earlier. For this reason, we argue in the next section that education *as* a right must be integrated with an education *in* human rights.

An education *in* human rights?

From the outset, the international human rights regime promoted education as a right *per se* and also as a means of facilitating a greater understanding of human rights in general. This second dimension, education *in* rights, is evident from A.26(2) of the Universal Declaration:

Education shall be directed to the full development of the human personality and to the strengthening of respect for human rights and fundamental freedoms. It shall promote understanding, tolerance and friendship among all nations, racial or religious groups, and shall further the activities of the United Nations for the maintenance of peace.[31]

Three years previously, the link between education and peace had been articulated in the preamble to the UNESCO Constitution, adopted in

London on 16 November 1945. This sentiment is conveyed strongly in the Constitution's opening sentence, which declares that 'since wars begin in the minds of men, it is in the minds of men that the defences of peace must be constructed'.[32]

The belief in the link between human rights and humane politics has persisted among those codifying the human rights culture. The World Conference on Human Rights held in Vienna in June 1993, for example, contained important clauses on human rights education in its Programme of Action:

The World Conference on Human Rights calls on States and institutions to *include* human rights, humanitarian law, democracy and the rule of law as subjects in the curriculum *of all learning institutions* in formal and informal settings.[33]

Clearly the standard set at Vienna is running considerably ahead of state practice. But crucially, statements like the one quoted above can add legitimacy to those educators, parents, politicians and other activists who seek to persuade their governments to include human rights values in the curricula of 'all learning institutions'.

This right to a 'democratic education' set out in the various covenants and charters of the post-war human rights regime has not been completely realised, even in developed states which have the resources to provide compulsory education for all children under sixteen. We identify three general explanations for this uneven commitment to deliver an education which promotes the democratic values of 'understanding, tolerance and friendship': 'national' priorities, cultural diversity and neo-liberal values.

'National' priorities

Traditionally, many developed states (particularly Commonwealth countries) held fast to the view that politics should be kept out of the classroom. This raises an issue that runs throughout any comprehensive discussion of education, namely whether 'politics' can ever be excluded from the classroom, and, if it cannot be, whether it should be explicit or left implicit. A brief comparison between the British and US approaches to a political education is instructive here. In Britain traditionally, the only politics a child was likely to learn was by osmosis – some would prefer to say insidiously – in a history lesson about empires or wars. A structure of meaning to politics was given by the character of the curriculum, but only implicitly. Although teachers are now more likely to provide informal guidance on political ideas, few schools offer distinct compulsory units on social or political education.[34] The pedagogic culture in the United States provides a sharp contrast to the ostensibly 'apolitical' character of British education. Most American states require a daily pledge of allegiance to the flag. Moreover, 120 minutes of social studies education is required in primary schools every week. In secondary schools, the majority of students have to take a course in politics and government.

There are two related explanations for the priority accorded to an education about liberal democracy in the United States as opposed to in Britain: first, the dominant 'melting pot' view of political culture in the United States, which implies the need to cement the social bonds of this 'nation' of immigrants; and secondly, the belief in the link between education and good citizenship which successive US presidents have advocated, from Thomas Jefferson to William Jefferson Clinton.

The way an apolitical education can explicitly serve injustice was blatant in the case of South Africa before the 1990s. During the colonial era, as in Britain's other former African colonies, all schooling glorified colonialism and was aimed at inculcating schoolchildren with British values and knowledge. Schoolchildren 'knew more about the mountains and monarchs of Britain than about the geographies and histories of their own land, or those of their neighbour'.[35] Later, during the apartheid era, no small part of the strategic licence which led to South Africa's minority government destabilising the region and imposing institutionalised racism at home rested on the inculcation of a particular version of the history and geography of the region. Generation upon generation of South Africa's white youth were taught the theory that their neighbours – not to mention black South Africans – were, at best, inferior and, at worst, manipulated by external powers.[36]

Nadine Gordimer has described the effects of such an education. The experience of growing up as a settler in South Africa in the first part of the twentieth century, she has written, was one of being born into a society that had 'long established its ruling accommodation with the indigenous people'; it was a 'society removed from all danger, that had made itself comfortable with injustice'.[37] In this South Africa most whites lived as outsiders in the world in which they were actually insiders. White children had a tenuous connection with the present, or ignored or did not see or understand the surrounding injustices. It was a life of freedom from danger, and created the luxury of a privileged 'apolitical' settler class. For Gordimer, '[t]his totally surrounding, engulfing experience was removed from one not by land and sea but by law, custom and prejudice'. Students of International Relations do not have this excuse of being ignorant and apolitical settlers in their 'totally surrounding, engulfing experience' – that of world politics. They know, and so must choose to be comfortable or uncomfortable with injustice, however far removed they are 'by land and sea'. In education, as in the rest of life, there is no escape from politics, whether the field of one's vision is local or global.

Cultural diversity

States differ greatly on the priority they accord to human rights, whether in public education or in political rhetoric. National priorities are always influential, as just explained, but at a deeper level cultural diversity represents a yet more serious challenge to the normative basis of the idea of universal human rights. This can be seen, in the local context, in the potentially conflictual relationship between education and multi-culturalism; for example, parents with fundamentalist Christian beliefs will have different views on the kind of values which should be promoted in comparison with Muslim, Hindu or atheist parents. Of course, religious convictions shape not just a true-believer's thinking on rights, but their entire view of the life world; this includes disputes about the origins of the universe, the sanctity of life, and the toleration (or otherwise) of those who do not share their faith.

Thinking about culture in a global context reveals that there are significant regional differences in the meaning and priority accorded to education. This can be seen in the radically different parent–child relationships evident in the developed North and some parts of the developing South. In the North, governments are expected to provide education and welfare, whereas in the South, children are often expected to be the providers of economic and social 'security' for their extended families.[38] This shows how governments in developing states face not only resource constraints when trying to comply with international human rights norms on education, but also cultural factors which serve to shape the commitment of parents to the education of their children. The question arises as to whether some cultural (especially religious) outlooks are directly incompatible with the spirit and practice of certain aspects of the human rights regime. What does 'universal' mean, in terms of implementation, if this is the case?

The ascendancy of neo-liberal values

The UN Charter, the UNESCO Constitution and the Universal Declaration of Human Rights were drafted at a time when the experience of world wars and the Holocaust cast a dark shadow over the immediate future. There was a strong sense that the 'international community' had to make a new start. In the intervening period, however, these solidarist sentiments have waned as a culture of individualism has taken hold, particularly in the Western world. The more recent hegemony of neo-liberal values is discernible in British documents on human rights. During the 1980s and early 1990s, the British Conservative party openly declared that '[t]he aim of the Government's education policy is to raise standards at all levels of ability, to increase parental choice and to make post-school education more widely accessible and more responsive to the *needs of the economy*.'[39]

By extolling values of flexibility, enterprise, individual responsibility for welfare and so on, the rightist governments in Western Europe and the United States found themselves in an uncomfortable position when it came to promoting traditional 'family values'. *Laissez-faire* economics is undergirded by a *laissez-faire* attitude to human flourishing: it treats labour as an expendable commodity to be discarded according to the imperative of 'downsizing'; it expects workers to 're-tool' and learn new skills irrespective of age or ability; and it also attaches no importance to the good of the local community, as individuals and their families are forced to move from one area to another in search of employment. Whilst giving enthusiastic approval to the spread of these labour market forces, conservative governments in Britain and the United States decried some of the consequences, such as the break-up of families (often related to unemployment or the pressures on women to work in low-paid part-time jobs) and the concomitant rise in crime rates and in social dislocation more generally.

In response to the above, it could be argued that this neo-liberal ideology was not the responsibility of individual governments. The economic reshaping of the world, now labelled 'globalisation', has come about in a way that no government ever intended (even if some have approved of it more than others). These forces, without doubt, are eroding the collectivism which underpinned the domestic and international institutions of the early post-1945 period. But all is not lost. As we will show in the next section, there are good reasons for thinking that there exist new opportunities for advancing 'the intellectual and moral solidarity' of humankind for which the UNESCO Constitution hoped.

The end of the Cold War triggered a wave of optimism among policy-makers and in public opinion alike about the prospects for a new world order, including enhanced compliance with human rights. Underlying the fall of communism in Central-Eastern Europe and the former Soviet Union, and the end of apartheid in South Africa, was the idea that individuals mattered. There can be no doubt that growing awareness about human rights played a significant part in delegitimising and top-pling these regimes, as dissidents in Central and Eastern Europe have testified.[40] It is a belief in the rights of ordinary citizens which, when mob-ilised against governments, can give power to the powerless. Although this optimism of the early 1990s has been tempered by the practices of illiberal regimes in Central Africa and parts of Asia – notably China – and elsewhere, certain progressive possibilities for including human rights values in education can be seen to be emerging.

New opportunities fifty years on

The year 1989 proved to be a false dawn for the optimists and propa-gandists of what President Bush called the New World Order. Never-theless, if international politics did not conform to his vision of a US-led 'international community', several new opportunities did open up for the further advancement of the human rights culture; for example, techno-logical developments allowing easier communication across frontiers helped to consolidate a global civil society interested in human rights. In this section we want to identify three political developments in the 1990s that have helped the growth of a human rights culture: democra-tisation, global awareness and the initiatives of international institutions.

Democratisation

Human rights and democracy have a synergistic relationship, for both have the concept of entitlements at their centre. It is not surprising, therefore, that a number of the post-communist 'democracies in transi-tion' have recognised the significance of a human rights education for their prospects for peaceful change. In Russia, the first major review of education policy undertaken by the Russian Federation noted that 'what the state and society most urgently need is the upbringing of Russian citizens who share democratic values and are capable of actively partici-pating in the formation of a state based on law'.[41] It is clear that the transmission of human rights values by educational institutions in Cen-tral and Eastern Europe is vital for democratic principles to become embedded in these societies which are undergoing so much change and are facing such social and economic stress. This is a reason for the support that Western governments and individual entrepreneurs like George Soros have given to curriculum reform in those countries where a particular version of Marxism-Leninism had penetrated into all aspects of cultural and academic life.

Older liberal-democratic societies have also been contemplating – at least to some degree – the significance of a more human rights-based education as a way of combating what is widely felt to be a declining sense of community. In 1996, the murder of a London head-teacher, Philip Lawrence, and the massacre of primary-school children in Dunblane, Scotland, prompted a reflection in British society about the teaching of morality in schools. The official response, evident in the argument made by the chief executive of the Government's School Curriculum and Assessment Authority, is to add the teaching of right and wrong as 'the two extra Rs'. The content of this particular interpretation of morality is one which stresses family values, and the importance of overcoming the 'morass of moral relativism'. For Mary Midgley, children do not need to be taught about marginal questions of cultural diversity; instead, she believes that morality in education should stress universal principles such as the 'Golden Rule', shared by all cultures, which maintains that 'you do not do to others what you would not want done to you'.[42]

A growing cosmopolitan awareness?

We noted earlier how the 'collectivism' of the early postwar years has been disrupted by global economic forces. These same forces also undermined Stalinist state socialism as an effective economic competitor – and so also as a systemic threat to the West. There is nevertheless a widespread dissatisfaction with major aspects of globalisation and anxiety about the dangers inherent in such globalisation issues as environmental degradation, economic injustice, weapons of mass destruction, political oppression and so on. Today's coalition of counter-hegemonic forces is extensive, though often fragmented and focused on single issues. Already in the late 1980s there were over 18,000 international non-governmental organisations creating what Elise Boulding called a 'global civic culture'.[43] This developing global civil society – committed to such principles as non-violence, human rights and environmental sustainability – is increasingly well organised and self-conscious.[44]

A major motivation for these voices arguing for a radical rethinking of global politics is what they perceive to be the destruction of the natural environment – something which 'threatens the very survival of life on our planet'.[45] The relationship between transnational environmental movements and human rights is an ambiguous one. On the one hand, some ecological opinion sees an exclusive emphasis on *human* rights as part of the same anthropocentrism which treats the earth as an expendable resource; on the other hand, learning about human rights is crucial to the development of a cosmopolitan moral awareness which will be sensitive to environmental problems. 'Ecological rights' are seen by some writers as the embodiment of human and environmental rights, both redefining 'the relationship of human beings with one another and of rich countries with poor countries, as well as of all mankind with its natural environment'.[46]

Those in any society actively supporting organisations committed to human rights and economic justice for all are always likely to be in a minority, and we would not want to exaggerate their power, or their attractiveness to today's students, the children of the era of Thatcher, Reagan, Kohl and their imitators. The 'culture of contentment' has shaped the outlooks of the young – today's students – as well as the older generation – those already supposed to be of a more comfortable political tendency. Nevertheless, those who doubt the emergence of a growing cosmopolitan awareness need only consider the extensive global support that exists for transnational social movements such as Greenpeace and Amnesty International; and, even if interest is patchy and commitment is short-term, popular opinion can be mobilised by awareness of the needs of distant strangers. This suggests that a human rights education does not need to be 'transmitted' to children and young adults as indoctrination; instead what is required is the nurturing of a latent cosmopolitan awareness. People around the world are already aware (to varying degrees) of the existence of practices of torture, political oppression, unfair imprisonment, domestic violence, capital punishment, degrading treatment of prisoners and so on. What needs to be grafted onto this elementary knowledge is an understanding of the causes of these practices of human wrongs, so that young people are able to evaluate opinions about them critically. This level of moral awareness goes beyond knowledge of a problem and its causes; it also requires a personal commitment to do whatever one can to secure compliance to human rights norms. This kind of cosmopolitan moral awareness demands action – in other words, joining campaigns, writing letters and potentially engaging in civil disobedience.

Institutionalising global education initiatives

The prospects for bringing human rights values into education have been improved by specific programmes sponsored by international institutions. The UN, in addition to standard-setting and sponsoring multilateral gatherings (such as the 1993 International Congress on Education for Human Rights), has a dedicated organ for promoting political education. UNESCO's Constitution, noted above, emphasised the causal connection between peace, education and the prospects for peace. Over half a century later, Frederico Mayer (the Director-General) reiterated this principle in his 1997 New Year's speech, which opened with the words: Lasting peace is a prerequisite for the exercise of all human rights and duties.'[47] In other words, peace requires human rights and duties to be exercised, and human rights and duties cannot flourish without peace.

At a practical level, UNESCO seeks to promote human rights values through its Associated Schools Project. Beginning in 1953 with only thirty-three schools as members, the Associated Schools Project now has over 3,300 members in 125 countries. The Project has four main themes: human rights; the activities of the UN and its responses to global challenges; knowledge and understanding of other peoples and their languages; and the environment. The idea of educational exchanges has been taken up by governments, regions and cities and towns in their transnational relations. It has also become a feature in regional forums such as the EU, the Asia Pacific Economic Council, and the Arab League. Such intensification of social contacts is, it should be noted, a necessary process in the building of 'security communities' between states.[48]

Perhaps the most forward-looking human rights education initiative to be promoted by a single country is Canada's global education programme, funded by the Canadian International Development Agency. The global education programme includes initiatives for teacher-training and curriculum development. The objectives of the programme are 'to promote a prejudice-free world, through understanding of global interdependence and solidarity between Canada and the Third World, and the encouragement of cultural enrichment through a better knowledge of other lifestyles and ways of thinking – to foster international understanding, tolerance, respect for the rights of others, and rejection of racism'.[49] Such programmes are the life-blood of a growing human rights culture.

The role of universities in a human rights education

It is hardly surprising that there is no explicit right to a university education laid down in the human rights regime. Access in all countries must be contingent upon the ability to benefit from higher education; in this sense universities are necessarily meritocratic institutions. Before articulating what those values should be, and how they might be promoted, it is important to confront the sceptics who argue that universities should keep values out of their mission statements.

The idea that universities should 'transmit' values that might be described as political is bound to provoke traditionalist resistances. The counter-case might be put, for example, on behalf of 'objectivity' and 'academic purity'. The problem is that even these values have political and not just scholarly implications. In South Africa during the apartheid era – to take a paradigmatic example – academics had three choices. They could be 'public intellectuals' espousing the universal case against racism; they could be comforters of the racist regime, through active support or friendly criticism; or they could stay ensconced in their ivory towers, ostensibly maintaining academic purity either by keeping away from controversial topics or by attempting to be 'balanced' or 'impartial' in their writing and public utterances. Some forms of 'purity' can serve injustice, and the latter is one of them. Each choice, and no choice, is to take sides in the great issues of politics. Instead of objectivity and purity we would question whether is it possible to have a value-free study of human society. The belief that we should aim for value freedom in academic life is a long and respected one in the social sciences, but it is one we think is fundamentally flawed.

Universities, like other institutions of learning, cannot avoid transmitting values. It is desirable, therefore, that those who work in them do not hide the values they think underpin their teaching. Self-criticism is as necessary as the application of one's 'critical intelligence and moral sensibilities' to other societies. If one is explicit, then students have reference points. The least justifiable position is that which smuggles in values in the guise of 'the pursuit of truth', the application of 'common sense', the exercise of 'idle curiosity', or claiming expertise in describing the world 'as it is'. In the study of the social world those academics who assert their own objectivity are always likely to be found the most wanting in terms of real critical distance from their subject matter.

What purports to be 'value-free', 'objective' or 'apolitical' analysis often is merely a cloak for status quo thinking, and, therefore, status quo values. This is not always at the conscious level, but even if it is not, it still serves to reinforce conservative thinking. One consequence of this is that those academics who want change in society are criticised by traditionalists for improperly bringing 'politics', 'values' – or even 'emotion' – into academic discussion. But in each case there is no escape. Eschewing values is itself a value, and being unemotional is a form of emotion. Attempting to be apolitical is a type of politics. We believe that the assumptions and epistemology of traditional theory in International Relations are untenable, given the parlous state in which many of the earth's inhabitants live. It leaves the world as it is and somehow tries to escape any responsibility for the outcome. How can one be value-free and unemotional when well in excess of 25 million people have died from wars since 1945, and 40,000 children die daily from preventable disease and malnutrition? So, against those who would argue: 'do not bring politics into the university, we are all good academics'; or 'our task as academics is to describe the world as it is, not discuss how it ought to be'; or 'what should guide our studies in universities is the pursuit of truth, not political programmes'; or 'academics should not use the lecture theatre as a pulpit in which to preach their political news' – we would say that there is no escape from politics; describing the world 'as it is' is a value-laden activity; attempting to rule out the discussion of 'what ought to be' is to dismiss a major part of political philosophy; the pursuit of 'truth' is not an unproblematical aim; and the worst preachers are those who smuggle in their political preferences under the guise of objective truth or talk of separating facts and values, power and morality.

The contrast between the two approaches just identified is well illustrated by the long debate between Strategic Studies and Peace Research. Since the former was the offspring of International Relations orthodoxy, its proponents won the day in a disciplinary sense. Strategic Studies was praised for its realist credentials – being objective, relevant, value-free and unemotional – whereas proponents of Peace Research were criticised during the Cold War for being preachers, peaceniks, other-worldly and the rest. In practice, peace researchers on the whole had an up-front commitment to the ideal of peace, together with specific opposition to the illegality, immorality and irrationality of nuclear weapons. The point we want to emphasise is that both Strategic Studies and Peace Research were infused with values, but one was seen as 'ideological' and 'political', since it was on the side of change and common humanity, whereas the other gained the reputation of being cutting-edge social science, embedded as it was in statist values. Strategic Studies was ethnocentrism writ large, and so was not seen as a problem in the national(ist) educational contexts in which it flourished. The disciplinary difference between orthodox Strategic Studies and Peace Research, in our opinion, was not that one was 'political', the other not, but that one normalised the status quo, whereas the other adopted a critical stance towards it. Teachers of International Relations have a similar choice with respect to the way they approach the study of the theory and practice of human rights.

If the argument above is accepted then we have no choice other than to be 'political'. If this is the case, the problem facing academics – students, teachers and researchers (if these categories can be distinguished) – is how we can be political in an academic way. To begin with, it is probably easier to assert what we mean by saying what 'being academic' about issues such as human rights is not. In the first place, ignorance is entirely inconsistent with an academic approach. That is, one needs to read and investigate what others have said about human rights, and to know the positions of practitioners. Secondly, there must be 'respect for evidence'. While the meanings of the evidence can be contested, somebody's 'facts' cannot just be wished away. Thirdly, it is anti-academic to refuse to listen to contending viewpoints, however unacceptable they might be. This does not mean that one must conclude that they be given political space, but that there are no grounds for refusing them some academic space (and a good test of whether one understands an alien position is to try and explain it, persuasively, to others). Finally, dogmatism, by which we mean conclusions based on prejudice rather than a sophisticated understanding of the complexities of issues, is inconsistent with an academic approach.

The anti-academic attitudes just summarised are particularly unhelpful in the study of world politics, which is an arena of multiple truths, differing perceptions, complexity, historical richness, multicultural variety, clashing national interests, power politics, contested norms and so on. If this thesaurus of our subject matter is valid, then an academic approach must be geared to dealing with complexity and different ways of seeing and being. In the light of this, the academic virtues begin with 'moderation' in approach, in the sense of being aware of, being willing to listen to, and trying to understand the enormous range of viewpoints about the complex issues that confront students of world politics. This invariably leads to the avoidance of simple analyses (resulting in monocausal explanations) and simple answers (derived from prejudice). A moderate approach is not synonymous with some trivial idea that the middle way or a 'balanced' approach is always the best one – a familiar British predilection. Whether truth or right or whatever is found in the middle depends entirely on the 'extremes' by one which one takes one's bearings.

It is of profound importance that some people in all societies – and universities are a key institution in this regard – devote time and energy to understanding the theory and practice of human rights. It is of profound importance because of the effects on peoples' lives of their society's attitudes and behaviour with respect to human rights, for human rights say something profound about the way we see ourselves as humans at this stage in our collective history. They are the front line of applied ethics in world politics, and it would be worrying if societies refused to devote resources to studying them in their universities.

Students of human rights have to face up to the problem that there will always be blurred edges, philosophically, politically and methodologically, with such an intensely controversial and important subject in a multicultural and interstate setting. But they should not allow the fear of doing something wrong prevent them from even attempting to do something right. Universities are important for human rights, and human rights are central to universities. Universities are important for human rights because they should embody – in their conception as the *universitas* – certain universals such as the search for knowledge, the practice of tolerance and freedom of speech. At the same time universities can be part of a global civic culture which can take a longer perspective than politicians, can try and unsilence the silenced, can attempt to expose the power plays of the powerful and use knowledge in the emancipatory interests of the victims of world politics. Human rights are important for the daily work of scholars because the principles they embody allow them to flourish, potentially, as a result of ideals such as freedom of speech and non-discrimination. Furthermore, engagement with human rights can change the way one thinks about the world. By focusing on individual victims of oppression – the litmus test of world politics – one can get a very different view of 'international reality' from that given by traditional state-centric perspectives. From the biography of a single insecure stranger we can learn at least as much about what makes the world go round, politically, economically and ideologically, as can be discovered in a file in a foreign ministry. We may teach human rights, but human rights also teach us. They teach, for example, that the majority of sovereign states do not guarantee security, and that they have the power to commit acts of genocidal violence, prepare for nuclear overkill, and commit acts of state terror on a scale that makes officially defined terrorists look like amateurs. The intensification and spread of the human rights culture, which puts people rather than sovereign states at the centre of concern is a key step in the invention of humanity.

A cosmopolitan education

The modern university, confronted by the pressures of globalisation, mass education and the demands of local politics, faces many problems. Universities also have to suffer a great deal of criticism, unable equally to respond effectively to multiple and sometimes conflicting demands. It is little consolation to know that universities have throughout their histories been the target of criticism (they must therefore have been doing something right). We appreciate here that we are adding another dimension to their already overburdened agenda. We also appreciate that we have been discussing primarily universities in democratic polities. In some countries being an academic is not simply a job or a vocation: it can be a matter of life and death. Words can kill and when tyranny cannot control truth, it invariably tries to punish its messengers. But words can also liberate, and if human rights are not nourished in these institutions, where can they be? And if human rights do not flourish, what does 'humanity' mean – other than what those with local power allow it to mean. This brings us back to our introduction, and to Daw Aung San Suu Kyi's plea that those of us in the privileged world – and privileged universities – use our liberty to help promote the liberty of those whose human rights are trampled upon. At this point, as with the South African illustration earlier, we have three choices. Each choice or no choice is both political and consequential. Clearly, our commitment to a human rights education is a positive choice for a politics of common humanity (subject to all the academic caveats we mentioned earlier). With respect to their role within departments of International Relations and Political Science we recognise that despite constituting a central element in global politics, human rights have only occupied a peripheral place in the teaching of the subject. In his introduction to the special issue of *Political Studies* on human rights, David Beetham argues that there has been a certain scepticism about human rights within the academy, its universalism being believed by many to be 'philosophically insecure, morally problematic and politically impractical'.[50] While granting the force of such criticisms, some earlier chapters in this volume attempted to counter them.

Given the importance of human rights issues, and the ways of responding to critics of universalism, we believe that the subjects of human rights and world citizenship merit a more secure place in the International Relations and Politics curricula.[51] There is obvious scope for discussion about how it might be done, but the literature is well developed and student enthusiasm is generally high. What we would suggest, to bring the subject home, is making the subject matter vivid in two main ways. First, try to show how human rights are important to students in their own lives. For the relatively secure in the West, this might well consist of showing how their lives would be different if certain rights were taken away. Secondly, there is considerable value in empathetic involvement, that is, encouraging students to try and feel what life must have been like – or is like today – when naked human beings stand defenceless before the juggernaut of state power. A focus on individual lives is often the most effective way of bringing such realities to life. This is evident in the teaching of the Holocaust which draws on the diaries of Anne Frank, the stories of Primo Levi, and the images of *Schindler's List*, each capable of stimulating an empathetic understanding of the needs of strangers in violent times. Reading the annual reports of human rights organisations, or their regular newsletters which focus on individual cases of abuse, is a valuable and realistic antidote to the lifeless accounts of world politics perpetrated by neo-realists. Furthermore, this sort of education – a cosmopolitan education – not only teaches us about others, but is also a crucial component of understanding the self and our immediate cultural referents.[52]

David Beetham offers a down-to-earth justification for a human rights education. 'In the final analysis', he argues:

the justification for human rights as a theme in the curriculum lies in its ability to engage our critical intelligence and our moral sensitivity together; and to develop a clearer understanding, not only of how the world is, but of what kind of world we might come to inhabit. In doing so, it offers a challenge to both idealism and scepticism alike. The subject exemplifies, that is to say, a recurrent feature of the political condition: not only the struggle for power and influence between competing interests, but the collective striving for human betterment in an imperfect world.[53]

In this spirit, we conclude with our belief that in order to expand moral awareness and so help in the task of our self-reinvention as humans, we should add a fourth 'R' – (human) Rights – to the 'three Rs' of the traditional curriculum. We support both education as a human right, and an education *in* human rights: both must be part of a politics of common humanity appropriate for the first truly global age.

Notes

1 Daw Aung San Suu Kyi, 'Please use your liberty to promote ours', *International Herald Tribune*, 4 February 1997.
2 Louis Henkin, *The Age of Rights* (New York: Columbia University Press, 1990), p. xiii.
3 'Social movements and world politics', special issue of *Millennium* 23.
4 UNESCO, *World Education Report* (Oxford University Press, 1995), p. 19.
5 Henkin, *The Age of Rights*; Eric Hobsbawm, *The Age of Extremes: The Short Twentieth Century 1914–1991* (London: Michael Joseph, 1994).
6 Richard Rorty, 'Human rights, rationality, and sentimentality', in Stephen Shute and Susan Hurley (eds.), *On Human Rights. The Oxford Amnesty Lectures* (New York: Basic Books, 1993), pp. 111–34.
7 Sophie Haroutunian-Gordon, 'Soul', in James W. Garrison and Anthony G. Rud, Jr (eds.), *The Educational Conversation* (Albany: State University Press of New York, 1995), p. 97.
8 H. Reiss (ed.), *Kant's Political Writings* (Cambridge University Press, 1989), p. 54.

9 It should be noted that universities have played an important role in institutionalising post-colonial authority. Mahmood Mamdani, 'Historical notes on academic freedom in Africa', in John Daniel *et al.*, *Academic Freedom 3: Education and Human Rights* (London: Zed Books, 1995), p. 16. For further discussion of this link between higher education and the forging of a post-colonial identity, see Kenneth W. Thompson, 'Education and human rights', in David P. Forsythe (ed.), *Human Rights and Development: International Views* (London: Macmillan, 1989).

10 Derek Heater, *World Citizenship and Government: Cosmopolitan Ideas in the History of Western Political Thought* (Basingstoke: Macmillan, 1996), esp. pp. 13–21.

11 Ralf Beddard, 'Rights and performance: economic and social rights in the UK', in R. Beddard and D. M. Hill (eds.), *Economic, Social and Cultural Rights: Progress and Achievement* (London: Macmillan, 1992), p. 132. There are signs of change in the British government's attitude towards human rights following the election of the Labour Party in 1997.

12 Martha C. Nussbaum, 'Patriotism and cosmopolitanism', in Joshua Cohen (ed.), *For Love of Country: Debating the Limits of Patriotism* (Boston: Beacon Press, 1996), p. 9. See also Martha Nussbaum, *Cultivating Humanity: A Classical Defense of Reform in Liberal Education* (Boston: Harvard University Press, 1997).

13 A. C. Grayling, 'To hell with all religion', *Observer*, 11 August 1996.

14 Quoted by Michael Barber, 'Left and right kept behind after school', *Guardian*, 12 September 1996.

15 Grayling, 'To hell with all religion'.

16 Edward Shils, *The Order of Learning: Essays on the Contemporary University* (New Brunswick, N.J.: Transaction Publishers, 1997).

17 Robert Nisbet, *The Degradation of the Academic Dogma* (New Brunswick, N.J.: Transaction Publishers, 1996).

18 Grayling, 'To hell with all religion'.

19 Henry Shue, *Basic Rights: Subsistence, Affluence and US Foreign Policy* (Princeton University Press, 1980).

20 'Extract from the Universal Declaration of Human Rights', in Norma Bernstein Tarrow (ed.), *Human Rights and Education* (Oxford: Pergamon, 1987), pp. 237–8.

21 The most significant of the various human rights codifications can be found in Article 13 of the International Covenant on Economic, Social and Cultural Rights (ICESCR), wherein 'State Parties' recognise the following:

(1) Primary education shall be compulsory and available freely to all.

(2) Secondary education in its different forms, including technical and vocational secondary education, shall be made generally available by the progressive introduction of free education.

(3) Higher education shall be made equally accessible to all, on the basis of capacity, by every appropriate means, and in particular by the progressive introduction of free education.

(4) Fundamental education shall be encouraged or intensified as far as possible for those persons who have not received or completed the whole period of their primary education.

(5) The development of a system of schools at all levels shall be actively pursued, an adequate fellowship system shall be established, and the material conditions of teaching staff shall be continuously improved.

International Covenant on Economic, Social and Cultural Rights, G. A. Res. 2200A, Article 13, para. 2.

22 By 'developing world', the UNDP means the two categories of 'middle-income' states (GNP per capita of $695 to $8,625) and 'low-income' states (GNP per capita of $695 and below).

23 UNDP, *Human Development Report* (New York: Oxford University Press, 1995), p. 4.

24 A term used by the UNDP to denote (presumably) 16+ education. Note that a discussion of the right to education easily slides into an exclusive focus upon children. But it must not be forgotten that education is not, according to the regime, the exclusive domain of the child. Adult education is referred to in the ICESCR; moreover, access to higher education should be unlimited by age.

25 *Human Development Report*, p. 16.

26 UNESCO, *World Education Report*, p. 47.

27 The following statistics are taken from Richard Carver, 'Malawi', in Daniel *et al.* (eds.), *Academic Freedom 3*.

28 'Human right to learning confirmed', *Times Higher Education Supplement*, 12 December 1997, p. 2.

29 George Walden, *We Should Know Better: Solving the Education Crisis* (London: Fourth Estate, 1996).

30 For example, Audrey R. Chapman argues that 'virtually all reports only present national aggregate data and thereby conceal significant discrepancies by gender amongst various groups'. 'Monitoring the right to education: reporting to UN treaty bodies', in Daniel *et al.* (eds.), *Academic Freedom 3*, p. 4.

31 'Universal Declaration', in Tarrow (ed.), *Human Rights and Education*, pp. 237–8.

32 UNESCO, *World Education Report*, p. 16.

33 Emphasis added. The Declaration goes on to add: 'Human Rights education should include peace, democracy, development and social justice, as set forth in international and regional human rights instruments, in order to achieve common understanding and awareness with a view to strengthening universal commitment to human rights.' The Vienna Declaration and Programme of Action, paras. 79–80.

34 In 1987, the figure was just over 20 per cent. See Tarrow (ed.), *Human Rights and Education*, p. 177.

35 Ken Booth and Peter Vale, 'Critical security studies and regional insecurity: the case of southern African', in Keith Krause and Michael C. Williams (eds.), *Critical Security Studies: Concepts and Cases* (Minneapolis: University of Minnesota Press, 1997), ch. 11, p. 331.

36 Ken Booth and Peter Vale, 'Security in southern Africa: after apartheid, beyond realism', *International Affairs* 71 (1995): 287, 291.

37 Nadine Gordimer, 'The other world that was our world', *Guardian*, 3 June 1995.

38 This argument is made by Abdullahi An-Na'im. He recognises that '[t]hese stereotypes are obviously not universal models of the situation in the South or North, but they certainly reflect dominant sociological norms and assumptions which appear to underlie public policy in these regions'. A. An-Na'im, 'Cultural transformation and normative consensus on the best interests of the child', in Philip Alston (ed.), *The Best Interests of the Child: Reconciling Culture and Human Rights* (Oxford: Clarendon / UNICEF, 1994), p. 66.

39 *Aspects of Britain: Human Rights* (London: HMSO, 1992), p. 84. Emphasis added.

40 See, for example, Václav Havel, *Open Letters* (London: Faber and Faber, 1991).

41 *The Development of Education: National Report of the Russian Federation* (Moscow: Ministry of Education, 1994). Quoted in UNESCO, *World Education Report*, p. 79.

42 Mary Midgley, 'Rights and wrongs', *Guardian*, 16 January 1996.

43 Elise Boulding, *Building a Global Civic Culture* (Syracuse University Press, 1988).

44 See, for example, Paul Ekins, *A New World Order* (London: Routledge, 1992); on the influence of one group, the Peace Movement, see David Cortright, *Peace Works: The Citizen's Role in Ending the Cold War* (Boulder: Westview, 1993).

45 David Ray Griffin, 'Preface', to J. Baird Callicott and Fernando J. R. da Rocha (eds.), *Earth Summit Ethics: Toward a Reconstructive Postmodern Philosophy of Environmental Education* (Albany: State University Press of New York, 1996), p. xii.

46 Nicholas M. Sosa, 'The ethics of dialogue and the environment', in Callicott and Rocha (eds.), *Earth Summit Ethics*, p. 67.

47 Declaration by the Director-General of UNESCO, January 1997.

48 Communication was at the heart of the concept: see Karl Deutsch *et al.*, *Political Community and the North Atlantic Area* (Princeton University Press, 1957).

49 UNESCO, *World Education Report*, p. 88.

50 David Beetham, 'Introduction: Human rights and the study of politics', in Beetham (ed.), *Politics and Human Rights* (Oxford: Blackwell, 1995), pp. 1–9.

51 *Ibid.*, pp. 8–9.

52 Nussbaum, 'Patriotism and cosmopolitanism'; Nussbaum, *Cultivating Humanity*. See George J. Andreopoulos and Richard Pierre Claude (eds.), *Human Rights Education for the Twenty-First Century* (Pittsburgh: University of Pennsylvania Press, 1996) for ideas about initiating, planning and implementing programmes for teaching people about human rights.

53 Beetham, 'Introduction', pp. 8–9.

Index